155.937
C436s

The Child and Death

THE CHILD and DEATH

John E. Schowalter, Paul R. Patterson,
Margot Tallmer, Austin H. Kutscher,
Stephen V. Gullo, and David Peretz,
editors

with the editorial assistance of
Lillian G. Kutscher

New York / Columbia University Press / *1983*

Library of Congress Cataloging in Publication Data
Main entry under title:

The Child and death.

(Foundation of Thanatology series)
Includes bibliographies and index.
1. Terminally ill children—Psychology.
2. Children and death.   3. Children—Death—Psychological
aspects.   4. Grief.   I. Schowalter, John E., 1936–
II. Series: Foundation of Thanatology series
(Columbia University. Press) [DNLM: 1. Attitude to
death.   2. Death—In infancy and childhood.
3. Terminal care—In infancy and childhood. WS 200 C536]
RJ249.C48 1983   155.9'37   83–1981
ISBN 0-231-04912-9

Columbia University Press
New York   Guildford, Surrey

Copyright © 1983 Columbia University Press
All rights reserved
Printed in the United States of America

Clothbound editions of Columbia University Press books are Smyth-sewn
and printed on permanent and durable acid-free paper.

· Contents ·

Preface		ix
Acknowledgment		xiii
I.	THE CHILD'S PERCEPTION OF DEATH	1
1	Changing Perspectives: Preparing for Life or Death ALBERT J. SOLNIT	*3*
2	Death and the Child MAX M. STERN	*19*
3	The Child and Fear of Death NELLI L. MITCHELL AND KAREN R. SCHULMAN	*27*
4	Children's Attitudes Toward Death APRIL R. ZWEIG	*36*
5	A Man Came and Killed Our Teacher BRUCE L. DANTO	*49*
6	The Grandparent Teaches the Child About Living and Dying PAUL R. PATTERSON	*75*
7	*A Course in Miracles* and Its Practical Application to Life and Death GERALD G. JAMPOLSKY	*79*
II.	CHILDREN'S REACTIONS TO PARENTAL DEATH	87
8	Parental Death in Childhood—A Review of the Psychiatric Literature TECLA CRITELLI	*89*
9	Children's Reactions to Parental Death RICHARD A. GARDNER	*104*
10	Children, When Parents Die MORRIS A. WESSEL	*125*
III.	CARING FOR THE LIFE-THREATENED CHILD	135
11	Dying Children and Their Families MELVIN LEWIS AND DOROTHY OTNOW LEWIS	*137*
12	Terminal Phase of Childhood Cancer: Home Care of the Dying C. M. BINGER, A. R. ABLIN, J. H. KUSHNER, AND G. A. PERIN	*156*

13	Home Care for the Child with Cancer IDA M. MARTINSON	172
14	Helping a Child with Leukemia to Die at Home JOAN TAKSA ROLSKY	180
15	Death in a Family of Hemophiliacs AKE MATTSSON	187
16	Hospice Care for the Dying Child ROBERT W. BUCKINGHAM	199

IV. STAFF, PARENTS, AND THE DYING CHILD — 207

17	On Facing Death: Perspectives of a Child Psychiatrist in a Medical School Setting JOHN E. SCHOWALTER	209
18	Emotional Support of the Pediatric Malignant Disease Treatment Team CHARLES R. KOCH	224
19	Psychosocial Interactions of the Dying Child, His Parents, and Health-Care Professionals GEORGE W. MARTEN AND ALVIN M. MAUER	235
20	Care for the Caregivers EDWARD H. PAKES	250
21	Children with Cancer in Group Therapy CLYDE H. FLANAGAN	266
22	The Child Life Worker's Contribution within an Oncology Setting CAROLYN A. LARSEN	293
23	The Child with Cancer Returns to School: Preparing the Teacher PATRICIA DESY-SPINETTA AND JOHN J. SPINETTA	303
24	Feeding the Dying Child—Ethical Decision-Making in a New Guise JAN VAN EYS	315

V. THE SUDDEN DEATH OF A CHILD — 329

25	Perspectives on Sudden Infant Death Syndrome RALPH A. FRANCIOSI	331
26	Predicting the Risk of Sudden Infant Death—Dilemma for the Practitioner SUSAN J. STANDFAST, BARBARA J. KUTER, SUSAN K. JEREB, AND DWIGHT T. JANERICH	335

Parental Mortification and Restitutional Efforts Upon the
Sudden Loss of a Child   WERNER I. HALPERN   *346*

VI. PARENTAL BEREAVEMENT AND GRIEF   355

28 Childhood Bereavement: Preventability and the Coping
Process   LARRY A. BUGEN   *357*

29 Mourning the Fatally Ill Child   EDWARD H. FUTTERMAN
AND IRWIN HOFFMAN   *366*

Index   *383*

Preface

Few children elude the protection of an environment established, with all good intentions, to support their physical and emotional survival until they reach an age when they are expected to suddenly become independent. Without much fear of contradiction, it can be said that children constitute an extremely large group of unenfranchised individuals. Control over their lives is exercised by paternalistic figures, either parents or caregiving surrogates; they are legally protected by the same laws that society has enacted to ensure the safety and well-being of all citizens. Before reaching a specified, arbitrarily set age, they are expected to respond to the commands and control of adults who make decisions of all sorts for them.

Nurturers of young people are committed to protecting them physically, to shielding them from physical and emotional trauma, to nourishing their body, mind, and spirit. In this sense, children are free to experience the magic days of childhood because the facts of their lives, their consummate control by others, relieve them of responsibilities. We can only hope that such relatively limitless "protective custody," within the context of death-related events, can yet be shown to be an imperative for them and appropriate for fostering their development to a stable and healthy maturity.

As this book surveys children's involvements in relation to death, it proposes two perspectives: the perspective of those who are life-threatened and dying and the perspective of those who will be survivors. Illness and death invade all lives as unwanted intruders and are most threatening when they affect those who have not yet fulfilled the promises offered by life itself. If caregivers and parents, as survivors, can offer children some comfort in their contemplation and interpretation of death's meaning, the structuring of children's lives will be made stronger and they will be prepared to share in the decisions ultimately to be made on their behalf.

Within the framework of their age-related ability to comprehend the world about them, children have a right to be made aware of the certainties of that world. For example, to the very young child, a parent's death can be understood only as the mysterious disappearance of someone who gave love and security, not as a true catastrophe that is poorly appreciated for the long range. For an older child, it can be misinterpreted as a punishment (or otherwise) and induce unremitting feelings of guilt for acts that most likely were never perpetrated. The contributors to this volume describe the impact of parental death and the process of adjusting, or not adjusting, as suggested by their clinical evaluations of the perceptions of children of all ages. Clearly, children's perceptions of both death and life are altered and shaped by the knowledge, experiences, attitudes, philosophies, and humanitarian instincts of those who provide them with the supportive care to which they are entitled.

Surviving losses of all natures is an inevitable task for everyone. Children who are physically healthy can learn adaptive mechanisms for coping with life stresses when the guidance offered to them is informed and sensitive. Children who are life-threatened can also be offered a supportive environment that will enhance the quality of their too-short lifespan by caregivers who can instill within its limited course both purpose and meaning. As some caregivers envision it, the environment in which a terminally ill child lives can be one that promotes growth to the very last, that permits uninterrupted attachments to loved ones to the very end. Ideally, such can be obtained by offering the highest possible quality care within the home as an alternative to institutional care, when resources permit. If therapeutic interventions require that the child be hospitalized, the institutional environment can be enriched by support given by and to caregiving staff. The usefulness and availability of the hospice approach for children can be contemplated but still has to reach general acceptance.

Parents and caregivers are both significant survivors when a child dies—as are a child's siblings and friends. These younger survivors represent another area of unenfranchisement of the child, where opportunities to mourn appropriately are limited. Such a bereavement seems almost unthinkable and is as unthinkable to the surviving adults as the concept of death is incomprehensible to a child. Yet parents must endure such losses and caregivers must suffer multiple losses if their professional role entails commitments to life-threatened children. As grief is worked through, adjustment to the loss can take place; and this is suggested by the contributors to the sections of this book that relate specifically to parents and caregivers. The grieving needs of siblings and young friends remain a major area for further research.

A primary purpose of this book is to offer a broad view of how we, as adults, can understand children's perceptions of death—those derived from fantasy and those derived from reality. Such knowledge can guide our actions and make us wiser and more effective caregivers for those who will die too young and for those who will survive them.

The Editors

· ACKNOWLEDGMENT ·

The editors wish to acknowledge the support and encouragement of The Foundation of Thanatology in the preparation of this volume. All royalties from the sale of this book are assigned to the Foundation of Thanatology, a tax exempt, not for profit, public scientific and educational foundation.

Thanatology, a new subspecialty of medicine, is involved in scientific and humanistic inquiries and the application of the knowledge derived therefrom to the subjects of the psychological aspects of dying; reactions to loss, death, and grief; and recovery from bereavement.

The Foundation of Thanatology is dedicated to advancing the cause of enlightened health care for the terminally ill patient and his family. The Foundation's orientation is a positive one based on the philosophy of fostering a more mature acceptance and understanding of death and the problems of grief and the more effective and humane management and treatment of the dying patient and his bereaved family members.

The Child and Death

· I ·
The Child's Perception of Death

· 1 ·
Changing Perspectives:
Preparing for Life or Death

ALBERT J. SOLNIT

Ironically, man's search for certainty is most discomforting when he is facing the end of life, especially from illness. The child who is dying of a fatal illness arouses in himself and his family, as well as in the physician and others who care for him, the most fearful and resentful awareness of uncertainty and loss. The insightful literature on the management of the dying child in the United States (Anthony 1940; Beecher 1962; Bozeman et al. 1955; Cannon 1942; Chodoff et al. 1964; Eissler 1955; Freud 1917; Green and Solnit 1964; Gunther 1949; E. Kris 1941a, 1941b, 1942, 1944, 1945; Lindemann 1944–1945; Mahler 1950; Nagy 1948, 1959; Nagy et al. 1960; Richmond and Waisman 1955; Richter 1957; Solnit and Green 1959; 1963; Toch et al. 1964; Vernick and Karon 1965; Wolf 1958) examines various facets of this tragic, inevitable experience of human destruction and loss—a life snuffed out before it has unfolded. Each author describes an approach that should enlist the active interest of other professionals in this area. Most of these studies have concentrated on the differing reactions of those who survive the dying patient, but a few have also approached the reactions of the patient himself (Eissler 1955; Gunther 1949; Nagy et al. 1960; Solnit and Green 1963).

Toward the end of the school-age period and just before puberty (ages 9–12) most children realize and can conceptualize the inevitability of death, not only for elderly people, but also for their parents and most painfully for themselves. Even with the support some children feel from religious or cultural beliefs and convictions, the concept that inevitably each of us has to die becomes a threatening, unpleasant, ineffable quality of the future. Most children are able to lay aside this oppressive sense of inevitability, denying the feel of it because it is so far off. More importantly, the juices of life and the joy of living help to block out the fearful, painful conviction about death. Normatively, with the satisfactions of life, and increasing competence, the inevitability of death pales and fades into a distant future as though it were an interesting science fiction.

When a child suffers from a chronic life-threatening illness, which in the recent past has been viewed as fatal, the family and the child often find themselves in uncharted waters (Green 1980). Children suffering from leukemia, lymphomas, sarcomas, and other malignancies, as well as certain inborn metabolic disorders (e.g., cystic fibrosis), are often in a situation in which the adults, parents, and professionals cannot provide firm guidance based on confident expectations. The adults and the children do not know whether to prepare for life or for death.

Developmental Concepts and Perspectives

In order to describe a child's susceptibility to the fear of dying, it is necessary to understand those developmental steps and perspectives that lead to the cognitive and emotional capacities and tolerances necessary to be able to conceptualize death as an inevitable human experience and the end of human experience. The concept of death is understood by most children just before puberty or at the beginning of puberty (Anthony 1940; Nagy 1948). At that time, the totality of his experiences, emotional tolerances, intellectual development, and sense of time, in retrospect and projected into the future, enable the child to conceptualize the implications of inevitability in a number of ways. Just as he finally is able to recognize the inevitability that there is a beginning to life and that certain natal physical characteristics, such as the sexual differences, will persist, the child finally also becomes aware of the inevitability that everyone will eventually die. This awareness of inevitability as a real—not imagined—concept is accompanied by other evidences of perceptual and intellectual development. For example, it is toward the end of latency, nine to eleven years, that the fullest awareness of constancy in size, texture, and weight of inanimate objects develops even when the object is absent.

Before this crystallization there are many partial concepts that the child has about death. The child under the age of three or four equates death with the absence of the human love object on whom he depends. The four- and five-year-old child is curious about burial, about the characterizations of dead animals and flowers, and about the accidental features of death. A clear example of this was recently told to me by Dr. Raymond Duff, an esteemed colleague and collaborator. "Recently, a four-year-old boy said, 'If you run in the street, my Mom says you might die. If you are dead, they put you in a big box and they put the big box in a big hole in the ground. And they put dirt over it. And you stay there!'" Thus, the preschool child experiences the fear of dying as a loss of the love and attention necessary for feeling cared for physically and emotionally. When the young child feels furious and frustrated by the limiting, prohibiting, or punishing powerful adult, this developmental experience often becomes associated with the child's wish that the loved adults would go away and never return. It is in this stage of development that the child experiences wishes and thoughts as magically potent. To wish or want strongly carries with it the risk and probability that the thought is father to the act. The child is not yet aware, as the older individual painfully learns, that there are many intermediate steps between a wish or thought and a thought-directed act.

For the child between the ages of five and nine years death is personified. The school-aged child postpones his direct curiosity and expresses through sublimated activities his curiosity about and fear of dying in a superstitious and investigative manner. For example, he jokingly holds his breath when he passes a cemetery in order not to be "spooked." He extends his scientific curiosity to the differences between organic and inorganic substances, and he classifies varieties of life as he normatively equips himself to face the future with hope rather than fear.

In the school-aged child (5–12 years of age), there is sufficient experience and maturation to place a psychological distance between magical and logical thinking. This allows the child to comprehend the distinctions between death and absence, between dying and going away, and to have an effective awareness of the difference between memory and fantasy. In this way, the school-aged child gradually acquires the basis for conceptualizing the inevitability of death as the end of the human experience. This notion probably receives a significant impetus from the dawning awareness that one is preparing for the unknowns of adolescence with its powerful biological drives. There is a reluctant realization that the relative stability of these middle years of childhood is now being replaced by the introduction to adulthood, the end of which is death. The upsurging quality of the sexual and aggressive drives in early adolescence is often experienced as magically powerful and may precipitate a regression to a belief in the magic of thoughts and wishes. If such a regression persists, the adolescent's development may be seriously blocked. At such times in early adolescence it is not uncommon to see depressed teenagers who not only are preoccupied with death as it is reported daily but also find it difficult to deny the sad closeness they feel to natural or man-made catastrophes.

Although this presentation is intended to describe the more usual situation, generalizations have their limitations when one is attempting to deal with highly individualized responses. The spectrum of reactions is understandably a broad one. For instance, Noshpitz (1960) has pointed out that the disturbed adolescent may demonstrate a complete denial and defiance of dying even when well aware of this possibility. Other adolescents with severe ulcerative colitis, recurrent diabetic coma, or anorexia nervosa have seemed to us to feel committed to dying. Such children appear to derive from this a feeling of power, and they resist, often in a passive manner, the physician's efforts to reverse this commitment.

The Child with a Fatal Illness

Hence, there is a developmental background against which we can focus on the reactions of adults and children to a child who is dying. Few useful observations are available in relation to acute deaths, though it is evident that the young child expresses his wish to be with the parental figure (to feel loved) and to avoid pain. When death comes acutely, the child's awareness is often obtunded because of delirium, stupor, or coma.

In the more gradual dying experience there is often evidence of depression, withdrawal, fearfulness, and apprehension. Although most children with a fatal illness do not directly ask if they are going to die, a few over the age of four or five years do ask such a question. In these cases, the parents (and physicians and nurses) may have their own reactions to and preferences in how to meet the child's curiosity (Solnit and Green 1959). However, such a question requires understanding before an appropriate answer is given. The child's own curiosity and capacity to conceptualize, as well as his familial and religious upbringing, are often expressed in this way. When such questions are raised, the physician can ask what the child means by dying and try to find out the meaning of the question and how to answer it usefully. It is usually not appropriate to answer the child's question in the affirmative without a prior discussion and agreement with the parents about how to answer the question usefully and with due respect for the parents' attitudes and preferences. They may wish to be the ones who answer this question; they may wish to have help in answering such questions; or they may prefer that the question be unanswered. Child and parents, as well as siblings, will be able to cope better with loss of health and life when family cohesion and integrity are strengthened and effective. Generally, the child is expressing three fundamental concerns by his behavior, by direct questions, and by questions expressed indirectly:

1. Will you make me feel all right? (Pain)
2. Am I safe? (Anxiety about body and life)
3. Will my mother or father stay with me? (Loneliness, Aloneness, Depression, Hopelessness, Helplessness)

Although systematic psychological studies of children suffering from fatal, terminal illness are lacking, it is useful to assume that children invariably sense at a significant level of awareness what is happening to them. They sense by "reading" faces and gestures, by feeling tensions and concerns, often quite accurately. The same is true even when a deliberate attempt is made to shield them from tragic, frightening, or complicated family affairs, including their own fatal illness.

Although each person and each group will experience dying in terms of their expectations and fears from the past, and in terms of preparing for what will happen next, the irreducible, unavoidable anguish of dying is that which derives from loneliness. Even the helplessness that characterizes the inevitability of dying is viewed as intolerable and overwhelming because no one can be with the dying person to the last. Dying can be imagined; death is unimaginable.

The intolerance and fear of such loneliness is often expressed according to the child's developmental resources (i.e., movement, talking, thinking, and remembering). The child's chaotic reactions are intertwined with the familial and cultural supports and rituals that are evoked in these circumstances.

As adults, mature and capable, we are a part of our legacy that more or less transforms chaos into order in a particular or patterned way, reducing what is intolerable to problem units of experience that are manageable. This is facilitated by classifying our perceptions and making choices between "either this or that." There is no either/or to the inevitability of dying and death for all animals, including man. But the reduction of the complexity of human dying to first steps and to a hierarchy of more and less important issues, personal and societal, enables each of us to deny what we cannot encompass, the whole of the journey to death. We consider or experience one part of it or another but almost never all at the same time.

Such a human defense, as either/or (A. Kris 1977), i.e., the defensiveness of classification, also leads us toward simplifications that become burdens. For example, there is the implication that either all children dying of leukemia should be told about their illness, its treatment, and the outcome probabilities or none should; or each parent of a dying child should be referred for psychotherapy that will be supportive and that will enable him or her to fully mourn the child who will die; or psychotherapy is contraindicated.

These simplifications—either do this or do that—are understandable, but, in fact, they tend to produce the dehumanization they were designed to prevent and overcome. Also, such an approach tends to interfere with each family's being able, according to their life style and value preferences, to use their preferred ways of deciding how to understand the "fatal" condition and to make choices about treatment when there are alternatives available.

For the dying child, the felt helplessness of his parents can, and often does, magnify the terror he feels from the pain, malaise, and sadness of the adults and the loneliness of being in hospital or the loneliness that often stems from the walled-off, warded-off feelings of his parents and siblings. There are three major tasks confronting the dying child and his family. These three tasks can be viewed as indices of how the medical, nursing, and allied professions are functioning in helpful or in nonhelpful ways. These three tasks are the following:

1. For parents and for their sick or dying child to recognize what the malady is in terms of their fears and wishes. These fears and wishes are usually communicated by the substance and timing of the questions raised or fears expressed. Such questions include how certain or uncertain the outcome of the illness and treatment is and what steps should be taken to further understand the nature of the threatening condition. The child's developmental capacities should be taken into account in anticipating what questions will be raised and in fitting the level of language and of abstract thought to the child's cognitive and emotional capacities. In a sense this is a variation of informed consent from parents and of developmentally appropriate assent from children in providing them with information and understanding about the child's illness.

2. For parents and their child to know what treatment or treatments are available, i.e., which choices are specifically indicated and which are optional. The most useful information should be available about the effects of these treatments in regard to primary aims of eradicating, halting, and relieving the pain and discomfort of the illness; and the secondary aims of minimizing the discomfort, weakening, or/and disfigurement caused by the illness and the primary effects of treatment.

3. To enable the parents to mobilize their resources and understand their choices in order to make those decisions they may wish to make about treatment and care of the child; to delegate other decisions to doctors or others if they so choose; and to plan for themselves and other members of the family in a manner that is appropriate and proportionate to their life experiences and value preferences (Duff and Campbell 1980).

Throughout, ambiguities, especially about preparing to die or preparing to live, will pose a challenge to those in the healing arts and to the child and his family. Presumptively, the least harmful attitude for those providing the medical care is that of cautious, reserved optimism (Tiger 1979). Such optimism is as realistic as restrained pessimism, since each child is unique and not to be treated as a statistical mean. This attitude acknowledges that our precision in making forecasts is limited. It also recognizes that where such limitations are in force, the hopes for and commitments to a life worth living can sensibly be given the edge, the weight of a feather on the side of optimism. Any more than a feather's weight would be like a promise; broken promises are damaging and distressing. This slight emphasis also supports the continuing interest and concern of professionals in the care of their patients, enabling patients to feel the psychological presence of caregivers in more supportive ways. Feeling hopeless or resigned before it is completely clear that there is no hope is usually perceived by patients and their parents as withdrawal, apathy, or insensitivity.

Is such an approach an either/or trap, one that comforts those who need it least (doctors, nurses, et al.) and deprives those, the child and his parents, who need it most, of an uncertainty, an ambiguity that is painful but realistic? Can one not know and be neither optimistic nor pessimistic? Will a preference for a slight optimism corrupt those who should lead with knowledge and humility, disillusioning the patient and his parents?

We all wish for certainty, knowing it is rare. When certainty is apparent, most frequently there is cynical disillusionment when it turns out not to be so. We are struggling with the painful dilemma that knowledge advances slowly, piece by piece, and our ability to put it to use is hampered and set back because all of us want new partial truths to be whole and absolute. This dilemma is increasingly difficult to avoid as our understanding about chronic and fatal illness in childhood is uncovered at what seems to be a slow pace, but by comparison to 40 years ago at a breakneck pace. How shall we guide ourselves when parents want to know if the pain and destructive effects of a new treatment, and the repetition of illness and treatment, are worth the candle for a child who is suffering from an acute lymphoblastic or myeloblastic leukemia, a child with no kidney function left, a child with an inborn error of metabolism or a congenital or acquired immunological deficiency? How shall we assist parents who are confronted with crises that threaten the child's life over and over and with their limited ability to provide hour-to-hour care?

In fact, psychoanalytic knowledge and its limitations have strongly suggested that such decision-making rest with the parents as we provide them with as much information and support as we can. On the other hand, parents may prefer to delegate the decision to clinical experts or the courts. We have suggested the following questions as guidelines to indicate the limits of parental autonomy in making such decisions:

1. Do medical experts agree that the treatment is nonexperimental and appropriate for the child?
2. Will the denial of treatment result in an early death?
3. Is the anticipated result of treatment what society would want for every child? Will the treatment lead to a life worth living, according to the family's values and in agreement with societal consensus (Goldstein et al. 1979)?

Parents who would not allow such a treatment when all three questions are answered affirmatively have justified intervention by the courts in order that such treatment can be provided under the authority of the state before the child is returned to his parents. Conversely, if any one of the three questions cannot be answered in the affirmative, there would be no grounds on which to interfere with the parents' preferences regarding treatment choice or the choice of no treatment. It is the responsibility of professionals to help parents know what their choices are and to support the parent and child in carrying out appropriate decisions about the choices they make (Duff and Campbell 1979; Schowalter et al. 1973; Lewis and Lewis 1979).

If a child suffers from a chronic illness that would constitute a threat to life if untreated, e.g., juvenile diabetes mellitus or severe repeated grand mal epilepsy, the parents' refusal or inability to provide the daily care and treatment that are necessary should also require court intervention to protect the child from being physically damaged.

With these three guidelines, the search for certainty is limited, and coping with uncertainty in regard to invariably fatal conditions (e.g., malignancy, no kidney function, an urgent need for a blood transfusion as in aplastic anemia) can be approached rationally. Statistical probabilities shift too rapidly and are too limited for guidance in the individual case to take the rights of parents and their children away with regard to living or dying unless all three guidelines are satisfied.

These issues are also raised to emphasize how complex the decision-making process is with regard to the newer treatments—radiological, surgical, and chemical. We must be prepared to accept our limitations in making predictions. This should also encourage us to share our knowledge with parents and to provide support for them as they participate in making decisions about treatment and treatment choices or delegate to us more or less of the responsibility for decisions to treat. In this formulation it is assumed that treatment ranges from specific therapy that will eradicate and cure, with or without toxic and other untoward side effects, to nonspecific therapy that provides appropriate symptomatic relief or as much freedom from pain, discomfort, and fear as possible. It is in this sense that choices of therapy can be presented for decisions by parents, by older adolescent patients, or when delegated, by the physician.

With such uncertainty and with increasing opportunities for parents and children to make choices or share in making them, how will they know what to expect? How will they know whether to prepare for dying or for a life worth living?

Perhaps we can stretch the human capacity to tolerate not knowing if we are aware of what to do about it and how to do it. Physical pain, loneliness, helplessness, and anxiety are still basic discomforts, each of which threatens to exceed the child's tolerances in damaging ways. Symptomatic relief is crucial. Enabling the patient and parents to know, at the level they want to know, can be relieving. Forming alliances with the children and their parents that enable them to have an active role in the decisions about diagnostic and therapeutic procedures, at the same time as the clinical expert is respectful of their preferences for denial, can be supportive (Duff and Campbell 1973). Enabling parents to meet and help each other in group therapy and group discussions has been reported as helpful (Adams 1978; Gilder et al. 1978). Coping with similar fears and uncertainties, these parents whose children are involved in similar painful and distressing treatments and uncertainties share the same hopes that their children, like Lazarus, will return to the living. However, such group experiences are not useful to everyone. They should be viewed as an option for parents to consider and to accept or reject as a preferred pathway of assistance.

Above all, the mantle that physicians have been invited to wear for so many years must be resisted and modified, especially those coverings that suggest fantasies of omniscience and omnipotence. Competence, compassion, and continuity of care are the key requirements for health professionals who are working together as a team and together with seriously ill children and their parents who are facing an uncertain outcome for the child. These three Cs will be eroded if certain principles are not followed. The first principle is that one member of the health team be the physician of record (Duff 1979), the one who provides the continuity and orchestrates the medical care so that competence is provided with compassion; the second principle is that the limitations of our knowledge, technology, and inner resources (Schowalter 1978) be recognized when we are working with children who have what may be a fatal disease. As one colleague (McCollum 1978) put it:

> Passing through a hospital playroom, a staff social worker paused near Dana, who, when he was five, had become blind from an inoperable brain tumor. Feeling a surge of sadness about this little boy's predicament, wishing to reach out and offer comfort, the social worker nonetheless hesitated awkwardly—what can you say to such a child? How can you talk to him?
> Sensing her nearness, Dana turned toward her and held out his hand. "Would

you help me go across the room to where the blocks are, please. I can't see, you know. I don't want to bump into something." His quiet explanation about his condition made possible a comfortable and spontaneous conversation. Child and social worker found their way across the room together, talking about the block building that Dana was planning (McCollum 1975).

I was that social worker. And late that afternoon, my family came home to find me seasoning the supper casserole with tears—tears shed for Dana. . . .

A clinical social worker becomes a finely tuned instrument—a receptive instrument that registers and resonates with nuances of her client's feelings. We call it empathy, without which there can be little, if any, therapeutic gain. At times, however, empathy can merge into identification with patient or client. When that occurs, the sense of separateness needed for a therapeutic perspective is lost. The client may be less effectively served, and the clinician may feel unduly burdened.

I experienced just such a loss of boundaries in my pediatric work. During prior years in child guidance settings I had been able fully to empathize with anguished parents of children lost in an autistic world, or severely brain damaged. But I never felt vulnerable. I knew that my own children were not congenitally brain damaged or psychotic or even emotionally troubled beyond what is normally expectable as development proceeds. In pediatrics, the boundaries between the patients' parents and myself became less clear. How could I assure myself that my children might not succumb to leukemia or nephrosis or some other deadly threat? I had, in fact, lost one child in his eighth month of intrauterine life. The grief of parents I counseled re-awakened my own mourning for that baby, and confronted me with the vulnerability of my two healthy children.

Again and again I resonated with the protest, the terror, the profound sadness of dying children and their families. So much energy was needed to contain and resolve those feelings that I became less available emotionally to my own family. After six years, it was clearly time to leave the medical center.

I left, but carried with me much guilt about abandoning such needful people, and I felt a loss of self-regard. Surely a competent, experienced professional should be able to cope with any challenge!

So it then seemed, [this colleague later reflected]. But in time this expectation came to seem tinged with grandiosity. Caretakers of the dying need to find channels through which support from colleagues, supervisors or consultants can flow. But even then, they must at times gain some distance from such painful, taxing work. The patients' needs are still served, although more obliquely, by the clinician's retreat to the laboratory, the auditorium, the library, even to the publisher!

It requires courage and healthy humility to acknowledge and accept the limitations that each of us has and shares with others. In fact, those who go beyond the limits of their own inner resources often become those who have invested in either/or approaches, insisting on unreal certainties that protect the caregiver but often expose the sick child and parents to oversimplifications, categorical imperatives, and formulae that tend to dehumanize the decisions and care for such children.

As we have become more familiar with openness toward dying, there have been many efforts to reduce the dehumanizing aspects of multiple specialists involved in treating children with a fatal disease. Once the treatment can be carried out on an ambulatory basis, for example, families can be given their choice of where their child will die, in hospital or at home. Candor and tact about diagnosis, prognosis, and treatment within the limits of our knowledge often foster innovation by parents and health professionals, and hence, more home care may be desirable and feasible. In a remarkable study (Fortunato and Komp 1979), it was demonstrated that children who died at home could receive the medical help and support they needed, that the families had made this choice freely rather than hospitalize their dying children, and that those 13 of the 27 who died at home (median age, 5 years 8 months) had survived on the average of 32 months as compared to the 18 months of the 14 who died in hospital (median age, 5½ years) and who were comparable in terms of illness, treatment, and distance from the hospital. They conclude, "The home environment can contribute much to the supportive care and comfort of a dying child. The long period of time from diagnosis to death in *all* can permit the family with the proper guidance to develop a more complete acceptance of the child's death."

Conclusion

This paper has examined the developmental challenges and risks for parents and siblings and the role and limitations of health professionals, when a child is under treatment for a disease that poses a serious, uncertain threat to life. The examination of these situations, in light of comparatively rapid changes in our knowledge of life and death issues for such children, points to the complications that arise when certainty is insisted upon by parents and by those who provide professional care and guidance for the sick child and his family. These complications deserve systematic study as a first step toward reducing and preventing them, as well as toward a better grasp of the painful question—preparing for life or death?

REFERENCES

Adams, Margaret. 1978. "Helping the Parents of Children with Malignancy." *Journal of Pediatrics* 93(5):734–38.

Anthony, S. 1940. *The Child's Discovery of Death.* New York: Harcourt Brace.

Beecher, H. K. 1962. "Nonspecific Forces Surrounding Disease and the Treatment of Disease." *Journal of the American Medical Association* 179:437.

Bozeman, M. D., C. E. Orbach, and A. M. Sutherland. 1955. "Psychological Impact of Cancer and Its Treatment. III. The Adaptation of Mothers to the Threatened Loss of Their Children Through Leukemia. Part I." *Cancer* 8:1.

Cannon, W. B. 1942. "Voodoo Death." *American Anthropolology* 44:169.

Chodoff, P., B. Friedman, and D. A. Hamburg. 1964. "Stress Defenses and Coping Behavior: Observations in Parents of Children with Malignant Disease." *Journal of the American Psychiatric Association* (Feb.), 743.

Duff, R. S. and A. G. M. Campbell. 1973. "Moral and Ethical Dilemmas in the Special-care Nursery." *New England Journal of Medicine* 289:390–94.

Duff, R. S. and A. G. M. Campbell. 1979. "Social Perspectives on Medical Decisions Relating to Life and Death." In J. Ladd, ed., *Ethical Issues Relating to Life and Death,* New York, Oxford University Press.

Duff, R. S. and A. G. M. Campbell. 1980. "Moral and Ethical Dilemmas: Seven Years Into the Debate About Human Ambiguity." *Annals, AAPSS* (Jan.), 19–28.

Duff, R. S. 1979. "Guidelines for Deciding Care of Critically Ill or Dying Patients." *Pediatrics* (July) 64 (1):17–23.

Eissler, K. R. 1955. *The Psychiatrist and the Dying Patient.* New York: International Universities Press, p. 338.

Fortunato, R. and D. Komp. 1979. "An Evaluation of Death at Home for Children With Acute Lymphoblastic Leukemia." *Virginia Medical Monthly* No. 106:124.

Freud, S. 1917. *Mourning and Melancholia.* Standard Edition, 14, 237. London: Hogarth Press and Institute of Psychoanalysis, 1957.

Gilder, R., P. R. Buschman, A. L. Sitarz, and J. A. Wolff. 1978. "Group Therapy with Parents of Children with Leukemia." *American Journal of Psychotherapy* (April) 32:276–87.

Goldstein, J., A. Freud, and A. J. Solnit. 1979. *Before the Best Interests of the Child* (Chapter 6). New York: Free Press (Macmillan).

Green, M. 1980. "The 'Vulnerable Child': Intimations of Mortality." *Pediatrics* (May) 65(5).

Green, M. and A. J. Solnit. 1964. "Reactions to the Threatened Loss of a Child: A Vulnerable Child Syndrome." *Pediatrics* 34:58.

Gunther, J. 1949. *Death Be Not Proud.* New York: Harper & Brothers, Pyramid Books, 1957.

Kris, E. 1941a. "Morale In Germany." *American Journal of Sociology* 47:452.

—— 1941b. "The 'Danger' of Propaganda." *American Image* 2(1):3.

—— 1942. "Mass Communication Under Totalitarian Governments." In D. Waples, ed., *Print, Film and Radio in a Democracy.* Chicago: University of Chicago Press.

—— 1944. "Danger and Morale." *American Journal of Orthopsychiatry* 14:147.

—— 1945. "Public Opinion and World Order." In G. Murphy, ed., *Human Nature and Enduring Peace,* p. 402. Boston: Houghton Mifflin.

Kris, A. 1977. "Either Or." *The Psychoanalytic Study of the Child* Vol. 32. New Haven, Conn.: Yale University Press.

Lewis, M. and D. Lewis. 1979. "Death and Dying in Children and their Families." *Archives of the Foundation of Thanatology* 7:9.

Lindemann, E. 1944–1945. "Symptomatology and Management of Acute Grief." *American Journal of Psychiatry* 101:141.

Mahler, M. 1950. *Helping Children to Accept Death.* New York: Child Study Association of America.

McCollum, A. 1978. *Coping with Prolonged Health Impairment in Your Child.* Boston: Little, Brown & Co.

—— 1975. Communication by Audrey McCollum, M. S., to the Association of Pediatric Social Workers in Oncology. December 1978.

Nagy, M. H. 1948. "The Child's Theories Concerning Death." *Journal of Genetic Psychology* 73:3.

—— (1959). "The Child's View of Death." In H. Feifel, ed., *The Meaning of Death.* New York: McGraw-Hill.

—— J. M. Natterson, and A. G. Knudson, Jr. 1960. "Observations Concerning Fear of Death in Fatally Ill Children and their Mothers." *Psychosomatic Medicine* 22:456.

Noshpitz, J. D. 1960. "Discussion of: Psychology of Physical Illness" by S. Little. *Pediatric Clinics of North America* 7:85–96.

Richmond, J. B. and H. A. Waisman. 1955. "Psychologic Aspects of Management of Children with Malignant Disease." *American Journal of Diseases of Children* 89:42.

Richter, C. P. 1957. "On the Phenomenon of Sudden Deaths in Animals and Men." *Psychosomatic Medicine* 19:191.

Schowalter, J. 1978. "The Reactions of Caregivers Dealing With Fatally Ill Children and Their Families." In O. J. Sahler, ed., *The Child and Death,* pp. 123–138. St. Louis: C. V. Mosby.

—— J. B. Ferholt, and N. M. Mann. 1973. "The Adolescent Patients' Decision to Die." *Pediatrics* 51:97–103.

Solnit, A. J. and M. Green. 1959. "Psychologic Considerations in the Management of Deaths on Pediatric Hospital Services. I. The Doctor and the Child's Family." *Pediatrics* 24:106.
—— 1963. "Pediatric Management of the Dying Child. II. A Study of the Child's Reaction to the Fear of Dying. In: *Modern Perspectives in Child Development*, p. 217. New York: International Universities Press.
Tiger, L. 1979. *The Biology of Hope*. New York: Simon & Shuster.
Toch, R. et al. 1964. "Management of the Child With a Fatal Disease." *Clinical Pediatrics* 3:418.
Vernick, J. and M. Karon. 1965. "Who's Afraid of Death on a Leukemia Ward?" *American Journal of Diseases of Childhood* 109:393.
Wolf, A. W. M. 1958. "Helping Your Child to Understand Death." New York: Child Study Association of America.

· 2 ·
Death and the Child

Max M. Stern

Thanatology, the science of the human response to death, has two distinct aspects: a more general one dealing with the effect of man's awareness of the existence of death on his behavior and one dealing with the behavior of a dying individual. Yet to understand the latter requires some knowledge of man's general response to the inevitable end of life. This paper is specially devoted to the influence of an insight into the existence of death on the child's mental development.

There is widespread belief that children are not concerned with death. Freud expressed this belief when he wrote in *The Interpretation of Dreams* (1900), "The fear of death has no meaning to a child . . . . children know nothing of the horrors of corruption, of freezing in the ice cold grave, of the terrors of eternal nothingness" (p. 254) and in 1926 (p. 130) ". . . nothing resembling death can ever have been experienced; or if it has, as in fainting, it has left no observable traces behind."

During the last decades, child psychology has proved this opinion to be a fallacy. Even before this, however, already in 1912, Hugh-Hellmuth pointed to children's concern about death. Child psychologists, among them Anthony (1940), Barnes (1964), Chadwick (1929), A. Freud (1960), Furman (1964), and McDonald (1964), have indicated that the child at the age of two or three starts to have some idea of death and that his concern about death is most often tied to the death of relatives or of animals.

What does the child know about death? From where does this knowledge come? What is the impact of his knowledge on the child's development and on the attitude of the adult toward death?

All knowledge originates in experience whether one's own experience or that won from empathy with other objects, even animals. In several papers (Stern 1951, 1961, 1968a, 1968b), I have maintained that in the first year of life, in the so-called maturational crises, every child goes through experiences of dying; that these experiences have a decisive influence on the development of the human mind; and that failure of adaptation to them results in neurosis. On the basis of my clinical experience, I have maintained that better understanding of the process of adaptation to these experiences may help to prevent this failure or, in case of an outcome of neurosis, may provide improvement of the therapeutic method used to correct such a failure.

To speak of adaptation to death is in itself a contradiction. Adaptation refers to changes in the interaction between a subject and an object for the purpose of self-preservation. In the instance of man neither the object, the fact of death, nor the human subject can be changed so that unlimited self-preservation would be accomplished. Adaptation to death has an antithetical aspect. It demands awareness of death on the one hand and denial of death on the other. While unlimited denial would endanger existence, unlimited awareness of death would paralyze any activity and thus would be just as harmful to self-preservation. Adaptation to death can refer only to a behavior that achieves optimal ability for preservation. In order to achieve a modicum of self-preservation, we need disavowal of death as well as awareness.

Maturational Crises

At the root of man's development is his immaturity at birth. According to zoologists, man is a prematurely born animal (Portmann 1956). In his first year, development and maturation interact. The latter occurs in dysjunctive hormonal and neuronal jumps that give rise to maturational crises, as observed by Spitz and Cobliner (1965), Emde et al. (1976), and Tennes and others

(1972). These are the postnatal crises that occur from two months to the fifth month and the eight months' crisis, usually called stranger anxiety.

The postnatal crises seem to originate in lack of adaptation to the sudden transition of the 2- to 4-hour sleep pattern to the 8-hour pattern, which produces a biotraumatic situation during sleep, that is, in applying Selye's concepts (1950) a process of dying and defense against it.

The eight months' crisis, called by Emde et al. (1976) the "eight month distress," originates in the uneven maturation of the memory and with it the anticipatory process. In this crisis, the child starts to respond to a stranger with anxiety: after a short exploration of his appearance the child turns away and cries. It is characterized by the pavor nocturnus attacks that make their first appearance at that period and in which the sleep is interrupted by intense terror personified by an attacking monster. It looks as if the sudden appearance of a stranger reactivates in the child's mind the sudden intrusion of the threatening objects into sleep. Through the maturation of memory and the anticipatory process, the experiences of that period have a lasting impact. This crisis must be regarded as decisive for the formation of neurosis or health (of course, in addition to other factors such as constitution and incidental events).

Clinical observation has shown that the child conceives of death as a repetition of the experience of pavor nocturnus. Most child observers stress that what the child is afraid of in fear of death "is not simply death"; it is fear of a hostile outsider, a burglar breaking into the house at night and killing the child while asleep (Nagy 1959). Children describe death in terms of pavor nocturnus, of paralysis of motility—"You cannot get up [and move] when you want to" (Barnes 1964); of insensitivity;—"you feel like a piece of wood"; of inability to breathe, to cry, and yell (Anthony 1940, Chadwick 1929, Kastenbaum 1959). Death is personified as a ghost, a skeleton, or a black angel coming at night and killing. The child's fear of a burglar attacking at night is a common effect of pavor nocturnus. Not only children but also adults conceive the state of death as being in a nightmare.

Patients have remarked: "Death is being dead and not dead.

... It is not being able to breathe, to talk, but you still can feel ... you can't do anything, you are paralyzed. I keep telling myself it is nothingness, but it doesn't help. I constantly dream of dying by suffocation, by suffocating under water. Perhaps my indecision comes from that." Even Freud reflects the same projection when he describes "freezing in the ice cold grave" (1900:254) as an expression of the fear of death. Hamlet describes his fear of death: "To die, to sleep; to sleep: perchance to dream: ay, there's the rub, *for in that sleep of death what dreams may come when we have shuffled off this mortal coil this gives us pause*" (Shakespeare 1602:73).

The first year pavor nocturnus attacks are signs and effects of the dysjunctive maturation of the mental apparatus at that period; the maturation of mental activity precedes the maturation of the sexual apparatus. The immaturity of the latter prevents the completion of its operation, which means biotrauma. That this occurrence reaches the quality of a lasting trauma stems from the activity of memory and anticipation. The pavor nocturnus attacks reappear later in dreams and in symptoms that are attempts at reparative mastery.

In the pavor nocturnus of adults, the infantile biotrauma reaches, like a fossil from the archaic past, into the individual's present. That later pavor nocturnus repeats early biotraumatic situations is confirmed by the phenomena of blank hallucinations such as the Isakower phenomenon (Stern 1961).

The behavior of the parental figures, especially of the mother, at this period is of great importance for the healthy development of the child. In his predicament, the child flees to her for protection against the danger. Her task is not only to relieve the child's anxiety. Like any strong emotion, the fright instigates premature sexual excitation that has to be gratified to a certain extent by her. Any inadequacy in her behavior, be it excessive frustration or excessive gratification or the acting out of the hostility of a frightened immature individual, is fateful for the child's further development. A healthy attitude fosters both requirements for mastery: acceptance and disavowal of the horrifying experience.

Disavowal

Pavor nocturnus is not only the precursor and prototype of the experience of dying; it is also the prototype of its disavowal: after having gone through the terror of dying, the child awakens back to life. This reversal is reflected in fairy tales, which tell about being lost in the wild wood, being eaten by a witch or a wolf, but which always end with the significant notion "And from now on they lived happily ever after." A similar turn appears in the myths of a child being abandoned in a box by the bad parents but saved by a good mother, as occurs in the myths of Moses and Oedipus.

The Biology of Disavowal

Disavowal or negative hallucination seems to be, like all hallucinations, an innate response: its purpose is to prolong life. It appears as retrograde amnesia.

According to Heim (1891) and Jaspers (1963) people who have gone through near death experiences report about two contradictory attitudes: one, of biotrauma consisting of a paralysis of motility and sensorium and two, of pleasant hallucinations that deny the fatal reality. A man who had fallen from a high rock reports:

> "A sudden peace flooded me like magnificent music. I floated quietly and tranquilly among small rosy clouds, enveloped in a marvelous blue sky," (Heim 1891, as quoted in Jaspers 1963:368) or a seriously wounded officer reports: "I lost all power of movement when I was hit by the bullet, but I felt quite comfortable and well"; the running blood gave me the feeling of a warm bath" (Jaspers 1963:369).

Similar descriptions are found in other publications, for example, in Pfister's paper (1930): ("Shock Thought and Shock Phantasies in Imminent Danger of Death.")

The experience of the child in acute traumatic situations is the prototype for man's response to the fact of the inevitable end. The threat on the one hand and disavowal on the other induce restless activity, an existential biodefensive agitation, fostered by the existential depression resulting as a response to the inevitability of death.

Disavowal is characteristic of children's behavior. In spite of the fact that childhood is a period of biotraumatic dependency, children are usually elated, jumping, dancing, playing, and disavowing this predicament. That childhood is regarded by adults as the lost paradise also originates in this disavowal.

The infantile dependence is finally dissolved by the separation individuation in adolescence. In cases of excessive biotraumata this development fails. The consequence is neurosis—a perpetuation of the infantile dependency. There is a clinging to infantile ways of defense against biotraumata, to protection by the omnipotent parents. The overpowering need for protection unconsciously assigns to every object the role of a parental figure. Thus, the infantile anxiety wishes and defenses are "acted out" in every object relation. In his object relations the neurotic uses his fixation to symbiotic dependency, which in infancy protected against trauma, to ward off fear of the inevitable final trauma. The amalgamation of the past's obsolete anxieties with the fear of the inevitable final trauma fosters the perpetuation of the impact of early conflicts and reinforces the clinging to infantile dependency.

This short study of the biological background of psychic adaptation to death may serve as a framework for prevention of neurosis and for its therapy. The insight that failures in the management of the interaction between mother and child in the crucial period at the end of the first year might indicate behavior that prevents the misdevelopment called neurosis.

During treatment, the patient should become aware of his clinging to infantile dependency, as well as of its inadequacy. This occurs through free association, including dreams. They reactivate the biotraumatic past that leads, on the one hand, to an adult's awareness of the obsoleteness of his infantile fears and defensive measures. On the other hand, it will lead to an establishment of a healthy disavowal of the inevitable and consistent threat of death.

REFERENCES

Anthony, S. 1940. *The Child's Discovery of Death: A Study in Psychology.* New York: Harcourt, Brace.

Barnes, M. J. 1964. "Reactions to the Death of a Mother." *Psychoanalytic Study of the Child* 19:334–57.

Chadwick, M. 1929. "Notes Upon the Fear of Death." *International Journal of Psycho-Analysis* 10:321–34.

Emde, R. N., T. J. Gaensbauer, and R. J. Harmon. 1976. "Emotional Expression in Infancy: A Biobehavioral Study." *Psychological Issues,* Monograph No. 37. New York: International Universities Press.

Freud, A. 1960. "Discussion of Dr. John Bowlby's Paper." *Psychoanalytic Study of the Child* 15:53–62.

Freud, S. 1900. "The Interpretation of Dreams." *Standard Edition,* 4/5. London: Hogarth Press, 1953.

Freud, S. 1926. "Inhibitions, Symptoms and Anxiety." *Standard Edition,* 20:87–172. London: Hogarth Press, 1959.

Furman, R. A. 1964. "Death and the Young Child: Some Preliminary Considerations." And "Death of a Six-Year-Old's Mother During His Analysis." *Psychoanalytic Study of the Child* 19:321–33, 377–97.

Heim, A. 1891. "Notizen über den Tod durch den Absturz." *Jahrbuch des Schweiz.* Bern: Alpen-Klubs 1892, pp. 327–37.

Hugh-Hellmuth, H. v. 1912. "The Child's Concept of Death" (translated from German by A. O. Kris) *Psychoanalytic Quarterly* 34:499–516, 1965.

Jaspers, K. 1963. *General Psychopathology* (translated from German by J. Hoenig and M. W. Hamilton). Chicago: University of Chicago Press.

Kastenbaum, R. 1959. "Time and Death in Adolescence." In H. Feifel, ed., *The Meaning of Death* pp. 99–113. New York: McGraw-Hill. (Paperback)

McDonald, M. 1964. "A Study of the Reactions of Nursery School Children to the Death of a Child's Mother." *Psychoanalytic Study of the Child* 19:358–76.

Nagy, M. H. 1959. "The Child's View of Death." In H. Feifel, ed., *The Meaning of Death,* pp. 79–98. New York: McGraw-Hill.

Pfister, O. 1930. "Schockdenken und Schockphantasien bei höchster Todesgefahr." *Int. Zeitschrift für Psycho-Analysis,* 16:430–55.

Portmann, A. 1956. *Zoologie und das Neue Bild des Menschen.* Hamburg: Rowohlt.

Selye, H. 1950. *Stress.* Montreal, Canada: ACTA, Inc.

Shakespeare, W. 1602. *Hamlet.* Leipzig: Tempel Verlag.

Spitz, R. A. and W. G. Cobliner. 1965. *The First Year of Life.* New York: International Universities Press.

Stern, M. M. 1951. "Pavor Nocturnus." *International Journal of Psycho-Analysis* 32:302–9.

Stern, M. M. 1961. "Blank Hallucinations: Remarks about Trauma and Perceptual Disturbances." *International Journal of Psycho-Analysis* 42:205–15.

Stern, M. M. 1968. "Fear of Death and Trauma." *International Journal of Psycho-Analysis* 49:457–61.

Stern, M. M. 1968. "Fear of Death and Neurosis." *Journal of the American Psychoanalytic Association* 16:3–31.

Tennes, K., R. Emde, A. Kisley, and D. Metcalf. 1972. "The Stimulus Barrier in Early Infancy: An Exploration of some Formulations of John Benjamin." In R. R. Holt and E. Peterfreund, eds., *Psychoanalysis and Contemporary Science,* 1:206–34. New York: Macmillan.

· 3 ·

The Child and Fear of Death

NELLI L. MITCHELL AND KAREN R. SCHULMAN

Death is synonymous with nothingness—a black cavern where one is not only alone but also loses oneself in the void. Religions, particularly, have sought to lessen the fear of nothingness with symbols and fantasies that permit us to repress our fears, at least to a point. To arrive at this state is the result of an evolutionary process. In the beginning these ways of dealing with death were not present. The primitive human being perceived a feeling of terror—nameless and innate—the "terror of not being." The authors propose that the child, like the primitive, has this nameless terror, which must be dealt with. We call it the fear of death. The primitive evolved religion to deal with it, and the child evolves his fantasies.

Choron (1964) states that the best subject for the study of the fear of death is the child rather than the "civilized adult." In this same vein Wahl (1976) hypothesizes that to reach the truth and understand the human meaning of the fear of death, the study of children is necessary. "Here in the child we are able to look upon our primordial selves naked of the overburden of years and the thick layers of repression and acculturation." Zilboorg (1943) reports that the child's inner world is filled with terror, with a pervasiveness of guilt and helplessness because of an immature ego. The child feels he has no real control over his environment. If adults persist in believing that children have little awareness of death, and hence cannot fear it, they fail to help children understand the void caused by death. In their dilemma children provide magical answers for themselves, utilize denial, or entertain a secret fear that they have been the instruments of this awful catastrophe. Koocher (1973:374) points out that it is far better to explore and attempt to respond to children's ideas than to allow magical or unspoken fear to play upon their imagination.

The central hypothesis of this paper is the universality of the innate terror of death in the human being and the position that the child is least of all immune to death fear and its symbolic representation. This terror cuts across all ages and developmental levels. We are not concerned with the development of the empirical knowledge of death, an area that has been extensively explored by others such as Anthony (1940), Nagy (1948), and Piaget (1929). These studies indicate the stages of evolution of a realistic understanding of death via year-by-year developments. For this paper it is not germane if the feelings and ideas acquired by learning significantly influence these basic attitudes toward death. Instead, as Rheingold (1967:1) states, "death is fantasied and felt not thought, and the images and emotions endow death with meaning." For Rheingold the emotional meaning of death is not open to intellectualization or abstraction, and he suggests that the most profound images of personal extinction and reaction to it take form long before the development of an empirical knowledge of mortality. Rheingold states further, "No theory of the child's attitudes towards death based on the learning process is tenable because the child shows dread of annihilation and mutilation before it has had an experience with death and mutilative injury."

Engel (1963), using a large battery of tests on borderline psychotic children, suggests that the projective material gives ample evidence of a basic preoccupation with survival and/or fear of annihilation. The test results show that these children have a tenuous grasp on reality and struggle to maintain contact with reality. Darkness and sleep are dangerous, for in some way sleep may be tantamount to death. The children find themselves vacillating between their fantasies and more realistic, less anxiety-provoking interpretations. This vacillation is characteristic of the "borderline" child. In Engel's report and in the clinical material, one can grasp the abject terror these children live in. Schilder (1942) found also that these children's thoughts are filled with ideas of terror and destruction, and everything unusual or unexpected is to be feared. Although these findings are from studies on disturbed children, qualitatively they do not differ from those discovered in "normal" children.

Certain assumptions regarding the child and death must be extinguished in order for empirical research to proceed. The most germane of these is that children do not understand death. As Kastenbaum and Costa (1977:288) suggest, this "preserves the image of childhood as a fantasyland where harsh realities do not and should not intrude." These attitudes in regard to the denial of the child's involvement with death-related phenomena fit all too well with our culture's death-denying system and the prevailing conceptions of cognitive development. Even Freud said that to the child death means little more than a departure or journey, and he felt that there was no unconscious correlate to the conscious concept of death.

The initial pioneering work on the child's understanding of death was done by Anthony (1940) in Great Britain and Nagy (1948) in Hungary. Both these investigative works had methodological problems that limited the generalizations being made (Kastenbaum and Costa 1977). In Nagy's study even the youngest child had ideas about death, primarily built around realistic, concrete perceptions. These findings are consistent with those of Hall (1915), who noted an abundance of perceptual detail on death in memories going back to early childhood. The most salient finding of Anthony was that children perceive death-related phenomena and actively try to understand them.

Other findings suggest that the child's discovery of death begins much earlier than cognitive theorists can accept. Spinetta et al. (1973:844) hypothesize that to equate the awareness of death with the ability to conceptualize it and express the concept in an adult manner denies the possibility of an awareness of death at a less cognitive level. Thus, if the perception of death can be present at some level that precedes a child's ability to talk about it, then this child can be said to be manifesting a nonconceptual anxiety in regard to death. Maurer (1961) suggested that the six-month-old's fascination for "peek-a-boo" and appearance /disappearance games is an attempt at mastery over being and nonbeing, separation and reunion. Koocher (1973) found that chronological age was not a reliable predictor of the child's level of death cognition but that a Piagetian classification of mental operations did predict it well.

Alexander and Alderstein (1958:108) observed that in their population (108 males between ages 5 to 16) death words generally elicit indications of increased emotional response. In the galvanic skin response (GSR) measure they used, two subgroups (5 to 8; 13 to 16) showed significant decrease in skin resistance. They interpreted their findings as indicating that "death has a greater emotional significance for people with less stable ego self-pictures than for people with an adequate concept of self." Ross (1967) found that the relationship between separation fear and fear of death was a specific dynamic one and not an instance of general fearfulness in children. Beauchamp (1974) suggested that awareness of death is an attribute of the human condition that children, as well as adults, must come to terms with. She found that the three-year-olds in her study showed far more fear than the older subjects. In commenting about the concept of causality, some three-year-old subjects included causes of death that were, in our culture, not realistic, for example, anger, bad behavior, and wishful thinking. Those children who exhibited more realistic perceptions were significantly less fearful than the other groups.

Two conclusions can be reached from this cursory review of the literature: (1) that even in childhood, loss, endings, separations, and death are core concerns of the individual; (2) that fear of death in children is intensified by the absence of the intellectual equipment and of the necessary defensive mechanisms essential for comprehending the experience of loss. As Formanek (1974) points out, the child is unable to allay his fears by means of denial or reassure himself that he will not be totally abandoned although only one person has gone.

In order to cope with and master his world, the child must evolve defensive fantasies. This is an attempt to suppress or limit the magical power of hidden wishes. Much as the primitive does with his rites and spells, the child uses words or ritualistic games to protect himself—for example, "step on a crack, you break your mother's back." To avoid this harm, the child must diligently avoid cracks. If he steps on a crack, then his fantasized aggressive wish against the parent may come true. Anthony (1940), citing the talionic law, equates the fear of death in children and its origin as a fear of retaliation—aggression of others.

According to Wahl (1976:63), one of the earliest symptoms manifested by the thanatophobic child is his obsessive blessing of persons at the end of prayers. The child's destructive thoughts are doubly frightening since the child reasons through his magical thinking and the law of talion "to think a thing is to do that thing"; to do a thing is to ensure an equal and similar punishment to the self and thus he fears not just the loss (death) of his parents but his own death as well. From this too we can understand no child escapes these hostile death wishes. Hence, no child escapes the fear of personal death in either a direct or symbolic form. However, "repression is usually so immediate and effective that we rarely see this process in its pristine form."

Rheingold (1967) views the psychology of death and the psychology of aggression as interwoven. Death, separation, loss, and trauma can be perceived as attribution punishment following the child's death wishes and aggressive impulses toward others.

Bloch (1974), as well as others, believes that rife in children's fantasies is a fear of being killed by their parents and of killing them in return. Since the child has the universal fear of being killed, Bloch believes that the parents' wish to kill the child must also be universal. Thus for Bloch, this fear of being killed, which reflects the parents' wish to kill, becomes the genesis of the fear of death in the child. Because these fantasies can be so disruptive to the child, we must take a look at his mental processes to see how he perceives inner and outer reality, particularly that pertaining to fear of death.

For these authors primitive man, the child, and the deepest strata (primordial) of the adult mind are synonymous. However, for the purpose of this paper we have elected to examine some of the components of the child's mind. This investigation should demonstrate the fear of death in its most visible, tangible, and disruptive form.

One of the most salient features of the child's world is animism, the tendency to impute life to inanimate objects. The distinction between animate and inanimate is of concern for this discussion.

Jean Piaget (1960) reported that animism is one of the earliest characteristics of the child's thoughts. It is based on a primitive mental structure. The child sees external objects in his own image: that is, he personifies them. The child attributes occurrences to his particular thoughts and feelings about them. If an angry or annihilative thought or feeling occurs, and an untoward occurrence follows, the child has verification of the power of his thoughts. To think a thing is to have it be so. For the child, reality exists within his thoughts and feelings. Death is never thought to result from chance or to be a natural happening. Guilt becomes one of the child's typical reactions to death. And yet, at the same time, he feels rage at the deceased who, he feels, has abandoned him.

Object and self nonconstancy are death-related phenomena. In infancy and early childhood, the disappearance or destruction of objects is experienced as a partial loss of the individual himself. Thus, in a sense, the child disappears too when the mother leaves the room. Consciously, separation or absence is tantamount to death. Although object constancy and self-constancy are established at a particular developmental stage, they need not be fixated, since the anlage remains. Thus, regression can occur at any time during life. According to Rheingold (1967:17), "Death is equated with willful withdrawal of the mother. Separation anxiety seems to be universal and is a major source of death anxiety throughout life, even among the aged, for like all early constellations, it remains long after the period of infantile helplessness and infantile interpretations."

It is relevant to examine the meaning of future time in relation to the child's fear of death. Since the child lives in the here and now, he has no real conception of the future. The adult conception of the future as a quantitative time different from past and present does not develop until about age 13 to 15 (Sturt 1957). When an object is not visible, even though temporarily, it is gone, irretrievably gone. With an awareness of the future, an adult can repress his anxiety about a temporary absence and the feeling of anxiety and terror associated with separation and loss. A child, with an awareness of present only, has the terror with no anticipation or hope. Hence, whatever happens in the present is real, complete, and final. Ghosts, malevolent spirits, all the imagery that beset them when separation occurs, are real since they exist at that particular moment. Since a child has not discovered objective time, his magical thinking has no boundaries, no time frame references. His thoughts and feelings are not under his control. He cannot influence events in his world. There is no process occurring of which he is aware. Hence, whenever a separation occurs, it is permanent and synonymous with nonexistence for the child. The way the child perceives the world makes this terror more formidable. This panic is death related.

In this examination of components of the child's cognitive structures, the most salient feature of his thinking is that his wishes have magical power to influence events: that is, his feelings are omnipotent and he is vulnerable to these and powerless to affect them. The child, like the primitive, is alien to the concept of chance. They both equate the symbol with that which is symbolized and are unable to differentiate between objective and wishful causation. Their death and the wish for another to die are superimposed.

> To primitive man, to children and in the deeper strata of the most rational adult mind, death is an enemy, an implacable destroyer. Death may be violent or nonviolent; due to internal or external causes, or agonizing or tranquil, but always it is imposed, not incurred naturally or contingently (Rheingold, 1967:20).

From this we can understand why children have recurrent nightmares and phobias. There is a time in childhood, considered a transient developmental crisis, when phobias and ritualistic behaviors occur and are considered healthy responses. We accept them as part of the normal maturation process, and we seldom analyze what it is or why it is. Becker (1973:19) states that

> in their tortured interiors radiate complex symbols of many inadmissible realities—terror of their world, the horror of one's wishes, the fear of vengeance by the parents, the disappearance of things, the lack of control over anything. It is too much for any animal to take, but the child has to take it so he wakes up screaming with almost punctual regularity during the period when his weak ego is in the process of consolidating things.

Death can be seen as a complex symbol involving aspects of reality inadmissible to the omnipotent and narcissistic self (Wahl 1976). Because of this, strong defenses are evolved against its recognition throughout the developmental process. The vulnerable child, particularly, is unable, for the most part, to defend himself from the magic and irrationality of his inner world. The process of maturing is caught up with defending the ego from the realities of life. When repression has triumphed, all the nightmares and memories of childhood, that is, pain, blood, darkness, aloneness, are put to rest in the conscious mind.

Becker and Zilboorg both indicate that repression takes care of the complex symbol of death for most people. Becker claims that a very favorable upbringing serves to repress the fear of death. This is made possible by the natural identification of the child with the power of his parents. The parents' powerful triumph over death becomes the child's. The whole argument for the universality of the innate terror of death can rest its case on just how effective repression is. The beginning of this process takes place in childhood. If this does not effectively occur around death fears, the seeds for later pathology may be sown. Madness can be seen as the presence of too much reality with the constant anxiety of nonbeing or annihilation. Searles (1961) and Feifel (1969) have both hypothesized that the schizophrenic's denial of reality may function as a magical holding back or undoing of death. As Feifel (1969) states, it is possible to act upon the death-defying logic that, since all living leads inevitably to death, the way not to die is not to live.

This whole field of the child's fear of death is full of contradictions and the absence of empirical knowldge. It is to be hoped this paper posits a premise for further research and clinical understanding.

REFERENCES

Alexander, I., and A. Alderstein. 1958. "Affective Responses to the Concept of Death in a Population of Children and Early Adolescents." *The Journal of Genetic Psychology* 93:167–77.

Anthony, S. 1940. *The Child's Discovery of Death*. New York: Harcourt, Brace.

Beauchamp, N. F. 1974. "The Young Child's Perception of Death." *Dissertation Abstracts International* 36(6-A):3288–89.
Becker, E. 1973. *The Denial of Death*. New York: The Free Press.
Bloch, D. 1974. "Fantasy and the Fear of Infanticide." *Psychoanalytic Review* 61(1):5–31.
Choron, J. 1964. *Modern Man and Mortality*. New York: Macmillan.
Engel, M. 1963. "Psychological Testing of Borderline Psychotic Children." *Archives of General Psychiatry* 8:426.
Feifel, H. 1969. "Attitudes Toward Death: A Psychological Perspective." *Journal of Consulting and Clinical Psychology* 33:292–95.
Formanek, R. 1974. "When Children Ask About Death." *Elementary School Journal* 75(2):92–97.
Hall, G. 1915. "Thanatophobia and Immortality." *American Journal of Psychology* 26:550–613.
Kastenbaum, R. and P. Costa. 1977. "Psychological Perspectives on Death." *Annual Review Psychology* 28:225–49.
Koocher, G. P. 1973. "Childhood, Death and Cognitive Development." *Developmental Psychology* 9(3):369–75.
Maurer, A. 1961. "The Child's Knowledge of Non-existence." *Journal of Existential Psychiatry* 2:193–212.
Nagy, M. H. 1948. "The Child's Theories Concerning Death." *Journal of Genetic Psychology* 73:3–27.
Piaget, J. 1929. *The Child's Conception of the World*. London: Kegan Paul.
Piaget, J. 1960. *The Psychology of Intelligence*. New York: Littlefield.
Rheingold, J. 1967. *The Mother, Anxiety and Death*. Boston: Little, Brown and Co.
Ross, R. P. 1967. "Separation Fear and the Fear of Death in Children." *Dissertation Abstracts* 27(8-B):2878–79.
Schilder, P. 1942. *Goals and Desires of Man*. New York: Columbia University Press.
Searles, H. 1961. "Schizophrenia and the Inevitability of Death." *Psychoanalytic Quarterly* 35:631–65.
Spinetta, J., D. Rigler, and M. Karon. 1973. "Anxiety in the Dying Child." *Pediatrics* 52:841–45.
Sturt, M. 1957. *The Psychology of Time*. New York: Pantheon.
Wahl, C. W. 1976. "The Fear of Death." In R. Fulton, ed., *Death and Identity*, Bowie, Maryland: Charles Press (rev. ed.).
Zilboorg, G. 1943. "Fear of Death." *Psychoanalytic Quarterly* 12:465–75.

· 4 ·

Children's Attitudes Toward Death

April R. Zweig

Children's attitudes toward death were explored to determine how children find out about death and to what extent their attitudes are a function of experience with death and selected demographic characteristics. The subjects were 115 black children and 23 white children, ranging in age from 8 to 12 years. A 62-item questionnaire was submitted to these children to assess their attitudes. The findings are interpreted in the context of previous research and suggestions are made regarding death education for children.

Introduction

Developmental psychology and psychoanalytic theory have dealt extensively with many aspects of childhood, but relatively little has been written on children's attitudes toward death. The available research has focused primarily on the developmental process (Anthony 1940, Nagy 1948, Alexander and Alderstein 1958, Melear 1973, Koocher 1973) as it relates to the child's ability to understand death. However, discrepancies referring to the

---

This article is based on the author's doctoral dissertation. The author would like to credit Dr. Margaret Lee, Dr. Gustave Rath, Dr. Claude Mathis and Dr. Kenneth Howard of Northwestern University for their assistance. Reprints of the questionnaire may be obtained by writing to the Institute for Juvenile Research, 1140 S. Paulina, Chicago, Illinois 60612.

time at which a child can conceptualize the meaning of death are found in the literature. These are due to many other factors that cannot be isolated from the maturational level of the child's cognitive processes. These include influences such as parental attitudes, discussion about death with adults, the child's past experiences with death, religious instruction, and the background and culture where the child grows up. This problem has been cited by Koocher (1973) in his reference to Nagy's (1948) finding that children's attitudes in the 5- to 9-year age group were characterized by personification-type responses. In contrast, not one child in Koocher's study gave a personification-type response. Koocher suggests that this may reflect cultural differences or different types of coping mechanisms that children use to deal with their thoughts about death.

Throughout this literature we find such discrepancies. Nagy's (1948) research also indicated that children view death as inevitable and universal after age 9, while Zelig's (1974) research indicates that at age 6 the child understands the irreversibility and finality of death. Such differences may be due to factors specific to each individual child and, therefore, such studies will not evidence a pattern characteristic of every child. These studies will only provide a framework within which specific circumstances affecting a child can be better understood.

The present study is directed to the following questions: (1) what are black children's attitudes toward death, and how do they compare to white children's attitudes; (2) how are these attitudes related to age, gender, and experience with death; and (3) what are the sources of these attitudes?

Method

Instrument

A 62-item structured-response questionnaire was developed in response to the need to clarify some of the contradictory results that previous studies have produced in relation to various aspects of children's attitudes about death. The items selected were based both on these empirical findings and on theoretical positions in this area. In addition to items measuring children's attitudes, demographic questions were also included in the questionnaire. The format for responses was for the most part multiple choice. The amount of time required to complete the questionnaire was approximately 20 minutes.

The 62 items were conceptually organized into the following categories: (1) death as temporary; (2) death considered as a person; (3) death as universal; (4) death as the cessation of biological functioning; (5) death as caused by aggression; (6) degrees of death; (7) death anxieties; (8) discussion of death; (9) learning about death; (10) expressive adaptation; and (11) knowledge of parents' views of death; and (12) parents' views of death.

Subjects and Procedure

The two samples of children used for data collection in this study are described below.

Black Sample 8 to 12. The subjects in the first sample were all enrolled in Chicago Youth Center programs during the summer. These are designed to provide social enrichment for inner-city children. This sample included 186 subjects, 80 males and 106 females, ranging in age from 8 to 12 years. Since this sample was predominantly composed of black children ($N=164$), the 22 other subjects were dropped from the analysis in order to tap a better defined population. Further analysis, to eliminate subjects who responded inconsistently, decreased the number of subjects in this sample to 115. Few significant differences were found between subjects who responded consistently ($N=115$) and those who responded inconsistently ($N=49$) to similar items in the questionnaire. Eliminating the subjects who responded inconsistently thus did not affect estimates of endorsement levels but did remove their adverse effect on interitem correlations. Table 5.1 describes the demographic characteristics of this sample, which was composed of 47 males and 68 females.

Black Sample 10 to 11. This sample included all the 10- and

Table 5.1.
Demographics of Black Sample 8 to 12

Age (years)	Percent
8	11.3
9	26.1
10	20.0
11	18.2
12	24.4

Religion	Percent
Catholic	24.4
Jewish	1.7
Protestant	5.2
Other (Baptist, Methodist)	68.7

Family Size (Number of Siblings)	Percent
0	5.2
1	14.8
2	13.9
3	20.9
4 or more	45.2

11-year-old subjects from the Black Sample 8 to 12. It was composed of 44 subjects, 15 males and 29 females. The purpose of constructing this sample was to have a comparison group for the white sample obtained.

White Sample 10 to 11. The White Sample was composed of 27 children, 21 males and 6 females, ages 10 to 11 years. These subjects all attended a Jewish Sunday School in Chicago and came from middle-class homes. A validity check was made to identify those subjects who were not motivated or who did not understand items on the questionnaire, and this sample was consequently decreased to 23 subjects. Though it is desirable to choose a sample that will be most generalizable to the total population, it is often difficult to obtain. The first sample represents black Christian children from lower socioeconomic backgrounds. The second sample represents white Jewish children with middle socioeconomic backgrounds. It is obvious that it would be impossible to make the results of this study applicable to all children.

But the N is large enough, especially in the first sample, to provide information about children's attitudes toward death that would be relevant to any broad sampling of children.

None of the children in the first sample were informed about the questionnaire prior to the day of its administration. The researcher was introduced and a brief introduction was read. Each item was read aloud because the younger subjects might have had difficulty in reading.

Following collection of the questionnaires, discussion was initiated by the researcher to outline the nature and purpose of this research, to answer any questions, and to discuss feelings and reactions to the idea of death.

Data collection with the White Sample 10 to 11 followed the same procedure. The principal difference was the researcher's visit to the Sunday School one week prior to the administration of the questionnaire. At this time the subjects were told that their assistance was needed for research being conducted on children's attitudes about death, that the questionnaire they would receive was not a "test," and that the following week the researcher would discuss in full detail the nature of this study.

Results

As described previously, this study deals with twelve aspects of children's attitudes about death. Total scores for these constructs were determined by intercorrelations of sets of items in order to develop internally consistent scores. Statistical evaluations involved analyses of variance and t-tests.

The analyses of variance evaluated the effects of age, sex, and "experience with death" on these attitudes. The Black Sample 8 to 12, used for these analyses, created the groups shown in Table 5.2. Each subject was asked if a parent, sibling, grandparent, other relative, or friend had died. If a subject said "Yes," he was put in the "experienced a death" group; if he said "No," he was placed in the "not experienced a death" group. In addition, the subjects were divided into groups by age (8 to 9 vs. 10 to 12) and gender. This created a 2x2x2 classification. A three-way analysis of variance (2x2x2) was computed for each attitude variable.

To compare the attitudes of lower socioeconomic black children with middle-class white Jewish children, a sample of 44 10- to 11-year-old black children and a sample of 23 10- to 11-year-old white children was used. T-tests were computed between the means for these groups for each variable.

A frequency count for the Black Sample 8 to 12 ($N=115$) showed that more than 75 percent of the subjects had experienced a death in their family and believed the following: that people die because someone is mad at them and wants them to die, that crying helps a person express his sadness over the death

Table 5.2.
Black Sample 8 to 12 ($N = 115$)

	Male		Female	
	8–9 yr	10–12 yr	8–9 yr	10–12 yr
Experienced a death	13	9	21	14
Not experienced a death	11	14	21	12

of someone he loved, that when they die their life will go on but not on earth, that after we die we are still in the memories of the people who loved us, and that a person goes to heaven when he dies. Moreover, they become scared and sad when they think about death, have been to a funeral, and tried to forget about death when they thought about it. Furthermore, they believe that when a person dies he can never come back to life, that when they die everything will stop, that it is important to be good so that when they die they can go to heaven, that death is a time when the heart and brain stop working, that all living animals and people must die, that having a memory of someone who has died is important, and that when a person dies he can dream.

Significant differences between black and white children were found with respect to several issues. The black children believed less in the finality of death; believe in a "deathman"; more often attributed aggression as a cause of death; learned more about death from available sources; expressed a greater fear of death; and believed more than white children that their parents view death as a long sleep and believe in heaven.

The analysis of variance for the Black Sample 8 to 12 ($N = 115$) showed significant differences on several constructs with respect to the age, sex, and "experience with death" of subjects. Younger black children believed more than older black children that death is caused by aggression; children who have experienced a death personify death more than those who have not; older children who have experienced a death discuss death more frequently than younger children and those who have not; females learn about death more than males; females who have not experienced a death learn more than other children; and younger children think that they know their parents' views about death more than older children do.

Discussion

Children's ideas about death ranged from believing that one's life goes on after one dies to the belief that when one dies everything stops. Children often think about death and yet are scared of death and try to forget about it. This confusion exists in children's thoughts about death for a variety of reasons. In part, it is due to the child's awareness of the mystery surrounding death that he observes in his parents. This impedes the child's learning and discussion of death. Also, the child's awareness of the effect of this topic on adults promotes the child's own anxieties.

No previous research has been done on blacks' views of death to identify reasons for this belief in the continuation of life after death. The majority of the black subjects participating (75 percent) in the present study had had some experience with death. This suggests that the belief in death as a transitory state is related, not to a cognitive understanding of death, but rather to cultural influences.

There were significant differences between the black and white samples in their belief about death as a temporary event. The black subjects viewed death more as a transitory state rather than as a permanent fact. The literature in this area suggests that the blacks' view of death as a transition is related more to their cultural norms than to a cognitive understanding of death. Jackson (1972) points out a view of death expressed in black literature—the themes of death as freedom, rest, departure, and as finding peace are common in both the spirituals and contemporary black literature. Jackson suggests that the magnitude and quality of death experiences among blacks give them a practical, worldly view of death. Blacks are prepared to accept death, and their familiarity with death is demonstrated in their view of death as another life on earth. In this sense, death provides a continuity with life.

A significant difference was found between black and white children on the construct measuring their belief in a "deathman." There were not any white subjects who gave an affirmative response to the belief in a "deathman." This construct was introduced because of Nagy's (1948) findings, which indicated that children between the ages of 5 and 9 personify death. None of the studies following her work though have had subjects reporting personification-type responses. A plausible explanation for such a response could be either that the stories children are told about death include the image of a person or that, as Koocher suggested, this is the result of cultural influences incorporated into myths about death and relayed to children on the occasion of the death of someone they knew.

A significant difference was found between black and white children's belief in death's being caused by aggression. To a much greater extent, blacks attributed death to aggressive causes. Sigel (1965) and McIntire et al. (1972) also found that children from lower socioeconomic backgrounds condoned aggression and saw death as a result of violence more often than other children did. The black child from a lower socioeconomic background is more often exposed to death and violence (Carter 1971). Also, Portz's (1964) research indicated that experience with violent forms of death appeared to be one of the most significant environmental influences on children's conceptions of death.

There was a significant difference between blacks and whites with respect to learning about death. The black subjects learned more about death from available sources than the white subjects did. All groups though learned more about death from reading than from any other source (television, school, or religious training). This finding is consistent with the notion that children have frequent thoughts about death but are reluctant to discuss them. Reading is a private experience, whereas gaining information from schooling or religious training implies sharing one's thoughts about death.

The total score measuring fear of death showed a significant difference between black and white children. This measure, however, looked at children's beliefs from two perspectives: fear of their own death and their perceptions of fear of death in others. In regard to their own fears of death, the subjects were directly asked, "How afraid of death are you?" and "If I think about death I get scared." The black subjects demonstrated a significantly greater fear of death than the white subjects on both of these items, though both groups clearly expressed a fear of death. With respect to their perceptions of fear of death in others, the black subjects believed all other groups, except criminals, have more anxiety about death than themselves. The white subjects also attributed greater anxiety about death to the other groups than they themselves felt, though in contrast to the black subjects, they believed criminals had more fears than any other group. Perhaps this is because white children believe that criminals should be punished for their acts more than black children do.

With regard to children's perceptions of their parents' views of death, it seems that these beliefs must come from the explanations given to them by their parents. The unrealistic beliefs that black children attribute to their parents suggest that parents are of little help in the child's formulation of ideas about death and that television is probably a greater influence on the development of these ideas.

Age was found to be a significant variable on several constructs. Younger subjects believed more that death is caused by aggression. Sigel's (1965) research also indicated that younger children's responses to death involved more ideas of aggression than was true for older children. Freud and Burlingham (1973) observed that guilt was a characteristic defense used by children to deal with anxiety caused by a separation; that is, children feel bad things happen to them because they did something wrong. According to Wahl (1959), the feelings of omnipotence characteristic of young children are their main defense against death anxiety, for this allows them to feel personally invulnerable to death. But at the same time it is these omnipotent feelings that are also responsible for death anxiety because it forces the child to take responsibility for these destructive thoughts, which he regards as magically fulfillable wishes. The idea of chance is foreign to the child; all motivation is personified, and he is unable to differentiate between objective and wishful causation.

The magical thinking about death, where the child's beliefs and myths rise, was hypothesized by Anthony (1940) to originate in an identification of death with birth (or prenatal life), while the expressions of death in fantasy appear to originate with suggestions of aggression. Anthony discusses how the process of changing conceptions of death is gradual. As the child gives up his magical thinking and accepts reason, he still may not be able to accept the absolute finality of death. Anthony points out the importance of the child's acknowledgment of his inability to escape death himself. In terms of his reacting to a death, the child's relinquishing of his magical powers allows him to be free of responsibility and of a sense of guilt with respect to the death of others.

A study conducted by Steiner (1965) showed that younger children tended to deny thoughts of death though they admitted to thoughts of death occurring in their play and dreams. The context of the idea of death in their play and dreams usually included aggression. Portz (1964) found that after the age of seven parental attitudes of nonavoidance in explaining death and experiences with violent forms of death appeared to be the most significant environmental influences on children's concepts of death.

The age variable was also found to be significant with respect to children's perceptions of their parent's views of death. Younger subjects believed more than the older subjects that they knew their parents' views of death. As was previously noted though, it appears that these beliefs come from explanations given to them by their parents. Often adults do not wish to pass their anxieties about death to their children, and in the event of a death a parent may find it easier to give the child a simple explanation, for example, Grandpa is sleeping in heaven.

Females, as a group, learned more about death than males did, while females who have experienced a death learn less about death than females who have not. Peck's (1966) research, involving only male children, suggested that experiences with death do not help the child learn about death, and Melear's (1973) study, using male and female subjects, also did not find that experiences with death serve to enhance the child's learning about death. In contrast to these studies, however, Gartley and Bernasconi (1967) and Bolduc (1972), concerned with both male and female children, found that an experience with death is a factor that enables the child to learn more about death.

It appears that an experience with death can be used by the child to further his understanding about death or provide him with an opportunity to express his thoughts about death, if his needs require and/or allow him to do this. For some children though, the need to repress such thoughts is paramount, and therefore, an experience with death does not affect the learning process.

Though the focus of the present study was an exploration of children's attitudes about death, the implications of the findings extend further than just serving as a description of children's ideas about death. The need for children to have opportunities available to them to discuss their questions and feelings about death has been made clear. It is difficult, however, for adults, as parents or teachers, to overcome their own fears in a way that would allow them to discuss the topic constructively. Consequently, direct understanding of the sources and organization of children's attitudes becomes of paramount importance in this area.

What we know about children's attitudes toward death is that children do not discuss death often, do not know their parents' beliefs about it, and yet, by age 8, have developed a fear of death. This fear is expressed in several ways: by denial, realistic expression, and/or justification through a belief that death happens only to bad people. We found that children who believe in heaven tend to attribute this belief to their parents. The important issue is how parents handle the explanation of death when someone dies. Whether or not a child attends a funeral does not have any particular effect on how the child views death. What is of importance is how death is discussed with the child.

The concern today with violence on television may be justified. Television appears to be a major source for educating children about death but, unfortunately, in a manner that does not give a realistic picture of death. Hence, repeatedly, the lack of communication between children and parents and teachers appears as the focal problem in helping children to understand death. It would be of great benefit to children if educators would attempt to correct the problem that has been evidenced by this appraisal of children's attitudes toward death.

REFERENCES

Alexander, I. E. and A. M. Alderstein. 1958. "Affective Responses to the Concept of Death in a Population of Children and Early Adolescents." *Journal of Genetic Psychology* 93:167–77.

Anthony, S. 1940. *The Child's Discovery of Death*. London: Kegan Paul, Trench, Trubner & Co., Inc.

Bolduc, J. A. 1972. "Developmental Study of the Relationship Between Experiences of Death and Age and Development of the Concept of Death." New York: *Dissertation Abstracts*.

Carter, W. B. 1971. "Suicide, Death, and Ghetto Life." *Life-threatening Behavior*, 1(4).

Feifel, H., ed. 1959. *The Meaning of Death*. New York: McGraw-Hill.

Freud, A. and D. Burlingham. 1973. *War and Children*. Westport, Conn.: Greenwood Press.

Gartley, W. and M. Bernasconi. 1967. "The Concept of Death in Children." *Journal of Genetic Psychology* 110 (March):71–85.

Jackson, M. 1972. "The Black Experience with Death: A Brief Analysis Through Black Writings." *Omega: Journal of Death and Dying* 3(3):203–9.

Koocher, G. P. 1973a. "Talking about Death with 'Normal' Children." Paper presented at the Annual Convention of the American Psychological Association, Montreal.

―――― 1973b. "Childhood, Death, and Cognitive Development." *Developmental Psychology* 9(3):369–75.

―――― 1975. Why Isn't the Gerbil Moving Anymore? *Children Today* 1(1).

McIntire, M. S., C. R. Angle, and L. J. Struempler. 1972. "The Concept of Death in Midwestern Children and Youth." *American Journal of Diseases of Children* 123:527–32.

Melear, J. D. 1973. "Children's Conceptions of Death." *Journal of Genetic Psychology* 123:359–60.

Nagy, M. 1948. "The Child's View of Death." *Journal of Genetic Psychology* 73:3–27.

Peck, R. 1966. "The Development of the Concept of Death in Selected Male Children: An Experimental Investigation of the Development of the Concept of Death in Selected Children from the Point of No Concept to the Point Where a Fully Developed Concept Is Attained with an Investigation of Some Factors Which May Affect the Course of Concept Development." New York: *Dissertation Abstracts*.

Portz, A. T. 1964. "The Meaning of Death to Children." New York: *Dissertation Abstracts*.

Sigel, R. S. 1965. "An Exploration into Some Aspects of Political Socialization: School Children's Reactions to the Death of a President." *Children and the Death of a President*. New York: Doubleday, pp. 30–59.

Steiner, G. L. 1965. "Children's Concepts of Life and Death: A Developmental Study. New York: *Dissertation Abstracts*.

Wahl, C. W. 1959. "The Fear of Death." In H. Feifel, ed., *The Meaning of Death*, New York: McGraw-Hill, pp. 16–29.

Zeligs, R. 1974. *Children's Experience with Death*. Springfield, Ill.: Charles C Thomas.

· 5 ·
A Man Came and Killed Our Teacher

Bruce L. Danto

November 10, 1976, was a cold and snowy day. Early that morning, children rushed to the C School to escape the bitter cold. Once there, they warmed to the heat and excitement of seeing friends and teachers who had prepared to spend the day with them. As was the case with most other days, the 30 children in Mrs. A's room listened to her stories, danced to music, and took in her lesson plan for the day. Then it was lunch time.

As lunch bags were about to be opened, an angry-looking stranger entered the room. He began talking to Mrs. A. She looked frightened, screamed, and shrank away from the man. Suddenly, he pulled out a dark blue revolver and began shooting at her. Room 213 was filled with terrible sounds. Bright red blood spurted everywhere and the teacher slumped forward over her desk. Without a word, the man fled.

In the tumult following the first shot, some children sat stunned and motionless in their seats. Others were catapulted into action. Some ran out of the room. Seven-year-old William dashed two blocks to his home without a coat. Speechless, he sat there on the floor, shaking violently. In the nights that followed, he spoke through his nightmares of that event in Room 213.

Back in Mrs. A's room, the English papers she was about to correct during the lunch hour lay on the desk under her body. In

Reprinted from Otto S. Margolis, et al., eds., *Acute Grief: Counseling the Bereaved* (New York: Columbia University Press, 1981), pp. 87–110.

the ears and minds of her 30 pupils, her screams continued to echo off the walls of that room.

This tragic scene was interrupted by Mr. B, the school's principal. Soon after his arrival into Room 213, snow-splashed police cars with their flashing lights and shrieking sirens appeared at the C School. The school filled with police, neighbors who had seen the commotion, and parents of children from all classes who rushed there after receiving notice of trouble. Among those present was Mr. D, Regional Superintendent of the city's public schools. The police immediately established an interrogation room, and frightened children were questioned by a battery of homicide detectives. (Detroit *News* 1976).

What happened to those children? Had any school staff ever anticipated such a tragedy? What can be done to deal with the nightmarish psychic trauma that such an event can produce for anyone, especially for children?

I believe there is a need to present the facts as they occurred. This is in keeping with the method of process recording familiar to social workers. Process recording reports details of events in the order of their occurrence. The interactions among those persons present are also recorded.

To serve as an aid for any future similar happening, I have written in detail the steps taken to deal with the traumatic effects of an overwhelming horror story.

This is what happened.

In the afternoon, about an hour following the shooting of Mrs. A by her estranged husband, I was returning from Monroe, Michigan, where I had lectured on the management of the violent person. I tuned in the news and heard the story. It left me as shocked as any other listener. For the next two days I followed the news with concern.

On the second day following the shooting, the teacher's estranged husband was accused of the killing and placed in custody.

It was learned that the teacher had just recently transferred to the C School and had changed her name to A in order to hide from her husband because she feared for her life.

Witnesses are vital to convictions. The only witnesses to this particular event were six- and seven-year-old children. These same youngsters, who had been traumatized by the horror of the killing and the death of their teacher, were now facing the fears of testifying in court.

Early in the afternoon on November 11, I received a call from Superintendent D. He asked if I would be willing to meet with his staff as soon as possible to map out a program to deal with the psychological problems that were appearing among the children and their families. I agreed to meet with the staff of the region early the next morning.

At the meeting, Superintendent D, a psychologist, a social worker, and a supervising educational psychologist shared with me some of the problems that had already appeared, for example, the tremendous anxiety of the parents and their children who had witnessed the event, the need for a new teacher to replace Mrs. A, the new room to which the students would be assigned (while the death room was being cleaned and repainted by volunteer parents), and finally, the approach to be used to help the children handle their anxiety and mourning.

I was opposed to advice, given by a social worker present at the meeting, that parents keep their children from talking about the event, watching television, and discussing and hearing news accounts. I believed they needed to talk about it and follow the story so that they could master the event psychologically and maintain the memory within a proper framework of reality. The children needed to straighten out the facts and learn what the police were doing, what the school was doing, and what was happening to the families of the children who had shared the fatal event.

I reviewed what is involved in mourning, for example, memories of the deceased, guilt feelings about not being able to say good-bye, fear of black people in this particular situation, possible fear of men, apprehension that grownups could not protect children from such danger, and the children's fear that a new teacher might suffer the same fate.

I talked with the staff about the need to teach children about death and ways to handle the various stories they would hear about what happened to dead people. Ghost stories and the like usually arise when children are confronted with a death experience.

Because some children had already contacted the social workers and social psychologists through their parents, I felt that I could best be used if I met the parents, the prosecuting attorney, the police, and the school staff. A meeting was scheduled for the evening of November 17 at the C School. The material that follows represents some detailed notes I made of that meeting.

Meeting at C School, November 17, 1976

There was much anxiety present during this first meeting, both on the part of school personnel and parents. Mr. D opened the meeting and introduced various staff members who would be involved. He then stressed that these people would be there to help the children; he assured everyone that the children would not be used as "guinea pigs." He introduced me and explained why I had been called in. Because nothing like this had happened before, there were no precedents to follow; therefore, it was felt that my expertise in this area would be extremely valuable. Mr. D also answered questions that parents had regarding the facts of the incident.

Mr. B, the principal of C School, then spoke and tried to clear up any misinformation parents had acquired as a result of newspaper accounts. Mrs. E, the new teacher for this class, was introduced to the group.

The precinct chief greeted us. He had little to add to what had already been said, but he did assure the parents that the police were trying to work cooperatively with them in order to minimize any anxiety the children might have when dealing with the police. The homicide detective, Mrs. F, spoke next and explained step-by-step to the parents what would happen in terms of court proceedings, as well as what would be expected of the children at the pretrial hearing.

Some parents were concerned about the lack of evidence (for example, the missing gun) and the fact that the children had been asked to testify. The parents were mainly concerned about the effects of the court experience on their children, as well as the inadmissibility or inaccuracy of the testimony of the children. In general, the majority of the parents worried that the killer would go free or not be prosecuted to the fullest extent. Some parents also expressed a fear that if the man were released, he would then seek out the children for revenge. Mrs. F reassured the parents that there was substantial evidence against Mr. A and that there were some adults who could positively identify him.

Then I spoke regarding some of the natural and most likely short-lived reactions the children might experience. These reactions could be considered natural for their ages (six and seven) and might have nothing to do with this particular trauma alone: sleep disturbances, clinging and dependent behavior, the need to be alone, bed-wetting, academic problems, reactions to violence on television. In general, these symptoms consisted of regressive behaviors or reactions that directly related to violence and were part of the natural experience of six- and seven-year-old children.

Then I talked about four basic learning needs underlying the management of these children:

1. Learning about death.
2. Learning about how totally unacceptable violence is.
3. Learning about one's responsibilities as a citizen to ensure that wrongdoers are brought to trial.
4. And learning, through the experience of the judicial process, that punishment is a consequence of violent action.

I told the group that these children could benefit from this experience if they were taught to understand it and to integrate it into the broader aspects of living. I explained that participation in the judicial process would also provide them with closure. I stressed the importance of explaining the events logically and rationally in order to serve the needs of the children.

While not emphasizing the trauma of the experience, I pointed out that the children needed to explore and understand why some persons became violent, what death entails, and that they needed to look at both the positive and the negative traits of their teacher so that she would not become deified.

I stated that if the children were to "work through" and integrate this experience, they needed to play a substantial role in the process of mourning. I suggested that the children should have a memorial service that would provide ideas other than a "trip to heaven." This would begin to provide them with closure. This was not done, however, because some parents objected to it.

I then asked the parents how their children were reacting. One parent said that her child (who had not exhibited this behavior before the shooting) was now pretending to shoot other children, using his fingers as a gun. He was one of the children who had been highly anxious after the shooting. I interpreted this behavior to the mother, saying that her child was trying to reverse the nature of the trauma by seeing that when he "shot" people, they did not die.

Another child was reported to be playing policeman almost constantly since the killing. I explained that this child may benefit from acting out the role of a policeman because he was identifying with that part of society that is helpful to others and brings wrongdoers to justice.

Another child had developed a fear of returning to school, began clinging to her mother, and complained of nausea.

Another child, who denied any shooting had occurred, also was clinging, nervous, and had become shy. Other children, like their parents, had fears because the man had not yet been convicted. They too worried that he would return to get them. Some parents thought that the children should not be treated as adults and, thus, should not have to go to court and be required to testify.

There was anxiety that some of the children could not identify the man in the lineup and that, therefore, he might not be found guilty. According to the police, only three out of eleven children positively identified the killer. Again the parents were reassured that three identifications would be sufficient for conviction.

Another group of parents who had fully explained the event to their children said their children were having no problems.

Some parents felt there was an overemphasis on the situation and that the children should forget what had happened. One parent was somewhat hostile about the intervention of the school social work service and the psychological service. He wanted the classroom situation to return to normal so that his child would begin to forget.

I explained that even if a child is *taught* to forget, he in fact does *not* forget; the knowledge is repressed. Thus he keeps the trauma intact, never learning to cope with it. Only by facing the situation directly and dealing with it openly can he learn to cope with it. And if he doesn't talk about it, he also gets the message that talking itself is dangerous and he never learns to verbalize what he feels.

The purposes of this meeting were to alleviate parental concerns about misinformation gained from newspaper accounts, to familiarize the group with police and court procedures, and to deal realistically with the overall effect on future emotional development of the children. By the end of the meeting, most parents appeared more relaxed and knew better how to respond to their children. Both the parents and the school staff learned about the legal work needed to bring the killer to court and to justice.

Finally, the meeting created an opportunity for me to insert myself as a spokesman and an interpreter who could see both the view of the parents and the view of the police. It allowed me to play a supportive role with the children, as well as with their parents, moving in the direction of aiding the police and the school in their work.

This first meeting was terribly important; it provided an opportunity to accomplish several things. The parents were able to share their concerns with school personnel and the police; in turn, school personnel and the police gained some valuable insights and awareness about how the parents were reacting to the shooting.

These goals were established; we were moving in a positive direction by the end of the first meeting. I was able to help the parents see that specific work and therapeutic tasks were necessary; their response was positive when they were assured that they would be consulted every step along the way. They were told that justice requires community participation, even for children, and that this experience could teach the children a valuable lesson in responsibility.

The reduction of anxiety in the group of parents, teachers, and region staff was obvious; everyone had agreed that working for the children was a possible and important goal.

The police were especially relieved because they did not know how to handle either the anger of the parents or their questions concerning what could be done for their children. The initial hostility felt by the parents toward the police and court was diminished by patient explanations and reassurance.

When I said there would be no fee for my work, all other parties felt more motivated to offer their assistance to these kids. There were fewer complaints about attending evening meetings and extra time involvement for the counseling staff, teachers, and the police officers.

After that most important first meeting, additional contact involved my receipt of notes from the new teacher, Mrs. E, who shared observations of the children. I also received calls from school social workers and psychologists who had problems and questions regarding particular children who had entered supportive psychotherapy with them.

The next meeting with parents took place on December 15.

Meeting at C School, December 15, 1976, 7:30 P.M.

Superintendent D offered a brief review of the previous meeting and then reintroduced the homicide detective, Mrs. F. She discussed the preliminary hearing, at which time the children had appeared in court and identified the defendant as the killer of Mrs. A. Mrs. F reported on how well the children behaved in court. Some of the parents of those children gave a different version of what happened. They felt that the children were brought into court cold, unprepared for what would take place. They thought the judge talked too rapidly to them, despite the fact that ordinarily he is a low-key and slow-talking man. Those who witnessed the event agreed that the judge and attorneys were kind to the children.

Mrs. F described how the killer was offered a plea of second-degree murder so that it would be unnecessary to have the children appear as witnesses; he would still face a life sentence for the murder of his wife. However, the defendant refused that plea. Mrs. F explained that, consequently, it would be necessary for the children to appear as witnesses. On hearing this, many of the parents were upset about having their children go through the court experience. One parent recounted how she had read that court officers had forced the children to touch the defendant as a way of identifying him. Mrs. F and other parents who had been present in the courtroom stated that the newspaper account was not true. All parties agreed to my urging that the children should be conducted through the court chambers and be introduced to the judge and the attorneys. Also they should be given some explanation of what was ahead for them. From what had been said, it was apparent that some of the children were most anxious about their court experience. One boy was not able to identify the defendant even though earlier he had clearly identified his picture from a newspaper and was able to accurately describe the clothing worn by the defendant on the day of the shooting.

Mr. B, the school principal, called upon the children's new teacher, Mrs. E. He said he wanted us all to see how she had decorated her new room for Christmas. He told us that Mrs. E's car, which had been laden with Christmas decorations for the class, was stolen right in front of the school and was still missing. Mrs. E, a plump, middle-aged black woman, exuded warmth. When she smiled, her face lit up. She described the adjustment of the children to her in terms of seeing how withdrawn they were in the beginning when she took over the class and how their quiet demeanor changed to a more affectionate relationship with her. At the time of this meeting, she felt the children were becoming more outgoing and verbal.

When she ended her presentation, one of the parents commented on how her child had identified the gray suit of the defendant rather than the man himself.

Another parent said that, because some of the children are now afraid of black men, he felt that racism would be used as an issue in the killer's trial; he said the defense would try to show the children were racially biased. Most of the other parents were indignant about this possibility; among those who were indignant were black parents. One black father expressed his resentment toward police officers based on his earlier contact with them and said that racism was a fact of life in the judicial and criminal justice system. His wife cringed as he said that, if his son were to be subpoenaed to appear in court, he would literally "head for the hills" rather than have his son face such racism and police abuse.

I said that I could understand his feelings but that he was offering the wrong model for his son and that respecting and trusting the police and the court were important; no parent should use his own bitter feelings as a model for his child. Otherwise, his child would never be free to develop an attitude of trust for any person of whom the parents did not approve. I said further that white parents would have to ensure that their children were not taught racist fears about black people for the same reasons. Most of the parents and school staff agreed with my statement. The black father fell into silence. It was my impression that he too agreed.

Mrs. E responded to my question about reports of the children's talking about ghosts in the school by describing how older children had reached the younger children of this particular class in which the shooting had occurred. She narrated how, at playtime in the school yard, the older ones had told the younger ones all kinds of tales about ghosts. The children returned to class from the playground and discussed how many ghosts must be in their old room where their teacher was killed. Mrs. E had tried to reassure them that there were no ghosts.

I asked her how she felt about leading the children on a tour of the old room so that they could be reassured about ghosts' not being present, see how fearless their teacher was about being in the room, and achieve a memory picture rather different from the blood-filled one they associated with the last scene of their former teacher.

One of the white parents immediately reacted with hysteria. She shouted she wouldn't permit her daughter to go to that room. Another mother indicated that her daughter would certainly not go there, since she did not even want to return to school.

I argued intensely for my plan. I discussed the mechanism of developing an action counter to the phobia as a means of helping the children not feel that contact with a room held magical properties such as a haunted house. I argued how necessary it was for them to have a different memory of the room, one that reflected how life had been brought back into a state of order. Others supported my argument and we were able to sway the reluctant parents. Another person suggested that the basement be included in the tour because the children believed ghosts were there too.

I asked for any observations made by parents concerning dreams and somatic symptoms in their children. All the parents eagerly shared experiences concerning their children who had developed sleep disturbances since the shooting. Some dreamed of ghosts, others had nightmares of being chased by large monsters. Because of the talk about ghosts when the children were playing, some of them remained close to home with a dependent clinging. Some feared loud noises. They were seen covering their ears with their hands when a popping noise was made while they played the game known as "perfection." Some of these children could no longer tolerate acid rock music. One of the children dreamed of his teacher smiling as he had seen her before she was shot. Two children claimed they had seen her eyeball shot out; this was clearly a distortion and not what the autopsy had shown. I was able to interpret how these children were showing signs of the traumatic anxiety and how the dreams helped them to dispel some of that anxiety. The dream of the smiling teacher was an example of denying her fate and an attempt to remember her as a living person.

Some of the children stopped watching television police programs. One of the children followed his grandfather through his house as he was cleaning his gun in preparation for a hunting expedition. Others were more upset about parents' leaving home for the night, even to attend a movie, and they became more dependent and more clinging. In class one day, a child brought in a toy gun and this startled the other children until they were assured that it was only a toy. One child suffered from stomach upset chronically after the shooting.

Another child suffered from dreams of someone breaking into his home. This was partly because the house next door to him was broken into a week after the shooting. The parents of this child spent much time discussing how they had reassured their son that it was safe to live in his home. The father had a gun and would lock up all the windows at night. He made a big production of how safe they were making it. I pointed out to them and all the other parents that, if they made such an elaborate effort to demonstrate how safe it was, they would be indirectly reinforcing the danger the child felt. After all, if it was so safe at home, why all the need to check each night to ensure safety and to have a gun around? The parents understood and agreed to check on security after the children were asleep.

This example illustrated how the general prevalence of violence in the community reinforced the traumatic event of the shooting in class. All agreed that such happenings made all of us feel a little paranoid about being out on the streets or even staying at home. Our anxiety is increased by watching violent television news and entertainment programs and we are feeling more and more apprehensive about leaving the safety of our beds.

When the problem of racial paranoia was raised, I suggested that contact between the children and black male teachers be fostered. In addition, a parent suggested that black female teachers could introduce the idea that they were married to black men who were not violent, who were fathers and cared about little children.

One incident was discussed that involved a white teacher's having lunch with a white child who became frightened when she saw a black male teacher in the gym. I suggested that the black male should have been invited to join them for lunch. Otherwise, the white teacher would be reinforcing the fear of blacks by saying, in essence, "Yes, you're right to be afraid, let's stay away from him."

Feelings of racial paranoia were strengthened by a report of another incident at the school. A black female bus driver had pulled a gun on children in the bus just about three weeks after the shooting of Mrs. A. The bus driver was arrested. The newspapers kept the fact that it had occurred at the C School out of the press account of the event because they rightly felt it would be harmful. But even so, most of the parents of this particular group were aware of the school connection and some of the children were also aware, since they were riding on the bus when this incident occurred. We responded by discussing the potential to globalize about black violence in the community and how important it was for parents to keep cool heads and assure their children that persons who were violent behaved that way because they were disturbed or had serious problems, and not because of any particular racial or ethnic identity. We instructed the parents to point out that black parents were equally concerned.

The meeting ended on a note of caution to parents not to express their anxiety about the need to attend court, if that was required, because that attitude would only make it more difficult for the children.

A Man Came

Following the meeting, Miss G, a school psychologist, and I went into a vacant office and discussed one of her cases involving a child in this group who had developed a school phobia following the shooting. His mother could not handle separation anxiety, because of her own anxiety, and she was unconsciously exploiting the shooting to find a way of keeping her son at home to meet her dependency needs. We discussed management of this mother in terms of bringing the parents into therapy and stimulating superego anxiety by confronting her with how destructive her behavior was for her son, for example, in his development of learning inhibitions, inability to form peer ties to his classmates, and inhibition of the ability to achieve self-sufficiency.

It struck me that the second meeting was attended by fewer parents, either because they thought they could handle their feelings and children without more help or because we could not offer them any real assistance.

I think that the parents who did not return were those who could handle their feelings and had been assured by the first meeting. Their children were the ones who had made a good adjustment to school and were relatively free of problems in their families. From what was stated at this second meeting, it appeared to me that most of the parents who did attend generally had difficulties in rearing their children. The killing was only one more problem to cope with.

This second meeting provided an opportunity for both black and white parents to express some racist feelings (if they had them) and concerns. My role made it possible to set limits on some of the more impulsive and more hysterical means of coping. Such control of negative behavior reinforced what the school staff was trying to do with the children and made coordination between home and school more effective. This meeting also helped some of the parents understand how thinking about the consequences of decisions was important.

I was not present at the third meeting, held on January 17, 1977. School staff had forgotten to notify me of the meeting until it had already started.

This is the report of that meeting written by Ms. H, a psychologist for the region:

C School Meeting of January 17, 1977

Most of the same parents were at this meeting as were at the previous one. Mr. D and Mrs. F were both absent because they were attending other meetings. Because of a mixup in communication, Dr. Danto was also absent.

Mr. B informed the parents that Mrs. F indicated that the trial date was scheduled for May 16, 1977. Authorities were trying to have Mr. A plead second-degree murder, but at this point, he was not willing to do so. It was also noted that all the children may have to be subpoenaed, which still concerned many parents.

Mr. B then asked parents what kinds of problems their children were having that appeared to be related to the shooting. One parent indicated that her older boy was having a reaction to the shooting while the younger child, who had been in Mrs. A's class, was adjusting well. She described her older child as "working on an ulcer," but indicated that he was a "nervous" child before this happened. She also said that the child was seeing the school social worker.

Another father described the following incident. He and his son were talking about the United States Tricentennial, and the father said that he would not be around. His son became concerned that his father was going to die now, and the father had to explain that he was not going to die at this point. This father also indicated that his son has been aware of the Gary Gilmore case and felt it was fair to kill Gilmore because he deserved it. In addition, this father said that his son was "jumpy" in his sleep and he wanted to get into bed with his parents, although they do not permit it.

This child was also questioning the concept of death and asking things such as: "Why is the body in the ground?" "Does a person come back to life?"

Mrs. E said that this child is fairly well adjusted within the classroom setting. She said he was fearful about going to the Christmas play because the last one had been based on "A Christmas Carol," and he remembered the ghosts of Christmas past, present, and future. He did, however, attend the play.

Another parent, who along with her child is seeing a psychologist, said that her child had developed a fear of open, crowded places such as parking lots and grocery stores because he was afraid of the killer. Also, this parent said that, for the past several weeks, her child had been wetting his pants at noontime. The pants-wetting was news to both Mrs. E and the psychologist; the mother had not previously mentioned it. But Mrs. E said that this child does not change clothes at noon. Therefore, the mother's reporting seems somewhat suspect.

Mrs. E said that the children have settled down and are doing better. She also related that one boy brought a 22-caliber bullet to school and showed it around. Some children told her about it and she sent the child to the assistant principal. Mrs. E thought the child did this to produce a reaction in the other children. Some children had told their parents about this incident and others had not. Mrs. E also said that while the boys were helping the janitor distribute paper towels to various rooms during the Christmas party, they passed by their

A Man Came 61

old room. Most of the children showed no reaction, while some said, "That's our old room." None showed an adverse reaction.

Another child told his parents that two policemen came in the room and sat down. He said that they were nice policemen. Having the policemen visit was part of the plan to prepare the children for the courtroom setting. This child's response was indicative of the benefits gained from this preparation.

This meeting, in general, seemed to revolve around the same issues as the last one and many of the incidents discussed were similar to the ones discussed at the December meeting. This meeting provided a small group of parents an opportunity to ventilate some of their concerns. They also decided to schedule another meeting closer to the trial date.

It was obvious that the parents of these children were still displaying considerable anxiety about the effect of the shooting on their children and themselves. Furthermore, the children were expressing anxiety about death in general and about separation anxiety concerning the deaths of their parents. This is psychological material that should have been dealt with at this third meeting and that should have been handled in general by discussion in the classroom. Any opportunity to handle it at home or in the school was lost because of the lack of understanding on the part of the teachers and because of my inadvertent absence from this meeting.

One thing became very clear to me: children need an opportunity at home and in school to discuss death, what it means, and its effect on survivors. This is important for all children, especially when they have witnessed a death or when someone they know dies.

The fourth meeting was held at the school on March 16.

Meeting at the C School, March 16, 1977

We did not need a meeting until tonight. Three sets of parents and five single parents were present. Three parents complained about a play Mrs. E wanted to put on. White parents defended her play, *Children of the World Say Good Morning,* in which greetings were given in different languages. The play was dropped because these three parents did not want their children to see an ethnic image different from their own. Some parents expressed their anger. The objecting parents were the same ones who have been negative to other suggestions, for example, having children watch television reports, talk about the shooting, the death room tour, and the like. Because of the negative response, Mrs. E dropped the play.

I urged that they go ahead with the play and encouraged a discussion that might possibly reverse this decision. I pointed out that, because a majority favored the play, giving in to a negative minority would not serve the democratic process.

A social worker was quick to point out that the democratic process was not an issue here. Rather, it is the responsibility of the teacher to make decisions about programs, since this is the power invested in her by the Board of Education.

A decision was made to continue the play.

Some teachers were upset when the custodian took some boys to bring chairs up to the death room. One teacher worried that parents would complain. However, it was reported that the children were not upset.

A parent asked how to discuss death with a child. I advised a casual approach to reassure the child that death is not magical or necessarily filled with horror. The death of a pet can serve as an example of death as a natural process.

Some of the parents shared concern about their children who are aggressive toward siblings.

Parents were unable to discuss their child's dreams. They were embarrassed at not being able to answer questions that the dreams evoked. They felt that discussing the dreams would reveal their own fears about death.

Some parents were upset by press and news media coverage, and they accused the school of giving their names to the press without permission. Mr. B said that all parents had been contacted, that they had made their own decision about granting interviews, and that those who wanted them called the newspapers themselves. The parent group decided against further news coverage and offered to support a letter to the region stating their decision.

They felt reassured that I would be at the trial with the children to ensure that nothing harmful would happen to them. Proposed was a request for a closed trial and a private trip to court for the children.

In this meeting parents expressed some conservative views about strangers. It was evident that some of the parents were anxious to maintain stability and avoid anything new and challenging. Their behavior was regressive; efforts to control change were redoubled because they did not want more responsibility. Their regressive dependence was expressed in terms of others' taking over and controlling the press and court process as far as their children were concerned. They did not want the pressure and responsibility of making important decisions.

However, there were times when they did support their children. At these times I felt that it was important to offer them my support and assistance, since it was imperative to keep them functional and capable of offering whatever support they could to the children. Obviously they needed some assertive leadership and direction to help them bind the anxiety created by the crisis of the tragedy at the C School.

Meeting at the C School, May 4, 1977

Four sets of parents and three single parents were present. The meeting was chaired by Mr. B. Mr. J of the prosecuting attorney's office attended.

The trial date was set for May 16. The authorities were uncertain about whether the trial could begin as scheduled because a new defense counsel had replaced the old one (who had withdrawn from the case). The meeting was opened for questions.

A parent asked where subpoenaed children would be kept and who would protect them from being badgered by the press. The prosecuting attorney was opposed to bringing them in for a visit to court, but the parents stood firmly for this request. He assured them that they would be with their children and he believed a jury trial would be waived. The group wanted me to be present at the trial and the prosecutor agreed. Parents were concerned about how much school would be missed. They wanted to know if the children who did not actually see the killing would have to participate in the trial. I explained that the children would have to appear when the people's case was presented and they would miss very little school. Secondly, I presumed that the defense would opt to prevent too many kids from testifying, since their reaction of fear of the defendant would adversely affect the jury.

One parent raised the question of how court personnel talk to children. There was concern that the court reporter had obscured a child's view of the defendant at the preliminary hearing. I cautioned parents to play down the protection and preparation of their children for the trial. A teacher broke the tension by saying that, while the adults were expressing so much anxiety about the upcoming trial, the primary concern of the children was how each would spend the $12 each was to receive for being a witness!

Vocabulary was discussed, and it was pointed out that blacks and whites sometimes use different terminology. It was stressed that both the court and the police should make sure that the children understand the words being used, and when colors were being used for description, it should be verified that the child actually knows colors.

Again, the parents expressed worry about whether the killer could be identified and consequently convicted because most of the children were unable to recognize him.

At the time of the shooting, some were so frightened that they immediately repressed what they had seen. Some were in a part of the room where they could only see his back. Some heard the shot and immediately closed their eyes and covered their ears. There was the one boy who ran out of the room and all the way home. In fact, there were only three children who could accurately describe Mrs. A's killer.

I reassured the parents that the three identifications would be sufficient for conviction.

I commented on how the children can have positive feelings about the act of identifying the killer if they understand that they are helping to bring a wrongdoer to justice. One parent told how her children had witnessed a holdup in a pet store. They saw this happen with other witnesses who testified against the robber. The children saw that, even though the witnesses had testified, they were not harmed. They saw that, despite their fears, the best thing did happen: the robber was convicted and the witnesses were alive and well. They learned that their being fearful did not mean that bad things would happen, and they also learned how to cope with their own fear.

Many parents were upset by stories in the press about their children. They objected to the press's taking pictures of the children.

There was some concern about the children's home addresses' being available to the defense and, therefore, to the defendant. One parent wanted assurance in writing that, if future problems were to occur because of the availability of their addresses, the Board of Education would offer their services. Mr. D reassured them.

A parent asked, "How can we say things will be okay? How can we help our kids to overcome trauma?"

I responded that we cannot tell them that disasters will not happen. We cannot always prevent them. But what we can say is that there will always be supportive persons who will help them work things out. This is what they needed to hear.

One mother revealed that her son had an asthma attack after the shooting. Another mother reported that her son urinates frequently in school and at home. Another child does not want to leave Mrs. E and is also sleeping now with seven dolls.

I explained that such behavior is normal for their age and is very possibly unrelated to the trauma. I cautioned them to guard against assuming that all such behavior is a reaction to the killing. I pointed out that these children are at an age when they are feeling tense and insecure about a number of things in their lives.

At this meeting, the parents were showing more anxiety. Although they mobilized forces to come up with some practical ideas on how best to handle their children in court, they were still very tense and looking for direction. Their need for psychological support from those of us working with them was strikingly apparent. From the questions they asked, it appeared that they were almost obsessed with the traumatic experience of their children.

Since almost all problems regarding their children were seen by these parents as being an outgrowth of the killing, it was important to point out that their children had other sources of anxiety beside the shooting of their teacher. Their request for assured counseling help was an expression of hope that they would not be abandoned. It was associated with marked feelings of dependency that had been generated by their regressive reaction to anxiety. It was of concern that the parents' problems with anxiety might spill over and reinforce the anxiety and fears in their children.

Before turning to the final aspect of this process—the trial itself—I would like to discuss some of the observations of the children made by school personnel.

I had asked staff to keep notes and observations about the children so that we could monitor what was happening on a week-to-week basis. As early as November 22, 1976, notes were kept.

Following are brief statements relative to the progress and behavior of Mrs. E's class as presented to me by Mrs. T:

Monday, November 22, 1976
Today was court day and ten children were absent. K wet his pants on the playground at lunch time. He was very upset by this. He said the aides wouldn't let him come back into the building. The class was a little restless after lunch, and so I had them rest with the lights off and played soft music. For some reason they were watching the door.

Tuesday, November 23, 1976
Five children were absent in the morning and four were absent in the afternoon. K was home ill. I do not know if this has anything to do with the wet pants or not. M, who is a hot-luncher, wanted to go home for lunch. She was crying because she saw a black male teacher in the gym. I let her eat lunch with me. She was okay then. N's mother came over after lunch. Someone knocked N down at lunch time. The mother started crying, but soon stopped after a little "t.l.c."

Wednesday, November 24, 1976
No problems today. Seven children were absent in the morning; five were absent in the afternoon.

Thursday and Friday, November 25 and November 26, 1976
Thanksgiving vacation.
I should add that I also received a Form 657, which is a request for social worker or psychological service, from one of the mothers requesting that Miss P, school psychologist, see her son U "regarding the incident at C School." At this time I do not know the concerns of the mother, but I will contact her and obtain further information and see that her request is followed up immediately.

January 31, 1977 (Monday)
Eight children were absent. R was sent home at 11:00 A.M. because he was ill. He had told Mrs. S that he was in Mrs. A's room. He has called me Mrs. A several times. There were no other problems.

Tuesday, February 1, 1977
Five were absent. T brought in a book called *Gus and the Baby Ghost*, which he wanted me to read to the class. U became very upset and said I wasn't supposed to read stories like that. He said that some of the children might have bad dreams. T said that Mrs. A was in the ground. V said that she wasn't in a casket at all, and some people were not put in caskets. W said that they were burned in an oven through a door, but Mrs. A was on a cloud in the sky. Everyone wanted me to read the ghost story. I could tell that some were afraid, thinking the worst about the book. I didn't read it, because I didn't know how the parents would react when the children told them I had read a ghost story in class. They all joined in telling of ghost stories on television and in the movies. I let them talk it out and then read to them from the book *Chinese Fairy Tales*.

Patrick knows some sort of "dirty" poem about his mother. He was saying it to the boys during math time. I removed him from the group and told him not to repeat it.

Wednesday, February 2, 1977
R repeated the "dirty" poem he was saying yesterday at lunch time. I had Ms. S talk with him. Two children were absent. No other problems. U is working extra hard; he wants to read to me several times during a day.

Thursday, February 3, 1977
Four were absent. No problems. X kept his head down.

Friday, February 4, 1977
Three absent, no problems. X kept his head down most of the morning. He can do the work, but he does not seem interested. I talked to his mother last week about this problem. She said he was ill with a cold. He didn't make a valentine for his mother during the art period today.

From the observations made by Mrs. E, it was plain to see that some of the children were still expressing anxiety about the shooting and the loss of their teacher two months after the event. One youngster was misidentifying his new teacher as the dead teacher.

Most of the children were discussing ghost stories despite being assured that there are no such things and that, therefore, the death room had no ghosts. It was apparent that they needed to discuss their fears openly. Their new teacher, Mrs. E, wisely let them deal with these fears in the group setting. She used the techniques of management that we had discussed in the evening parent meetings, as well as during interim meetings and phone consultations. The school, the parents, and the children were indeed fortunate in having such a sensitive teacher and staff.

From Mrs. E's notes of February 1, when she repeated the imaginings of the children about what becomes of a person who has died, it can be seen that fear of death and cremation was present independent of the death of Mrs. A.

Out of Mrs. E's experience using the C School trauma as an opportunity to ventilate feelings and learn about death, we see that the subject of death can be aired safely and openly.

The unfortunate aspect is that there has been no sensitivity on the part of the Board of Education in recognizing the need to institute a policy regarding death.

Before the trial, an unfortunate conflict occurred. I had been planning to be available for the trial. Arrangements had been made and approval received for me to be with the children during their court appearance. The children had expressed a wish to meet me, for there had been much publicity about my work with a task force to capture a child killer who had been at large.

It was planned that my meeting with the children was to take place on the morning preceding the trial. But there always seemed to be a postponement of the trial. Finally, when the day came for the trial to get under way, I was leaving for meetings in Helsinki and Moscow. I never did make it to the trial.

However, I had talked with Ms. H, one of the psychologists from the region, and we went over procedures for helping the children through the trial. I had advised protecting them from the press and television media, which had been so uncooperative. They had persisted in following the children to and from school, asking them questions concerning their feelings about the "killer," reminding them of their terror, and then taking pictures of them in a frightened state.

We decided to have the psychologist refuse to permit interviews or pictures of the children. They were to be kept in a room to which the media could not gain entry.

The parents were permitted to remain in the court, separate from their children but within their view, so that each could reassure the other. It was agreed by the judge and attorneys that care would be exercised in how the children would be questioned and that Ms. H would be able to caution them openly if she felt there were psychologically harmful or stressful questions or comments being made. The children were taken to the courtroom in advance of the trial. They met with the attorneys and the judge and saw where they would be seated. They used the microphone so that it would be familiar to them.

Here is Ms. H's report to me about this pretrial experience:

Report on the C School Incident, July 29, 1977
by Ms. H, region psychologist
Prior to the court date, most parents became anxious about how the children were going to react and the procedures that would be used for having the children testify. The anxiety the parents felt appeared to be proportionate to the anxiety they had initially experienced after the shooting. As a result, one parent spoke to the prosecuting attorney shortly before the trial date and asked that his child be excused from testifying. He felt that the court experience would produce much anxiety in the child and would be detrimental to his development. In some respects, the court date had heightened the child's anxiety and more regressive behavior was noted. In addition, some paranoid tendencies were noted; for example, the child wanted to listen to every newscast regarding the kidnapping of the children in Holland and was afraid this would happen to him.* The prosecuting attorney excused the child from testifying because his testimony was not crucial to the case.

On the trial date the parents and children were sequestered in a large room, away from the media. Here they waited until taken down in groups of five to the witnesses' waiting room. Many of the parents appeared anxious regarding procedures, the media, and how the children would react. Mrs. E, Mr. B, Mrs. Y, the counselor, and I were there. The parents and children tended to rely on the support from peers more than on our support, with the exception of that of Mrs. E.

The children brought pop and candy with them, as well as activities to do;

*Terrorists had entered a school in Holland and held the children hostage. They were eventually released unharmed.

for the first hour or so they were fairly well behaved. As the day wore on, however, the children became bored. Most of them displayed an appropriate amount of anxiety; they did not seem preoccupied with testifying. It appeared that the field trip was beneficial to them because they knew what to expect (which may have reduced their anxiety). Most of the children did not cling to their parents but interacted instead with their peers.

The children who were highly anxious appeared to have parents who were also highly anxious. I felt that much of the parents' anxiety was transmitted to the children. These children appeared preoccupied, clung to parents, or began to feel ill. Some of the older girls (eleven years) appeared the most anxious. Perhaps it was because they were aware of the event's implications. In general, the older the child or the more anxious the parent, the more anxiety the child appeared to display.

As stated before, when the time came to testify, the children and their parents were escorted through a back passage to the witnesses' waiting room. This was done in order to avoid contact with the media. Mrs. E and Mr. B were in the waiting room in case the children needed any reassurance. Although I was not in the waiting room, from what I gathered, the atmosphere was tense, and at this point, most of the children's anxiety began increasing.

The parents and Mr. J escorted the children into the courtroom. The parents were allowed to sit at the prosecutor's table facing their children. The judge then spoke to the children, emphasizing the need for telling only what they saw. The judge explained the concept of truth to the children in concrete terms they could understand and tried to reduce any anxiety they might have. The children were then questioned by the prosecution, and at this point, many were visibly anxious. When a child positively identified Mr. A, the child was cross-examined by the defense attorneys. These children displayed a great deal of anxiety at this point, some became confused, and some began to cry because of the defense attorney's implication that they were lying. During the questioning, a few of the mothers also began to cry.

Three older children also had been subpoenaed to testify: one boy and two girls. The boy handled himself quite well, even under intense cross-examinations. The two girls (who were sisters) were highly anxious and began to cry. Although they had seen Mr. A, they had difficulty identifying him or remembering details of the event.

In general, it appeared that most of the children had difficulty remembering the details of the event. They had repressed much of what they had seen or felt. Other children appeared to have distorted the objective facts of the shooting.

When they were through testifying, the children were allowed to go home. Again, they were escorted through a back passage out of the building in order to avoid contact with the media.

In general, most of the parents and children handled the court experience well. Children and parents, however, who evidenced high anxiety levels prior to the trial appeared to have the most difficulty. It was felt from talking to these highly anxious parents that much of their anxiety was due to a misperception and distortion of the objective situation. These feelings and misperceptions, therefore, were passed on to their children. Parents who were low in anxiety appeared to have a more realistic perception of the situation and thus passed this on to their children. One overall conclusion I came to was that the parents' reaction to the shooting had a significant influence on their child's reaction—which tended to mirror their own.

From Ms. H's report, it was clear that anxiety ran high for many parents and their children; 30 children had been witness to the traumatic situation and few were scarred. Of those anxious as the time for trial approached, there was ample clinical evidence that these parents and their children had problems arising from causes other than the trauma itself.

To what extent was my absence at a critical time a factor in the failure of some of the parents to cope more effectively with their anxiety? This question is undoubtedly hard to answer, but it should be asked. An important support that had been promised was removed from them at a time when they needed it. This was unfortunate. None of us had anticipated that the trial would be postponed and then rescheduled to a time that was in conflict with the international meetings to which I had already commited myself.

What would I have done if I had been present? I know that I would have done everything possible to urge that the child who had been frightened of the hostage situation in the Netherlands be at the trial. To have permitted him to remain at home at such a crucial time was to encourage him to run from a source of anxiety and to develop a direction of flight from fear. Such a decision might well be costly to this child. Almost everyone knows that, following an auto accident, the driver of a car is urged to master the trauma by driving again. Most people would not urge him to stay at home and give up driving.

This same principle applies to children who develop school phobias. They should be handled firmly, and one should insist that they go to school. They must, if necessary, even be dragged to school because school attendance is vital to overcoming school phobias.

The child who feared going to the trial should have been treated in this same manner. He should have been forced to attend the trial. This is the only way he could have overcome his phobia.

What about the parents themselves being at the trial? Did it help or hurt? I think that it helped neither the parents nor their children. I think it would have been better not to have had the parents there. Some of them wept in court as their children cried. Such behavior did not lend support to their children at a time when they needed it. In their general living situations, these same parents failed to lend support to their children. This could be seen in the pretrauma histories of the families. Their presence would not be permitted if I were to be involved again in a similar experience. It would have been better if the parents had waited for the children in the waiting room upstairs or outside the court.

Justice triumphed. Mr. A, the estranged husband and killer of Mrs. A, was convicted of second-degree murder. The children who were witnesses made their appearance in court and were safe. Everyone connected with the case sighed with relief as summer vacation got under way. There was no more murder trial to anticipate. It was all over.

The small group of teachers, administrators, social workers, psychologists, and I had never been through such an experience. No guidelines had been laid down by either the experiences or the theories of others. Although most of us feel good about what we did, it would be fair to say that it may take many years before we get to see how successful we were in terms of the growth and development of the children who saw their teacher killed.

After the C School event occurred, *Clinical Psychiatry News* (1976) carried a story about 50 children in Elmhurst, Illinois, who witnessed a fatal stabbing of a father by his son on May 3, 1976. The killing happened as the elementary school children were on their way home for lunch.

A psychiatric social worker was called in to consult with the school counseling staff in regard to the psychological management of the children. He advised the teachers that the children should be encouraged to express their feelings about their obviously traumatic experience through art as well as through verbalization. Small group psychodramas were staged; he felt that, in this way, fantasy could be cut away and the children would be able to stick to reality.

Parents were involved, and within 36 hours, a PTA meeting was called. The social worker explained how their children's feelings should be handled and how parents could assist their children in dealing with angry feelings. Unfortunately no explanation was offered of why the social worker felt that angry feelings were involved with the homicide. Little, if anything, was mentioned about anxiety and other symptoms of trauma.

The social worker advised against separate child and parent vacations and recommended that, instead, families should be together for the summer because of the experience. He offered no rationale for this advice. Why he felt camp would not be helpful to the kids is unclear to me, since in the C School situation, it was apparent that, on the day of the trial, peer support of one another was a key factor in helping the children bind their anxiety. Peer support proved to be more supportive than anything coming from the parents at the trial.

The Elmhurst report mentioned nothing about working with the court and the police to help the children who were witnesses. Contact to help those parents with actual problems was not discussed.

In my opinion there was nothing in the reporting of the Elmhurst experience that was basically of assistance to us, even though the Elmhurst killing preceded the A killing.

As a result of my experience with the C School event, I feel the following guidelines can be suggested for future traumatic situations involving children who witness a homicide in or around a school. School staff should be used, along with any competent outside consultant skilled in the art and application of crisis intervention management techniques, thanatologic principles, or forensic psychiatry or psychology. Such a consultant should be able to work with lay or parent groups and should have had experience working both with the police and with the court. The consultant should instruct the staff with whom he works about the use of the process recording method to keep records and observations of contact with the children, as well as with their parents and teachers. This person should be available for consultation as needed and should prepare to meet with parents at their convenience. This means at night for the most part.

Parents should be in the decision-making process concerning the policy of voluntary treatment of children and concerning what will be shared with the press in terms of knowledge about what is happening to the children. It is important that the consultant establish a policy with the school staff that ensures that parents are not drawn into the traditional bureaucratic structure in which they are told what to do.

Finally, the consultant should be with the children and/or parents at the time of the trial, when they may have to testify in open court. It would have been helpful in the C School situation if the court had been more cooperative about working out a docket so that I could have been there. But fortunately, the parents and children had been capably prepared, and staff members were there to help offer support and control in an effective and meaningful manner.

Looking back, I see that this tragedy provided an opportunity for various community resources to work together toward helping these children to learn to cope with trauma. In particular, we were able to teach some psychological principles to the court and to the police for the handling of young children in a stressful situation.

In summary, we learned that not all the anxiety expressed was solely related to this one event. We found that there were recurring worries evoking recurring questions. The questions mainly involved anxiety concerning death and mourning. These concerns did not just develop at the time of the killing—they were there all along.

What occurred here points to the need for educational institutions to address themselves to the subject of death. Another important fact to remember is that the children were not the only ones traumatized; we also found that the parents were overwhelmed with anxiety generated by the killing. They felt guilty about not having fulfilled their sociological role as protectors of their offspring. They also suffered from feelings of inadequacy because they were unable to answer many of the questions that their children asked.

The parents also feared that, if the criminal justice system did not find the killer guilty, he might revengefully harm the children. Those expressing the most anxiety were the persons who experienced the most anxiety prior to the C School tragedy. It was undue anxiety expressed by the parents that created undue anxiety in the children; of great significance is the observation that the children who did not cope well had parents who did not cope well. Those children who did cope well had parents who coped well.

The most effective parents had children who were able to identify the killer. Consequently, we might conclude that an effective rearing enabled children to see reality.

We must remember that children are always imitating their adult role models, especially during a crisis. Role models affect others both positively and negatively. Adults in positions of authority are role models for children in their charge as well as the parents of those children. When sensitive parents pattern their behavior after supportive authorities, they reinforce positive role modeling for their children. Teachers, school counselors, and administrative staff must be aware of this enormous effect they have in assigning their own attitudes to others. The police and court personnel also share in the process through their own behavior role modeling.

Finally, I would suggest to the consultant who takes my coordinator position in any similar situation that he or she stress to all adults involved the importance of their behavior. The consultant must always be aware of his or her own importance as a role model, not only for the children, but also for all those adults involved who will in turn serve as role models for the children.

REFERENCES

"School Fears Teacher's Killing Could Scar Her Pupils for Life." *Detroit News*, November 11, 1976.

"How School Dealt with Children's Trauma of Witnessing Murder." *Psychiatry News*, November, 1976.

· 6 ·

The Grandparent Teaches the Child About Living and Dying

PAUL R. PATTERSON

Certain regressive attributes have been associated with the behavior of the aged such as, "Grandpa certainly has become childish." "I have to treat and feed Grandma as if she were a child." "As one gets older, one becomes shorter but one's stories become longer."

Perhaps our aging parents have recaptured the enthusiasm of childhood. Maybe their prolonged, detailed stories of the past are really an expression of their freedom from the daily worries that beset us and of their joy of living again in the past or of remembering pleasures that they might not have had the time to enjoy when those days were being experienced.

Only when we are older do we say that our youth was the happiest time of our life. Perhaps as children or as adults, we need to be reminded that we should be happy with living at any stage of life. Even as adults we forget that we are our parent's children, no matter what our age. Our parents always look upon us as their children.

What a blessing it is for children to have a grandparent close to them, to spoil them, take their side when scolded, slip them candy, and relate those long, detailed experiences of the past. In turn, aren't these grandparents fortunate to have someone who loves them and will listen to them? Many people pay money to professionals by the hour just to have someone listen. Grandma pays only a cookie or two! So what if our parents have become childish? That terminology may be a misnomer for being capable of living with happy memories and having the capacity to retreat from the responsibilities of decades of living.

A good parent is one who can relate to the child and the adolescent. Parents with poor memories of their own childhood and adolescent days are poor providers of understanding and acceptance. Pediatricians know that many a child's emotional development is stunted by parents who are so enmeshed in business or other demands that they are unable to regress sufficiently to relate to their children as children. We have learned from institutions for the mentally retarded that by using retarded adults as caretakers we are able to advance the retarded child into interpersonal relationships more readily and with a greater degree of patience than when a nonretarded adult is the supervisor and companion.

Bonds of understanding and love do develop between a child and an aged companion and have positive effects on the child's personality. Perhaps parents should be pleased and shocked into reality when their child asks, "What did you do in the olden days?"

My own father always told me that I should read the newspaper every day because if I did this, within ten years I would be a historian. Our elders, therefore, with their years of reading, as well as their life experiences, are keepers of history, thought, and philosophy—the caretakers of culture and beliefs. Our elders maintain our religious beliefs and traditions and reinforce ideals of morality. Many children have learned about God's love, caring, and the concept of heaven from grandparents.

Upon reaching a certain age, one may become more concerned about dying and in fact may become preoccupied with reading the Bible, attending religious services, and making attempts to assuage fears of dying and death. We have heard older people maintain they hardly slept a wink all night, night after night, to such an extent that a diagnosis of insomnia could be made. We do find that many insomniacs have a fear of dying, and it has been suggested that there is an association between this fear and insomnia. However, insomnia can also result from depression in the lonely elderly who have been shelved by their children.

From the elderly, small children learn about their families, their roots, and receive answers to their questions about God and heaven. Granted, grandparents' stories may be filled with embellishment, but how fascinating these tales are to eager minds! Grandparents can take a child into their confidence and, with an admonition "not to tell Momma or Daddy," talk about their plans to be with God. They may even describe what they think heaven is like and tell how wonderful God is, and that He's always in our presence and will look over all of us and take care of us all of our lives. How blessed is the reassurance of these secrets told to us!

Older people complain about today's youth and wonder what this present generation is coming to or what is happening to this world. Perhaps this disillusionment with the world as it exists is God's final gift to the elderly. When older people pray and talk about God, we can feel their close rapport. The only analogous experience that I know of would be the sincerity that small children express when they pray or relate their religious beliefs.

The association of the child and the grandparent serves a purpose for both. How nice it is to have someone willing to listen to you, believe in you, and love you. The alpha and omega, the beginning and the end of life, are joined together in mutual understanding and love.

For many, the death of a grandparent is the first experience with the meaning of loss and the reality of loneliness when someone loved has gone for good. Explanations of why Grandpa died are given to children to prevent them from having anxiety about their own death; they may be told that he died because he was old and tired and had lived his life and because God wanted him to be with Him.

Many have been blessed with a grandparent so loving he or she was looked upon as divine and immortal. Such assumptions reflect the special relationship between the child and grandparent. Even after it is understood that grandparents are mortal, the memories touched by a shared and warm love can influence individuals throughout their own lives.

It may be said that children who were blessed with grandparents have gained much to sustain and enrich their lives. They have learned that death can be regarded as a peaceful completion of life, rather than something to be feared. They have stabilized their religious beliefs. And with the ritual of the funeral, they have experienced a symbolic farewell. Children of any age—from 6 to 50—in grieving are unconsciously expressing gratitude for the gifts from the past given to them.

· 7 ·
A Course in Miracles and Its Practical Application to Life and Death

Gerald G. Jampolsky

My interest in catastrophic illness—and in those persons facing life and death situations—began during my internship in Boston in 1949. I was then becoming conscious of my own fears of death. At the same time, I was fascinated to observe in the hospital wards that "the will to live" could dramatically affect the longevity of a person with a so-called terminal organic illness. Most physicians agree that this phenomenon is a medical truth—yet it has not been possible to take "the will to live," put it under a microscope, examine it, measure it, and replicate it so that it can be recognized as a scientific truth.

Perhaps the time has come for us to change our so-called scientific criteria for determining what is factual. And perhaps the time has come for all of us to recognize that what is real does not have to be seen or measured to qualify as truth.

Most of us allow reality to be established for us by the opinions of the majority in our culture. Hence, the reality that most of us subscribe to is a limited one, confined by our physical senses and restricted to sequential time, and a thinking process that experiences time and space as real. With this limited reality we experience a world that is filled with pleasure and pain, birth and death, and events are understood by cause and effect. Today there seems to be a growing change of consciousness and the recognition that we seem to be destroying each other and the world in which we live. Many are feeling a sense of emptiness inside which has aptly been called by Mother Teresa "spiritual deprivation."

More and more people are looking within themselves for a sense of fulfillment. In the field of medicine, as well as in all walks of life, people are beginning to take a new look at their values, their motivations, and their goals. Reality is constantly being reevaluated and concepts of living and dying are undergoing great change.

More and more faith is being expressed that it is possible to transcend our physical senses and experience a reality where minds are joined as one universal mind and where there is no separation, where there is no space or time, no cause and effect and birth and death, and where there is only eternal love continuously extending and expanding beyond our farthest imagination.

It was in May 1975 that I first really began to look inward, after which my life began to change dramatically. I came across some writings—three books called *A Course in Miracles,* published by the Foundation for Inner Peace in Tiburon, California. Before that time I had not been even remotely interested in the subject of God or a spiritual pathway. To my surprise I became totally immersed in these writings and found myself experiencing periods of peace of mind that I had not thought possible. I then began to relate these writings to both my personal and professional life.

The course suggests that there are only two emotions, love and fear: love is our true essence and natural inheritance; fear is something our mind makes up and is illusory. The writings suggest that what is real is eternal and all inclusive. Only love can fit that definition and that truth. What we see with our physical eyes is not lasting, is perishable and transitory, and hence, not real.

The course can be summed up simply in the following way:
"Nothing real can be threatened."
"Nothing unreal exists."

In 1975, wanting to demonstrate the practical applications of *A Course in Miracles,* I founded The Center for Attitudinal Healing in Tiburon. The center was based on an educational model that was a supplement to and not a substitute for the medical model for people who wanted to take responsibility for their own health, their own inner peace. The theme of our center became "As you learn to help others, you learn to help yourself," and "This instant is the only time there is."

At our center, health is inner peace, and our goal in healing is to bring about peace of mind by letting go of fear. This is different from the conventional medical model, which is concerned about changing and modifying cells and bodies.

Some of the concepts we use at the center are the following:

1. Being a "love finder" instead of a "fault finder"
2. Being a "love giver" rather than a "love seeker"
3. Choosing peace of mind instead of conflict

There are no patients or doctors. We are all there to heal ourselves of our misperceptions of being separate; we are all student-teacher, teacher-student to each other. Age and experience are not factors in determining who our teacher is. We are actually psychotherapists to each other, helping each other to redetermine what is real and what is false. We are determined to see each other and ourselves as guiltless and blameless.

Our initial guidance for establishing a group process for children with various forms of cancer, leukemia, and traumatic illness was the observation that these children rarely had a vehicle or an environment where they could talk freely about their concerns about their illness and their fears of death. Our thought was that perhaps children would be better able to help each other than both professional and nonprofessional adults counseling them on a vertical axis.

In our group process the lay volunteers and I interact horizontally and equally with the children, and we are there to learn from each other. Each of us has a single purpose of getting rid of fear as a way of learning to have peace of mind. We find this happens when we are totally concerned and focused on giving to rather than on getting from each other.

The ages of the members of the group range from 6 to 19 years, and we meet two times a month for an hour and one half. I, and almost all of our staff with children, volunteer our time and no fee is charged. Incidentally, we do have a sibling group because siblings have their own problems about death, such as, "Thank God it's not me that has cancer;" guilt, envy of all the attention that the ill sibling is getting, and then, at times, guilt about their feelings of "I wish my brother/sister would hurry up and die so I can get attention from my parents."

Although our center is founded on a spiritual basis, no religious dogma is fostered, and we tend to act as catalysts to each other for clarification of our own fears, fantasies, and thought processes. The children help each other with problems such as the following:

1. "How do you handle the situation at school when you have no hair and the kids are teasing you?"
2. "How do you get over the fear of shots?"
3. "How do you deal with pain?"
4. "What do you do when you are bored and lonely and scared at the hospital at night?"
5. "What do you do when you are scared and thinking about dying and you want to talk to your parents but you don't 'cause you want to protect them and don't want to make them cry?"

The following is a specific example of how the children use "active imagination" (positive mental pictures in their mind) as a way of getting rid of fear and guilt. Before going to bed each night, they close their eyes and get a mental picture of themselves putting all their guilty feelings, fears, and painful experiences into a garbage can. Then they visualize a helium-filled balloon being attached to their garbage can. They then watch their garbage disappear beyond the horizon.

As the children became involved in helping each other with these serious questions, they decided to write a book composed of their writings and pictures to help other children who may develop a catastrophic illness. This book is titled *There Is a Rainbow Behind Every Dark Cloud* and is published by The Center for Attitudinal Healing, Tiburon, California. In this book are a number of pictures of children's associations to death. For example, one child's perception of death was a picture of himself jumping into a swimming pool and just disappearing. Another child drew a picture of himself as an angel floating up into heaven and with a small devil at the bottom of the page saying, "We lost another one."

Greg, an 11-year-old child, died of leukemia in August 1977. When no more drugs were to be used and physical death seemed imminent, the others asked Greg what his thoughts were about dying. Greg replied, "I think that when you die, you just discard your body which was never real in the first place, and then you are in heaven at one with all souls. And sometimes you come back to earth to act as a guardian angel to someone." And then he added, "I think I'll come back some day to be a guardian angel to someone."

To me, these children seem like wise old souls in young bodies, here to teach everyone they touch the truth.

It has been my experience that very young children do not fear death unless they pick up the fears of the adults around them. These young children have the advantage of seeing the world as one and have been fortunate in not picking up the adult belief system of sequential time that states there is a past, present, and future—a cause and effect—that implies we are all separate beings.

We have found that frequently children over the age of five and six begin to demonstrate a pattern that Dr. Kubler-Ross has described in adults, namely, anger at the world, anger at God, and "Why me?"

In a taped interview, Ed, a 16-year-old boy who died from leukemia in 1978, stated:

> Can you see my knuckles, right there? Well, that was broken because I banged my hand against the wall. That was a few months ago, and that was just out of frustration from the disease.
>
> I am at peace now; I live a lot more now than I ever did. If everyone felt the way I do right now, the world would be a nice, very nice place to live.
>
> I have just accepted death. I am trying to live each day, I just experience that day—there is a lot in a day. I don't think about time too much. I am not afraid of dying. I know that at least my spirit will go somewhere and it won't be dying—I will just go on.

In our group children and adults alike have found that perceptions and fears of death have greatly changed by having a free, totally accepting, nonauthoritarian interchange.

In the conventional model, the child in the terminal phase of leukemic disease is frequently isolated from other children because of his low resistance to infection and the fear that a common cold might cause his death. We have noticed that this is the very time when the child seems to need, and wants to feel, a connection to others. We then found that, when the terminally ill child, his physician, and his family have agreed to this premise, there were a number of children in our group who chose to continue their visits during the terminal phase of the illness, and this experience seemed beneficial to all.

We have developed a group interaction based on the principles of *A Course in Miracles* for children who have to face life-and-death situations. In this process we have endeavored to learn to let go of the fears and guilty experiences of the past, to let go of our attachments to our past values, experiences, and the intellectualization of endless "why" questions. We are focused on letting go of the fears of the future, as well as the temptation to want to control the future and predict it.

The vehicle we have used is total forgiveness with no exclusions. In addition, we have concentrated on focusing on not making condemning judgments, not blaming others or ourselves, and giving love to and accepting each other with no limits, boundaries, or expectations.

The result has been an experience that has been most difficult to articulate. Simply said, working with these children has changed my life. It is an experience of love and joy. It is a conviction for both child and adult that minds are joined and we are one self. It is the knowledge that, when one experiences love as one's only reality, life is then experienced as eternal.

When we allow children and others to be our teachers, it is possible to look past what we see with our physical eyes and, instead, through the vision of love, see only light radiating from others—and then know that that light is but a mirror of ourselves; that light is but the reality of ourselves; that light is love.

We can choose to let the innocence in children remind us of the purity of love. By identifying with this innocence in children, the fearful child in all of us can disappear, and we can learn to recognize innocence that has always been inside of us, an innocence that emanates a light that dissolves all the intellectual, perceptual shadows that make us feel that we created the universe, that make us feel that bodies are real, that birth and death are real, and that we are separate from each other and God.

The experience of this light allows us to have a universal experience that we are one.

As mentioned earlier, the theme of our center is "As you learn to help others, you learn to help yourself" and "This instant is the only time there is."

Our work and our concepts about life and death and the illumination of light can be summarized by one sentence from *A Course in Miracles:*

TEACH ONLY LOVE FOR THAT IS WHAT YOU ARE

REFERENCES

A Course in Miracles. 1976. Tiburon, California: Foundation for Inner Peace.
Jampolsky, G. G. and P. Taylor, eds. 1978. *There Is a Rainbow Behind Every Dark Cloud.* Tiburon, California: The Center for Attitudinal Healing.

· II ·
Children's Reactions to Parental Death

· 8 ·

Parental Death in Childhood—
A Review of the Psychiatric Literature

TECLA CRITELLI

Introduction

An estimated 5.2 percent of children younger than 18 years in the United States have lost either parent by death, that is, 3.5 percent paternal orphans, 1.5 percent maternal orphans, and 0.1 percent full orphans (Statistical Abstract of the United States 1977, Dennehy 1966). Although there is a considerable amount of circumstantial evidence to suggest that early parental death is associated with subsequent adult psychopathology, childhood bereavement reactions have been relatively unstudied. Orphanhood is more than 200 times as common among children as is the specific syndrome of childhood autism (Rutter and Hershov 1976), which has been investigated intensively. Many aspects of the complex of reactions in response to the loss of a loved one by death in adults have been studied (Parkes 1972, Epstein et al. 1975). One can only speculate about which factors differentiate normal effective bereavement in children from morbid responses and about the significance of normal effective mourning for the child with respect to short- and long-term consequences.

Normal adult grief characterized by distress, impairment of functioning, and a predictable clinical course (Lindemann 1944, Wretmark 1959) has been likened to the physical morbity following a bodily injury, for example, a burn (Engle 1961). Is there an age-appropriate parallel complex of reactions in children? Understanding that many symptoms of depressive states are regular features of uncomplicated adult grief (Parkes 1972, Lewis 1938), what can we learn about depressive symptomatology in children from their responses to the loss of a parent by death?

Childhood Bereavement and Adult Psychiatric Disorder

The retrospective case report comparison of psychiatrically disturbed adults having a history of childhood bereavement with different control groups has been the strategy used almost exclusively in studying the long-term effects of early bereavement. Although adult dysfunction is equated with psychiatric hospitalization, it is possible that early bereavement affects patterns of use of health care facilities, in addition to mental health. Parental death in childhood is a relatively discrete and readily identifiable life event. Several factors determined from individual case reports to have affected long-term outcome have been selected for study. Clearly determining the significant factors associated with unfavorable long-term outcome requires an enormous data pool. There are serious methodological problems in many of the retrospective studies, including the following: differences in data gathering, failure to consider demographic data, and inadequate use of statistical tests of significance, and these shortcomings and others are reviewed elsewhere (Dennehy 1966, Markusen and Sutton 1971, Gregory 1958, 1966a, Birtchnell 1973).

A number of studies have examined the role of parental death in the development of specific psychiatric disorders reflecting an environmentally influenced, developmental view of mental illness. Several early studies demonstrated an increased incidence of early parental bereavement in adults with varying psychopathology as follows: schizophrenia (Barry and Lindemann 1960), sociopathic personality (Brown 1966a, Earle and Earle 1961), hysterical personality (Fitzgerald 1948), and psychoneurosis (Barry and Lindemann 1960, Ingham 1949). These results have not been replicated in more rigorously controlled studies. Indeed, several studies have reported no significant difference in rate of occurrence of early parental death between psychiatric patients and controls (Pitts et al. 1965, Brill and Liston 1966, Granville-Grossman 1966, Gregory 1966b, Munro 1966), underlining the wide differences among samples studied.

Depressive illness, unlike other adult psychiatric disorders, has been convincingly associated with an increased incidence of childhood bereavement. The initial study compared depressed psychiatric and medical patients (Brown 1961). Several studies have confirmed the finding of increased rates of early parental bereavement among seriously depressed adults by using different kinds of control groups (Beck et al. 1963, Sethi 1964, Munro 1966, Hill and Price 1967, Birtchnell 1970).

The criteria used for the diagnosis and ratings of severity of depression varied widely in these studies; however Beck et al. (1963) and Birtchnell (1970) both used formal rating scales and demonstrated similar findings. In addition, Hill (1969) and Birtchnell (1970) both demonstrated an increased rate of early parental bereavement among seriously depressed patients having attempted suicide in comparison to other psychiatric patients. At present one can only speculate about the relative importance of genetic endowment and parental dysfunction prior to death in the later development of depressive illness, for no systematic inquiry into parental psychopathology preceding death is available.

There has been a good deal of speculation regarding the stage of development, reflected in age, of greatest relative risk for unfavorable outcome following parental death. While younger children are dependent upon parents for physical wellbeing, older children use their parents as role models. There is no uniform age breakdown between studies, and none has broken down age by consecutive years, limiting the comparison between studies. The following studies have reported significant findings with respect to ages of greater vulnerability: Barry and Lindemann (1960), mother's death prior to age 5; Norton (1952), father's death prior to age 10; Archibald et al. (1962), death of either parent prior to age 14; Brown (1961) and Dennehy (1966), parental death between the ages of 10 and 14 years; and Birtchnell (1970), death of a father for a daughter prior to age 10 and death of either parent prior to age 4. While there is no agreement between studies regarding the ages at which a child is potentially most at risk for the long-term adverse consequences of parental bereavement, it appears, in general, that early childhood is the period of greater vulnerability. Moran (1968) demonstrated that the increased incidence of parental bereavement in his sample of psychiatric patients could not be explained by increased maternal age, suggesting that the unfavorable long-term outcome of early parental bereavement is not determined primarily by the adverse influences of advanced parental age.

As parental death disrupts family functioning, potentially leading to redefinition of the individual's role in the family, various speculations have been made with respect to the import of parent loss on the development of gender-appropriate behavior. There is no agreement between studies about the relative risk for loss of either parent for male or female children, and indeed one study of a large series of homosexual males failed to document an increased incidence of paternal death before age 15 (Abe and Moran 1969). Sibship structure and the surviving parent's coping style do appear to influence adult functioning. Birtchnell (1971) demonstrated that being the eldest child of the same sex as the dead parent was associated with unfavorable long-term outcome while the presence of an older sib of the same sex as the dead parent alleviated the adverse effects of bereavement. From their comparison of sibships of a larger sample of psychiatric patients and normal population controls, Hilgard et al. (1960) contrasted normal and emotionally disturbed adults with a history of childhood bereavement and found the following factors were associated with favorable adult adjustment: (1) a strong surviving parent who kept the family together and managed to cope with the extra burdens of bereavement; (2) available community and/or family resources; (3) a good relationship, including a clear definition of roles between parents prior to death, and (4) a history of the development of separation tolerance by experience with a series of smaller separations from parents prior to death.

Early parental death has been implicated as a determining factor in the development of social deviancy. Brown's (1966) finding of an incidence of criminal activity among men with a history of early bereavement has not been convincingly replicated. Markusen's (1971) preliminary study documented a nonstatistically significant increase in criminal activity and divorce among men with history of parental bereavement. Promiscuity, illegitimate pregnancy, and drug addiction have not been studied in this fashion.

Enduring personality characteristics associated with early psychic trauma have been difficult to document. The initial case reports of passive traits in early bereaved individuals (Barry 1965) have not been convincingly reproduced in later, larger controlled studies (Wilson et al. 1967, Birtchnell 1975, 1978).

It appears clear from these studies that serious depressive illness is associated with increased rates of early parental bereavement in comparison to normals. In addition, age at bereavement and family composition and circumstances are factors influencing outcome.

Theories of Adverse Consequences

Orphanhood carries with it a magnitude of intrafamilial, sociocultural, and financial stresses, in addition to parent loss. I will attempt to organize some of the relevant theories of adverse consequences in the areas of intrapsychic dynamics, learned coping styles, and family disruption.

Intrapsychic Dynamics

Karl Abraham (1911) drew a distinction between grief as a response to a life experience—the loss of a love object—and depression, the consequence of repression and unconscious conflict. Freud (1917) presented an adaptive model of normal mourning dynamics in *Mourning and Melancholia,* in which he outlined the intrapsychic work of giving up lost objects seen as a necessary task before taking on new love objects. The editor's footnote to this work (1917:243) indicates that the German *"Trauer"* like the English "mourning" can mean both the effect of grief and its outward manifestations. Deutsch (1937:13) made the connection between the inability to mourn and the development of psychopathology, stating "unmanifested grief will be found expressed to the full in some way or other."

Many theorists have worked to understand the child's ability to experience grief, to understand death, and to perform the intrapsychic work of mourning in a developmental framework. Observations of sadness and grief of considerable duration and intensity in very young children and infants have been described by several writers. Spitz (1945, 1946:324) described depression in response to the loss of mother as "a specific disease in infants living under specific environmental conditions." Mahler (1961) has hypothesized a certain development of intrapsychic structure necessary in order for a child to experience grief and states "as soon as the ego emerges from the undifferentiated phase, the mimetic, gestural and physiologic signs of grief do appear." Finally Bowlby (1953, 1960, 1961a, 1961b, 1963) drew his comparison between children's reactions to separation from their parents and pathological adult mourning states from children as young as six months old. It appears that children begin to demonstrate the capacity to experience sadness and grief following the loss of important objects from six months of age.

Children's understanding of death has been assessed by use of interviews and projective tests. Furman's (1974:50) group found that normally developed children above the age of two years can achieve a basic understanding of "dead" if they have been helped to use their daily experiences with this goal in mind. Several authors, who have interviewed and tested children who have not experienced parental bereavement, suggest that children have little or no concept of death before the age of three (Anthony 1940, Schilder and Weschler 1934, Nagy 1948). The child's later ideas about death are a reflection of his physiologic and psychological maturation (Dunton 1970). It appears possible for very young children to understand the irreversible cessation of life functions quite apart from having a discrete concept of death itself.

Psychodynamic theorists have attempted to define the stages of maturation at which children develop the ability to perform the intrapsychic work of mourning. As effective mourning is recognized as adaptive and necessary for further development, theories of adverse consequences crop up along the developmental spectrum.

Klein (1940) hypothesized the normal mourning of the depressive position in the first three to five months of life that is interfered with by separation from mother and is not a response to separation from mother. Klein's theory of psychic development postulates a relatively complete intrapsychic structure quite early on, one aspect of which is normal mourning, and differs quite strikingly from the other authors cited herein who postulate a gradual development of intrapsychic structures with an attendant development of the abilities to perform intrapsychic work.

Freud and Burlingham (1943) cared for a large series of children separated from their families because of war conditions. They observed that "the childish grief is short-lived, mourning of equal intensity in an adult person would have to run its course throughout a year: the same process in the child between one and two years will be over in 36 to 48 hours. It is a psychological error to conclude from the short duration that the reaction is only a superficial one and can be treated lightly" (p. 51) and that "after three years of age children will not normally forget their parents" (p. 61). Although the intrapsychic dynamics of childhood mourning are not more explicitly detailed, it appears clear that these workers recognized that mourning was occurring, despite its difference from the adult process.

Furman's group (1974) places the ability to mourn effectively, with the help of an adult, to the developmental stage of object constancy, given an understanding of "dead," which they have found in children older than two years.

Other theorists have hypothesized that the psychic structure of the child is not sufficiently developed to accomplish the task of effective mourning and that this immaturity necessarily leads to developmental interference (Nagera 1970), a tendency toward regression (Scharl 1961), inadequate development of self-esteem (Roshlin 1961), an inability to master the oedipal conflict (Meiss 1952), and other morbid responses (Shaumbaugh 1961).

Wolfenstein (1966) concludes from a series of 42 early bereaved children in psychotherapy that successful mourning is not possible until the individual has negotiated the intrapsychic work of adolescence. This conclusion is quite strikingly different from Furman's. The theories cited here were developed from work with disturbed, bereaved children, and understandably the method of investigation, individual analysis, does not lend itself to the study of normal children for confirmatory evidence.

Learned Coping Styles

Depression has been likened to the animal model of learned helplessness (Seligman 1972) in that the reduced response initiation and the outlook of helplessness regarding one's ability to effect change are cognitive characteristics of depression (Birtchnell 1969); Brown et al. (1977:13) suggest "a person deprived of important sources of value can develop a feeling of helplessness. From this relatively specific feeling of hopelessness related to a particular event or difficulty a main general feeling of profound helplessness may develop, and this may form a central feature of depressive disorder itself."

Family Disruption

Family disruption following parental death is most probably not equivalent to that following divorce, for bereavement is not necessarily associated with antecedent family disharmony. Parental death may, however, be associated with chronic illness in a parent, affecting his ability to care for his children. Childhood psychiatric disorder has been shown to be associated with chronic illness in the parents (Rutter 1966). A parent's grief, after the death of a spouse, with all the inherent dysfunction, may be quite long-lived (Parkes and Brown 1972a, 1972b), and various coping styles employed by grieving parents have been described and studied (Hilgard et al. 1960; Lifshitz et al. 1977). Rutter (1971, 1972) has comprehensively reviewed the concepts of maternal deprivation with respect to the impact of a parent's death on the family. Finally, Marris (1958) has described the social intrafamilial and economic hardships experienced by a large sample of widows and their families following the death.

Short-Term Consequences of Bereavement

Several investigations have looked at the short-term consequences of adult bereavement, and numerous case historical and theoretical conceptual works have been reviewed elsewhere (Parkes 1972, Epstein et al. 1975, Maddison 1967). Lindemann (1944) undertook the first clinical study of adult grief, described the psychological and somatic symptomatology of normal grief, and presented case reports of morbid grief reactions. Other studies followed, as well as attempts at classification of adult morbid grief reactions (Bergan 1977, Liebermann 1978).

The short-term consequences of childhood bereavement have not been systematically studied. One can only speculate about the normal symptomatology or clinical course of grief in normal children. While the impact of a parent's death is certainly not equivalent to that of the death of a spouse (Clayton et al. 1969), perhaps a comparison with some data from adult studies may be useful. Parkes (1972) and others (Engle 1961) have employed structured interviews in prospective controlled studies of recently bereaved individuals at varying periods following the death. This approach has not been used with children and parents. Unstructured interviews and classroom observation have been used in two studies of children exposed to death of persons other than parents. McConville et al. (1972), interviewing a sample of psychiatrically disturbed children at varying periods shortly following the death of the director of the residence where the children were in treatment, reported various noneffective mourning reactions, including aggressive outbursts, regression, denial of feeling, and excessive guilt. Barnes (1964) observed nursery school children following the death of a classmate's mother.

Bereaved spouses have been shown, when compared with married controls, to demonstrate increases in sleep disturbance; appetite disturbances; weight loss; depression; restlessness; sense of strain; consumption of tobacco, liquor, and tranquilizers; and hospital admission rate for acute mental problems during the bereavement process (Parkes 1972, Barnes 1964, Clayton et al. 1972, Parkes and Brown 1972a, Clayton 1973, Cox and Ford 1964). These symptoms are present in adult depressive states as well (Lewis 1934).

There are two reports of increased rates of occurrence of parental bereavement among child psychiatry patients demonstrating prevailing sad mood in comparison with other child psychiatry patients (Caplan and Douglas 1969, Seligman et al. 1974).

Arthur and Kemme (1964) reviewed the symptomatology of 83 emotionally disturbed children, aged 4½ to 17 years; 35 percent of them appeared sad during the interview and were referred to child psychiatry at varying times following parental bereavement. They reported transitory disturbances of eating, intense separation fears, threatened and attempted suicide, phobic reactions, night terrors and nightmares, hopelessness, and apathy.

Kliman (1968) reported a series of 18 normal orphans, 14 years old and younger, from seven families, using interviews with the surviving parent done one day to five months following the other parent's death. Among the symptoms appearing one month following the parent's death were enuresis, learning disturbances, phobias, separation anxiety, hypochondriasis, conversion symptoms, and antisocial acts. In this sample, the youngest children, girls losing mothers, and adolescent boys losing fathers demonstrated the poorest postbereavement adjustment.

Stein and Susser (1969) documented a significantly increased incidence of and hospitalization for mental illness during the process of bereavement for widows.

Rutter (1971) has done the only systematic controlled study of bereaved child psychiatry patients using children from medical and dental clinics as controls. He found a significantly increased incidence of parental bereavement among the child psychiatry patients. The highest proportion occurred in the third and fourth years in this sample. Because the parents' death rate in this age period was so much higher than in earlier or later years, this study provides some evidence for a period of increased vulnerability. Rutter documented no significantly increased rates of occurrence for particular forms and disorder in the bereaved children. A few children, mostly adolescents, developed symptoms of depression or antisocial disorders closely following bereavement; however, almost one-third of the children developed symptoms after five or more years, suggesting that the consequences of parental bereavement play an important role in the development of subsequent disorder.

Conclusion

A systematic inquiry into normal bereavement reactions in children of various ages would permit a clearer definition of morbid grief reactions. The considerable evidence for an association between childhood bereavement and adult depression is reviewed. The methodology for systematic child assessment is developing, and a study of normal children's bereavement responses, similar to those available for adults, is possible. At present it is unclear to what extent the symptomatology demonstrated in normal childhood bereavement overlaps with that of childhood depressive states. One can speculate that a further classification of the symptomatology of childhood bereavement would usefully lend itself to the study of childhood depressive states.

REFERENCES AND BIBLIOGRAPHY

Abe, K. and P. Moran. 1969. "Parental Age in Homosexuals." *British Journal of Psychiatry* 115:313–17.

Abraham, K. 1911. "Notes on the Psychoanalytical Investigation and Treatment of Manic Depressive Insanity and Allied Conditions." In *Selected Papers on Psychoanalysis,* New York: Basic Books, 1960, pp. 137–56.

Anthony, S. 1940. *The Child's Discovery of Death.* New York: Harcourt, Brace.

Archibald, H., D. Bell, C. Miller, and R. Tuddenhorn. 1962. "Bereavement in Childhood and Adult Psychiatric Disturbance." *Psychosomatic Medicine* 24:343–51.

Arthur, B. and M. Kemme. 1964. "Bereavement in Childhood." *Journal of Child Psychology and Psychiatry* 5:37–49.

Barnes, M. J. 1964. "Reactions to the Death of a Mother." *Psychoanalytic Study of the Child* 19:334–57.

Barry, H. 1965. "Dependency in Adult Patients Following Early Maternal Bereavement." *Journal of Nervous and Mental Diseases* 140:196–206.

Barry, H. and E. Lindemann. 1960. "Critical Ages of Maternal Bereavement in Psychoneuroses." *Psychosomatic Medicine* 22:166–81.
Beck, A., B. Sethi, and R. Tuthill. 1963. "Childhood Bereavement and Adult Depression." *Archives of General Psychiatry* 9:295–302.
Bergan, L. 1977. "Human Grief—A Model for Prediction and Intervention." *American Journal of Orthopsychiatry* 47:196–206.
Birtchnell, J. 1969. "The Possible Consequence of Early Parent Death." *British Journal of Medical Psychology* 42:1–11.
Birtchnell, J. 1970. "Depression in Relation to Early and Recent Parent Death." *British Journal of Psychiatry* 116:299–306.
Birtchnell, J. 1971. "Early Parent Death in Relation to Size and Construction of Sibship in Psychiatric Patients and General Population Controls." *Acta Psychiatrica Scandinavica* 47:250–70.
Birtchnell, J. 1973. "The Use of a Psychiatric Case Register to Study Social and Familial Aspects of Mental Illness." *Social Science and Medicine* 7:145–53.
Birtchnell, J. 1975. "The Personality Characteristics of Early Bereaved Psychiatric Patients." *Social Psychiatry* 10:97–103.
Birtchnell, J. 1978. "Early Parent Death and Clinical Scales of the MMPI." *British Journal of Psychiatry* 132:574–79.
Bowlby, J. 1953. "Some Psychological Processes Set in Train By Early Mother-Child Separation." *Journal of Mental Science* 99:265–72.
Bowlby, J. 1960. "Grief and Mourning in Infancy and Early Childhood." *Psychoanalytic Study of the Child* 15:9–52.
Bowlby, J. 1961a. "Process of Mourning." *International Journal of Psychoanalysis* 42:31–40.
Bowlby, J. 1961b. "Childhood Mourning and Its Implications for Psychiatry." *The American Journal of Psychiatry* 118:481–98.
Bowlby, J. 1963. "Pathological Mourning and Childhood Mourning." *Journal of the American Psychoanalytic Association* 11:500–541.
Brill, N. and E. Liston. 1966. "Parental Loss in Adults with Emotional Disorders." *Archives of General Psychiatry* 14:307–13.
Brown, F. 1961. "Depression and Childhood Bereavement." *Journal of Mental Science* 107:754–77.
Brown, F. 1966. "Childhood Bereavement and Subsequent Psychiatric Disorder." *British Journal of Psychiatry* 112:1043–48.
Brown, G. W., T. Harris, and J. R. Copeland. 1977. "Depression and Loss." *British Journal of Psychiatry* 130:1–18.
Caplan, M. and V. Douglas. 1969. "Incidence of Parental Loss in Children with Depressed Mood." *Journal of Child Psychology and Psychiatry* 10:225–32.
Clayton, P. 1973. "The Clinical Morbidity of the First Year of Bereavement: A Review." *Comprehensive Psychiatry* 14:151–57.
Clayton, P., L. Desmarais, and G. Winokur. 1969. "A Study of Normal Bereavement." *American Journal of Psychiatry* 11:341–64.
Clayton, P., J. Halikas, and W. Maurice. 1972. "The Depression of Widowhood." *British Journal of Psychiatry* 120:71–78.

Cox, P. R. and J. R. Ford. 1964. "The Mortality of Widows Shortly After Widowhood." *Lancet* 1:163–64.

Dennehy, C. 1966. "Childhood Bereavement and Psychiatric Disorder." *British Journal of Psychiatry* 112:1040–69.

Deutsch, H. 1937. "Absence of Grief." *Psychoanalytic Quarterly* 6:12–22.

Dunton, H. D. 1970. "The Child's Concept of Grief." In B. Schoenberg et al., eds. *Loss and Grief,* New York: Columbia University Press.

Earle, A. M. and B. V. Earle. 1961. "Early Maternal Deprivation and Later Psychiatric Illness." *American Journal of Orthopsychiatry* 31:181–85.

Engle, G. 1961. "Is Grief an Illness?" *Psychosomatic Medicine* 23:18–22.

Epstein, L., L. Weitz, H. Robach, and E. McKee. 1975. "Research on Bereavement: A Selection and Critical Review." *Comprehensive Psychiatry* 16:537–46.

Fitzgerald, O. W. S. 1948. "Love, Deprivation and the Hysterical Personality." *Journal of Mental Science* 94:701–17.

Freud, S. 1917. *Mourning and Melancholia.* Standard ed., 14:237–58.

Freud, A. and D. Burlingham. 1943. *War and Children.* New York: Medical War Books.

Furman, E. 1974. *A Child's Parent Dies.* New Haven, Conn.: Yale University Press.

Granville-Grossman, K. L. 1966. "Early Bereavement and Schizophrenia." *British Journal of Psychiatry* 112:1027–34.

Gregory, I. 1958. "Studies of Parental Deprivation in Psychiatric Patients." *American Journal of Psychiatry* 115:432–44.

Gregory, I. 1966a. "Retrospective Dates Concerning Childhood Loss of a Parent." *Archives of General Psychiatry* 15:362–67.

Gregory, I. 1966b. "Retrospective Dates Concerning Childhood Loss of a Parent." *Archives of General Psychiatry* 15:354–61.

Hilgard, J., M. Newman, and F. Fisk. 1960. "Strength of Adult Ego Following Childhood Bereavement." *American Journal of Orthopsychiatry* 30:788–98.

Hill, O. 1969. "The Association of Childhood Bereavement with Suicide Attempt in Depressive Illness." *British Journal of Psychiatry* 115:301–04.

Hill, O. and J. Price. 1967. "Childhood Bereavement and Adult Depression." *British Journal of Psychiatry* 113:743–51.

Ingham, H. V. 1949. "A Statistical Study of Family Relationships in Psychoneurosis." *American Journal of Psychiatry* 106:91–98.

Klein, M. 1940. "Mourning and Its Relation to Manic Depressive States." In *Contribution to Psycho-Analysis, 1921–1945.* New York: McGraw Hill, 1967, pp. 311–38.

Kliman, G. 1968. *Psychological Emergencies of Childhood.* New York: Grune & Stratton, pp. 59–94.

Lewis, A. 1934. "Melancholia: A Clinical Survey of Depressive States." *Journal of Mental Science* 80:277–378.

Lewis, A. 1938. "States of Depression: Their Clinical and Aetiological Disorders: A Critical Review." *Omega* 2:107–17.

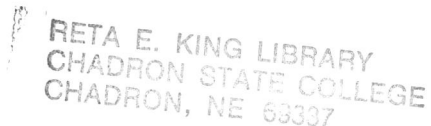

Liebermann, E. 1978. "Nineteen Cases of Morbid Grief." *British Journal of Psychiatry* 132:159–63.

Lifschitz, D., G. Berman, and D. Gilod. 1977. "Bereaved Children—The Effects of Mother's Perception and Social System Organization on Their Short Range Adjustment." *Journal of American Academy of Child Psychiatry* 16:272–84.

Lindemann, E. 1944. "Symptomatology and Management of Acute Grief. *American Journal of Psychiatry* 101:141–48.

Maddison, D. 1967. "Factors Affecting the Outcome of Conjugal Bereavement." *British Journal of Psychiatry* 113:1057–67.

Mahler, M. 1961. "On Sadness and Grief in Infancy and Childhood." *Psychoanalytic Study of the Child* 16:332–51.

Mahon, E. 1977. "The Painted Guinea Pig." *Psychoanalytic Study of the Child* 32:283–303.

Markusen, E. and R. Sutton. 1971. "Childhood Bereavement and Behavior Disorders: A Critical Review." *Omega* 2:107–17.

Marris, P. 1958. *Widows and Their Families.* London: Routledge and Kegan Paul.

McConville, B., L. Boa, and A. Purohit. 1972. "Mourning Depressive Responses of Children in Residence Following Sudden Death of Parent Figures." *Journal of American Academy of Child Psychiatry* 11:341–64.

Meiss, M. 1952. "The Oedipal Problem of a Fatherless Child." *Psychoanalytic Study of the Child* 7:216–29.

Moran, P. 1968. "Maternal Age and Parental Loss." *British Journal of Psychiatry* 114:207–14.

Munro, A. 1966. "Parental Deprivation in Depressive Patients." *British Journal of Psychiatry* 112:443–57.

Nagera, H. 1970. "Children's Reactions to the Death of Important Objects." *Psychoanalytic Study of the Child* 25:360–400.

Nagy, M. 1948. "The Child's Theories Concerning Death." *Journal of Genetic Psychology* 73:3–27.

Norton, A. 1952. "Incidence of Neurosis Related to Maternal Age and Birth Order." *British Journal of Social Medicine* 6:253–58.

Parkes, C. M. 1972. *Bereavement: Studies in Grief in Adult Life.* New York: Universities Press.

Parkes, C. M. and R. J. Brown. 1972a. "The Depression of Widowhood." *British Journal of Psychiatry* 120:71–78.

Parkes, C. M. and R. J. Brown. 1972b. "Health After Bereavement: A Controlled Study of Young Boston Widows." *Psychosomatic Medicine* 34:449–61.

Pitts, F., J. Meyer, M. Brooks and G. Winokur. 1965. "Adult Psychiatric Illness Assessed for Parental Loss and Psychiatric Illness in Family Members." *American Journal of Psychiatry* 121: Suppl. I–X.

Rochlin, G. 1961. "The Dread of Abandonment: Contribution to the Etiology of the Loss Complex and to Depression." *Psychoanalytic Study of the Child* 16:451–70.

Rutter, M. 1966. "Children of Sick Parents. An Environmental and Psychiatric Study." *Maudsley Monograph,* No. 16, London: Oxford University Press.
Rutter, M. 1971. "Parent-Child Separation: Psychological Effects on Children." *Journal of Child Psychology and Psychiatry* 12:233–60.
Rutter, M. 1972. *Maternal Deprivation Reassessed.* Middlesex, England: Penguin.
Rutter, M. and L. Hershov. 1976. *Child Psychiatry—Modern Approaches.* London: Blackwell Scientific Approaches.
Scharl, A. 1961. "Regression and Restitution in Object Loss." *Psychoanalytic Study of the Child* 16:471–80.
Schilder, P. and D. Weschler. 1934. "The Attitudes of Children Toward Death." *Journal of Genetic Psychology* 45:406–51.
Seligman, M. E. P. 1972. "Learned Helplessness." *Annual Review of Medicine* 23:407–12.
Seligman, R., G. Glaser, J. Rouk, and L. Harris. 1974. "The Effect of Early Parent Loss in Adolescence." *Archives of General Psychiatry* 31:475–79.
Sethi, B. 1964. "Relationship of Separation to Depression." *Archives of General Psychiatry* 10:486–96.
Shambaugh, R. 1961. "A Study of Loss Reaction in a Seven-Year Old." *Psychoanalytic Study of the Child* 16:510–22.
Spitz, R. 1945. "Hospitalism: An Inquiry into the Genesis of Psychiatric Conditions in Early Childhood." *Psychoanalytic Study of the Child* 1:53–74.
Spitz, R. 1946. "Anaclitic Depression: An Inquiry into the Genesis of Psychiatric Condition in Early Childhood." *Psychoanalytic Study of the Child* 2:312–42.
Statistical Abstract of the United States. 1977. No. 555, 98th Annual Ed. Washington, U.S. Department of Commerce, Bureau of Census, p. 352.
Stein, F. and M. Susser. 1969. "Widowhood and Mental Illness." *British Journal of Preventive Social Medicine* 23:106–10.
Wilson, I., L. Alltop, and W. Buffaloe. 1967. "Parental Bereavement in Childhood: MMPI Profiles in Depressed Population." *British Journal of Psychiatry* 113:761–64.
Wolfenstein, M. 1966. "How Is Mourning Possible?" *Psychoanalytic Study of the Child* 21:93–123.
Wretmark, G. 1959. "A Study of Grief Reactions." *Acta Psychiatrica et Neurologica Scandinavica,* pp. 134–39; Supplementum, pp. 292–99.
Young, M., B. Benjamin, and C. Wallis. 1963. "The Mortality of Widowers." *Lancet* 2:454–56.

Acknowledgment

The author thanks Dr. David Shaffer and Dr. Rodman Gilder for their help in preparing this review.

· 9 ·

Children's Reactions to Parental Death

RICHARD A. GARDNER

Now I lay me down to sleep.
I pray the Lord my soul to keep.
If I should die before I wake,
I pray the Lord my soul to take.
Also, God, please take care of my Mommy,
my Daddy, my brother, my sister, grandma Annie,
grandpa Joe, etc., etc.

This prayer, and many variations of it, have been heard in assorted societies throughout the world. It is usually taught to very young children and is so ancient that its origins are unknown (Wahl 1958). The fact that it has been learned by generation upon generation of children is testimony to our compelling need to deal with the painful awareness of our mortality. Two of the most common defense mechanisms that people have used to avoid dealing with their awareness of their ultimate demise are communicated to the child in this prayer: the denial of death's finality (in this case via the survival of a soul) and the appeal to an omnipotent entity (God) to protect and maintain one's life as well as that of dear ones.

By avoiding the death issue ourselves and by teaching denial to children, both parent and child are handicapped in their abilities to cope effectively with death. When children become old enough to think about the world around them, they ask two fundamental questions: Where did I come from? and Where do I go from here? Until recently, both questions were taboo. Now, most educated parents speak honestly and directly with regard to sex, but many are still reluctant to answer freely questions about death. Consequently, our children today are growing up with healthier attitudes toward sex, but they are often not equipped to deal with death as well as they might when they have the misfortune of being confronted with it firsthand. They may thereby suffer a variety of unnecessary psychological reactions that could have been avoided if healthier attitudes about death had been imparted. The therapist and other adults with whom children are involved have a unique opportunity to provide such preventive counseling. Here, I discuss one aspect of such counseling, namely, the situation where the child is confronted with the death of a parent.

Early Life Exposures and Experiences That Can Help Children Deal More Effectively with Death

A child's first contact with death usually comes through exposure to dead insects, worms, and other animals. As early as the age of two a child can appreciate the irreversibility of the death of a bug, bird, or domestic pet (Furman 1974:50). Such experiences provide the child with the opportunity to observe firsthand the fact that the dead animal does not move spontaneously and cannot be brought back to life and with concrete knowledge of the nature of death (Kliman 1968:90). Parents who protect their children from such exposures deprive them of healthy growth experiences. The parent who surreptitiously replaces a dead goldfish or hamster with an identical live one in order to protect the child from experiencing the painful loss is doing the child a disservice. It would be better to help the child express sorrow over the loss and seriously assist in the burial or disposal of the animal in a special place or in a special way that is agreeable to the child (Fraiberg 1958:273; Arnstein 1962:186–89). Learning, even secondhand, about the death of an adult may also be helpful in preparing the child for the death of someone closer. Parents who mistakenly assume that children are too fragile to bear such news and who protect their children from such information are depriving them of a salutary exposure that brings death into their scheme of things and lessens the shock effect when someone they love dies.

Helping the Children Deal with the Impending Death of a Parent

This is a complex issue. If the parent has accepted the fact that he is going to die and is willing to discuss it, then the child may have the opportunity to adjust slowly to the imminent tragic event. The fact of death, then, is not sudden to the child; he has had the opportunity for some desensitization and anticipatory mourning and is in the best position to deal with the trauma. However, when the dying parent uses denial mechanisms to deal with his impending death, this should be respected and the parent should not be confronted with statements about his inevitable demise. The young child of such a parent cannot, however, usually be relied upon to join with older children and adults in supporting such defenses and is liable to say such things as, "Daddy, Mommy says you're going to die. Is that right?" Therefore, it may be preferable to withhold information from the child or tell him what is being told the patient. Clearly, it is the humane course of action even though the parent's needs are being given priority over those of the child (Gardner 1971:617, Furman 1974:19).

The Mourning Process in Children

For the purposes of this discussion I use the term *mourning* to refer to the series of psychological reactions that a person may experience in response to and in the attempt to deal with the death of someone who has been meaningful. The questions of whether the child mourns and, if so, at what age he develops the capacity to do so have involved many investigators. I concern myself here with only a brief statement of some of the more common positions.

Most agree that the child must be old enough to have differentiated himself from the dead person in order to mourn the loss of that person. During the first six months of life, the child is still psychologically fused with the mother (or her surrogate) and cannot specifically experience her loss. He may, however, feel distress about any deterioration of or change in care that may result if the mother dies during this period (Nagera 1970:367–69). During the second half of the first year of life the child develops the ability to differentiate himself from his mother. A. Freud (1952:43–45) believes that the child can mourn only when he has developed object constancy, that is, when he can differentiate a whole, discrete, satisfying object who is independent from himself and separate from others as well. This ability generally occurs during the second half of the first year of life. S. Freud (1959:159) considered the acceptance of the fact that the loved one no longer exists to be the first step necessary to begin the mourning process. Without this realization the child cannot withdraw libidinal energy from the lost object and invest such energy in others. Nagera (1970:375–76) contends that the child cannot mourn until he can appreciate the irreversibility of death.

Most agree that the aforementioned capacities must be present before meaningful mourning can occur. There are, however, disparate investigative opinions about when such ability develops. The range varies from the first year of life to the late teens (Wolfenstein 1969: 432; 1973:433; Nagera 1970:262–63, 283; McConville et al. 1972:362). R. Furman (1968:53) and E. Furman (1974:270–75) contend that very young children can mourn if given a proper environment. It should be one in which the child is helped to deal realistically with the death and to express his thoughts and feelings (without denial or avoidance). The author concurs with the Furmans. Probably the most important factor determining when children can appreciate death (first with regard to others and then with regard to themselves—the two do not occur simultaneously) is the parental attitude toward death. The child who grows up in a home where the subject of death is taboo is not likely to acquire the necessary awareness for a meaningful mourning experience. Those who contend that a child cannot mourn until early or even late adolescence are likely to deprive younger children of a healthy psychological experience that can prevent the formation of subsequent psychopathology.

Facilitating Healthy Mourning

The mourning process cannot begin if there are reality problems that are of immediate concern and demand first consideration (E. Furman 1974:22, 164). If the child is afraid that he will no longer be provided with food, clothing, shelter, and other necessities of life because of the death of his father, he may not be able to involve himself meaningfully with mourning. Accordingly, the surviving mother should make every effort to provide the child with appropriate reassurances regarding such fears quite early so that mourning can get underway.

When children learn of someone's death, they are likely to respond first with fear regarding their own survival. Adults have the same response. Someone else's death confronts us most poignantly with the reality of our own mortality. We cannot mourn the loss of someone else until we have been reassured that our own death is not imminent. Therefore, the surviving parent does well to reassure the child that he is very young, has a long life ahead of him, does not suffer with the disease that took the life of his parent, can generally avoid such fatal accidents, and so forth (E. Furman 1974:96–97).

Well-meaning parents often avoid communicating to children their real views regarding death from the fear that such harsh truths will be psychologically detrimental. They may tell their children about a blissful afterlife in heaven without any conviction that this is so. Or they may give long theological and philosophical explanations, beyond the child's comprehension, in the attempt to avoid a direct disclosure of the facts or their own convictions. Generally, the child appreciates that such a parent is being evasive or dishonest. This produces unnecessary confusion and distrust at a time when the child is most in need of a secure and trusting relationship with the surviving parent. The parent does well, therefore, to tell the child exactly what he believes to have taken place (Maurer 1966:65, Arnstein 1962:185, 196). If the parent genuinely believes in some type of survival after death (whether in the form of body, or soul, or both), he should impart this belief to the child. If he is dubious about the existence of a hereafter, he does well to impart this notion in the proper setting. Or if he does not have a particular conviction, this should also be communicated (Gardner 1971:616): "Some people believe that Mommy is now in a place called heaven. Others say that that's not true. Daddy just doesn't know. As you get older you'll be able to make up your own mind about it." The child may wonder whether the dead parent is in pain. Reassuring the child that this is not the case can also lessen some of his anxiety.

Many children will view the parent's death to be an abandonment and may fear that the remaining parent will either die or abandon them as well. It can be useful, therefore, to reassure such a child that the surviving parent is healthy and well and that he will be taking care of the child (Clark 1972:709–11). Mourning is best accomplished as a shared family experience. The loss of the dead parent is best relieved when the child has a warm and close experience with the remaining members of his family (E. Furman 1974:57, Fleck 1972:194).

The Question of Whether the Child Should Attend the Funeral

Parents often fear that the child's attending the funeral will be excessively upsetting to the child and result in untoward psychological consequences. One of the most compelling arguments for allowing the child to attend the funeral is that it can provide him with the most meaningful firsthand information about what death entails. Children learn best from concrete experiences, and the funeral (its morbid aspects notwithstanding) can most effectively provide such an experience. Furthermore, observing the expression of emotion that usually occurs at the funeral makes it easier for the child to express his own feelings. Such release is central to the mourning process (Gardner 1978:216–21). If the parent fears that the child is so young that he may disrupt the services, then the services might be shortened or arrangements made for the child to attend only a portion, for example, the services and not the burial (E. Furman 1974:21, Gardner 1971:617–18).

Grieving

Grieving provides a piecemeal desensitization to the trauma of loss of a loved one. Every time the survivor thinks about the dead person, the pain becomes less and the loss more bearable. The process allows for a slow and continual release of the emotions produced by the loss. Blockage of such emotional expression prevents grieving and is one of the most common causes of psychological problems following parental death.

Providing the child with a photograph, a treasured possession, or other memorabilia of the dead parent can facilitate the expression of grief (E. Furman 1974:24, Gardner 1971:618–19). It is as if the object itself catalyzes the emotional response. The child may repeatedly ask the same questions about the dead parent: how did he die, will he return to life, where is he now? The surviving parent should be helped to appreciate that such repetition aids the resolution of reactions to the parent's death. Squelching them interferes with the healthy grieving process. In addition, such questions help the child correct the various cognitive distortions he might have about death, especially in the family where the subject has been taboo. The child may become preoccupied with a particular story (sometimes self-created) that is related to the parental death, and it may even be acted out in little plays (Bergen 1958:410). These are generally of great psychological significance. They help the child desensitize himself to the loss and serve other purposes in the grieving process. The therapist of the grieving child should have deep respect for these stories, and the surviving parent should be advised of their significance and encouraged to have the greatest tolerance for their indulgence by the child.

Anger

When a parent dies, the child is deprived of one of his most treasured possessions. The child becomes deeply frustrated over the loss and is bound to feel angry (although he may not allow expression of resentment). The anger may be revealed in boisterous and noisy play (Arnstein 1962:196), in nightmares (Gardner 1973:136–37, Chethik 1970:633–34), symbolically (for example, in soiling) (Chethik 1970:629–30), or projected onto others—for example, the surviving parent (Scharl 1961:474; E. Furman 1974:169). The surviving parent should be helped to accept and even to encourage expression (but not acting out) of such angry responses (to a reasonable degree) and should be helped to appreciate that they are part of the healthy child's response. Squelching expression of anger can contribute to the formation of symptoms that are indicative of a maladaptive reaction to the parental death (Clark 1972:709–11).

Identification with the Dead Parent

Psychologically incorporating the dead parent is a primitive mechanism for compensating for the loss (E. Furman 1974:25). It is as if the child were saying: "My daddy is not really gone; I have him here inside of me." Seven of the eighteen bereaved children studied by Kliman (1968:79, 87–88) showed evidence for such incorporation via identification with parental interests, mannerisms, and behavior. Although the acquisition of parental traits often exists in fantasy only, it can serve to motivate the child to gain real competence in a field that the dead parent was interested in at a rate that would not have occurred if the parent had remained alive. Accordingly, it can contribute to the child's mastering the deprivations he suffers from the trauma of parental death, and it can assist the child in acquiring other useful traits (Gauthier 1965:484–85). Sometimes the identification process is enhanced when the child acts out in play the parental attributes he is trying to acquire. It is as if he were practicing those attributes in an attempt to gain greater proficiency in their use. Such identifications can be helpful if they are confined to the healthy qualities in the dead parent and do not restrict the child from relatively autonomous development.

Forming a Substitute Relationship

One of the fundamental purposes of the mourning process is the decathexis of or disinvolvement with the internalized image of the lost love object (S. Freud 1959:154, R. Furman 1968:52–53). One cannot hope, however, for total decathexis. The closer and more meaningful the relationship with the lost parent has been, the greater the likelihood that there will be some residual cathexis—some lingering feelings of affection, respect, and involvement. The goal of the mourning process is not, however, merely the liberation of a significant degree of emotional investment from the image of the dead parent; rather, the ultimate purpose of mourning is for the child to have meaningful involvement with a substitute. This is the healthiest adaptation to the death of a loved one and the most predictable way to avoid the development of untoward reactions to the loss (Gardner 1978:223–25). If the child fails to free himself from the dead parent and remains preoccupied with him, he will not be likely to form meaningful relationships with surrogates. Some children may feel disloyal about affectionate feelings for the surrogate parent, and such guilt should be relieved by helping the child appreciate that his feelings are normal, healthy, and predictable (Kliman 1968:81–82).

Early Pathological Reactions to Parental Death

Parental death does not necessarily cause a child to develop psychopathological reactions. One must differentiate between psychopathology that results from the lack of a successful mourning experience and the psychopathology that results from the deprivation caused by the absence of a parent. In this section I discuss the former reactions, which usually manifest themselves in the period soon after the death of the parent. In the next section, I discuss briefly the latter group of reactions, which may take many months or years to manifest themselves (and when they do, they are generally more deep seated).

Denial

Especially during the period immediately following the parent's death a certain amount of denial on the child's part is normal. Since the child is prone to primitive thinking, he is more likely than the adult to use denial as a defense mechanism. The adult, however, readily uses the mechanism as well. Because the defense is so commonly invoked, it may be difficult to determine at what point normal denial ends and pathological denial begins. Generally, the greater the reality distortions and the longer they are maintained, the more it is likely that pathological denial is present.

Generally, the child reacts less grievously than the adult to the parent's death. The child may use play, however, to work out his feelings symbolically. Therefore, he seems to be reacting less strongly than he really is. The desire to avoid painful effects also contributes to the child's calmer reaction. In the eighteen children studied by Kliman, all of whom were told about the death of their parents, denial existed for as long as a week (Kliman 1968:81–82).

In one common mechanism, the child may say something that seems to indicate acceptance of the reality of the parent's death and then follows such a statement with one implying nonacceptance: "I know father's died, but what I can't understand is why he doesn't come home for supper." S. Freud describes this as a splitting of the ego (1953:254). The denial mechanism here is so strong that the child does not seem to be uncomfortable with the impossible contradiction. Nine to ten year olds typically use humor for the purpose of denying the painful affects associated with their awareness of death. Most children of that age laugh heartily at this parody of the traditional bedtime prayer:

> *Now I lay me down to sleep,*
> *A bag of peanuts at my feet.*
> *If I should die before I wake,*
> *Give them to my brother Jake.*

Pathological denial in the child is commonly caused by denial by the surviving parent or failure by the surviving parent to impart information to the child (Brown 1968:445). Cultural and social attitudes that discourage the family from talking about the unpleasant may also contribute to the child's use of denial.

Suppression and Repression

A common way in which the mourning process is prevented from taking its natural course is the child's suppression (conscious) or repression (unconscious) of his grief. Generally, parental and cultural influences play a significant role in producing such inhibition. The family may support the view that expression of feelings is somehow primitive or improper and that those who deal with pain stoically and with composure are more admirable. The child whose father has just died may continually hear people compliment his mother regarding how well she is bearing the strain. If she does "break down" (clearly a pejorative term) and cry, she is consoled until her tears cease. Such observations can have a powerful influence on a child and can inhibit his mourning process without any more active interference on the part of the surviving family and friends.

The child may, however, be exposed to more direct communications that may block his grieving. He may be told that "boys don't cry" or encouraged to "see how brave" he can be. The child may be complimented for being "grown up," that is, not "crying like a baby." Significant adults may consider the child's ability to inhibit his tears as a sign of "maturity" and "good adjustment." Overprotective parents may operate on the principle that everything must be done to prevent the child from experiencing pain. The child of such a parent may early inhibit his own painful expression because he recognizes that such expression causes the parent discomfort. He may come to feel guilty about expressing painful affects because his parents view such expression as proof of their failure to produce a happy child. The therapist who can convince the surviving family how unhealthy these attitudes are can perform a valuable service for the child whose parent has died.

Guilt

There are many ways in which the bereaved child may come to feel guilty. Although common, the guilt reaction is generally pathological and can add an unnecessary burden to the child at this already unfortunate period of his life. Guilt is associated with the anxiety alleviation that accompanies the common "there but for the grace of God go I" reaction to the death of someone close. This is especially true when death has been caused by an accident in which the survivors are among the grievers. To have the thought "I'm glad it was he, rather than I" would make most of us feel guilty. The child in such a situation should be helped to appreciate that such reactions are common, if not universal, and that he is not loathsome for having them.

As mentioned, children generally do not react to death with as much overt grief as adults. A child, observing how painfully the adults around him are reacting to the death, may come to feel that he is deficient because of his less pained reaction and that he may not have loved his deceased parent as much as he should have. Such a child has to be helped to appreciate that most children react that way and that his love of the dead parent is not being questioned (the situation in most cases).

The young child's cognitive egocentricity is so great that he tends to see himself as the cause of many of the phenomena around him (Piaget 1954:219–319). With such a sense of self it is not surprising that the child may consider a parent's death to have been the result of some wish or thought on his part, and this is likely to result in feelings of guilt. All children harbor angry feelings toward their parents, and at times these may be exhibited in the form of wishes that the parent go away and even die. Accordingly, the child may view the parental death as the fulfillment of such wishes and may consider the death to be his own fault. Also, thinking in accordance with the primitive law of talion (an eye for an eye, a tooth for a tooth), the child may fear that the dead parent will return to wreak vengeance on the person who caused his death. The child may fear that the parent's ghost hovers over him, waiting for the moment (usually at night) when he can kill him in retaliation. Such a child has to be helped to appreciate that all children have angry thoughts toward parents and those feelings cannot per se cause anyone any harm. Providing the child with specific information about the cause of death can also be reassuring in such situations (Gardner 1978:228–29).

The child may feel guilty about the anger he feels toward the deceased parent for having died and "abandoned" him. He may believe that such anger demonstrates some deficiency in his love, that no good and worthwhile child would have such angry feelings toward a dead parent. If he hears repeated words of praise about his dead parent, his feelings of self-loathing may intensify. Again, such a child has to be helped to appreciate that such angry feelings are common and predictable and that he does not differ from others for having them. He has, in fact, been deprived of one of his most treasured possessions and it is understandable that he would be frustrated and therefore angry about it.

A bereaved child's guilt can also be a manifestation of the attempt to gain a sense of control over a situation that is clearly beyond his control. The child may become preoccupied with the belief that he caused his parent's death, for example, "He died because I didn't treat him well. I was very bad and that upset him and made him sick." Implied in the notion of "It's my fault" is the concept of control. If the child harbors the delusion that he caused his parent's death, then presumably he has the ability to bring the parent back to life, or at least to prevent death in others (such as the surviving parent) (Gardner 1971:619; 1969a:146–55; 1969b:82–90; 1970:124–28). Such a child has to be helped to differentiate between those things in life that he can control and those that he cannot. He has to learn to resign himself to his impotency in certain areas. However, he also has it within his power to form deeper relationships with surviving adults, as well as new ones with substitutes, both in the present and future.

The surviving parent may produce guilt in the child by comments like, "What would your mother think if she were alive to see what you've done?" "Your father will never rest peacefully in his grave as long as you continue being so bad," and "Your mother would roll over in her grave if she knew what you said today." Instilling in the child the idea that the spirit of the dead parent is still somehow hovering about observing him or that in the grave the parent can still react to what the child does and says may be very effective ways of getting a child to comply with parental requests and demands, but they can also be the most predictable ways of producing pathological guilt.

The guilt induced in such children may not only interfere with the natural mourning process but may also contribute to the formation of various symptoms. For example, the child may attempt to reduce the guilt through antisocial behavior in the hope of getting caught and punished. He may become accident prone in the attempt to hurt (punish) himself and thereby lessen his guilt. Obsessive preoccupations with feelings of unworthiness associated with self-denigration for the most minor indiscretions may be another way of dealing with such guilt.

As the reader can appreciate, there are a variety of ways in which the child of a deceased parent may become inordinately guilty. The therapist does well to determine the causes in each case and attempt to alleviate those causes in the manner most appropriate to each situation. It is only in this way that the therapist can hope to alleviate such guilt, prevent its interference with mourning, and prevent its contribution to the symptoms that are often formed to deal with guilt. The author has elaborated elsewhere (Gardner 1977:45–50) on these and other forms of guilt that children may exhibit in response to parental death.

Regression

Most children will regress to some degree in response to the death of a parent. The child may become more infantile and more demanding of food and attention, may want more cuddling, may reinstitute babytalk, and so forth. Such regression, when it is mild and transient, should be considered normal. In addition, the surviving parent probably should indulge it to some degree because it can provide the child with reassurance that others are available to satisfy his needs. Regression as a reaction to parental death is generally more common in young children than in older children.

When the regression is severe, the child does not proceed along the "developmental track" but remains fixated at an earlier level or at the level he had attained at the time of the parent's death. The child may regress or become fixated with regard to ego functions as well, so that his intellectual and social functioning may become impaired and retarded. In therapy as well, the child may exhibit regressive phenomena and it is up to the therapist to create a proper balance between its indulgence and resolution (Shambaugh 1961:513–19).

When the regression reaches pathological proportions, the ways in which the surviving parent has handled the child have often contributed. For example, the parent may have become overprotective, in part to compensate the child for the loss. The parent may have tried to instill a maturity in the child that he is not capable of achieving. Repeatedly telling the child "You have to take on many extra duties, now that Mommy's gone" may be anxiety provoking to the child and he may regress in order to avoid those extra responsibilities. (A certain amount of increased responsibility after parental death can be salutary; it is when excessive pressures for such maturity are applied that the child may react pathologically.) The parent may unwittingly evoke oedipal anxieties that the child may react to with regression. For example, the mother who says to her son "Now that Daddy's gone, you're the man of the house" may provoke great anxieties in the boy over the awesome responsibilities he is being asked to assume (Gardner 1971:619).

Depression

In spite of the previously mentioned tendency of the child to react less strongly to death than the adult, the death of a parent is certainly something a child is likely to get depressed over.

S. Freud (1959:152–70) described mourning as the normal reaction to the loss of a loved object and considered melancholia to be the result of the bereaved person's failure to decathect his libido from the internal image of the lost object. He related the self-derogation that is typically seen in depression to anger that the bereaved feels toward the deceased and redirects against himself. Depression can then occur when mourning has not taken its normal course.

E. Furman (1974:191–97), in her extensive study of bereaved children, could not find an invariable relationship between depression and inhibited anger. Those children who became depressed, however, often suffer concomitant losses. Many bereaved children did not become depressed, and she could not find any particular factor that could be of predictive value in determining which children would become so after parental death. Many children were not even conscious of their sadness.

In severe cases of depression the child may become apathetic. He loses interest in the world about him and appears to be insensitive to stimuli, both internal and external. In such a state the child desensitizes himself to the painful affects associated with the loss of the parent, especially the sadness (E. Furman 1974:191–97). In extreme cases the bereaved child may attempt suicide. Identification elements may be present in such cases, as well as the attempts to reunite with the dead parent. One of E. Furman's patients ingested the same pills her mother had used in her (the mother's) suicide. Here both identification and reunion elements were present.

Late Pathological Reactions to Parental Death

The pathological reactions to parental death that can occur beyond the mourning period can often be divided into two categories: those that result from the failure of the child to have had a successful mourning experience and those that are the result of the deprivation the child suffers because of the loss of a parent. Of course, there can be overlap between the two groups.

With regard to the first category, I have described in the previous section the common ways in which the mourning process can be inhibited. Clearly, the therapist does best for the bereaved child by counseling the surviving parent early so that the various kinds of inhibitions do not occur. When the therapist is consulted after some of the deleterious influences are already operating, he can still aid in preventing their perpetuation. Often, however, the therapist is asked to see a child months, and even years, after the death of the parent and it becomes apparent in some cases that the child has not mourned and that a belated mourning experience may be salutary. It appears that in some children the passage of time does not seem to preclude the value of a belated mourning experience. Elsewhere (Gardner 1971:620–22) the author has described a four-year-old girl whose brother had died six months before her first visit. She had never been told the circumstances of her brother's death or allowed to have a mourning experience. She presented with a constellation of phobic symptoms all of which appeared to be related to her failure to have worked through her reactions to her brother's death. When the parents provided her with information about the brother's death, and with various memorabilia, and encouraged her questioning them about the brother's demise, she underwent a belated mourning experience and her symptoms cleared. In some cases the patient may profit from such belated mourning; in others the pent-up feelings contribute to the formation of other psychological difficulties and a simple mourning experience will not be completely therapeutic.

The appearance of symptoms related to the loss of the parent is also common. New symptoms appeared within one month of bereavement in all eighteen children studied by Kliman (1968:78, 80). The most common symptoms observed were fearfulness, separation anxiety, insomnia, and eating disturbances. The child may develop significant loss of trust. After all, if one's parent can abandon one, who can really be trusted? Symptoms may develop that symbolically represent a search for the lost parent (Wolfenstein 1969:140, 447). For example, the child may become very materialistic or even steal—the acquired objects symbolizing the lost parent. The child's ambivalence toward the lost parent may be split. The positive feelings may remain with the dead parent and the negative ones directed toward the surviving parent or a surrogate (Wolfenstein 1969:432–33, 449, 459).

Idealization of the dead parent is common. It is not considered respectful to speak ill of the dead, especially to their children. Such withholding of information can contribute to the child's idolizing the dead parent. All children do best with a balanced view of their parents, with accurate recognition of both their assets and liabilities. Without such experiences the child is likely to have unrealistic views of and expectations from others. The child who idealizes a dead parent and grows up believing that there was never anyone else who matched him or her in benevolence, virtue, honesty, and the like is bound to be disappointed with all other human beings he may encounter because they inevitably reveal their weaknesses. Accordingly, surviving parents do well to avoid such idealization and should describe the dead parent in a truthful and balanced way. Sometimes such idolization may serve as a reaction formation against unconscious angry feelings that the child harbors toward the dead parent—feelings that he is too guilty to express. In such cases attempts should be made to assuage the child's guilt and encourage expression of the anger. Sometimes the surviving parent has pathological needs of his or her own to idolize the dead spouse. In such cases these have to be worked out first; if not, the child is not likely to discontinue his own idolization.

The surviving parent may be a pathologically dependent person who parentified the dead spouse and related as a child to him or her. Such a parent may try to place the child in the parental role after the death of the spouse (Arnstein, 1962:198). Some children react to such pressures with regression. Others, however, may not only take on the caretaker role but may also remain at home long beyond the time when their peers have achieved independence. Through guilt induced by the surviving parent they remain both protector and dependent child and never assume an independent existence. Finally, the death of the surviving parent may become a formidable trauma from which the child may never recover, because he may never have learned to live an adult, self-sufficient, and independent existence.

The younger the child at the time of the parental death and the longer he is not provided with a surrogate, the greater the likelihood that he will be psychologically traumatized and that the chances of his developing psychopathology will be enhanced. However, such pathology can, in my opinion, most often be prevented by adequate affection and attention from the remaining parent. The literature is replete with articles describing the relationship between parental loss and the development of subsequent psychopathology. Many have described a relationship between parental death in childhood and a variety of psychiatric disorders in later life, the most common being schizophrenia and other forms of psychosis, juvenile delinquency, psychopathy, alcoholism, depression, and suicide. Bowlby (1952) and Kliman (1968:59–74) provide good reviews of the literature on this relationship, which in the opinion of most therapists has by now been firmly established. Most therapists agree, however, that many of these disorders can be prevented by the remaining parent's providing meaningful concern and involvement.

REFERENCES

Arnstein, H. S. 1962. *What to Tell Your Child.* New York, Pocket Books, pp. 186–89.

Bergen, M. E. 1958. "The Effect of Severe Trauma on a Four-Year-Old Child." In *Psychoanalytic Study of the Child,* Vol. 13. New York: International Universities Press, p. 411.

Bowlby, J. 1952. *Maternal Care and Mental Health.* Geneva: World Health Organization.

Brown, F. 1968. "Bereavement and Lack of a Parent in Childhood." In E. Miller, ed. *Foundations of Child Psychiatry,* p. 445. London: Pergamon Press.

Chethik, M. 1970. "The Impact of Object Loss on a Six-Year-Old." *Journal of The American Academy of Child Psychiatry* 9(4):633–34.

Clark, M. B. 1972. "A Therapeutic Approach to Treating a Grieving 2½-Year-Old." *Journal of The American Academy of Child Psychiatry* 11(4):709–11.

Fleck, S. 1972. "Some Basic Aspects of Family Pathology." In B. Wolman, *Manual of Child Psychopathology,* p. 194. New York: McGraw-Hill.

Fraiberg, S. H. 1968. *The Magic Years.* New York: C Scribner, p. 273.

Freud, A. 1952. "The Mutual Influences in the Development of Ego and Id." In *Psychoanalytic Study of the Child,* Vol. 7. New York: International Universities Press, pp. 43–45.

Freud, S. 1959 (1917). *Mourning and Melancholia.* In *Collected Papers,* Vol. 4. New York: Basic Books, p. 159.

Freud, S. 1900. *The Interpretation of Dreams.* In *The Standard Edition of the Complete Psychological Works of Sigmund Freud,* Vol. 4 London: The Hogarth Press, 1953, p. 254.

Furman, E. 1974. *A Child's Parent Dies.* New Haven: Yale University Press, p. 50.

Furman, R. A. 1968. "Additional Remarks on Mourning and the Young Child." 18: *Bulletin of the Philadelphia Association for Psychoanalysis,* 18:53.

Gardner, R. A. 1969a. "Guilt, Job, and J. B." *Medical Opinion and Review* 5(2):146–55.

―――― 1969b. "The Guilt Reaction of Parents of Children with Severe Physical Disease." *American Journal of Psychiatry* 126(5):82–90.

―――― 1970. "The Use of Guilt as a Defense Against Anxiety." *The Psychoanalytic Review* 57(1):124–28.

―――― 1971. *Therapeutic Communication with Children: The Mutual Storytelling Technique.* New York: Jason Aronson, p. 617.

―――― 1973. *Understanding Children.* New York: Jason Aronson, pp. 136–37.

―――― 1977. "Children's Guilt Reactions to Parental Death: Psychodynamics and Therapeutic Management." *Hiroshima Forum for Psychology* 4:45–50.

―――― 1978. *The Boys and Girls Book About One-Parent Families.* New York: Putnam Sons, pp. 223–25.

Gauthier, Y. 1965. "The Mourning Reaction of a Ten-and-a-Half-Year-Old-Boy." In *Psychoanalytic Study of the Child,* Vol. 20. New York: International Universities Press, pp. 484–85, 489.

Kliman, G. 1968. *Psychological Emergencies of Childhood.* New York: Grune & Stratton, pp. 79, 87–88.

Maurer, A. 1966. "Maturation of Concepts of Death." *British Journal of Medical Psychology* 39:35.

McConville, B. J., L. C. Boag, and A. P. Purchit. 1972. "Mourning Depressive Responses of Children in Residence Following Sudden Death of Parent Figures." *Journal of The American Academy of Child Psychiatry* 9(2):362.

Nagera, H. 1970. "Children's Reaction to the Death of Important Objects." In *Psychoanalytic Study of the Child,* Vol. 25. New York: International Universities Press, pp. 367–69.

Piaget, J. 1954. *The Construction of Reality in the Child.* New York: Basic Books, pp. 219–319.

Scharl, A. E. 1961. "Regression and Restitution in Object Loss." In *Psychoanalytic Study of the Child,* Vol. 16. New York: International Universities Press, p. 474.

Shambaugh, B. 1961. "A Study of Loss Reactions in a Seven-Year-Old." In *Psychoanalytic Study of the Child,* Vol. 16. New York: International Universities Press, pp. 513–19.

Wahl, C. W. 1958. "The Fear of Death." *Bulletin of the Menninger Clinic,* 22(6):219–21.

Wolfenstein, M. 1969. "Loss, Rage, and Repetition." In *Psychoanalytic Study of the Child,* Vol. 24. New York: International Universities Press, pp. 432.

Wolfenstein, M. 1973. "The Image of the Lost Parent." In R. S. Eisner, ed. *Psychoanalytic Study of the Child,* 28:443. New Haven: Yale University Press.

· 10 ·

Children, When Parents Die

Morris A. Wessel

Five percent of American children lose a parent through death before they reach the age of eighteen. Meeting the needs of these bereaved children is a formidable task. I often wonder why so little consideration is given them. Possibly the reason is that it is so distressing when a child suffers a tragic loss. How much a person extends himself to help bereaved friends or patients depends on the magnitude of the bereaved person's distress, one's confidence in his own ability to cope with this distress, and how worthwhile one believes it is to become involved.

The death of a child's parent may recall an adult's painful losses during childhood, or evoke fantasies of how one would have felt if the death of a parent had occurred in one's own childhood, or make one realize how one might feel about dying and leaving one's own young children. These reactions make it difficult for adults to comfort and support a child who is struggling to adapt to the loss of a parent. Too often, adults assume that a child is "too young to understand" and cannot realistically grasp the finality of the loss. However, this assumption permits one to avoid the poignancy of a child's struggle, which is painful to observe. This is unfair! How a child copes with the death of a loved one depends to a great extent on how adults who take care of his needs support him as he grapples with this crucial loss. Furthermore, how the important adults who care for a child function may depend on how members of the helping professions help them to understand a child's needs at this moment of stress. It is important to remember that health caregivers do not provide daily care for a bereaved child and are not available when he needs comforting. Most, if not all, of our energy should be given to supporting and helping the adults who nurture a bereaved child and are with him on a minute-to-minute basis.

The loss of a parent in early life places an enormous burden on a young human being. Usually a child invests almost all of his feelings in his parents. The death of a parent deprives him of a major opportunity to love and be loved and, particularly when a mother dies, disrupts much of his daily care. To what degree this experience remains an unmasterable burden, interfering seriously with psychological development, and to what degree it becomes a stressful experience with which a child copes and integrates depends largely on how the significant adults in his life help him to recognize, verbalize, and tolerate his feelings and reactions. There is no average response of a child to the death of a parent. Each child's life experience and stage of development presents a unique basis for the manner in which he or she adapts to and deals with the tragic loss. It is important to listen carefully to what a child says. All too often, adults familiar with theoretical conceptualizations may superimpose upon a child formulizations that reflect their knowledge but are premature at the particular moment.

The preparation for the death of a loved one begins long before the loss occurs. Parents and teachers should help a child understand the distinction between being alive and being dead. Many opportunities arise that can be used in teaching these concepts. Finding a dead bird or animal in the woods, experiencing the death of a favorite pet, or learning about the death of a TV soap opera character or of a prominent person are common life experiences that should be used by adults to acquaint children with the meaning of life and death. Although common topics of conversation, these events lack the intensity and personal pain experienced when a close family member dies. By the age of three, and sometimes earlier, children can grasp the concept of death if adults help them to integrate their perceptive observations of the world about them. Of course, coping with death as it applies to a pet, a TV character, or a public figure is enormously different from dealing with a realistic loss when a parent dies. Nevertheless, past experiences with these life-and-death situations serve as a basis for a child to understand the death of a parent or other loved one. "Cessation of life" or "no longer living" or "resting at peace" are descriptive terms for presenting to a child what happens when death occurs. Another approach is to say that when someone is dead, "he will no longer eat, or sleep, or run, or play, or feel, or be sad, or happy, or angry." It is unwise to equate death with "going to sleep." The suggestion that the deceased went to sleep only adds to a child's burden, for he wonders if he too might die while asleep.

A child often feels deserted as members of a family become preoccupied and withdrawn as the tragic moment of the death of a family member approaches. He loses the attention of the person who is ill. Other family members, preoccupied with their own reaction to the critical illness, also become less and less available to him. A child may become angry with everyone around him. He feels abandoned at a time when he needs more rather than less attention.

The solemnity and palpable gloom in a home as a family anticipates a death is frightening to a child. Yet whisking a child away to neighbors or banishing him to his room without explanation is bewildering and confusing. Health caregivers should suggest to the adults caring for a child that explanation for the sadness and preoccupation are important. Adults may be able to share the fact that "Daddy is very sick and the doctors and nurses are doing everything they can to make him comfortable. He may die soon. I want you to know that's why we're all so sad." A child may not be able to grasp fully, any more than many adults do, the reality of what is taking place. However, the conversation establishes grounds for discussion later on when one might say, "You remember I said Daddy was awfully sick and might die? I'm very sad now to have to tell you that Daddy did die."

When the primary caregiver, such as the mother, is the patient, it is wise for health caregivers to help a family designate one person who will assume the major care of the child. This may be a father, aunt, grandparent, close friend, older sibling, or housekeeper. As a mother becomes increasingly incapacitated, a child wonders who will provide for his needs. Consistency during a mother's illness and afterward in who assumes the nurturing responsibility is important. Whenever possible, a child should be maintained in his own home where the familiar surroundings, his toys, his own bed and furnishing offer support at this time of stress.

A child experiencing the loss of a loved one wonders whether this could happen to other people who love and take care of him—or to himself. Reassurance must be realistic, for who knows when any of us will die? It is best to say, "I don't think it will happen for a long, long time, and I'll be here to take care of you for many years." When it is a mother who dies, it is appropriate to approach the matter by saying, "We will miss Mommy very, very much. We will be sad for a long time. I will see to it that someone will care for you and do the things Mommy used to do for you."

It is by no means easy for a grief-stricken parent to assume this approach, but it is important to do so. It reassures the child that his nurturing needs will be met yet at the same time acknowledges his need to be sad. There is no way to protect a child from the loss when it occurs. A child needs support and comfort in being sad. He may, upon observing adults crying and their continued sadness, consider it as permission to release his own tears and feelings of desolation. It can help him to begin the process of grieving, which is appropriate and necessary when a loved one dies.

Parents often ask whether a child should attend a parents' funeral. I believe a child of four or older can make this decision for himself. One should describe the service and mention that the relatives and friends who will be there will be very sad. An appropriate way of presenting what will take place might be, "We're all very sad because we miss Daddy so much. I will be sad too. There will be music and prayers. Our minister (rabbi, priest) will talk about Daddy. If you would like to come with us, I'll ask [a relative or close friend] to join us. Or if you would rather stay home, that is all right too. Someone will stay there with you."

A child may find the gathering of relatives and friends and the ritual of the service supportive. On the other hand, he may anticipate that the experience is more than he can cope with, and he may wisely decide to remain at home. When a child attends a funeral, it is important that someone, preferably a person who is not intensely grief stricken, be with him. Nothing is sadder than the sight of a bewildered, grieving child standing alone during a funeral service, ignored by adults who are preoccupied with their own grieving. An adult companion should be assigned the specific task of caring for the child and be ready to leave with him should the experience become overwhelming.

Words should be carefully chosen when one is explaining to a child what happens after death. The discussion should portray honestly the family's philosophic and religious beliefs. The concept of life hereafter is, however, difficult for a young child to comprehend. A child may think of heaven as a place far away but accessible and a place from which people can return or, at least, telephone or send a letter. Nevertheless, if the family has this belief, it is wise to present the idea to a child of any age in honest terms. One can say, "The body of a person who dies is placed in a special box in the cemetery. I'll show you where that is. The body rests there. I like to believe that part of the person, the spirit, the things we love him for, rests in a place called Heaven—far, far way, where there's no pain, or hunger, or suffering."

Explanations involving a description of how God needs the deceased to work in heaven, or of God's coming down to take the deceased to Him, may offer comfort and solace to an adult. However, in a child who loves and wants the deceased person right here and now, this explanation is likely to arouse distrust of a God who swoops down to carry a beloved adult to heaven. The "I like to believe" presentation allows a child to accept or reject the philosophic point of view.

Every child is quick to sense dishonesty and insincerity. A disbelieving adult who presents a concept of life hereafter, hoping that somehow this will aid a child, only creates confusion and stimulates distrust. It is better just to say, "I do not know exactly what happens after death, but I know that Daddy will no longer be with us."

A child who does not attend a funeral may ask to visit the

cemetery at a later date. It is wise to grant this wish. The sight of a grave serves as documentation of the event and often helps a child to begin the painful process of adapting to the reality of the loss. It provides a focal point for future discussion.

When a loved one dies, certain patterns of behavior appear among many children. At first, a child may present a pensive posture, often with sadness and anger. After a short period, he may—to the consternation of adults—return to play with his toys or watch TV. This short sadness span is not a matter of unawareness nor is it disrespectful. Rather, it is a matter of denial, which allows the child to postpone having to deal with the loss. It is comparable to a bereaved adult's disbelief of a tragic loss, which is a normal reaction in the initial phases of grief.

An informed child, even after participating in a funeral, may believe that his loved one will return. Erna Furman reports the comments of Bess (three and a half) who, though well aware of her mother's death, announced to her father, "Mommy called and said she'd have dinner with us." It is at moments such as these that trusted adults have the arduous and awesome task of helping a child deal with the realities of the death. It is difficult to use these moments constructively, as did Bess' father who said, "I think you wish Mommy would call and have dinner with us. When we miss Mommy very much, we like to think that she's not really dead. I guess it will be a sad dinner for both of us tonight."

Adults who have suffered the loss of a loved one in their childhood have memories of crying alone at night in a closet or under the bedclothes. They often remember being very aware that a grieving parent would also be weeping behind closed doors. Those in the helping professions need to remind adults that a child's observation of a sad and crying adult may be a crucial factor in helping him to begin to express his own feelings of sadness. It can serve as permission for expressing these natural feelings. The feelings of intense loneliness and desolation, and at times terror, that arise when a child retreats and weeps alone may be diminished. At these moments a child should have somebody he loves comfort him.

Prolonged longing and wishing for the return of the deceased are normal in childhood, just as in adulthood. Knowing and understanding that a loved one has gone forever are only initial phases of accepting the permanence of loss. Like an adult, a child must grapple for a long time to adapt to a significant loss. All too often what happens is that the adult, finding the child's struggle painful, turns away and avoids dealing with his anguish. Health professionals, teachers, and the clergy can share with adults who care for a child how important it is to provide continuing support.

When family members are away, bereaved children become anxious, fearing that they too might fail to return. A bereaved child should be informed where a departing loved one is going and when he will return. Telephone contact should be maintained if the return is delayed.

One may anticipate that a child will regress to behavior formerly abandoned during his period of bereavement. He may become anxious at bedtime and be fearful of leaving home. He may lose bladder and bowel control. He may be restless and out of sorts. Common symptoms are poor school attendance as a result of bodily complaints and a decrease in ability to meet educational challenges.

A bereaved child dreads illness, even a minor one. He imagines that he may be about to die. Hence, every call to a physician concerning a child's symptoms merits prompt response and careful consideration. It should also be remembered that illness does occur in bereaved children. Gastrointestinal complaints may reflect an early phase of malabsorption syndrome, peptic ulcer, or ileitis. However, the bereaved child who presents behavioral symptoms may be far healthier than the child who denies the loss and is unable to deal with it in any manner.

The death of a parent during adolescence has unique effects on the child. At one moment, a healthy adolescent is extremely independent, setting off with great determination to make his own way in the world. Old relationships are discontinued and new associations are sought. If confronted by stress, an adolescent often reverts to a less mature state, seeking parental care, sympathy, and advice. At any other time of life these fluctuations would be considered abnormal. During adolescence, vacillation and restlessness are expressions of the normal process of maturation. The two-parent family constellation allows the adolescent to break away gradually on a trial basis, to thrive at an activity outside the family setting. Yet during these phases of intense independence when the adolescent is often critical and openly hostile to parents, there remains the comforting fact that the option of returning to home base still exists. Even during intense bursts of independence, an adolescent will live at home or, if living away, return home periodically to enjoy his parents and the opportunity to be cared for.

These alternating ways in which a young person relates to parents must be considered when an adolescent is coping with the loss of a parent. It is one experience to be struggling to free oneself and to become independent, knowing that both parents are available when needed. It is quite a different experience when death removes a parent while this struggle for emancipation is taking place.

More than the young child, a bereaved adolescent may dread any illness, for adolescents are deeply concerned about their bodies and life-threatening illness. Any call to a physician merits prompt response and careful consideration. This is usually reassuring, for it reinforces the idea that the doctor really cares about his young patient and that, in most instances, the imagined disease can be ruled out.

Adults and children mourn at different paces. A parent may mourn completely over time and be free to remarry, while a child or adolescent is still dealing with this process. A new wife who assumes the maternal role with warmth and love may be unprepared for the reactions of a child who is grieving for his mother. Once the child expresses appreciation for what his new mother is trying to do, he will be able to openly express sadness over the loss of his natural mother.

Bereaved children need to know that their doctor cares about them. A phone call, a brief comment at the time of the first meeting after a death, or a letter are ways of letting a child know that his doctor understands what he is experiencing. Parents and others caring for the child need all the support the physician can give them.

The suggestion that a physician's role is to "cure sometimes, to relieve often, to comfort always" is as true now as when enunciated by Dr. Edward Trudeau more than 50 years ago. This concept provides a model for the caregiver to follow, particularly when a child or adolescent suffers the loss of a parent.

· III ·
Caring for the Life-Threatened Child

· 11 ·

Dying Children and Their Families

MELVIN LEWIS AND DOROTHY OTNOW LEWIS

The dying child creates anxiety in the doctor because of at least three major reasons: the feelings of impotence, failure, and anxiety on being confronted with one's own limitations and mortality; the regressive pull evoked by the child's loneliness, abandonment, neediness, and insecurity; and the difficulty of dealing with the parents' anxiety, depression, anger, resentment, and denial. The situation is compounded because dying is a transitional state, and each case seems different; at first sight there is no readily apparent, orderly way to deal with the child, the family, oneself, and one's colleagues. The physician may at first seek to protect himself or herself by avoiding the dying child and cover his avoidance by such rationalizations as the child does not want to talk about his or her condition or he will get upset if it is discussed. Yet the child and the family look to the physician for understanding, support, and direction.

There is probably almost nothing that the child or parent fears, imagines, feels, or experiences that cannot be discussed with him or her in some honest way, and the basis for that discussion is a trusting relationship. Children in particular soon learn whom they

---

The authors thank the following publishers for their permission to use some of the material from the following publications:
Lewis, M. 1971. *Clinical Aspects of Child Development*. Philadelphia: Lea and Febiger.
Lewis, M. and D. O. Lewis. 1973. *Pediatric Management of Psychological Crises*. Chicago: Yearbook Medical Publishers, Inc.

can trust and hence whom they will open up to. Indeed, the child often senses more accurately what the adult can tolerate than the adult recognizes how much the child can assimilate, and the child acts accordingly.

How then should a physician proceed? A knowledge of how children and parents understand and react to dying and death in different circumstances provides us with a foundation for a sound clinical approach.

Basic Information

The Child's Concept of Death

The child's reaction to his own dying or the death of others is related in part to his concept of death (Anthony 1940, Gartley and Bernasconi 1967, Schilder and Wechsler 1934, Wolff 1969), which in turn is related to his developmental stage. (See tables 11.1–11.3.)

During the first few years, the child has virtually no concept

Table 11.1.
Reaction of Child, Parents, Siblings, and Staff Before Death of Child

Subject	Ideas on Death	Reaction to Death
Child, 0–5	abandonment, punishment	fear of loss of love
Child, 5–10	concepts of inevitability, confusion	fear of pain and/or bodily harm
Child, 10–15	reality	control of body and other developmental tasks
Parents	—	When cause is *acute:* anxiety, concern, hopefulness When cause is *chronic:* premature mourning, anticipatory grief, guilt, reaction formation and displacements, need for information
Siblings, 0–5	—	reactions to changes in parents (sense of loss of love and withdrawal)
Siblings, 5–10	—	concern about their implication, fearful for themselves
Siblings, 10–15	—	generally supportive
Staff	—	anxiety, conspiracy of silence

Table 11.2.
Reaction of Child, Parents, Siblings, and Staff During Death of Child

Subject	Sudden	Acute	Chronic
Child, 0–5	—	avoidance of pain, need for love	withdrawal, separation anxiety
Child, 5–10	—	guilt (bad) regression, denial	guilt (religious), regression, denial, depression, despair, anxiety, anger
Child, 10–15	—	depression, despair for future	depression, despair, anxiety, anger
Parents	anger, disbelief, displaced rage, accelerated grief, prolonged numbness	desperate concern, denial, guilt	denial, remorse, resurgence of love
Siblings, 0–5	reactions to changes in parents (sense of loss of love and withdrawal) in all instances of death		
Siblings, 5–10	concern about the implication, fearful for themselves in all instances of death		
Siblings, 10–15	generally supportive in all instances of death		
Staff	reaction: withdrawal in all instances of death tasks (in all instances of death): 1. correct distortions, e.g., "am I safe?"; "will someone be with me?"; "will I be helped to feel better?" 2. comfort parents 3. allow hope and promote feeling of actively coping 4. protect dignity of patient		

Table 11.3.
Reactions of Parents, Siblings, and Staff After Death of Child

Subject	Sudden	Acute	Chronic
Parents	guilt, mourning	anger at M.D., need for follow-up, over-idealizing, fantasy loss	remorse, relief, and guilt
Siblings, all ages	in all instances: (1) respond to reaction of parents, (2) experience survivor guilt		
Staff	in all instances: need to provide for aftercare of survivors, tact when requesting autopsy, and accurate information regarding disposal of the body; billing should be delayed		

of death other than a disappearance. Children between 5 and 10 years of age (approximately) are beginning to clarify their concepts but are still at times confused. For example, a child may say, "When I die, my heart stops, I can't see, and I can't hear. But if I'm buried, how will I breathe?" Some of the difficulty in thinking clearly is developmental, but some of the difficulty is emotional. If the child has a heightened concern about his body and its functions at this time, he may tend to think of death in terms of the harm to that part of his body and its function, the more so because he also tends to think in concrete terms at this stage.

Somewhere between 10 and 15 years of age, the child acquires a grasp of the meaning of mortality (Kastenbaum 1959). His reaction to death at this time is influenced more by his emotional struggles than by his intellectual capacities. Thus, a young adolescent who is concerned, among other things, with sexual performance, control of his or her impulses, physical intactness, and separation from parents may react with anxiety if any one of these sensitive conflict areas is aroused by the dying process.

Child's Reaction

The dying child experiences a variety of reactions. The very young child is mostly preoccupied with the discomfort of the illness, whether acute or chronic, and the separation and withdrawal that occur when hospitalization is necessary. A somewhat older child, although also troubled by pain and separation, interprets the illness according to his level of cognitive development and emotional conflicts. Thus, he may interpret the illness as an act of "immanent justice" for the guilt he feels about some misdeed, real or imagined. Usually, there is regressive behavior in the face of the illness, hospitalization, treatment techniques, and the fear of mutilation. Occasionally there is a denial of discomfort or dread (Solnit and Green 1959, Solnit 1963). An older child who is aware of the finality of death may deny his anxiety but also exhibit a depression, occasionally mixed with outbursts of anger and anxiety. This is especially common in adolescents. We now know that depression in children is similar to that in adults.

Withdrawal from ward activities, diminished appetite beyond that induced by the fatal disease or by its treatment (e.g., chemotherapy, radiation), and difficulty sleeping may alert the astute clinician to the existence of a depression beyond the expectable normal reactions of fear and sadness in relation to the illness. When such a depression occurs, especially during a lengthy relentless illness, the pediatrician may wish to consider a trial of antidepressant medication. The pediatrician might benefit from consulting a child psychiatrist in such a situation. Some children are astoundingly courageous and steadfast in the face of death.

The range of reactions is great. In a sense, all that has gone before contributes to the child's understanding of, and reaction to, death. Each child is an individual, and a myriad of variables influence the ultimate behavior of the child, his family, and the helping persons around him.

Reaction of Others

An important determinant of the child's reaction to death is the reaction of those around him. These others may be parents, siblings, or hospital staff. Parental reactions may be general or specific. Specific types of reactions may vary according to whether the death is sudden, acute, or chronic (Friedman et al. 1963).

Reaction of Parents. The general reactions of parents have a chronological sequence, starting before and continuing during and after the moment of death. Initial shock and denial of the diagnosis may last from a few seconds to a few months. This may be followed by anger ("Why my child?") or guilt ("If only I had . . ."). Sooner or later, the parent starts to bargain ("If he could only live to . . ."). This is followed by a normal grieving and mourning over impending loss and the beginning of separation. Finally, a stage of resignation or acceptance can be reached.

When the death is *relatively rapid* (e.g., perhaps as a consequence of a brief illness), the period before death is filled with anxiety and concern. The parents may be desperately hopeful, but they may also experience feelings of guilt and have a need to deny the possibility of death as an eventual outcome. After such a death the parents may again feel some diffuse anger that may be displaced onto the physician. (When one is angry at the gods or fate, one is likely to express rage at a figure perceived as powerful.) This may occur whether or not the physician has been diligent, but it is more likely to fester and be prolonged if the physician fails out of his own discomfort to show consideration at the time and provide the opportunity for a followup interview. Over a period of time the parents will then undergo their own characteristic mourning process. This may include some identification with the lost person and occasionally an over-idealization of the lost person (particularly when parents also experience the loss of fantasied expectations they had for the lost child). Further possible reactions may include a displacement of attitudes toward the dead child onto one or more of the surviving children, attempts to fill the loss by another pregnancy, or a period of withdrawal. These and other normal reactions should be respected and left alone.

When the period of dying is *prolonged,* a *premature mourning* may occur, with anticipatory grief and withdrawal of interest in the dying child, perhaps accompanied by a displacement of warm feelings onto an infant child in the family. Often, unacceptable thoughts arise. For example, a parent may find himself wishing that the child would finally die and relieve everyone of the emotional and financial burden and suffering. Such a wish might horrify a parent and lead to the immediate mobilization of certain defense mechanisms. One defense mechanism that is seen commonly is that of reaction formation: the parent becomes extra protective in caring for the dying child. Guilt may also be experienced. Such guilt (and anxiety) may be expressed in repetitive questions that require tactful answers.

As a chronically ill child nears death, the parents may be filled with remorse, and a resurgence of love occurs. Rarely, a denial of the imminence of death may remain in force. After the death of a chronically ill child, parents may feel a mixture of relief and guilt, with perhaps feelings of remorse uppermost in some instances.

Reaction of the Siblings. Siblings who are very young, especially under the age of five years, sense the withdrawal of the parent intensely and consequently experience a loss of love. Such young children may view the death of significant other persons as an abandonment, punishment, the realization of unacceptable wishes—or all three. Children between about five and ten years of age are generally somewhat more concerned for the dying child and may also be fearful for themselves. They also resent the attention given to the dying child. Although it is expected that older children can usually muster a supportive attitude and temporarily assume parental roles for the younger siblings at home, even teenagers feel and react to parental withdrawal and may "act up" during these trying times. They, too, require special attention. Children, as well as adults, may experience survivor guilt after the death of a child (Lifton 1967). Some children suffer serious symptoms and subsequent distortions of character structure (Cain et al. 1964).

Reaction of the physician. Hospital staff naturally also experience anxiety when in the presence of a dying child or a grieving parent (Solnit and Green 1959) and tend sometimes to deal with that anxiety by withdrawal and a conspiracy of silence. This reaction may hamper their optimal care of the dying child and his family and prevent the staff from carrying out certain essential psychological tasks. Besides comforting the parents, such tasks involve providing the child with an optimum feeling of being active in his attempts to cope with anxiety and allowing the child some hope. Furthermore, the privacy and dignity of the child require protection. Lastly, certain distortions require correction. A child may, for example, be quite concerned about questions such as "Am I safe?" "Will someone be with me when I need them?" "Will I be helped to feel better?" The continuing need for tact carries through into the period of aftercare for the survivors.

With this foundation we can now suggest a practical approach for helping the child and the family when a child is dying and finally dies.

Clinical Management of the Dying Child

Talking with the Parents About Fatal Illness

The hardest task for the physician is to tell the parents that their child is fatally ill. The physician should take the parents into a private office and allow at the very least half an hour, uninterrupted by telephone calls or other tasks. He can begin by telling them the nature of the diagnosis. He might then go on to describe the treatment that is available to offer some relief for the child's symptoms. He will, at some point, have to tell the parents that there is no treatment that can cure the child of the illness. Throughout this interview he should pause and give the parents every opportunity to express their feelings and ask questions. He must resist his understandable impulse to "shut off" their grief. If they ask if the child will die from this illness, he will have to confirm that this is so. If they do not ask, he should at some point attempt to clarify that this is an illness that is progressive and that the child will die. This, by the way, does not imply that the parents will necessarily comprehend or accept what they have heard.

The physician should not end the interview then but should stay with the parents as they experience their shock and perhaps anger and grief. He might then tell the parents how he plans to treat the child and help them feel some measure of participation and control of the treatment.

He is obliged to tell the parents what to expect as the illness progresses. This need not be completed in the first interview but rather should be done in stages over an extended period. The goal is to give the parents information that will enable them to anticipate the child's needs at each stage. The parents will usually indicate by their questions what they need to know.

Regular contact with the parents should then be planned—not just passing comments but time set aside to talk, review, and listen in the privacy of an office. The physician should resist the natural impulse to avoid the parents or avoid the subject. In order to do this, he must recognize his own feelings of impotence and anger when faced with a dying patient. The parents will come to trust the physician and feel safe to express, if they so wish, some of their less acceptable feelings if they can be sure of his availability and readiness to listen. During these planned interviews, the physician can discuss with the parents their child's behavior, their management of the child, what to tell siblings, and whether and in what way they would like their minister, priest, or rabbi involved. The parents should be reassured about their own handling of the situation, and the physician should feel free to share his admiration for how well they are meeting the child's needs.

The physician may be asked for advice regarding religious sacraments. Although intended to comfort, the practice of offering prayer with the child and administering the sacrament of the sick may arouse anxiety. Although it is possible for the sacrament to be given without the parents' consent, or even knowledge, most priests nowadays prefer to involve the parents and family first and also have the family present in the room. However, this practice may cause upset as much in the family as in the child. The current modification of the Sacrament of the Sick does not alter very much the way in which the child might experience the ritual.* Indeed, there are no specific modifications for children other than the judgment of the particular priest. The physician should discuss with the parents and the priest the child's needs and how the child might experience the prayer and sacrament before any ritual is actually undertaken.

Talking with the Child

When it comes to talking with the child, especially the young child, the parents' feelings and wishes must be respected; some parents, for example, do not wish the child to be told that he is going to die, whereas others do. For some families, some degree of denial is an important protective device that the family needs.

There is no simple answer to the question of whether or not an individual child should be told. One useful approach is to discuss with the parents how they anticipate they might respond if their dying child asks them whether he is going to die. There are several stages that might be suggested for their response to such a question. First, the reason for the question must be understood; the child may be responding to the parents' or the hospital staff's anxious behavior, or the child may be concerned about pain, mu-

---

*Ordo Unctionis Infirmorum Eorumque Pastoralis Curae," Rituale Romanum, (Roma, Typis Polyglottis Vaticanis 1972, pp. 10 and 15.

tilation, loneliness, the needs of others, and so forth. The child can then be given repeated opportunities to talk about what he might be worried about. Second, if the parents decide that they want the child to know that the illness is lethal, the process of telling the child about the illness and impending death should have more the characteristics of a dialogue than an announcement. Some children simply cannot understand and do not want to hear; they should not be told. Others have to arrive slowly at the realization of the significance of their illness; it is too much to be understood and grasped at one time. Third, the child must be given hope. Even when he is told that the illness is one that causes death, he can and should be told that the physicians will do everything they can to fight the illness. The adults must agree not only on how but on who should be the first to tell the child. Sometimes the physician is not the appropriate person at first to communicate this information. A parent or clergyman who is close to the child may have a more sensitive understanding of the child's needs.

A discussion of this kind with parents often helps them to express some of their own concerns. It also promotes a feeling of trust and of being understood, as well as a feeling of at least some sense of control and mastery in the care of their child. Nothing is so painful as the feeling of helplessness as life slowly ebbs away.

Most important, the physician who has engaged in a dialogue with the parents is now prepared to have a dialogue with the child, always keeping in close touch with the parents. The physician can, for example, convey assuredness as he imparts to the child as much of the truth as the parents want and the child seems ready to know. There is no blueprint answer.

The ward staff should be clear about who has the primary responsibility for talking with the parents and child. When it has been agreed by the parents that the physician should tell the child, the physician should first establish a relationship of trust with the child. When he does tell the child, he should make sure that someone is available to be with the child after he has left the room if the child so desires. Involved staff should be clear about the child's level of awareness so that the child does not receive conflicting and therefore puzzling information. Ward staff also experience anxiety when in the presence of a dying child or his family. Their natural inclination to avoid these feelings may cause them to stay away from both the child and the grieving family. Such impulses may be handled better when the opportunity to explore and share feelings is provided through ward staff meetings (Lewis 1962).

Specific Management of the Child Who is Dying

Kübler-Ross (1972) gives a beautiful description of a dying boy expressing his thoughts and feelings:

> A little boy tried to paint what he felt like. He drew a huge tank and in front of the barrel was a tiny little figure with a stop sign in his hand. This to me represents the fear of death, the fear of the catastrophic, destructive force that comes upon you and you cannot do anything about it. If you can respond to him by saying it must be terrible to feel so tiny and this thing is so big, he may be able to verbally express a sense of smallness or impotence or rage. The next picture he drew was a beautiful bird flying up in the sky. A little bit of its upper wing was painted gold. When he was asked what this was, the boy said it was the peace bird flying up into the sky with a little bit of sunshine on its wing. It was the last picture he painted before he died. I think these are picture expressions of a stage of anger and the final stage of acceptance.

This description captures the essence of one aspect of the care of the dying child: with the parents' permission and in the privacy of his own room, the young child should be given the opportunity on different occasions through drawings or play with toys and dolls to express his concerns. If necessary, and if agreed on by the parents, the collaboration of a child psychiatrist is useful here. The opportunity for expressive play enables the child to exercise some mastery over his anxiety. If the child expresses concern about pain, loneliness, or fear through this play, this should be noted mentally by the physician. At a different time it may be possible to reassure the child, without reference to the prior play session, that the physicians will make sure that he does not have pain, that there will always be someone available to help him, and that everything will be done to help him feel better. Such an interpretation during the play itself may cause a child to feel tricked and exposed and, as such, inhibit future play.

Patients, adults and children alike, feel threatened by the passivity imposed on them by illness. Every effort must be made to give the child a feeling of active participation in his treatment. He should be informed at each stage what is being done and why and what he can expect. Some feeling of hope needs to be provided. Lastly, the dignity of the child requires protection, and privacy should be ensured.

Denial of death in a child, as in an adult, is a defense against anxiety and should be respected. Each person must be allowed his own way of dealing with the dread of death. At the same time, certain distortions should be corrected. For example, the child may require reassurance that the illness was not brought about by anything the child thinks he may have done. Reactions that generate further anxiety, such as regression, should be gently but firmly controlled by the parents, as well as by the hospital staff; excessive regressive behavior is uncomfortable for a child, as well as for those caring for him.

Children vary in their capacity to deal with the impending inevitability of their own death or the diagnosis that implies impending death. Some children, particularly older children, want to know, whereas others do not want to know or cannot comprehend.

The Moribund Child

In a situation in which a child has no brain activity and is being kept alive only by artificial methods, with no hope of spontaneous respiration or recovery of brain function, the physician must proceed with tact. First, before any decision is made to stop artificial supports, the parents must be fully informed and prepared. The physician might first tell them that at present the child is being kept alive by machines but that there is no possibility of spontaneous respiration or recovery of brain function. He should explain why this is so. In some instances, the parents have already considered the issue and will have come to the decision to discontinue artificial life supports. Such parents may also have decided whether they want to be in the room at the time. Other parents may experience great anguish at the burden of deciding to discontinue artificial respiration and may also prefer not to know exactly when it will be stopped. In a tactful way the physician can say to such parents that there is nothing more that can be done. Then when the parents do come to the decision to discontinue artificial life supports, the physician should ask the parents where they would prefer to be when this is done.

The parent's wishes must at all times be respected; it is their child. Parents should not be rushed. It is always their decision to make, and they need all the support and help they can get.

It is essential also that the parents experience a sense of unanimity and security in the total ward staff. Therefore, the staff physician should first discuss with the total ward staff the steps just outlined and encourage them to express their thoughts and feelings prior to implementing the plan. Patients tend to seek different answers from different staff members, and it is essential that all staff be aware of the way in which an individual case is being handled so that their responses do not conflict.

If the child dies suddenly without the parents' being present, they should be informed immediately, no matter what the time of day. The sense of guilt at not being present when a child dies is an enormous burden.

Management of Parents During Prolonged Illness in the Child

The constellation of reactions that may occur in parents when the period of dying is one of prolonged suffering necessitates sensitive patient management. Some parents may request other opinions regarding prognosis or treatment. Often they should be given this opportunity. Sometimes, however, a futile search for a magical cure may devastate a family emotionally and financially. The physician should then gently attempt to encourage a more realistic and helpful way of coping with the frustration of impotence. The physician can help parents by giving them opportunities to talk about their feelings in an accepting, nonjudgmental way. For example, parents often experience relief if the physician reassures them that they are doing everything they can and that he knows how hard it is for them. He can also say: "Many parents have told me how at times they had wished it would all finally end and then felt bad about thinking that. But it's a natural thought to occur. We all have all kinds of thoughts. What is important is that you have done everything that could possibly be done."

Questions may arise about child rearing during the long period of time during which remissions occur and treatment is administered. While the situation is far from "normal," there is often a wish on the part of the child to feel "normal." Perhaps this represents in part the child's wish that he no longer has the disease, that there is no longer a need for painful treatments, and that he can at least talk freely with others about feelings of frustration, anger, and resentment.

At the same time, parents may feel in a quandary about how to rear the child; siblings, about how to relate to the child and deal with their guilt; and teachers, about how to educate and deal with the child and the other children in the classroom. Once again, there is no blueprint answer; indeed, preset "solutions," such as "treat the child normally," may only burden the parents with more conflicts and guilt. One must think out and manage each situation individually, taking into account the many needs of the child, the parents, and the siblings.

Management of Siblings

Part of good medical management is the awareness of the effect of dying and death on siblings. Siblings of all ages need support and explanations, and the physician can help the parents provide this. He may suggest that the parents may wish to gather the family together and give a simple explanation to all the children. It would include the facts that Johnny is very ill and everyone is doing his best to make him as comfortable as possible; the illness he has could not be prevented and it is no one's fault; it is necessary to figure out together how everyone can help. Later, individual children in the family may be given additional information as they give evidence that they require it. If children are told that death is near, they will also need help on how to conduct themselves in the presence of the dying child. The dying child needs their support, and they can give this by making drawings, bringing messages from others, or getting things the child may need. If the dying child asks them whether he is going to die, they can say: "I don't know. I know it's a serious illness. Would you like me to ask Mommy and Daddy, or do you want to ask them yourself?"

When the child dies, in order to avoid hurt feelings, all the siblings should be told at approximately the same time, if possible. A simple account of the death can be given if the children ask questions. It is better to avoid such statements as "He died in his sleep," especially when young children are present, because of the danger of engendering a fear of sleep.

A visit to the home by the physician is nearly always deeply appreciated by the parents and siblings who are mourning the death of a child (or by the spouse and children who are mourning the death of a parent). If the physician has had a longstanding relationship with the family, he should inquire about any funeral or memorial service and attend. A physician who has provided extended care to a dying child may be remembered only for his failure to attend a service or to convey his personal condolences.

Sometimes a parent will ask whether a child should attend the funeral. The physician should first find out whether the parent will be in control of himself and who will be available to support the child. For children under the age of about five years the funeral can be a puzzling experience unless explained and unless there is a great deal of support. Attendance also depends on cultural practices. Children above the age of five years can often use the funeral ritual in the same way as adults do, especially if they have before them the model of adults who can also explain to them their feelings and describe what is taking place. If a child does not wish to attend the funeral, he should not be made to feel guilty. Rather, arrangements should be made for him to be in the company of an understanding adult during the funeral.

Older children should be encouraged to attend whatever rituals are followed by the adults since, again, these practices usually serve in part to help a person deal with the reality of death. If the older child chooses not to attend, his choice should be explored, but if he still feels that he does not want to come, this should be respected. Each person mourns in his own way. In no circumstance should the subject of the dead person be closed off. A wall of silence hampers the child as he struggles with the feelings about, and reality of, death. Some of the specific ways of helping children understand the many facets of death have been described by Wolf (1958).

Other questions involving siblings may arise later. A younger sibling may ask to have some of the dead child's toys. This can be done in a helpful way by suggesting perhaps that the dead child would have wanted his younger brother or sister to have the toys. Other decisions, such as changing the dead child's room or considering giving a younger sibling the room previously occupied by the dead child, might be deferred until most of the mourning has been worked through. Such decisions might then be made on a rational basis, less affected by the emotions of mourning.

Requesting Autopsy Permission or Organ Donation

A difficult task for the physician is requesting autopsy permission or organ donation. Because of its difficulties, it is frequently done in a hasty, tactless manner. The physician must be aware that many families have strong feelings against such procedures. For example, Orthodox Judaism prohibits the permanent removal of organs. Despite the physician's medical curiosity and zealousness to learn, he must resist his wish to pressure a family into agreeing to a procedure to which it basically objects. On the other hand, he may legitimately present an autopsy as a postmortem internal examination in order to determine the cause of death and the effects of previous treatment. He can honestly present the possible potential benefits of such procedures to others. If asked whether the child will be cut open, he must answer honestly even if he knows that the autopsy or donation may subsequently be refused. If families are reluctant to agree to such procedures, they should not be made to feel guilty at their decision.

When a Parent Dies

The Children

When a parent dies, the physician should anticipate with the surviving parent what reactions he may expect from the children. Children, particularly young children, are unable to tolerate and therefore complete the painful task of mourning the reality of the death of a parent. Sad feelings are often curtailed, and often the child quickly returns to everyday activities as if nothing had changed. Although mourning in extremely young children is brief, it is difficult to assess the impact on future personality development. Occasionally, a child may express hostile feelings toward the surviving parent. The child may actually be angry at the parent who died and abandoned him. Since such feelings are usually experienced as unacceptable, he displaces them onto the living parent. The expression of hostile feelings toward the surviving parent unfortunately invites punishment when it is misunderstood. Frequently, a child, by virtue of his still somewhat primitive way of viewing the world, is convinced that he caused his parent's death, either by not being a good child or by wishing the parent dead at one time or another. When he provokes the surviving adult, he may in part be seeking punishment to assuage his guilt. Therefore, it is necessary to prepare a parent for these reactions, as well as to attempt to correct the child's fantasy.

The child who has lost a parent is a child at psychiatric risk. This is particularly true of the child who loses a mother. Impairments in the child's capacity to form new, lasting relationships may show up later. Shame at being different may be experienced. Impaired sexual identity and conscience formation may also occur (Neubauer 1960, Bonnard 1962). In addition, the loss of a parent during childhood may predispose a child to attempted suicide during adolescence.

The family disruption and reactions of the surviving parent may result in a depression in the child. The presenting symptom may be a school learning problem or a behavior difficulty. Another hazard that sometimes occurs is a morbid attachment of the surviving parent to a child of either sex, particularly an adolescent. The adolescent may then have great difficulty in separating from the parent or may develop along homosexual lines.

On the other hand, as development proceeds, the child may be able to carry out more of the work of the mourning on a piecemeal basis. As his cognitive capacity matures and his reality testing is strengthened, the child may at some later date be able to express some of the feelings that hitherto have been repressed. These feelings may include yearning and sadness, as well as anger and resentment.

The physician can help most if he can enable the parent, who is also in a state of mourning and withdrawal, to recognize the needs of the child. The child needs to know that there is someone on whom he can depend to have his needs met and to express his feelings. In some instances, the physician may appropriately buttress this role of the parent by making himself available to the child, if the parent agrees. The pediatrician should not hesitate to suggest a consultation with a child psychiatrist if he is especially concerned about the child's behavior.

The Surviving Parent

The death of a parent almost always disrupts a family, no matter whether it is the mother or the father. As far as possible, the physician should try to help maintain the family stability and avoid making hasty decisions while members are in a state of acute grief. The services of a relative or homemaker may be helpful during this acute period. Some tact is required as the physician tries to steer a course that will not be experienced by the parent as either intrusion or abandonment.

The disruption in the family caused by the death of a parent is not confined to the period of mourning. Loss of income, reduction in the amount of time that can be spent with the children, changed roles in the surviving spouse, caretaking responsibilities for the older children in the family, and altered social relationships are some of the repercussions that continue to affect the family. The physician should remain available to the members of the family. Sleep difficulties, psychosomatic disturbances, or school learning difficulties are some of the common signs of continuing distress. Referral for psychiatric evaluation may then be indicated.

REFERENCES

Anthony, S. 1940. *The Child's Discovery of Death.* New York: Harcourt, Brace.
Bonnard, A. 1962. "Truancy and Pilfering Associated with Bereavement." In S. Lorand and H. L. Schneer, eds. *Adolescents,* New York: Hoeber Medical Division, Harper and Row.
Cain, A. C., I. Fast, and M. E. Erickson. 1964. "Children's Disturbed Reactions to the Death of a Sibling." *American Journal of Orthopsychiatry* 34(4):741.
Friedman, S. B., P. Chodoff, J. W. Mason, and D. A. Hamburg. 1963. "Parental Behavior Before Death of Child." *Pediatrics* (October) 32:610–25.
Gartley, W. and M. Bernasconi. 1967. "The Concept of Death in Children." *Journal of Genetic Psychology* 110:71–85.
Kastenbaum, R. 1959. "Time and Death in Adolescence." In H. Feifel, ed. *The Meaning of Death.* New York: McGraw-Hill.
Kübler-Ross, E. 1972. "On Death and Dying." *Journal of the American Medical Association* 221 (2):174.
Lewis, M. 1962. "The Management of Parents of Acutely Ill Children in the Hospital." *American Journal of Orthopsychiatry* 30:60.
Lifton, R. J. 1967. *Death in Life.* New York: Random House.
Neubauer, P. B. 1960. "The One-Parent Child and His Oedipal Development." *The Psychoanalytic Study of the Child* 15:286.
Richmond, J. B. and H. A. Waisman. 1955. "Psychological Aspects of Management of Children with Malignant Disease." *American Medical Association American Journal of Diseases of Children* 89:42.
Schilder, P. and D. Wechsler. 1934. "The Attitudes of Children Toward Death." *Journal of Genetic Psychology* 45:405–51.
Solnit, A. J. 1963. "The Dying Child." *Developmental Medicine and Childhood Neurology* 7:693.
Solnit, A. J. and M. Green. 1959. "Psychological Considerations in the Management of Deaths on Pediatric Hospital Services. I. The Doctor and the Child's Family." *Pediatrics* 24:106.
Wolf, A. W. M. 1958. "Helping Your Child to Understand Death." New York: Child Study Association of America, Inc., pp. 7–44.
Wolff, S. 1969. *Children Under Stress.* London: Allen Lane, The Penguin Press, pp. 53, 66, 75–93.

· 12 ·

Terminal Phase of Childhood Cancer: Home Care of the Dying

C. M. Binger, A. R. Ablin, J. H. Kushner, and
G. A. Perin

Introduction

Although recent advances in pediatric oncology have led to an increased number of long-term survivors, the fact remains that about half of the children and adolescents afflicted with cancer die of their disease. The stress on the patients and their families is immense and leaves in its wake widespread psychological and social problems (Binger et al. 1969). The crisis of initial diagnosis and hospitalization begins the period of family stress. This is followed by the complexity of the ongoing management of the disease, remissions and exacerbations, the terminal phase, death, and resultant grief and mourning by the survivors.

The terminal phase is particularly stressful for all concerned—patient, family, friends, and professionals. There is no longer a chance for long-term survival. Although further chemotherapy, surgery, or radiation may prolong the patient's life, side effects and complications may seriously diminish the quality of the remaining days. Medical decisions are complex and difficult. Psychosocial issues are horrendous.

Ours is a culture wherein most deaths occur in the hospital. This is related to advances in medical technology and specialty care. Relatively few families have experienced an actual death in their own home. Death remains a taboo topic. It is not accepted as a natural part of the life cycle. Yet this has not always been so (Aries 1974). In the past, the dying were cared for in their own homes surrounded by family and friends. Is it not possible that this relatively recent phenomenon of our culture has contributed to the psychosocial morbidity of such families and lessened the quality of life for the patient? The recent development of the hospice movement for care of dying adults has taken this into consideration (Stoddard 1978). In the United States the majority of hospices are staffed by interdisciplinary teams committed to caring for people at home. Some include visits to nursing homes, hospitals, or wherever the patient may be at the time. Many such patients are cared for in special facilities designed on hospice principles.

Hospital care of the terminally ill child or adolescent places a very heavy load on hospital staff. They often feel relatively helpless. Their own anxieties and fears concerning death are reactivated. While they can and do provide supportive medical care focused on alleviating pain and suffering, they find it difficult to support the dying child and parents psychologically.

Parents, upset and depressed, often feel helpless. As they struggle with their own anticipatory grief reactions, they find it arduous to support their dying child or adolescent. They find it difficult to assist each other and to be loving, attentive parents to their other profoundly concerned children. The hospital, with its unfamiliarity, rules, multiple personnel, and all its technology, further contributes to this.

Siblings are particularly prone to the stresses of the terminal phase and death (Binger 1973). Normal family functions and discipline are disrupted. The parents are physically and emotionally involved with their dying child. Siblings are rarely allowed to visit the hospital. Their last contact with their brother or sister is usually the day he or she was taken to the hospital for terminal care. Their own process of grief and mourning is hindered.

Clinical experience has demonstrated that during this most stressful period the essence of supportive care and enhancement of quality of life is that psychological support provided by family members to each other. If we, as professionals, have done our psychological work well throughout the illness, we have catalyzed and fostered positive, supportive, family relationships.

At the University of California Medical Center (San Francisco), an interdisciplinary pediatric oncology team has been working together to provide psychosocial support to such patients and their families from the time of initial diagnosis through the period of grief and mourning. In the context of such ongoing support it has become clear that, for many families, caring for the dying child or adolescent at home may have important advantages for the child and family. Medical treatment is focused on alleviation of pain and suffering. The major therapeutic goal becomes enhancement of the quality of life for the dying and prevention of residual emotional illness in the survivors.

This paper summarizes the experience of six families who elected to care for their dying child or adolescent at home. The support of the professional team was maintained.

Retrospective Study

The Study

The pediatric oncologists recalled a total of six patients they had treated for various types of cancer in recent years wherein parents chose to care for their dying child or adolescent in the home. Professional personnel—which included physicians, specialized nurses, and social workers—collaborated in providing ongoing medical and psychosocial support.

Each of these parents was asked to come to the medical center to be interviewed by a child psychiatrist regarding the impact of the total illness and their feelings concerning home care of their dying child. All accepted. Although the interviews were unstructured, there was a major focus on various aspects of the terminal phase and home care.

We were concerned about how and why the parents decided on home care; parental concerns; required medical care; nature of communication within the family; impact of home care on the patient, siblings, and parents; sources of psychosocial support (including extent and nature of that by professionals); nature of the death; immediate and subsequent adjustment of the family; and possible clinical applications to other families.

In the six families there were a total of 12 parents and twenty-one siblings. All were Caucasian and middle class. At the time of death the patients ranged in age from four years to 16 years. The duration of the illness, from diagnosis to death, ranged from six months to five years.

The ages of the children, duration of illness, types of cancer, and treatment were as follows:

1. Mary was age 3½ at the time of diagnosis and 4 at time of death. She had an abdominal tumor (neuroblastoma). Treatment included surgery, radiation, and chemotherapy.

2. Diane was age 4 at time of diagnosis and age 6 at time of death. She had a brain tumor (medulloblastoma). Treatment included neurosurgery (with resultant hemiparesis), radiation, and chemotherapy. Because of severe back pain she underwent a laminectomy with resultant paralysis of both legs. She knew about and talked of her eventual death.

3. Patricia was age 10 at diagnosis and 12½ at death. She also had a brain tumor (medulloblastoma). Treatment included neurosurgery (with resultant mild hemiparesis), radiation, and drug therapy. She did not talk openly of her eventual death but did know that she was dying. The mother regretted the lack of open communication.

4. Bonnie was age 5 at diagnosis and 6½ at death. She had an eye tumor (retinoblastoma). Treatment included radiation and drug treatment. She knew she was going to die and spoke openly of death.

5. Katherine was age 14 when she underwent surgery for an abdominal mass. She was found to have an inoperable tumor (osteogenic sarcoma). From the beginning she knew there was no hope for survival. She died at age 16.

6. Jean was age 13 months at diagnosis and six years at death. She had an abdominal tumor (Wilms tumor). Treatment included surgery, radiation, and drugs. There were many ups and downs. The family rushed to the hospital at the time of death.

Observations

In reviewing the experience of medical personnel involved in the care of these children and families and the material from the interviews, a number of observations and clinical impressions were gathered.

REASONS FOR HOME CARE

In all cases, the possibility of home care was initially raised by the professional staff. This occurred when it became clear that the child's condition was terminal. With help from the professional staff, the parents had accepted that there was no realistic hope for survival and that the focus of terminal care related to the quality of life. In the oldest patient this was apparent at the time of the initial abdominal laparotomy. In the other families this point was reached after a period of time following various surgical, radiological, and medical treatments.

The parents were willing to consider home care for a variety of reasons. In three families, this occurred as a result of discussions with other parents who had lost children to cancer. In some families there was general dissatisfaction with previous hospital care. "We did not like the routine." "It is a place of doom and gloom." Several parents said their decision was based on the feeling that it was the "natural thing to do," "we felt we could offer more to our child at home than the hospital could," "there is nothing like being in one's own home with one's own family," "even if our entire family moved into the hospital, it wouldn't be the same." More than half the parents were not adamant about keeping their child at home. "If we couldn't control the pain, bleeding, or convulsions, we would have taken her back." "All that we were concerned with was the quality of our child's remaining life."

PARENTS' CONCERNS

The parents expressed concerns about medical aspects of caring for the child or adolescent at home. "How would she die?" "I needed to know what to expect so that I could take care of her." "I wondered if I would be qualified to care for her." "I had no nursing background."

REQUIRED MEDICAL CARE

In actuality all parents were capable of learning the medical aspects of home care and became almost as proficient as professionals. This occurred through the instruction of the physician or visiting nurse. The medical nursing procedures involved preventing bed sores, administering oral and intramuscular medication for pain, and administering oxygen and rectal enemas. In essence, all the procedures were supportive and for relief of pain and suffering. In five of the cases, management of pain became a major aspect of terminal treatment. There was no need for heroic life-saving measures.

OPENNESS OF COMMUNICATION

These parents were quite open and truthful with all their children about the seriousness of the illness. Four of the children knew that they were going to die and talked of it with their parents and siblings. The other two gave indirect evidence that they knew but did not talk directly about death. In retrospect, the parents of those two children wished they had been more open with their children. Such discussions concerning death focused on separation, loss, and religious conceptions. These children were particularly communicative and upset by alterations in appearance resulting from the disease or treatment—loss of hair, Cushingnoid appearance, disfigurement, and paralysis.

NORMAL FAMILY ACTIVITIES

Even with all the complications of the disease and treatment, these families were determined to carry on as normally as possible. Their routine included vacations, continuation of school, use of a home teacher, visits with friends, and celebration of holidays. "We learned to take one day at a time."

PARTICIPATION OF SIBLINGS AND PEERS IN CARE OF THE DYING

Of particular note in these families was the participation of the siblings in the care of their dying brother or sister. Such assistance included taking their sibling outside in a wheelchair, spending time reading and playing games, and running errands. (This was in marked contrast to situations wherein terminal care is in the hospital and the sibs neither see nor help their ill brother or sister in his or her last days.) Most parents felt that the siblings had gained in being able to participate in the care of their dying sib to the very end, being allowed to communicate openly in their own way their fears and concerns about death and to participate in the family grieving process at home, both at the time of death and subsequently. Several parents remarked that the siblings seemed reassured in seeing the parents support the dying child or adolescent to the very end.

We were also impressed with the support provided by peer relationships. Through home care such relationships can be maintained. Such peers often need help from significant adults such as school teachers and their own parents.

SOURCES OF SUPPORT

The sources of outside support for these families varied. For all families there was ongoing involvement with the oncologist, specialized nurse, and social worker. Other sources of support included grandparents and friends who came to live in the home during the terminal phase, the clergy, parent groups such as Candle Lighters, and many professional personnel who assisted these families in a concerned and humane manner during the child's illness. This humanitarian approach by many professionals, however relatively brief in relation to the total duration of the illness, was remembered as a source of support.

Regardless of the cumulative support of many professionals it was obvious that these families relied on one physician for continuous and ongoing support. In most of these families this person was the pediatric oncologist. In other cases it was the family doctor who worked in collaboration with the oncological team. Such support included home visits, talks with the child and family, and general availability. "Even a two minute phone call helped." In three of the cases considerable time was spent on home visits by the physician. Such home contacts were supplemented by the specialized nurse or social worker. In other cases such professional contact mainly centered around office visits and phone calls. These contacts focused not only on the supportive medical treatment but also on various aspects of humane emotional and supportive counseling.

PARENTAL ATTITUDES TOWARD DEATH

In deciding on home care, the parents had accepted the reality that their child's condition was terminal. Most looked at death as a "natural process." This attitude toward life and death was conveyed to the dying child or adolescent and to the siblings.

DEATH

It was no surprise to learn that these families coped well with the emotionally painful process of death. A six-year-old child had a birthday party with her invited friends the day before death. Shortly before death she slipped into coma and died in her mother's arms. A 12½-year-old child slipped into coma on her last day and died. All the family, including grandparents and four siblings, were there and grieved together. A 4½-year-old child became increasingly weak and died while being read to. The entire family grieved together. There was one exception. This was the family whose daughter had lived for five years following diagnosis of Wilms tumor at 13 months of age. Several times they had understood that the cancer was cured, only to have it recur.

Even in the end they had not given up hope for a cure. Although the child quietly died at home in the father's arms, the mother became frantic and both parents rushed with the dead child to the emergency room.

DISPOSITION OF THE BODY

The handling of the body following death varied from calling the mortician, who immediately came and took the body, to leaving the body in the home for varying lengths of time (up to seven to eight hours), during which time members of the family grieved together and talked of life and death. Three of the families had made prior arrangements with the mortician about disposal of the body and nature of the funeral.

FOLLOWUP

At the time of the retrospective study (one to two years following the death), one of the siblings manifested emotional problems that seemed directly related to the death in the family. One set of parents manifested marital problems aggravated by the life crisis. All the other were coping well.

Case History

The following is a summary of one typical family. Mary, aged 3½, lived in a middle-class community that was more than a two-hour drive from the university medical center. Her sister Susan was age six. Her mother and father, in their early thirties, were both college graduates. The family was close, and life had been going well for all of them.

In early December Mary developed symptoms of loss of appetite and weight. She was examined by her pediatrician who felt an abdominal mass. Mother recalled the look of serious concern in the pediatrician's eyes. She thought to herself, "It must be malignant." They were referred to the university medical center for further studies and treatment. Both parents recalled having controlled their emotions in front of the doctor but crying together that night.

The next day the maternal grandmother came to care for Susan while the parents took Mary to the hospital.

Following appropriate diagnostic studies Mary underwent abdominal surgery. The surgeon found an inoperable tumor. Biopsy revealed the tumor to be malignant (neuroblastoma). The surgeon related that there was a small chance of survival if radiation and chemotherapy were effective in shrinking the tumor so that it could be removed.

The family next met with the pediatric oncologist, a specialized nurse, and a social worker, who worked in collaboration with the oncologist. They spent considerable time with the parents discussing the usual course of such a cancer, the treatments to be used, as well as the psychological factors faced by the entire family and gathering a psychosocial history (Ablin et al. 1971). Both parents recalled this discussion as being very helpful in that they had some idea of what to expect and felt confident in the professional staff. In essence a therapeutic alliance was developed between the professional staff and the family. By late December Mary was discharged from the hospital. She returned to the medical center regularly for radiation therapy and chemotherapy. The tumor had shrunk to a size that was believed operable. "We were all excited."

From the beginning the parents told Mary she had a cancer that was very serious. During these initial weeks, she seemed depressed and kept to herself. The specialized nurse made home visits and engaged Mary in puppet play along with other play therapy activities. This relationship seemed to help her emotional status.

In early February she was again admitted to the hospital for surgery. The surgeon was unable to remove the entire tumor. Soon it was evident that the cancer had spread to other parts of the body.

The parents expressed many negative feelings related to the hospital care. "We felt helpless." "The radiologist didn't relate well to Mary." "The routine was upsetting." "It was a place of doom and gloom." "We were furious when the nurse woke her up just after she finally went to sleep." "Everything was so impersonal." On the other hand they recognized that this was a most distressing time for themselves and that they handled their internal pain through criticism.

Following recovery from the surgery, Mary was discharged from the hospital and continued on chemotherapy. It was during this period that her appearance began to deteriorate. She lost weight. Her hair began to fall out. "She wouldn't look at herself in the mirror." "She was embarrassed in having her friends visit."

Both parents remained open and supportive with Mary and Susan. There was still an outside chance that the cancer could be controlled.

However, in March, following further diagnostic studies, the oncologist told the parents that there was no chance of recovery. This marked the beginning of the terminal phase. Both parents accepted the reality that it was just a matter of time. There was no hope for cure.

The oncology team gave careful consideration to raising the possibility of home care with the parents. Factors taken into consideration included the reality that there was a close therapeutic alliance between them and the family, which would be ongoing; that there were multiple sources of community support; that the family was stable and coping well; and that there was openness in communication. The parents readily accepted this suggestion and felt comfortable with it.

They resolved to make Mary's remaining days as comfortable as possible. "We felt that this could best be done in our own home and by our own family." "We wanted to get her out of the hospital." They all took a trip to Disneyland. Upon their return, they learned from the oncologist that there was a new experimental drug that might offer some hope. They returned to the hospital for further tests. Each test showed more and more complications of the cancer. A trial of the new drug did not result in improvement. The parents resolved to carry on at home and continue with outpatient visits at the oncology clinic.

In early May they all celebrated Mary's fourth birthday. Later that week she developed weakness and pain in her legs. The oncologist offered to readmit her to the hospital for further treatment. Both parents were determined not to take her back to the hospital. "We felt we could do more for her at home." They consulted with their local pediatrician, who advised them to do what they felt best. He offered his help in collaboration with the oncology team. The specialized nurse continued with home visits, which were supportive to Mary and the parents. A wheelchair was arranged so that Mary could be out of bed. The nurse and physician instructed them in the use of pain medications.

By this time it was evident that Mary knew she would die. She stopped talking of the future. One day when she appeared dejected, her father asked her what was wrong. She said she was worried about dying and saw death as a monster who comes and takes you away. She demanded that a routine be maintained.

Susan was also told that Mary would die. She had been jealous of all the attention Mary received. "I want to be sick like Mary." On the other hand, she had to be reassured that she wouldn't develop cancer herself. She received support from her parents, grandmother, and teacher at school.

The family received help from many close friends. The pediatrician prescribed pain medication, called periodically to ask how all was going, and made several home visits. Grandmother remained in the home and helped care for both children along with doing general household chores. Susan participated in the care of her sister by taking her out in her wheelchair, reading to her, and playing games with her. The parents did manage several days off while grandmother took over.

Mary died in early June. The morning of her death her pulse rate became very rapid and she appeared extremely weak. She did not want to leave her room. She wanted someone with her at all times. Grandmother and the parents took turns being with her, reading stories, and playing games. At one point mother cried while reading to her. Mary said she understood. In the early evening, while being read to, she gave a gasp and died. The family pediatrician was called and pronounced her dead.

Susan had been away for the weekend visiting friends and she returned to the home several hours later. In the meantime, the parents had placed Mary's body on the cot in their room. When Susan arrived, all the family gathered around the body. The parents focused on the reality that Mary was alive in her body one moment and dead the next. "Death is part of the life process." All grieved together. Before Mary's death, the parents had arranged for cremation of the body. They had also made legal arrangements to take the ashes to a friend's ranch. They all participated in spreading the ashes over the ranch land. "We all have a pleasant memory of this." "It seemed natural."

In the letter to the oncology staff written several days after Mary's death, the mother stated, "So even in death Mary was still very much a part of our family, and it wasn't until we placed her in the box to take her to be cremated that I realized that for me Mary's spirit had indeed left her body and that now we were disposing only a shell, an outward form without any essential substance. And yet, memories will never be enough. When friends in their efforts to comfort and console say, 'Well, I'm glad the end finally came because she was so sick,' we find that our response is that we would choose a million days with a very sick Mary over one day without her. And of course, we no longer have that choice. The finality of death is all too real and painful. I know the hardest days are yet to come. No one can replace my Mary. All the 'I want her back' cries will not make her appear. So, please, if you can, keep sending your letters of news or your thoughts and responses to life and living, for they help us so much to go on and live."

Members of the oncology staff remained in contact with the family through the period of grief and mourning. The surviving family members adequately worked through the period of grief and mourning and were all functioning well at the time of the followup. They felt they had grown as a result of this tragic experience.

Discussion

This paper has focused on the home care of the dying child or adolescent. Clinical experience, plus material from a retrospective interview with six families who elected home care, has been reviewed. None regretted their decision to care for their child at home. As a whole, they expressed feelings of having themselves matured and grown as a result of this tragic experience in their lives. This is in marked contrast to a number of previous studies wherein families had lost a child from cancer. Binger and colleagues reported that in 11 of 20 such families, one or more members required psychiatric help following the death of their child (Binger et al. 1969). Kaplan and his colleagues reported that three months after a child's death from leukemia, 14 of 40 families had a member undergoing psychiatric care (Kaplan et al. 1976). Friedman and associates described the adverse consequences to families having a child die from cancer (Friedman et al. 1963). On the other hand, Futterman described a series of families who coped well with such a life crisis (Futterman and Hoffman 1973). None of these studies involved home care of the dying child. A study at the University of Minnesota described home care for children dying of cancer (Martinson et al. 1978). In that group, only 1 of 32 families had a member who received psychiatric care following the death of the child. In that particular study, home nursing service was provided during the terminal phase.

Our approach is different in that the interdisciplinary team providing support for home care of the dying child has been intimately involved with the family since the time of initial diagnosis. Such involvement continues through the period of grief and mourning. It is in the context of such a long-term, therapeutic alliance between the patient, family, and professionals that consideration is given to home care once the terminal phase is reached. A number of clinical variables are involved in the decision to approach the subject of home care with such families. Obviously the professionals involved must feel comfortable supporting such a decision, as must the parents and the children involved. The professionals must be able and willing to continue providing psychosocial support to such families. Consideration should be given to family cohesiveness, support systems, stability of family members, coping strategies, and other life stresses.

In our own study and in a number of subsequent cases, we

found that most of these families had come to terms with the reality of death. There were no longer heroic medical treatments to be implemented. Medical care was focused on alleviation of pain and suffering. The essence of care was the psychological support provided by family members to each other in the environment of their own home. These parents were able to provide unique psychological support to their own children that could not be as effectively done by anyone else. As a result they felt good about themselves. Siblings were likewise able to participate in a meaningful way. Peer relationships were maintained. Within the family there was an openness in communication, which further enchanced the mutual supportive efforts. Both anticipatory and subsequent grief occurred in a family setting. The quality of the children's final days was enhanced. They felt most comfortable being cared for in their own home with their own possessions, surrounded by their own family and friends. It was our clinical impression that these multiple factors together, which occurred in the context of ongoing support from an interdisciplinary group of professionals, were influential in helping these families cope with this tragic experience in their lives. We were further impressed that for the survivors there was emotional growth of family members, increased family cohesiveness, and positive redefinition of values. Although this remains a preliminary study, we feel from further clinical experience of our own that home care of the dying child or adolescent should be considered as a viable alternative within the total longitudinal, comprehensive, psychosocial care of selected patients and their families.

REFERENCES

Ablin, A. R., C. M. Binger, J. H. Kushner, C. Mikkelsen, R. C. Stein, and S. Zoger. 1971. "Initial Conference with a Family of a Leukemic Child." *American Journal of Diseases of Children* (October).

Aries, P. 1974. *Western Attitudes Toward Death from the Middle Ages to the Present*. Baltimore and London: The Johns Hopkins University Press.

Binger, C. M. 1973. "Childhood Leukemia—Emotional Impact on Siblings." In E. J. Anthony and C. Koupernik, eds. *The Child in His Family: The Impact of Disease and Death*. New York: Wiley.

Binger, C. M., A. R. Albin, R. C. Feurstein, J. H. Kushner, and C. Mikklesen. 1969. "Childhood Leukemia—Emotional Impact on Patient and Family." *New England Journal of Medicine* (February) 280:414–18.
Friedman, S. B., P. Chodoff, J. W. Mason, and D. A. Hamburg, 1963. "Behavioral Observations on Parents Anticipating the Death of a Child." *Pediatrics* 32:610.
Futterman, E. H. and I. Hoffman. 1973. "Crisis and Adaptation in the Families of Fatally Ill Children." In E. J. Anthony and C. Koupernik, eds. *The Child in His Family: The Impact of Disease and Death.* New York: Wiley.
Kaplan, D. M., R. Grobstein, and A. Smith. 1976. "Predicting the Impact of Severe Illness in Families." *Health Social Work* 1:72.
Martinson, I. M., G. D. Armstrong, D. P. Geis, M. A. Anglim, E. C. Gronseth, H. MacInnis, J. H. Kersey, and M. E. Nesbit. 1978. "Home Care for Children Dying of Cancer." *Pediatrics* 62(1) (July).
Stoddard, S. H. 1975. *The Hospice Movement—A Better Way of Caring for the Dying.* New York: Stein and Day.

· 13 ·
Home Care for the Child with Cancer

Ida M. Martinson

The Home Care for the Child With Cancer research* has been an explorative and descriptive study looking for the answers to two questions: Is it feasible to have a child die at home? Is it desirable to have a child die at home?

Since 1972 I have been involved with research to identify and evaluate the nursing care required for the family of a child who is dying from cancer at home. Beginning with the basic philosophical approach that the parent becomes the primary caregiver, the nurse becomes the facilitator, and the physician becomes a consultant, the study has several aims:

1. to provide the option of home care to the family of a child with cancer;
2. to assess the home as an alternative care setting for the child with cancer;
3. to determine the role(s) of the nurse in the home care of the child;
4. to identify the most immediate problems of the family and child during home care;
5. to identify the supportive mechanisms required by the child, the family, and the nurse during their experience of caring for the dying child at home;
6. to identify, through interviews, the benefits and limitations of

*Funded in part by DHEW, National Cancer Institute, Grant CA 19040, July 1976.

home care as perceived by the child, the family, nurse, and other health professionals;
7. to identify the difference in health care costs between care in the home and care in the hospital;
8. to explore the interface of this project with existing health agencies giving services in the home;
9. to assist health care agencies in implementing home care delivery service for a child with cancer.

We return to the two questions: Is it feasible to have a child die at home? Is it desirable?

From August 1976 through June 1978, sixty-four families were involved with our project.

As we have families referred to us, we look at the following: (1) Is the child's cure-oriented therapy discontinued? I think none of us wanted to get into the situation where home care would be an alternative to therapy. At the time of referral to us, the child has usually been through the last experimental protocol available or desired. (2) We look at the child's desire to be at home. We have yet to find a child who does not want to be at home, but it is important that we always check for that. There might be a child who really has become more dependent on health care in the hospital and would really prefer to be in the hospital. (3) We look at the parents' desire to be with the child at home. The child's desire is by far the most important factor. If you ask parents, "Do you want to take your child home to die?" they are probably going to say, "No." They don't even hear the word "home." They perhaps are saying, "No, I do not want my child to die." We are finding parents are willing to give home care because of the child's desire to be at home. (4) By far the most crucial part, we feel, is the "parents' recognition of their own ability to care for the child." We have yet to find a family where neither of the parents have the ability, but we do find the majority of the parents do not recognize their own ability to care for the child. That would be a basis for another study: What are the factors involved? What happens to parents' recognition of their own ability when they are involved in our health system year after year?

We then move into the situation of "perceived feasibility and desirability of the child dying at home." We really did not say "no" to anyone. We accepted all referrals to the project. In the study we were looking at the roles of the nurse, the physician, and other professionals, including the clergy. We were getting demographic data and the history of the child's disease and attempting to identify family and community support.

Moving into the next stage, we were beginning to see it is the ratio between the perceived benefits of a child dying at home minus the problems of the child dying at home. Frequently, the professionals involved count up the problems and may even reach a point where the problems are so many and of such magnitude that it is felt necessary to admit the child to the hospital. It is at that point that parents are usually quite articulate about what the benefits of home care are from their point of view.

During the first 24 months of the study we worked with 58 families where a child died; 46 (79 percent) died at home, 1 died in an ambulance on the way to the hospital, and 11 died in a hospital.

The families live throughout Minnesota, North Dakota, and Wisconsin. About half of them have been from the Twin Cities–Seven County metropolitan area.

Where are our referrals coming from? The University of Minnesota referred 31 patients (53 percent); eight other hospitals and one clinic referred 27 (47 percent). I had expected the University of Minnesota Hospitals to make referrals to us, but through word of mouth other hospitals heard of our project and also made referrals. At the University of Minnesota we have worked with 15 physicians. Nine additional physicians represent the nine other health care institutions.

The ages of the children with cancer who have died at home while a part of our study were as follows: mean age of 9.2, median age of 8.5 years, with a range of 1 month to 17 years. A question sometimes asked is "Is there some age where it is more feasible to care for the child at home?" We have had seven children under the age of 2; nine children 3–5 years; seven children 6–8 years; six children 9–11 years; four children 12–14 years; and thirteen children aged 15–17 years. In the latter group of 15–17 year olds, some thought the children would not want to be at home. However, that has been the largest single group dying at home.

The ages of children with cancer who have participated in our study and returned to the hospital to die are as follows: four children 3–5 years; one child 6–8 years; two children 9–11 years; three children 12–14 years, and two 15–17 years.

Diagnoses of the children covered a rather wide range. We had decided we would not limit our study to leukemia. If we were going to look at the feasibility of home care, we needed to cover all children with cancer. Any children under the age of 18 who had cancer who have been referred to us have been accepted in the study. At this point we are unable to say that there is any one type of cancer that cannot be cared for at home and another that can. Home care has been possible regardless of the diagnosis. Of the 46 children who died at home, 19 had leukemia, 4 had lymphoma, 10 had central nervous system cancers, 4 had neuroblastoma, 6 had bone tumors, and 3 had other forms of cancer.

When we look at the pain medications given during the last 48 hours of life for the 46 patients who died at home, we found 8 children in whom there apparently had been no pain. Most of the children did, however, have pain. Pain control is an important element in the success of home care. Parents have also commented that their child has had more pain relief at home than in the hospital.

We had considerable trouble trying to control the pain of one of the children early in the study. The physician involved contacted the Seattle Pain Clinic, who suggested the use of methadone. It worked so well with that first child that we have continued to use methadone for children with severe pain. It is as effective as morphine sulfate and has other advantages. It is effective for 8 hours. If one has a child who has pain relief for 8 hours, one has the potential of the child's sleeping through the night, which in turn allows the parents to sleep through the night. I think it is apparent that allowing parents to get sufficient rest can be a critical variable in whether parents are able to keep their child at home.

When we started the program, one of the things we wanted to do was to make sure we could give the quality of care that the child would have in the hospital. Of the 11 children who received injectable medications, the parents of 9 of these children were taught how to give injections and were able to give them to their child. We did not say "no" to any hospital-oriented equipment. We really thought that it was important to attempt to bring whatever was necessary to the home. We did have children who needed oxygen essentially for comfort. We knew from the literature that parents who have children with cystic fibrosis have for years been handling oxygen tanks at home, but what about a family with the acute crisis of having a dying child? Would they be able to remember all the safety precautions, for example? I can remember that first family and how closely we supervised them when the oxygen was in use. I think that the motivation of these families is so high that they have not had difficulties in learning the safety techniques of any of the hospital-oriented equipment.

Four of the children had to have intravenous equipment. When we began, we found that public health nurses, because of some rules they had, could not supervise an intravenous (IV) medication at home. We thought about it, discussed it, and then decided, "We'll supervise the IV," and we did. Because of our experience in this area, several of the public health nursing rules and regulations have been changed to allow their nurses to supervise an IV at home. It is interesting to us when we conduct the six-month postdeath interviews that we find the parents commenting that they were frequently counting the drops and occasionally changing the bottles for the IV while the child was in the hospital. Other hospital-oriented equipment included the indwelling urinary catheter, gavage feeding tube, wound-drainage tubing and, a nasotracheal suction machine. The suction machine was one that bothered me personally. I thought, "That will be one for sure that will have to be done in the hospital!" However, we have had 4 children who have required suctioning, and the families were able to perform this task at home successfully.

Among the 46 families, 24 of the children required no hospital-oriented equipment. That was something that surprised us because we were prepared and willing to bring all these things into the homes as necessary.

We also look at the hospital-oriented furnishing and supplies needed. Nine of the children used wheelchairs; seven used overbed tables. However, one mother commented, "Now, Dr. Martinson, why bring me an overbed table? An ironing board works much better, and besides, it doesn't look like the hospital." Five families had a hospital bed. In the pilot study most of the families had a hospital bed, but we found a wheelchair was perhaps more useful. After obtaining a hospital bed for one child, the next week the mother came back and said, "Oh, could I have a wheelchair instead?" We got the wheelchair and she later said, "We were able to take our child camping over Labor Day weekend." Other families had similar experiences. "He was able to be with his father, who is a mechanic, during the hours that he was feeling good." "I was able to take her grocery shopping. She can't talk anymore, but she can nod her head at foods she wants me to buy." These experiences point to another whole area to look at: the type of activity that a child can participate in during the days and hours before death.

Other hospital-oriented furnishings and supplies included Chux, ABD pads, and the like for 18 families; flotation pad, 12; alternating air mattress, 5. Here again, 11 of the children did not require even these supplies or furnishings.

A total of 58 primary or coprimary nurses were involved. In several instances a nurse could not give a 24-hour commitment to the family, and we then had a coprimary nurse who took over the commitment when she was not available. The average age of the nurses was 35.9 years, with a range of 23 to 63 years. Time elapsed since receiving diploma or degree was a mean of 13.6 years, with a range of 1 to 44 years.

The educational level of these 58 nurses has varied. Since this is a research study, we attempted to get nurses with a master's degree because of the need for intensive data collection. However, in Minnesota only 3 percent of our nurses are master's prepared, and so we did well to get 7 nurses (12 percent) who had a master's degree. Twenty-nine (50 percent) had a baccalaureate degree; 1 (2 percent) had an associate degree; 17 (28 percent) had a hospital diploma. Four (7 percent) were not registered nurses. Three of these 4 were licensed practical nurses and 1 was a nursing student. With the latter, we were able to have a faculty member supervise her work, and it worked out very well. For most of the nurses, it was their first time caring for a child dying at home.

We compared the basic costs for home and hospital care and the number of days of final care. For our home care group of 46, the average number of final days was 38.9, with a median of 20.5 days and a range of 1 to 256 days. For the hospital comparison group, we used the University of Minnesota Hospitals and received a list from their computer of 22 children who had died in the hospital. We went back 3 years to get the 22, because since our project began, fewer children have died in the hospital. Here we found an average of 29.4 days of hospitalization before death, which is very close to the 38.9 days for home care. The median was 21.5 days versus the 20.5 days for home care, and a range of 1 to 89 days in the hospital compared with the 1 to 256 days in the home.

The cost estimate for home care was a mean of $1,213, a median of $705; with a range of $55 to $7,280. These figures are based on the cost of nursing service at a rate of $10 to be on call 24 hours a day and for telephone consultation, $45 per home visit; and $10 per clinic visit. Both public health nursing agencies and hospital home care services in Minnesota were charging $35 per home visit.

The hospital control group had a mean cost estimate of $5,880, median of $4,300, and a range of $200 to $17,800. Those figures are based on the cost of nursing service and room and board at the rate of $200 per day, which was about the cost in Minneapolis.

The actual hospital cost figures are considerably different. Instead of $5,800, which is the base cost estimate, the actual cost of hospitalization for the 22 children in the control group was a mean of $13,016, median of $8,236, and a range of $68 (this for a child who died in the emergency room) to $58,833.

There are always four major participants involved in home care. The child, the family, the nurse, and the physician need to know that home care is feasible and that home is desirable. They must also realize that pain and other symptoms can be controlled at home, as well as in the hospital. There is involvement between parents and child. The parents are the primary caregivers, and it is important for them to realize this. The nurse has been a facilitator, and the physician has been a consultant.

With our 58 families in the first two years, we have completed interviews with the families one-month postdeath and at 6 months postdeath. Some have been completed at one-year postdeath, and we are now beginning to follow up with the last scheduled interview at 2 years postdeath. At this point all of the parents of the child who have died at home have said, "Yes, we would do it again."

The nurses involved in home care have said they would do it again. Most of them, whether they are public health nurses or hospital nurses, feel that on the whole it has given them a different outlook toward home care. Few of them had ever been on call 24 hours a day, 7 days a week, before this experience. They found it tougher in some ways, and yet at the same time, they have been willing to do it again. One nurse summed it up: "Any doubts I had about the wisdom of caring for such a critically ill child were erased in that last hour. This is what the child wanted and we did it." I also think it's that "we did it" sense of accomplishment that we are hearing from the parents.

The physician response has been good. Work was started back in 1972 with one physician, and in getting to know other physicians before I began the funded project, much groundwork had been done. The physicians now have come out very strongly in their support of having this service institutionalized as part of the University of Minnesota Home Health Services Department. That institution has already begun providing services, and so have St. Louis Park Medical Center in suburban Minneapolis and Children's Health Center in Minneapolis. Public health agencies in the seven-county metropolitan area have also agreed to provide home care services and are doing so.

· 14 ·

Helping a Child with Leukemia To Die at Home

JOAN TAKSA ROLSKY

When it is clear that nothing can be done to control the progression of a potentially fatal childhood disease such as leukemia or cancer, the question arises about where the child's last days should be spent. Each family must deal with this issue individually, arriving at a decision that is in the best interests of the child, as well as of other family members. At some point in the social work counseling that is part of the hematology-oncology program at St. Christopher's Hospital for Children (Philadelphia), this subject has probably been discussed with parents, either in individual or parent group meetings. Therefore, most families have given this issue some thought before the time arrives to make a decision. In the case of any particular child, further discussion between the medical staff and the family is best initiated early in the terminal phase of illness, before the stresses of the imminent death of the child are upon them.

It is important for parents to understand that they do have a choice; it is perhaps the only phase in the treatment of their child over which they can exercise control. Parents need support in accepting the transition of the therapeutic goal from one of maintaining life and seeking cure to one of keeping their child as comfortable as possible with no prolongation of suffering. Once parents can realize that there is no longer hope for comfortable life, they can understand that the hospital may not be the best place for their child. Many parents agree that their child's physical and emotional well-being can best be provided for in the familiar surroundings of the home.

Such a decision is often at first an intellectual one. However, as parents confront the imminent death of their child, the anxiety they experience is often expressed as concern that they will be inadequate to provide good care during the child's last days. The medical staff should expect this anxiety and be prepared to deal with it. Since one major cause of anxiety is fear of the unknown, it is the responsibility of the medical team to inform families as fully as possible about what problems might arise during the terminal phase of their child's illness. Development and management of symptoms such as bleeding, progressive weakness, infection, difficulty in breathing, seizures, and coma should be discussed, along with explicit instructions about what to do and when to call the physician. Even though some of these symptoms may not appear, families have reported that they felt more secure knowing what might happen. When these symptoms do appear, parents who have been fully informed do not experience the panicky need to do something to stop them but can concentrate their energies on providing relief for the child. Open discussion of symptoms during the dying process also reinforces the idea that our therapeutic goal for the child has changed to one focusing on keeping the child comfortable.

We must give parents the assurance that there are drugs to help alleviate the pain and discomfort that such new symptoms may produce. Parents are relieved to learn that several oral medications are available to reduce discomfort yet keep the child alert. Such drugs may be easily administered by parents, reducing their feelings of dependency on the medical staff and enabling them to feel they are active participants in the care of their child. Parents can receive instruction on how to inject stronger pain relief medication, if the need arises. Parental anxiety and sorrow at this point can create a desire among staff members to overassure families. It is important to be sure that parents do not interpret discussion of pain medications as a guarantee that the child will not suffer. Some discomfort is almost inevitable as the disease progresses, and parents are better able to deal with this if they are prepared.

In addition to the medical issues there are also emotional issues to discuss. The social worker and physician must attempt to prepare parents for what they and their child may feel at this time, including the anger, fear, sadness, isolation, anxiety, and disbelief that commonly occur. Written material can be helpful; placing parents in contact with others who have gone through this experience may also be very beneficial. Throughout the early treatment process, parent-to-parent contact is encouraged, both individually and in parent group meetings. So, too, when the issue is helping the child to die at home, the opportunity to share with parents who can relate to the difficulties involved is invaluable.

Another major area of concern for parents is what effect caring for the dying child at home will have on their other children. With the help of the staff, parents can decide to what extent siblings should be involved. Information about how children of different ages deal with death helps families make decisions appropriate for them. The death of a child in a family is a traumatic experience, whether it occurs at home or in the hospital. There are definite advantages for the siblings in having a brother or sister die at home.

When children can witness the progression of the terminal illness of their sibling, this affords them the opportunity to develop some understanding of the concept that death will bring peace and an end to suffering. The separation imposed on them when the patient dies in the hospital encourages fantasies about the dying process that can be more frightening than the reality. In addition, when the dying child is at home, siblings can be included in the caretaking by interacting with him in positive ways on a daily basis and thus feel they have been able to help. The fact that their parents are available to them for discussion or reassurance is particularly important. We have found that the adjustment of siblings has been easier when the child has died at home.

The question of what to tell the patient himself is of prime importance. Throughout the illness, parents are encouraged to keep open the lines of communication with their child and to answer questions as honestly as is appropriate for any particular child. Although there are guidelines about how children of different ages assimilate knowledge of their illnesses, individual decisions are made about each child. Often the most appropriate guide is the child himself. Children of various ages are capable of discussing their impending deaths, particularly if parents and staff have been receptive to such discussions earlier in the illness. However, if parents or staff members are uncomfortable with such open communication, children will pick up the cues, and a mutually protective atmosphere will be created. The staff must consider the needs of the whole family when dealing with this issue, being careful that their own anxieties do not take precedence over what is in the best interests of the family.

Once the parents have decided to keep their child at home, they may experience some concern about lack of contact with the hospital. Arrangements should be made to give the families the home phone numbers of pertinent staff members. They should be encouraged to call with any questions they may have. At St. Christopher's Hospital for Children, both the social worker and the physician who has assumed primary responsibility for treatment of the child during his illness keep in close touch with the family by telephone or home visits.

Some families prefer to make regular outpatient visits, often weekly, to the hematology clinic, even though specific therapy for the child's disease has been stopped. Physical examinations and blood counts done at these times help parents follow the progress of the disease. For the patient these visits maintain an established routine and reaffirm that the staff is still interested. As death becomes imminent, clinic visits may no longer be feasible; the frequency of contact by phone or home visits may need to be increased. If at any time the parents feel they would be more comfortable if their child were in the hospital, this option is left open.

When death is fairly near, the family should be informed about what to do when the child dies. They must know which physician to call to the home to complete the death certificate. They should also be encouraged to discuss in advance what funeral arrangements they wish to make. Parents often discover that their ideas about this issue differ; it is best if they can resolve any conflicts before the death occurs. Some parents choose to consult with a funeral director and their clergyman, who can offer assistance in making decisions. Parents should also be informed that a request for an autopsy will be made. Most parents will have considered the question of autopsy before its mention by medical staff. A discussion of the reasons for an autopsy is usually easier for parents when it comes before the child dies.

We need to inform parents that they may handle their child's body after death. Many parents wish to hold, bathe, or change the clothing of their child. The opportunity to provide this kind of care after death is very meaningful to parents. Even though such discussions in advance of death are painful, they relieve anxiety by reducing parents' fears of the unknown.

Any discomfort parents may feel about asking questions while their child is still alive is minimized when the medical staff assumes responsibility for initiating these discussions. We can also help by preparing parents for the initial feeling of relief they may experience at the time of the child's death. This acknowledgment and acceptance of such feelings does much to prevent unnecessary guilt.

The responsibility of the medical staff does not terminate immediately upon the death of the child. During their child's illness, parents have established important relationships with the various staff members who have shared this experience with them. Feelings of sadness are compounded if the loss of the child means the additional loss of these relationships. At St. Christopher's Hospital for Children, we assure families that we will maintain contact with them. When possible, the social worker and physician attend the funeral as a concrete demonstration that they are still concerned about the family. The director of the hematology-oncology department sends a personal note of sympathy to the family. The social worker maintains closest contact with the family by continuing to provide counseling during the grief period. This is accomplished by telephone, as well as by home and office visits, which generally decrease in frequency toward the end of the first year after the death has occurred. Once again, if the parents so desire, they are put in touch with others who have lost a child. If intensive counseling is necessary, an appropriate referral is made. The ultimate goal of the medical effort is to help the family deal as well as possible with their child's illness and death and to facilitate their working through the grief process and resuming normal family functioning.

A letter received from a mother who had cared for her dying four-and-a-half-year-old child at home reads, in part:

> When you first talked about the fact that we might be given the choice to have Bobby at home, it was in a group meeting. Bobby was doing well and I didn't think in terms of his really dying. I looked at the question idealistically and said of course I would want my child at home (wouldn't every good mother!). I didn't really think of all the other things that enter into this decision.
>
> When Bobby relapsed I had to look at the question differently. I don't think I really had a choice. I couldn't think of Bobby dying in the hospital. He didn't like it there. He needed to be home as long as he could.
>
> But then came the day that they told us there was nothing more they could do for Bobby. I knew Bobby needed to be home, but I was scared. I don't think this fear was of physical things—how I would react if Bobby bled, if he went into a coma, if he were in great pain—I would have to face those things in the hospital as well. It was a fear of my own inadequacies—that I wouldn't be able to do enough or what was right for Bobby without a doctor or nurse to say I was right. I know we were told we would handle whatever came along and doctors were just a phone call away. We understood all this, but couldn't really believe it until we started living it.
>
> We did get through those two weeks. I was really scared sometimes, especially at night when Bobby would wake up in pain. But most of the time, I was so glad we didn't have to be in the hospital.
>
> We were still a family. Bobby could stay in the bedroom and be quiet when he wanted, but when he felt better he came out with the other children. He rode his motorcycles, watched TV and played with his baby brother. We even went to the store and he picked out exactly what he wanted to eat. He couldn't do these things in the hospital. I could devote myself completely to Bobby and still be there for the rest of the family. We really needed to be together!
>
> When Bobby lay dying, I really appreciated having him at home. He was in his own bed. He felt secure. We had him on our own home ground. We were in charge. We could walk out of his room and walk away from it a little (we were not in a sterile hospital). Bobby knew he was dying, but he was not really unhappy. He could still smile at us and was content.
>
> Johnny and Tina (Bob's older brother and sister) got some understanding of why Bobby had to die. They watched him get weaker and they saw his pain. They faced the reality that his body was worn out and needed to rest. I think this really helped their acceptance of his death. They were glad he didn't hurt anymore.

I was glad John and Meg (the physicians) were there with us when Bobby died. It seems strange. Two weeks before, I was afraid to take Bobby home and that morning I was so scared we'd have to take him back to the hospital. Meg came with morphine and John with an I.V. setup. I was surprised, but so relieved; at that moment I realized just how important it was to all of us to have Bobby here.

Bobby died in his own room, in my arms. When we all said good-bye to him I put him to bed—his own bed. We all went out into the kitchen and sat around the table and talked for almost three hours. Bobby lay dead in his bed and we talked—about Bobby and about other things—but it was the right thing to do. We could never have done this in the hospital.

· 15 ·
Death in a Family of Hemophiliacs

ÅKE MATTSSON

This chapter describes the impact of death and of fears of dying in a family with two hemophilic boys. Hemophilia, a lifelong serious illness afflicting males almost exclusively, is characterized primarily by bleeding into the soft tissues and joints. The bleeding tendencies are due to clotting defects transmitted as sex-linked recessive traits by a carrier mother to a recipient son. Consequently, half of a carrier's sons are hemophiliacs and half of her daughters are carriers. The defects in clotting are caused either by a deficiency in the plasma antihemophilic factor (factor VIII) in classic hemophilia or in the Christmas factor (factor IX) in Christmas disease. Clinically, the two types of hemophilia are practically indistinguishable. Most patients with hemophilia show an onset of symptoms in early childhood and are subject to repeated bleeding episodes, often causing severe pain and requiring immobilization, hospital admissions, and various treatment procedures. Despite recent improvements in the treatment of acute hemorrhages with concentrated plasma fractions and greatly increased chances for a normal life span, the constant threat of a bleeding episode that might prove fatal looms over the young hemophiliac and his family.

Working as a liaison child psychiatrist to pediatrics, I was in-

"Death in a Family of Hemophiliacs," by Dr. Åke Mattsson, from the book *The Experience of Dying* by E. Mansell Pattison, © 1977 by Prentice-Hall, Inc. Published by Prentice-Hall, Inc. Englewood Cliffs, N.J. 07632.

troduced to the family when their two hemophiliac sons, Andy and Bill, were 8 and 10 years old. Both boys showed a high clinical severity of hemophilia—that is, their antihemophilic titer was less than 1 percent of normal. A sister, 11 years of age, complemented the family. They were devout Catholics. The father worked long hours as a security guard, and the mother augmented the family income by a weekend job as a supermarket clerk. Both parents were in their late thirties. Bill was found to be a hemophiliac at 8 months of age, and his family history showed that his maternal grandfather and two maternal cousins were known hemophiliacs. During Bill's first ten years of life, he required about thirty hospital admissions, mainly owing to hemorrhages into his large joints. Some of these admissions had lasted for several months because of protracted orthopedic treatment. Bill's bleeding episodes were more serious than those of his brother. Both Bill and Andy showed cycles of increased bleeding tendency several times a year. From the time that Bill was 8 years old and Andy 6, they would increasingly assist each other in taking care of minor bleeding and bruises. Bill was described as calmer, less daring, and less active than Andy. After both boys started elementary school, they used to play outside by themselves, and the mother ceased to watch them constantly as she had done earlier, worrying about their hurting themselves and sustaining hemorrhages.

Andy, the younger brother, had experienced twenty hospital admissions at the time he reached 8 years of age. Most of his bleeding episodes involved the soft tissues and muscles—infrequently the joints, in contrast to his brother Bill. The mother stressed that Andy seemed more happy, more alert, and spirited than Bill, even during the episodes of painful bleeding.

The developmental milestones of both boys were described as normal. The parents had tried to raise them as normally as possible and had allowed them a fair amount of physical activities with their peers after age 3 or 4. The boys had always related well to other children and often joined in neighborhood baseball games, using plastic bats and balls in order to minimize the risk of injuries.

The mother was the main disciplinarian in the family, even if both boys often expressed fears of causing their father to get angry at them during his brief periods of time with the family. No behavior problems were reported in either son. With a certain pride, the mother mentioned that Bill and Andy often took care of small injuries themselves by applying ice packs to bleeding sites and assisting each other. Indeed, from about age 6, both boys showed much evidence of a good psychosocial adjustment to their chronic illness.

Before her marriage, the mother was aware that she was a possible carrier of hemophilia, for her father was a hemophiliac and her two sisters had hemophilic boys. In the presence of his sister, she had told her future husband of the possibility of their having hemophilic sons, "so that all would be out in the open and honest before we got married." In retrospect, both parents felt that they had counted "a little too heavily" on the odds of having boys who were not hemophiliacs. Occasionally, the father would mention his wish for healthy boys with whom he could rough-house. Clearly, the mother had assumed most of the childrearing responsibilities and had allowed the father to work long hours away from home. She also excused the father for his infrequent visits to their sons during their hospital admissions for hemorrhagic episodes.

The mother often spoke in glowing terms about her hemophilic father's stoic attitude toward his serious illness. She recalled his telling her how he, as a teenager, unaware of what was ailing him, would often go to the slaughterhouse to drink fresh blood from killed animals in the belief that this would cure his bleeding disorder. The mother's father seemed to have minimized physical discomfort and fears associated with his hemorrhages all through his life. He had managed his life situation quite well until he died of cancer of the stomach at age 63. The mother's admiration for her father and his seemingly adaptive denial of his chronic disease was probably reflected in her own tendency to minimize her sons' disorder and remain hopeful even at times of critical bleeding episodes.

When observed in the hospital, visiting one of her ill sons, the mother always seemed calm, cheerful, and efficient in attending to the child. In addition, she had been remarkably successful in soliciting blood donors in order to replace the large amounts of plasma that often were required to treat her sons.

At 9 years of age, Andy had enjoyed a good year with no serious bleeding and had become proficient in many age-appropriate sports and games. Following a strep throat infection, he was admitted to the hospital for the care of bleeding into the soft tissues of his pharynx, which caused breathing difficulties and soon required a tracheotomy. After a few days, exchange transfusions became necessary, because Andy developed circulating anticoagulants. He remained alert and cooperative, despite the tracheotomy and strict bedrest, and appreciated any opportunity to engage with various ward staff members in playing games, reading, and watching television. Andy's cooperative attitude seemed to be sustained by the parents' assurance that both they and Andy should leave "things in God's hands," which included assisting the doctors and nurses in carrying out their duties. During this serious bleeding crisis, which lasted for ten days, Andy remained in a cheerful mood most of the time, to the point of being prankish on occasion. On the tenth day of his admission, an attempt was made to remove the tracheotomy tube because of considerable bleeding around it. Profuse bleeding ensued, and after a few hours, Andy died from aspiration of blood and subsequent asphyxia.

At the time of Andy's death, Bill was 11 years old. The parents declined our offer to provide some psychological assistance to the family in their mourning process, and for the next year and a half we had contacts with them only at times of some of Bill's bleeding episodes. To the surprise of both my pediatric hematology colleagues and me, the mother then called me and reported that Bill was showing problems in the parochial school he attended. His male teacher had become concerned about Bill's declining grades. He had impressed the teacher as "miserable if not depressed," and his reply to the teacher's admonitions was, "Why should I bother to study? I'm going to die anyway." The teacher's immediate response had been, "God will take you when he wants to," whereupon the teacher had tried to elicit more information about what he felt was Bill's misconception about hemophiliacs dying at a young age, as had been the fate of Bill's brother.

The parents and the teacher were shocked by Bill's repeated references to his brother's death "such a long time later." The mother had tried to reassure Bill about his future by telling him about the steady medical progress in the treatment of hemophiliacs. She admitted, however, that she and her husband had tried to avoid any discussion about Andy's death and had never openly recognized the possibility that Bill might worry about his own condition and safety.

During my interview with the mother, which preceded the brief psychiatric intervention with Bill, she recalled how Bill had cried upon learning about Andy's death. At the funeral, Bill went up to the casket, looked at his brother, and remarked, "He seems to be sleeping." Following the funeral, Bill had asked few questions about his brother. Occasionally, the mother would show Bill a picture of Andy taken a few days before his death, portraying Andy lying in bed, with a smile on his face, and displaying his tracheotomy tube to the surgeons. The mother had continued to carry this picture in her purse at all times and she also showed it to me during the interview. Whenever friends of the parents brought up the subject of hemophilia or referred to Andy, Bill would listen with interest, make no remarks, and often leave the gathering with his eyes filled with tears.

Before Andy's last hospital admission, he and Bill had shared a bedroom. Upon learning of Andy's death, Bill moved into his sister's room and for several weeks shared her bed. Three months later, Bill told his mother that he was ready to sleep by himself in his old room.

Following Andy's death, Bill had become more open, more daring, and more involved in play activities with friends in the neighborhood. He enjoyed roller skating, bicycling, playing baseball, and even practicing football with caution. When ice packs were necessary, he would apply them to his bleeding sites, and he seldom complained about pain and immobilizations. Obviously, at age 13 he showed a healthy independence in terms of self-care.

Commenting on her and her husband's reluctance to allow any family talks about all the memories surrounding Andy's last bleeding crisis, the mother recalled that only once during the intervening two years had the father broken down and cried about the demise of his son. At this time the father had been under the influence of alcohol. Religion had continued to play an important role in the family's life. The parents frequently told their children and their friends, "We have two children here and one angel in heaven." The parents had felt that Bill accepted these parental views and he often prayed to Andy in order for Andy to intervene, "because Andy is now closer to God, and he can help me when I am bleeding." Bill also seemed to share the notion that all of them would sooner or later join Andy after death.

At this point in my interview, the mother spontaneously wondered whether she should have spoken more directly to Bill about Andy's death in the intervening years. She added that she had continued to rely on her cheerful, matter-of-fact approach in regard to hemophilia, the approach she seemed to have learned from her own father. At the same time, she was definitely in tune with Bill and his upset feelings, and she had acted immediately upon the alerting signals from the schoolteacher.

When I saw Bill a few days later, he seemed well prepared by his mother for his visit with me. Bill was a cooperative, verbal 13-year-old, and he readily told me about his present school situation, minimizing his academic difficulties, particularly in science, saying, "I don't like to read so much about the human body." This provided me with an early opening into the area of hemophilia, and Bill complained, "I haven't been told much about hemophilia by anybody." Bill thought he had been about 6 years old when his mother first tried to explain to him about the disease, relating his frequent black-and-blue marks and joint swellings to a blood disorder. He then asked me many questions about the healing of cuts, of oozing tooth sockets, and of sprained joints. Bill knew that hemophilia was hereditary and mentioned the long life of his hemophilic grandfather. He then remarked that his two older cousins, both suffering from hemophilia, seemed to do fairly well, being in their late teens.

In my second meeting with Bill, we could approach the death

of his younger brother, a topic that Bill introduced by telling me that he missed Andy a lot, that they had been very close, and that "God wanted it to happen." Bill recalled his sad and frightened feelings immediately following the death of his brother, and his refusal to sleep in the room that he and his brother had shared. For a long time Bill had held on to a big teddy bear that used to belong to Andy, and he had imagined that the bear was his deceased brother. Especially at night, before going to sleep, these thoughts had helped Bill "to make it easier missing Andy." Everybody at home seemed to have missed Andy very much, according to Bill, so "it was too hard for us to talk about Andy's death and his and my illness." Bill then recalled situation after situation in which Andy and he had played together, had helped each other out when one of them was bleeding, had stood up for each other to other children, and also had allied themselves against their parents and their sister.

Bill felt uncertain about his chances to live a normal life span because his brother had died at a young age. He remembered visiting Andy once in the hospital and seeing the tracheotomy tube, and he also mentioned the mother's photograph of Andy. Bill knew that this fatal bleeding episode had not been related to physical injury but was caused by a throat infection. No wonder, Bill said, that he had been very scared several times in the intervening years when he had suffered from colds and sore throats. He had imagined the worst outcome—a complication of pharyngeal bleeding that might lead to his death.

In the subsequent four interviews, Bill repeatedly asked many questions about his clotting defect and the effects of plasma transfusions, about the progress of research dealing with improved treatment of bleeding disorders, and about the possibility of a "once and for all cure" of hemophilia. In addition, he wanted to learn more about hereditary illnesses and the specific genetic explanation of hemophilia. He went over his family background in great detail and recalled many early memories of his hemophilic grandfather and two hemophilic cousins and, of course, of his deceased brother. Bill remembered his mother's telling him about her role as a carrier, which was followed by a reflection on his part about the likeliness that his mother had "sad feelings" about this fact. Toward the end of these sessions, and also a few years later when I again met Bill, he stressed that his mother had three healthy brothers who did not have hemophilia. This important fact convinced him that his possible future sons would not have the disease.

Toward the end of the short period of psychiatric intervention, Bill began to speak about his interest in a trade school after high school graduation, and more specifically about learning to become a baker, a job in which "you can both make good money and don't have to be afraid of getting hurt." Any attempt on my part to bring up the likelihood that, on occasion, Bill and Andy had had their scuffles, and that Bill might have resented his brother, resulted in incredulous and irritated responses, such as "So what? It doesn't matter now; he is dead. . . . Andy was my best friend, we had the same illness. . . . I think he is alive in heaven and knows what's happening to me. . . . I can pray to him, too, and he can hear me, I think. . . ."

When I arranged for a followup two years later, Bill was a healthy-looking fifteen-year-old, doing satisfactory work in school; remaining physically active in biking, baseball, and softball; and enjoying many friendships. With a certain pride he told me that he seemed to be in much better shape than most of the other hemophilic teenage boys he knew in our area. At this time he had an excellent recall and understanding of the clinical and hereditary characteristics of hemophilia. He admitted to still worrying at times about "bleeding around my throat" as a complication to throat infections. Otherwise, memories of Andy seldom occupied Bill's mind. Bill, his sister, and his mother seemed to be able to speak about the years when Andy completed the family without any of them experiencing undue distress or a wish to avoid the topic. The father, however, continued to resent any mentioning of Andy except for the perfunctory ones included in the family's religious practices. Consequently, the father's psychological isolation had deepened, which the other family members were keenly aware of but felt unable to change. As Bill remarked, "Dad can never accept Andy's death. . . . Sure, it was a bad blow to me and Mom, but I think we have licked it; Dad still can't talk about it."

Discussion

The effects of Andy's death on his family and on his brother Bill in particular are similar to those reported in several studies of children's reactions to a death in the family. Binger's reports contain a summary of these studies in addition to accounts of his own observations of emotional disturbances in children who have suffered the loss of a sibling owing to leukemia (Binger et al. 1969, Binger 1973). Following his brother's death, the 11-year-old Bill showed an incapacity to sustain a mourning process, just as his parents did, with strong attempts at denial and suppression of his sad and frightened feelings, and an inability and unwillingness to accept the reality of Andy's death. Andy continued to "live on" in a highly personalized way, being able to communicate with Bill, in accordance with the family's religious beliefs. Bill's slowly developing learning problems were directly related to his feelings of futility regarding schoolwork, because he saw himself doomed to repeat Andy's fate.

Bill's scholastic problems and despair finally conveyed to those in his environment his long-standing sadness, worries, and confusing conceptions of hemophilia and the relationship of these problems to Andy's fatal bleeding crisis. The impact of the death on Bill had overtaxed his ability to cope mentally with his own chronic disorder and attendant psychologic stress. Particularly noticeable were inefficient—that is, maladaptive—use of the essential coping techniques offered by various cognitive functions (for example, memory, speech, judgment, reality testing) and his crippling reliance on certain psychologic defenses, such as denial, avoidance, and identification with his deceased brother, rather than with living and well-functioning hemophilic and healthy peers (Mattsson 1972).

Bill's failure to mourn Andy's death and to maintain a hopeful, positive outlook on his own future could largely be related to his family's conscious efforts to avoid any relevant, interpersonal sharing of memories and emotions related to Andy and his hemophilic condition. It was striking to observe how Bill's release of a host of pentup feelings and bewilderment in regard to his brother and his brother's death promptly enabled him to remobilize his good cognitive resources to cope successfully with the past and the present stressful situations. Simultaneously, with a lessening of his denial and avoidance of distressing feelings and of his overidentification with Andy, he demanded and could retain many facts about his familial disorder in all its ramifications. Subsequently, he began to look to his future academic and vocational goals, clearly viewing himself as a potentially independent and productive young adult.

Bill was confused by Andy's death on many levels. His strong dread of some of his bleeding episodes was partly related to his environment's failure to provide him with factual and sensible explanations about his illness, its complications, and its medical management. On a deeper level, Bill wondered why he had been spared while Andy had succumbed. A reference to guilt feelings plaguing Bill seems an inadequate answer in view of the unique closeness that had existed between him and Andy. The early and deep feelings of solidarity between hemophilic brothers are remarkable to watch in their behavioral expressions: from age 6 to 7, most brothers watch out for each other in play and games, assist each other in home treatment of hemorrhages, discuss their symptoms and treatment, and as they get older, increasingly share views on dangerous, reasonably risky, and safe activities, including vocational choices and family planning (Mattsson and Gross 1966). In other words the boys seem to gain substantial emotional support from each other, which is especially impressive at times of bleeding crises. Competitive, resentful, and hostile attitudes toward each other, as seen among healthy siblings, mostly appear only in subdued and sublimated fashion in hemophilic brothers who are over 6 or 7 years of age. These observations suggest that the mourning process of a surviving brother with hemophilia will differ from our expected "norms" in terms of its observed and subjectively felt manifestations of guilt and ambivalent attitude toward the deceased brother.

During the two years following Andy's death, the mother had been well aware of the family's deficiencies in not heeding Bill's many references to his frightened and sad state. Her reluctance to listen and respond to him, as she normally had done to both sons before, was related to her great concerns about the father's emotional fragility, increasing drinking habits, and steadfast refusal to allow himself and others to vent any expressions of grief about Andy. For years, the mother had accepted her husband's means of absenting himself from the family and providing minimal assistance in raising their two boys because of the lingering blow to his self-esteem inflicted by his begetting two "not normal" boys. The mother wanted to protect the father, and she was also openly afraid of his becoming unable to support the family if discussion about hemophilia and Andy's death were to make him seriously upset. Her many attempts at getting him interested in psychiatric counseling had been futile.

As soon as Bill signaled his distress through his teacher, the mother was able to assume an active role in opening up some communication among the family members in regard to hemophilia and its effects on the two boys. An additional helpful factor behind Bill's rapid psychologic improvement seemed to have been his mother's early acceptance of herself as a carrier of hemophilia. She had not hidden from her family her fearful, at times self-accusatory, feelings about her genetic responsibility for her sons' serious illness. Finally, her experience in growing up with a hemophilic father, who had stoically coped with his serious physical condition, made her prone to minimize the emotional impact of Andy's death on Bill and the other family members. She expected Bill to continue his satisfactory psychosocial adaptation to his disorder, just as her father had in the past. Despite these complex earlier experiences with hemophilia, the mother became an important ally in the brief psychiatric work wih Bill, and she gained much satisfaction from watching him change to a better-adjusted, more content, and hopeful teenager who wanted to strive toward achieving social and scholastic goals for himself as he learned to cope with his chronic illness in a realistic, adaptive way.

REFERENCES

Binger, C. M. 1973. "Childhood Leukemia—Emotional Impact on Siblings." In E. J. Anthony and C. Koupernik, eds., *The Child in His Family: The Impact of Disease and Death*, pp. 195–209. New York: John Wiley and Sons.

Binger, C. M., et al. 1969. "Childhood Leukemia: Emotional Impact on Patient and Family." *New England Journal of Medicine* 280:414–18.

Mattsson, A. 1972. "Long-term Physical Illness in Childhood: A Challenge to Psychosocial Adaptations." *Pediatrics* 50:801–11.

Mattsson, A. and S. Gross. 1966. "Adaptational and Defensive Behavior in Young Hemophiliacs and Their Parents." *American Journal of Psychiatry* 122:1349–56.

· 16 ·

Hospice Care for the Dying Child

ROBERT W. BUCKINGHAM

The hospice movement in the United States is making the process of dying easier and more humane for both terminally ill patients and their families. By integrating medical care with emotional and psychological care, home care with hospital or inpatient care, and family care with patient care, hospice has evolved a comprehensive program that attempts to meet the specific needs of the dying in every respect. Regular general hospitals are places one goes for diagnosis, treatment, and cure—to recover from diseases, to be rid of various physical ailments. It is natural that patients are treated from the point of view of their illnesses; it is a matter of disease first, patient later, for as soon as the disease is done away with, the patient is restored to as close to normal as possible and can go on as before. Hospital and medical treatment are primarily geared toward the patient's future—and that is probably how it should, or must, be in our busy, impersonalized society.

But this is not the case with the dying. Since their future has been definitely limited, what is important is the present. Since there is no more possibility for cure, emphasis must be placed on comfort and immediate symptom control. Since there is no returning to the past and to the normal way of life, primacy must be given to sincere individual attention and making the best of the given situation now.

Dying is not a disease—its manifestations are not merely temporary and physical. Instead, dying affects every possible aspect of human existence; it is a physical, a psychological, an emotional, a spiritual, and a social process. Adequate treatment for the terminally ill must deal with this final and ultimate process of dying as a whole and not merely concentrate on one of its aspects alone. By incorporating multidisciplinary teams of various medical, health care, and social workers, hospices can give a patient total care where and when it is needed. The crucial distinction between the contexts, and more importantly, the needs, of the normal hospital patient and the dying patient has been appreciated by hospices and acted upon to form methods and programs for better and more comprehensive care for the dying.

Hospice care attempts to provide the following:

relief from distressing symptoms of the disease

security of a caring environment

sustained expert medical and nursing care

assurance that patients and their families will not be abandoned.

I shall not dwell further upon the goals, methods, and achievements of the hospice movement here. The subject to be discussed is hospice care for the dying child. Hospices are a relatively new development in terminal care, especially in the United States, where the few existent hospice programs are not more than three or four years old. At this point the benefits of the hospice programs are limited to adults, those eighteen and older. But what about children with terminal illness; do they not also need the special comprehensive and individual care that hospice could bring them? Admittedly, the needs of children and their families are different and more varied than those of adults, and integrating child care into a regular hospice program could be a laborious endeavor. However, it seems that children, too, and their families, should have the possibility of receiving the adequate and intensive total terminal care that can rarely be found in today's large hospitals.

The term *child* covers such a wide range of stages in emotional, psychological, physical, social, and intellectual development that it is difficult to speak about the "child" as opposed to the adult.

However, to generalize, one could state that a child has not yet reached the levels of emotional, psychological, and intellectual maturity that are expected in most normal adults. The children's actual levels of development between the ages of birth and eighteen years vary much more drastically than adults' levels between the ages of eighteen and ninety. Thus, children are less in control of their own situation in the world (the amount of control increasing with age) and are, to varying degrees, dependent on a parental or other adult figure (the degree of dependence decreasing with age).

For the most part children are much more egocentric than adults, demanding and needing much more individual attention. Children have not learned to control the world around them as adults have, nor have they learned to conceptualize and objectify themselves and their situation. Again, these factors vary drastically with age and stages of development. One must keep in mind that growth, change, and development are the very essence of childhood, and for this reason it is much more complex than adulthood. Although the distinctions pointed out between child and adult are simplistic indeed, even these play a significant role in determining the different relationships child and adult will have with impending death and the different methods of care needed to deal with each respectively.

It seems self-evident that terminally ill children need and would benefit from hospice care as much as, if not more than, terminally ill adults. Children's and their families' needs differ from those of adults in several respects, and it is just such a comprehensive program as that of hospice that could help fulfill those specific needs. First of all, children are not expected to take part (again depending on age and maturity) in the decision-making process of their own terminal care. It is usually the family of the child that takes the responsibility of decision-making, although the consequences will affect the child; *thus a hospice's customary practice of regarding the patient and family as a single unit of care would be especially beneficial in caring for the dying child.* Since terminal illness in children is less frequent and seems more "unjust" than terminal illness in adults, families of child patients have even more difficulties in dealing with and accepting the situation. As Dr.

Morris Green states, "there are few human experiences so shattering as a child's death" (1967). Therefore, the family would need trained emotional and psychological advice during and, most importantly, after the course of terminal illness.

Children demonstrate a broad range of reactions to their own impending death. The difference between the reactions and needs of two children of different or even the same age can be as great as that between child and adult. Therefore, an effective care program would require staff trained to deal with children not only on the medical level but also on psychological and emotional levels. Because most children (depending on age and maturity) usually cannot be directly confronted with the fact of their own death, it is even more important that their daily lives retain as many aspects of their previous normal lives as possible. This too may put a greater burden on the parents, who may often feel the need to pretend that everything is all right with their child. Since the child is so dependent (related to age) on the family and because of the need for a semblance of normality, it seems that whenever at all possible, terminal care should take place in the home. Something like the hospice home care programs, with the addition of specially trained staff to meet the psychological and emotional needs of children of all ages, would appear to be the ideal answer to children's terminal care.

Green specifies some suggested "principles of management" for terminal child care (1967). He emphasizes the following eight points:

1. competence of the physician, who should give special attention to the child's complaints and minimizing pain
2. availability of the physician in case of prompt need
3. continuity of care via a continuing relationship between physician and patient
4. personalized care through frequent contact with and interest in the child and attempting to understand the child's fearful reactions and treat him/her as a person
5. preparation: the physician must always try to tell the child what is going on so that the child can have trust in the physician; he must give explanations of his procedure
6. allowing the child an active role, the physician should discuss

treatment with the child in a manner appropriate to his age so that the child can feel partially in control of his situation
7. permitting questions of the child to the physician, and informing and preparing the parents so they can know what questions to expect and how to deal with them
8. being supportive; the physician should maintain an optimistic outlook without unwarranted reassurance and without letting himself be engulfed by the family problems.

Green also believes that, in addition to these eight major guidelines for care of the terminally ill child, a physician should have a knowledge of the development of the child's concept of death and of the individual child and family, and the child's developing understanding of death may help him to deal satisfactorily with the specific questions and needs of child and parent. Although these methods of care for the dying child put forth by Dr. Green are very impressive and commendable, I question how effective a single physician or pediatrician could be in trying to carry them out alone. The very thoroughness and diligence of these eight major guidelines illustrate the necessity for a coordinated team of medical, social, and home care workers to effectively meet the needs of the dying child and support the need for hospice care.

The crucial and inherent bond between child and parent and the deep anxiety evoked in an adult by the dying child are two major factors that indicate the dire necessity of incorporating care for the family along with the care given to the child. As Green points out, the dying child often awakens one of man's deepest fears—death before fulfillment (1967). The experience of a child's terminal illness probably causes more psychological and emotional problems in the family members who are aware of the situation without being able to share it with the child (again, this depends on age and maturity) than in the child himself. Friedman points out what he feels to be most important in helping the family deal with its situation (1967). According to Friedman, the physician should be consciously aware of the common modes of adjustment used by parents, for only in this way will he be able to anticipate their needs, problems, and sources of anxiety. He should be able to give the parents emotional and psychological guidance and recognize the diverse forms of coping behavior that parents often manifest through denial. It is very important that the doctor demonstrate his willingness to answer all the parents' questions, that he clearly discuss the disease with the parents, and that he explain the various possible courses that the illness could take.

The parents' participation in the child's care may also need to be guided; they may wish to stay with the child day and night if he is in the hospital, or through denial they may be reluctant to acknowledge how the child is feeling. Parents will naturally impose their own fears or preconceptions of death on the child, and the physician should be aware of this while helping them to do the most and best that they can. He should also help them understand the common reactions of the child, who may be angry that his parents cannot get rid of the pain and make him well. Finally, the relationship between doctor and family should be a continuous one and not come to an end with the death of the child; as Friedman emphasizes, the physician can be of great help to parents months after the death of the child by rediscussing issues or answering other related queries. This careful attention devoted to the family of the patient is similar to regular hospice procedures in caring for the terminally ill. Again, it seems that a hospice care program would be better equipped and coordinated to fulfill the needs of a dying child's family than the overburdened physician who cannot be expected to be adequately trained in giving the psychological and emotional care and advice that are of foremost importance nor expected to go into the home and guide the family's treatment of the child.

Where one or two physicians alone cannot be expected to give comprehensive care and guidance to both patient and family in and out of the home, a hospice program could—and does for adults. With few additions to the present terminal care programs, hospices could guarantee to uphold the standards of care for dying children and their families put forth by Dr. Green and Dr. Friedman. The coordinated team of diversely trained staff, the care given to both patient and family together and individually, and the home care program so integral to hospices would be of infinite value to the dying child and his parents. A necessary addition to present hospice organizations would be the incorporation of staff trained specifically to deal with the emotional and psychological needs of children from infants to adolescents and staff with experience in working with families of terminally ill children. Such additions would not pose any major problems. If hospice care for children were to be extended to inpatient facilities, difficulties might arise in attempting to create a suitable environment for the children.

Maintenance of the family as a cohesive, supportive unit; provision for the relief of loneliness, separation, and anxiety; and symptom controls for the maximum comfort and alertness of the dying child patient are the key objectives for an inpatient or home care hospice program.

REFERENCES

Friedman, S. 1967. "Care of the Family of the Child with Cancer." *Pediatrics* (September) 40: 498–507.
Green, M. 1967. "Care of the Dying Child." *Pediatrics* (September) 40: 492–97.

BIBLIOGRAPHY

Benchenal, J. 1975. "Current Commentary I: Childhood Cancer." In C. Pochedly, ed. *Clinical Management of Cancer in Children*. Acton, Mass.: Publishing Sciences Group.
Benoliel, J. 1975. "The Terminally Ill Child." In G. Scipien, M. Bernard, M. Chard, J. Howe, and P. Phillips, eds. *Comprehensive Pediatric Nursing*. New York: McGraw-Hill.
Bluebond-Langner, M. 1978. *The Private Worlds of Dying Children*. Princeton: Princeton University Press.
Buckingham, R. 1976. "Living with the Dying: Use of the Technique of Participant Observation." *Canadian Medical Association Journal* (December).
Buckingham, R. 1978. "Care of the Dying." *Journal of Health Concerns* (May).
Buckingham, R. 1980. "Hospice and Health Policy." *Journal of Health Policy and Education,* (December), Amsterdam: Elsevier Scientific Publishing Co.
Chinn, P. 1974. *Child Health Maintenance*. St. Louis: C. V. Mosby.
Glaser, B. and A. Strauss. 1965. *Awareness of Dying*. Chicago: Aldine.
Graner, A. 1976. "The Effects of Pain on Child, Parent, and Health Professional." In Martinson, ed. (1976).
Gyulay, J. 1978. *The Dying Child*. New York: McGraw-Hill.

Kastenbaum, R. 1967. "The Child's Understanding of Death: How Does It Develop?" In E. Grollman, ed. *Explaining Death to Children*. Boston: Beacon Press.

Kulenkamp, E. 1976. "Eric—A Mother's Recollection." In Martinson (1976).

Martinson, I. 1976. "Introduction to the Home Care Project." In Martinson, ed. (1976).

Martinson, I. ed. 1976. *Home Care of the Dying Child—Professional and Family Perspectives*. New York: Appleton-Century-Crofts.

Richmond, J. and H. Waisman. 1971. "Psychological Aspects of Management of Children with Malignant Diseases." In R. Noland, ed. *Counseling Parents of the Ill and the Handicapped*. Springfield, Illinois: Charles C Thomas.

· IV ·
Staff, Parents, and the Dying Child

· 17 ·

On Facing Death: Perspectives of a Child Psychiatrist in a Medical School Setting

JOHN E. SCHOWALTER

Many questions, problems, and opportunities arise for the child psychiatrist who works clinically with dying children and who, directly or indirectly, teaches thanatology to medical students, pediatricians, and other hospital staff. This paper is a personal summary of what I have learned from doing work of this nature for the past 15 years at the Yale–New Haven Hospital. During this time, the field of thanatology has evolved from what was considered a very strange interest to what has almost become a fad.

For either to be done well, teaching and service must be intertwined. Although this meshing will be obvious in this paper, for ease of exposition these two components are discussed separately, following an introduction.

Introduction

Death is often accepted as the opposite of success in regard to the treatment of a patient. It seems that some students enter medicine to conquer their own death fears through others (Livingston and Zimet 1965), and while it is probably true that the field of medicine is the best approach available to study how to thwart death, medicine not only does not always work but also eventually always fails. Even when a physician is not more fearful of death than is usual, he or she will have to deal with it and its stresses much more than the average person will. In addition to the stress inherent in the situation are the impossible self-expectations of the medical student and physician. Some of these are intrapsychic in origin, but others come from the public and from how students are taught. In most medical schools, for example, it is rare to have lectures on what to do when you cannot do anything more for the patient's disorder. One is taught to fight but not face death. Denial is a common defense not only toward patients' problems. Physicians are themselves notoriously poor at looking after their own health, and it is surprisingly common for doctors to believe they cannot catch their patients' diseases.

An increasing factor in determining the emotional makeup of physicians is a general change in medical treatment approaches. There has been a burgeoning of developments in the field of medical engineering and of favoritism shown medical school applicants who possess training or degrees in the "hard" sciences. As medicine has become more sophisticated technically, it seems as though "things" have often tended to supplant concern for people. These changes have, however, caused medicine to become more complicated morally, as well as mechanically. It is not always taught that we should be concerned with ends, as well as means. Just because a thing can be done, we are not obliged to do it, and the more we can do, the more we have to think about what we wish to do.

Medical training has not always kept pace. Feelings and empathy are seldom discussed except in psychiatry, and psychiatry teaching that is not biologically based is often considered impractical by medical students and by the scientific investigators on the faculty who represent the students' most powerful role models. There is a common faculty-student collusion that if one only learns enough, there will be no need to worry about patients' not getting well.

The death of a child is especially painful for physicians and other staff. In one study of events that cause doctors' anxiety, the death of a child was ranked considerably higher by the physician respondents than the death of an adult was (Crammond 1969). In another study, in which English and American adults were asked to scale 61 life events as to how upsetting each event would be to them, the death of a child was rated first by the populations on both sides of the Atlantic (Paykel et al. 1976). It seems as though the belief that only old people die develops early in one's life and remains forever. There is also a common belief that children are "simpler" than adults and therefore those who work with them require less training, skill, and compensation than those who work with adults. When a child patient does not respond therapeutically, the novice may feel especially bad that he or she could not even cure a child. Solnit (1973) has noted that some health workers choose to work with children because they wish to avoid the deteriorating in favor of the developing and to avoid the end of life in favor of the beginning. Such individuals may find a dying child impossible to care for.

Service Situations

Compared to dying adults, dying children represent three special disadvantages and problems for caregivers. Dying patients tend to turn away from the dangerous future and toward the past for solace, but children and even most adolescents do not have this ability. By their cognitive inability to master the adult's sense of time, they are trapped in the present. Second, ultimately, and most literally at death, everyone is alone. Since children require parental closeness to be happy and to survive, to witness the loneliness of a dying child is especially painful for adults. Finally, the premature death represented by a fatally ill child brings home forcefully the fact that no one is guaranteed a long life, only a life time.

One situational variable that pertains to all caregivers is how close they are psychologically to the age of the patient. This closeness may be brought about by knowing another child or children who died at a similar age or by having a sibling, son, or daughter of the same age. Especially hard for young caregivers is the dying adolescent. Not only is adolescence the time for strength, beauty, and independence developmentally (and death is especially anathema to these goals) but also the proximity of the caregiver's age awakens a kinship with fatally ill adolescents that is very powerful. The dread of death before fulfillment is particularly pervasive among medical students who have had to endure inordinately long periods of training and who are looking forward to now obtaining the professional and financial benefits of their study.

One way of looking at the situation of the dying child is to divide the problems associated with care into three time periods (Schowalter 1970). Although each period has its particular difficulties, no period is as clearly demarcated in practice as on paper, and a number of issues such as denial, grief, guilt, and anger are common to all three.

The first is the period of impact. Being the first to know the diagnosis and prognosis, the pediatrician is the first to feel the impact of the tragedy. Telling the parents is very difficult, and although it is not unusual for the family's physician to rationalize having the hospital "expert" do this chore, in fact, most parents prefer to hear important medical news from the physician whom they know and who knows them best. The disclosure to the parents that their child has a condition that might prove fatal usually triggers a series of reactions that include shock, disbelief in the diagnosis, disbelief in the prognosis, anger, guilt, acceptance, and anticipatory mourning. It is not unusual for parents to find this event more overwhelming than the eventual death. The parents may blame the physician for making such a serious diagnosis, but more often they turn their anger on themselves and/or onto the nursing staff. Since a child's death is a threat to one form of parental immortality, there may also be anger toward the child. Being so unacceptable under the conditions of impending death, this anger must be placed elsewhere. Friendships, marriages, and religious faith often bear the brunt of such displaced anger.

While it is generally accepted that parents should know the facts of the case, it is much less easy to know how much should be told the child. Obviously, hope should never be completely withdrawn from anyone. Most fatally ill pediatric patients do not ask whether they will die, but most know that something terrible is wrong with them. In fact, once parents know the prognosis, their reactions to the child change so dramatically that it is impossible for the child not to realize that something very worrisome is occurring. It is extremely important to maintain an atmosphere of openness that allows the patient to ask as much or as little as wished. The more painful a decision is, the more people wish to establish a rule to cover it, and it would be easier if there was an age, type of diagnosis, family circumstance, or other marker that could be relied on to determine correctly what to tell the child. The only true marker, however, is the child, and the only measurement is the caregiver's sensitivity. Grief is painful not only for the sufferer but also for the observer, and this is a major reason why we frequently err in believing children know less and feel less than they do. It is not unusual, for example, for dying children to tell caregivers that they are dying but to add that parents or pediatrician should not be told, because the patient knows he or she is not supposed to know.

When a patient seems aware of what is happening but is reluctant to talk about it, there are facilitating questions that may be asked. For example, "You must sometimes worry about dying?" or even less direct, "You must sometimes wonder if you are ever going to get well?" Some children who know they are dying still do not want to be told. An adolescent once explained this to me when she said "If *you* tell me I'm dying, it's a fact, but if only I think it, I can believe it or not believe it depending on how I feel that day." It is crucial that caregivers know what questions the patient is asking whom and what the answers have been. Although all caregivers should be available to the patient and parents, it is mandatory that one person be in charge to coordinate the child's care. It is all too common that hospital care of dying children is diffused and confused by frequent staff changes or the lack of a single person who is responsible for the care being given in a complete and consistent way.

The second phase of care may be termed the period of battle and consists of the time of management until the child is in extremis.

Along with anger, guilt is ubiquitous when people are working with a dying child. Parents must be assured and reassured that their child's illness is not their fault. Caregivers also tend to feel guilty. This may be because their treatment is not working, their counseling is less than completely successful, there is a feeling of anger toward the child for not responding, there has been withdrawal from patient and family, and so forth. Guilt often leads to a variety of reactions that are problematic. Secrets may occur in regard to diagnosis, prognosis, physical tests, procedures, and drug side effects. Guilt may also cause parents and staff to become overly permissive, while dying children respond best when there is structure and when their schedule is kept as routine as possible.

Anger is an important factor in the reactions of caregivers, as well as of the family. A child's death is a threat to physicians' feelings of omnipotence, and working with a patient who does not respond is difficult for all the staff. Becoming angry is a common substitute for depression, and when working with dying patients, one senses that some caregivers look for reasons to criticize others in order to feel less bad themselves.

The reactions of caregivers are often affected by other situational variables. Patients who require severe dietary or fluid restrictions, who suffer remissions and exacerbations, who become progressively debilitated over a long period of time, or who are very demanding tend to bring out anger from the staff. Caregivers' reactions may include blaming the parents as overintrusive or underinvolved, treating the dying child as inferior, or allowing hospital routines to take primacy over dignity, respect, and humanity.

The third and final phase of care is the period of defeat. This includes the terminal phase of treatment, the death, and the period of contact with the family thereafter. Whenever there is a high census of dying children or there are multiple deaths over a short period of time, the staff is likely to become quite depressed. With multiple deaths, even the most experienced and competent caregivers admit to an unrealistically severe scrutiny of their own role in the children's care.

The length of time the staff has known the child influences the emotional intensity they feel. Children who are preverbal or who die quickly tend to cause less personal anguish than adolescents or those who are cared for over a protracted period of time. Patients whose deaths are due to accidents are sometimes an exception to the finding that quick deaths have relatively little impact on caregivers. Accidents are the most common cause of death during all but the earliest part of the pediatric age range. It is striking how little has been written about the reactions of caregivers toward children who die because of accidents. This paucity is partly due to the fact that many of these patients die before arriving in the hospital, die in the emergency room, or die following only a brief stay on the ward. Staff contact is therefore brief. I believe there are also emotional factors that have influence on the lack of attention to accidental deaths. Compared with staff reactions to children who die from illness, reactions to children dying from accidents contain more anger than guilt. There is less a feeling of medical failure and a greater sense of blame, either at parents for not protecting the child adequately or, more often in adolescence, at the patient for causing the mishap. A focus on blame sometimes causes the staff to resent caring for the patient and affects adversely the quality of care given.

In the literature, the most frequently described reaction of caregivers toward children during this terminal phase is withdrawal. Although withdrawal is a natural part of anticipatory mourning, and the patient may exhibit it as well, staff withdrawal should be neither abrupt nor extensive. Staff withdrawal from the patient is often accompanied by withdrawal from the family as well and at the time they need support most. It is important for all staff to follow the old adage that the fewer the treatments available to the physician, the more the physician must be available.

Following a death there may be a feeling of relief, as well as defeat, especially if the child has suffered for a long time. It is common for the tendency in staff to withdraw to become even stronger, but it is crucial that the family not be abandoned. Staff members' presence and willingness to listen are usually more important than what is said. In fact, much of the content of what is said is not heard. Oftentimes parents complain that once their child has died, the staff forgets about them and their child. Contact in the following weeks or months by the pediatrician, child psychiatrist, social worker, psychologist and/or chaplain to see how the parents and siblings are reacting to the death is very useful but seldom done.

With our ability through technology to keep patients' lungs oxygenating and their hearts pumping, the question of how long to keep patients alive has become an increasingly difficult one. In addition, especially with cancer patients, there is the dilemma of how long to press aggressive treatment during the terminal phase. On the one side are the possibilities of a remission and of gaining important new knowledge, while on the other side are the possibilities of providing unnecessary pain and of prolonging death rather than life. Again, there are no pat answers, and the patient and family should be included in the decision making as much as possible. In general, those closest to the physical care of the patient are the least willing to prolong the terminal phase. Staff friction sometimes occurs when attending pediatricians, radiologists, or oncologists continue to prescribe uncomfortable treatments to children in extremis. Unless the rationale for the treatments is well communicated, other caregivers may in various ways undermine the patient's and parents' confidence in the care they are receiving. When this sort of staff split occurs, anger and depression are the common sequelae for all involved.

A prolonged terminal phase causes individual staff members considerable emotional pain. The wish to avoid this pain is strong but is confounded by the realization that a wish for the pain to go away may include the wish for the child to die. For some these wishes are conscious, but for most they are not, since there is at the same time the wish that the child will not die. The usual response to such ambivalence, especially on the part of pediatricians, is to reject any course but to keep the child alive for as long as possible. With increasing frequency, however, and usually among caregivers who are not physicians, there is seen a very different reaction. This is an enthusiasm for "allowing" the patient to die or even a definite push for the use of some type of euthanasia. Carried to an extreme, both approaches get rid of a dying child whose presence is anxiety provoking. In the first approach the child, a treatment failure, is changed into an interesting medical exercise in keeping an organism alive, and in the second approach the child and the painful situation are removed through the hastening of death. There is no one formula or timetable, but the vigor applied in keeping the patient alive during the terminal phase is better based on the wishes and needs of the parents and patient than on those of the caregivers. By the midteens and with the appropriate information, the patient can often become a full partner in deciding what approaches should be used and for how long.

Teaching Situations

Given these common clinical situations and problems, there are various approaches and techniques through which a child psychiatrist can be helpful as a teacher. The first part of this section focuses on the teaching of staff, the middle portion on approaches to aiding parents in a way that will allow caregivers to work more effectively, and the final part of the section is a discussion of various techniques that promote better communication and interaction among staff members.

At present there is not much teaching done in thanatology preparatory to one's becoming a medical caregiver. This is changing somewhat in some schools. Pediatricians, however, are often action-oriented individuals who tend to avoid anything that smacks of passivity or defeatism.

In spite of resistance, a significant education in thanatology can be provided medical students with only a modicum of curriculum change and time. The expectations of perfection and that a physician's job is to stamp out death are now quite routinely conveyed in most schools. This is not necessarily said overtly, but it is absorbed by the student through a conspiracy of silence regarding physicians' professional and personal mistakes and problems. Teaching students that they and their peers will make mistakes and that death is something that must be faced as well as fought removes some of the pressure generated by unrealistic expectations. This knowledge also helps to modify the cold, ineffective routines that hospitals have traditionally used to protect staff from feelings and from patients.

Oftentimes when thanatology is taught, it is done through one or more didactic lectures. This is relatively ineffective unless accompanied by direct interaction with dying children and/or through rounds or discussions with staff who are caring for these patients. In general, medical students accept teaching about the care of the dying best from physicians. This is due not only to elitism but also to identification. With this subject, as with others, the best teachers are often those who are not more than a few years ahead of the students. A pediatric or child psychiatry house officer who is articulate and interested in the problems of the fatally ill can be a very valuable teacher. It is interesting how the urgency transmitted from experiences of a colleague who is just senior to the student can have credibility through the experience alone, while the far more extensive experiences related by a much older practitioner or professor may be dismissed as so much prattle.

A number of specific points should be stressed with students regarding working with fatally ill children and their families. None pertains exclusively to the dying, but all are especially important in these cases. The most general point concerns the maintenance of continuity of care. Many terminally ill patients require, or at least obtain, the services of a multitude of specialized caregivers. Each person has charge of a part of the child, but often no one is in charge of the whole. We all know that such fragmentation leads inevitably to poor care, but the phenomenon can be corrected only if looked for. The fact of the possibility of this danger must be repeated and repeated to students. Secondly, it must be stressed that in working with the dying, listening may be much more important and helpful than acting. This is especially true in the impact and the terminal phases. Finally, the student must be made aware of the ubiquity and power of the feelings of guilt and anger. The anger may be at the wasted past; at the absent future; at the cost in time, energy, and money; at the narcissistic injury; at Fate; at God; at one another; or at the self. There is also the powerful existential anger that encourages the belief that something so repugnant as a child's death must be somebody's fault.

The response of parents to their dying child has a major effect on the reactions of caregivers, and there are ways of working with parents that direct their grief into constructive rather than destructive actions. During the period of impact, it is useful to warn parents not to hurry to tell others of the tragedy. Until they have had a chance to begin to assimilate the news along with its meanings and demands, it is better to tell as few people as possible. When parents do seek solace by immediately informing family and friends, the result is usually counterproductive. They are not yet able to respond to the multitude of questions, to the outpouring of sympathy, or to the covert rebuke that accompanies some peoples' tendency to "blame the victim." It is better for the parents to first have some idea of how they feel and what they are going to do before they face the additional problem of explaining the situation to others.

We have found that a good way to help parents face the diagnosis and prognosis is not only to have professionals convey the information repeatedly but also to have available and encourage parents to meet together in groups. These groups may consist of parents of children together on the ward at the same time, parents of children having the same medical condition, or parents of patients who all are dying. The makeup seems less important than the skill of the leader in providing an atmosphere of mutual support and comfort. A common difficulty with such groups, however, is that parents seldom remain after their child dies. Although the postdeath period is one in which they could use the continuity of care provided by the group and the group could benefit from hearing of their experience, the feeling of having been let down or of having let the group down is common and frequently strong enough to keep the parents from continuing.

The helpfulness of drawing parents into the care and planning of their child's treatment cannot be overstressed. Mothers are usually better able to do this than fathers, who tend to be more fearful of hospitals, but it is best when both are involved. When parents feel they are part of the plan, their feelings of guilt and anger are reduced. Anger and guilt are emotions that often generate one another. They may also trigger similar reactions from the caregivers and reduce staff efficiency. There are constructive ways to channel parental anger, and one of the best is to encourage parents to join, if appropriate, a society to help raise money, lobby, change laws, educate, and aid in other ways to further the understanding of leukemia, sudden infant death syndrome, cystic fibrosis, or whatever condition their child suffers from.

We now come to approaches with staff who work with the fatally ill child. Techniques that promote better communication and interaction among staff members are most useful. Communication with the patients can be enhanced through patient meetings. Some patients would rather write their concerns than speak them, and this option should also be made available. We accomplish this through a ward newspaper (Schowalter and Lord 1972). It is especially important with adolescent patients to provide opportunities for them to maintain their self-esteem (Schowalter 1977).

Who supports the caregivers? Here, as experts in communication, is where child psychiatrists can often be most helpful. Besides communication of information, communication of personal feelings is important. Regular ward meetings are essential, and the child psychiatrist is often the most effective leader. Such groups can be formed from the staff of a ward or a specialty clinic. Physicians tend to have the most difficulty in these groups because their training and status often tend to encourage a suppression of feelings and a wish to give a definitive answer. It is also difficult when a member of the staff, no matter what the discipline, is considered an expert in thanatology. When this occurs, the person tends in the extreme either to be looked to for exact answers that will alleviate staff anxiety and pain or to be avoided as an unwanted reminder of death.

Although child psychiatrists may be looked to as caregivers to the caregivers, it is important that they have someone, most often peers, with whom they can talk. This brings up the final point that must be stressed. This is that teaching personnel about thanatology does not make difficult problems or emotions go away. Understanding and skill allow an impossible job to be done better, but after all we say and do regarding the fatally ill patient, the child still dies, and being human, we still mourn.

REFERENCES

Crammond, W. A. 1969. "Anxiety in Medical Practice—The Doctor's Own Anxiety." *Australia-New Zealand Journal of Psychiatry* 3:324–28.
Livingston, P. B. and C. N. Zimet. 1965. "Death Anxiety, Authoritarianism and Choice of Speciality in Medical Students." *Journal of Nervous and Mental Diseases* 140:222–30.
Paykel, E. S., B. McGuiness, and J. Gomez. 1976. "An Anglo-American Comparison of the Scaling of Life Events." *British Journal of Medical Psychology* 49:237–47.
Schowalter, J. E. 1970. "Death and the Pediatric Houseofficer." *Journal of Pediatrics* 76:706–10.
——— 1977. "Psychological Reactions to Physical Illness and Hospitalization in Adolescence: A Survey." *Journal of the American Academy of Child Psychology* 16:500–516.
Schowalter, J. E. and R. D. Lord. 1972. "On the Writings of Adolescents in a General Hospital Ward." *The Psychoanalytic Study of the Child* 27:181–200.
Solnit, A. J. 1973. "Who Mourns When a Child Dies?" In E. J. Anthony and C. Koupernik, eds. *The Child in His Family: The Impact of Disease and Death*, pp. 245–54. New York: John Wiley.

BIBLIOGRAPHY

Adams, M. A. 1976. "A Hospital Play Program: Helping Children with Serious Illness." *American Journal of Orthopsychiatry* 46:416–424.
Anthony, S. 1940. *The Child's Discovery of Death*. New York: Harcourt, Brace.
Aradine, C. R. 1976. "Books for Children about Death." *Pediatrics* 57:372–378.
Binger, C. M., et al. 1968. "Childhood Leukemia: Emotional Impact on Patient and Family." *New England Journal of Medicine* 280:414–418.
Bowlby, J. 1960. "Grief and Mourning in Infancy and Early Childhood." *The Psychoanalytic Study of the Child*. New York: International Universities Press, 15:9–32.
Bozeman, M. F., C. E. Orbach, and A. M. Sutherland. 1955. "Psychological Impact of Cancer and Its Treatment. III. The Adaptation of Mothers to the Threatened Loss of Their Children Through Leukemia: Part I." *Cancer* 8:1–19.
Bright, F. and M. L. France. 1967. "The Nurse and the Terminally Ill Child." *Nursing Outlook* 15:39–42.

Cain, A. C., I. Fast, and M. E. Erickson. 1964. "Children's Disturbed Reactions to the Death of a Sibling." *American Journal of Orthopsychiatry* 34:741–752.

Duff, R. S. and A. G. M. Campbell. 1976. "On Deciding the Care of Severely Handicapped or Dying Persons: With Particular Reference to Infants." *Pediatrics* 57:487–493.

Evans, A. and S. Edin. 1968. "If a Child Must Die . . . ." *New England Journal of Medicine* 278:138–42.

Freud, A. 1960. "Discussion of Dr. John Bowlby's Paper." *The Psychoanalytic Study of the Child*. New York: International Universities Press, 15:53–62.

Friedman, S. B., P. Chodoff, J. W. Mason, and D. A. Hamburg. 1963. "Behavioral Observations on Parents Anticipating the Death of a Child." *Pediatrics* 32:610–625.

Furman, R. A. 1973. "A Child's Capacity for Mourning." In E. J. Anthony and C. Koupernik, eds., *The Child in His Family*, pp. 225–231. New York: Wiley.

Gartley, W. and M. Bernasconi. 1967. "The Concept of Death in Children." *Journal of Genetic Psychology* 110:71–85.

Goggin, E. L., S. B. Lansky, and K. Hassanein. 1976. "Psychological Reactions of Children with Malignancies." *Journal of American Academy of Psychiatry* 15:314–325.

Green, M. 1967. "Care of the Dying Child." *Pediatrics* 40:492–497.

Gyulay, J. 1975. "The Forgotten Grievers." *American Journal of Nursing* 75:1476–1479.

Karon, M. and J. Vernick. 1968. "An Approach to the Emotional Support of Fatally Ill Children." *Clinical Pediatrics* 7:274–280.

Knudson, A. G. and J. M. Natterson. 1960. "Participation of Parents in the Hospital Care of Fatally Ill Children." *Pediatrics* 26:482–490.

McCollum, A. T. and L. E. Gibson. 1970. "Family Adaptation to the Child with Cystic Fibrosis." *Journal of Pediatrics* 77:571–578.

McIntire, M. S., C. R. Angle, and L. J. Struempler. 1972. "The Concept of Death in Midwestern Children and Youth." *American Journal of Diseases of Children* 123:527–532.

Nagy, M. 1948. "The Child's Theories Concerning Death." *Journal of Genetic Psychology* 73:3–27.

Orbach, C. E., A. M. Sutherland, and M. F. Bozeman. 1955. "Psychological Impact of Cancer and Its Treatment. III. The Adaptation of Mothers to the Threatened Loss of Their Children Through Leukemia: Part II." *Cancer* 8:20–33.

Schilder, P. and D. Wechsler. 1934. "The Attitudes of Children Toward Death." *Journal of Genetic Psychology* 45:406–451.

Schowalter, J. E. 1970. "The Child's Reaction to His Own Terminal Illness." In B. Schoenberg et al., eds., *Loss and Grief: Psychological Management in Medical Practice*, pp. 51–69. New York: Columbia University Press.

———1973. "Drugs, Fatally Ill Children, and the Pediatric Staff." In I. Goldberg et al., eds., *Psychopharmacologic Agents for the Terminally Ill and Bereaved*, pp. 296–306. New York: Columbia University Press.

———1976. "How Do Children and Funerals Mix?" *Journal of Pediatrics* 89:139–142.

Schowalter, J. E., J. B. Ferholt, and N. M. Mann. 1973. "The Adolescent Patient's Decision to Die." *Pediatrics* 51:97–103.

Solnit, A. J. and M. Green. 1959. "Psychologic Considerations in the Management of Deaths on Pediatric Hospital Services. I. The Doctor and the Child's Family." *Pediatrics* 24:106–112.

———1963. "The Pediatric Management of the Dying Child: Part II. The Child's Reaction to the Fear of Dying." In A. Solnit and S. Provence, eds., *Modern Perspectives in Child Development*, pp. 217–28. New York: International Universities Press.

———1965. "The Dying Child." *Developmental and Medical Child Neurology* 7:693–795.

Spinetta, J. J., D. Rigler, and M. Karon. 1973. "Anxiety in the Dying Child." *Pediatrics* 52:841–845.

Spinetta, J. J. and L. J. Maloney. 1975. "Death Anxiety in the Outpatient Leukemic Child." *Pediatrics* 56:1034–1037.

Vernick, J. and M. Karon. 1965. "Who's Afraid of Death on a Leukemia Ward?" *American Journal of Diseases of Children* 109:393–397.

Yudkin, S. 1967. "Children and Death." *The Lancet* 1:37–41.

· 18 ·

Emotional Support of the Pediatric Malignant Disease Treatment Team

Charles R. Koch

The treatment and management of the malignant diseases of childhood have become increasingly complex and now involve many personnel from various specialties. For certain malignancies, the results are curative. Although most malignant diseases remain eventually fatal, many productive and rewarding years can be achieved by energetic treatment. The treatment itself is dangerous and may be fatal. It becomes obvious that the treatment team becomes involved for months, even years, with families whose child is being treated. Inevitably, the vicissitudes of remissions, relapses, intercurrent complications (infection, chemotherapeutic side effects, and social disabilities) forge close relationships among the team, the patient, and his parents or siblings. A dependent relationship evolves encompassing the medical care and psychological needs that the team is called upon to meet.

Because of the intense nature of the family's realistic dependency and the team members' reciprocal personal, humane involvement, the treatment team finds the emotional-psychological aspect of the complete management the most demanding.

Ironically, the smooth and effective course of this relationship

---

The author acknowledges with gratitude the cooperation of the Division of Oncology, Children's Hospital of Philadelphia; its staff and trainees, its patients and their families, and the support given by Career Teacher Award NIMH T01 MH 11380-01 and the National Cancer Institute Grant #T-12-CA-08147.

requires the team to extend itself to a point of personal vulnerability to provide the level of support needed by the patient and the family. Once that point is reached, the team becomes prone to difficulty in management of their individual and collective reactions to the inherent stresses of empathy with a family coping with malignant disease and the eventual death of the child.

To achieve and maintain the goal of total psychosocial care concomitant with the delivery of comprehensive treatment from the initial phase of diagnosis, energetic therapy, and the terminal phase that culminates with the death of the child, the nuclear family unit needs to be conceived as the unit of intervention. If this comprehensive care is to be given, the reality of vulnerability to loss in the lives of those who provide service cannot be ignored.

The concept of the nuclear family as the unit of intervention cannot be underestimated. First, it is necessary for the comprehensive care of the family. Most important, however, is that it enlarges the scope of intervention of the entire staff; the patient may (or will) die but the family survives. Their survival may be in the direction of growth, or it may involve them in a morbid, nongrowth state. Great satisfaction can be achieved by the treatment team when, integrating their loss, a family continues to become stronger and more stable. For the treatment team, death is not an endpoint of involvement. There is vital, necessary work to sustain the family unit that promotes future growth, works for the amelioration of the effects of the loss on other children in the family, and thus enables the parents to emerge with a sense of having managed an essentially intolerable crisis in a growth-enhancing manner. A common, mutual experience of enduring the ordeal of the treatment and the ultimate death of one of their members provides them with a life bond that remains unique to their family fabric and history.

With the education of physicians, nurses, and medical ancillary personnel oriented toward cure of disease, there is little or no formal or structured training in dealing with the terminal phase of illness and treatment of the family of the dying child. When disease cannot be cured, a sense of loss of competence may affect the caregivers, usually manifested by a feeling that they have failed. Fantasies of omnipotence are not surrendered easily, despite the reality, and can be a source of painful loss. When empathy leads to identification with either of the parents, loss by death can be qualitatively the same for the team although the grief period is very much abbreviated by comparison. Where the identification is with the patient, the caregiver can be threatened by his own sense of mortality and unresolved fears of his own death. The team member's individual life experiences with loss and grief inevitably influence his reactions. For many of the younger staff, it may be their first encounter with loss by death. For them, it is understandably more difficult, but it can be both personally and professionally growth enhancing. When the team struggles with their own reactions in isolation and without support of realistic praise for performance, they may feel that their work is futile and hence that the painful experience is worthless and something to be avoided. On one occasion when I was acutely upset by the death of a child, I mentioned it to a colleague (one who was not a team member). His response was, "All your patients die." I was furious and demoralized.

People who elect to make the health care of children their life career because they like children so much may also unconsciously select that part of the life cycle in an effort to avoid confronting the issues of death and dying popularly associated with the latter stages of life. For them the experience of learning how to deal with their own reactions and to care effectively for the child and his family is especially trying.

Structure

The most effective structure for ensuring a common philosophy regarding treatment, management, and emotional-psychosocial care is a division treating malignant disease. This division should be devoted to the management of all malignant disease. Surgery, radiology, pathology, nursing, social work, and psychiatry coordinate with the director of oncology. In training centers, the director is responsible for all training related to malignant diseases and designates areas of responsibility to collaborating disciplines, while maintaining primary control over program design.

This structure affords vertical and lateral definition of responsibility and function. The benefit to the patient and his family from such a unified approach is obvious. The benefits to the staff and team function are less clear but critical for role definition and the achievement of mutual interdependency among the various roles. The individual team member's expertise and competence is the foundation for his contribution to the team effort. As one approaches the limits of disciplinary expertise, working familiarity with other team members' skills easily directs the problem for consultative help or for that team member to handle the problem. When the problem is an emotional one, the nurse may discuss it with the social worker and/or the psychiatrist. They may advise the nurse, enabling her to deal with it, or they may deal with it themselves. The structure provides clarity of direction, boundaries for use of skill, and mutual support. Paradoxically, this structured interdisciplinary collaboration leads, not to role diffusion, but to role clarity, and enhanced awareness of one's particular expertise and confidence in its use in the team effort become an essential component for the experience of effectiveness. This experience is self-rewarding and contributes to the sustenance of self-esteem and good morale.

Smaller centers can achieve this structure more easily, and the ease with which it occurs in a small team renders the structural aspects less visible. The informality and intimacy can often achieve the same morale-sustaining atmosphere. However, owing to the complexity of treatment of many malignant diseases and the expense of the required support equipment and resources (laboratory and staff, radiotherapy, pulmonary, and other essential special services), referral to larger, regional malignant disease centers becomes the major structural arrangement for the delivery of these services. At these centers with correspondingly larger staff-patient ratio, the internal structural design does not always spontaneously support the caregiving staff. It becomes necessary to include in the structure obvious and well-identified positions, conferences, and activities to ensure the support and to enable the team to use it.

The Setting

The settings for the delivery of care are determined by the philosophy and goals of the director and associate director. With an emphasis on the enrichment of the patients' "living" and the maintenance of the integrity of the family, all efforts support a major thrust toward maintaining the child in his home, in his school, and in his premorbid social milieu. This inevitably affects the character of the settings at different times and at different stages of the disease.

The inpatient setting is crisis ridden. Staff and parental stresses are intense. Ideally, a small unit or area of the hospital ought to be designated for the care of malignant diseases. Here the newly diagnosed patients, along with their families, are in a state of shock. The child is usually physically uncomfortable, frightened, and often away from home for the first time in his life. The parents appear variously dazed, numbed, unable to think clearly, often angry, emotionally labile, and helpless.

The second category of inpatients are those in for treatment of complications ranging from infection, relapses that cannot be managed in the outpatient clinic, or problems from chemotherapy or for the administration of chemotherapy too complex or dangerous for the usual outpatient clinic. Each patient and his family again find themselves in a state of disruption and crisis. (Parents have stated that the first relapse in the leukemic diseases is more terrifying than the initial diagnosis was.)

There are patients in the terminal phase of their disease for whom it is their last hospitalization. The supportive medical and the emotional-psychologic management assume primacy, and the goals of remission or further cure attempts are relinquished. For the patient the physicians' aim is symptom alleviation. No attempt is made to prolong the "dying"; suffering is controlled as well as it medically can be. No heroic measures are employed. The families are, or have been before this point, included in this decision-making process by the senior oncologists. The team irrespective of discipline devotes their energies to enabling the family to proceed through this intolerable period.

The outpatient clinic is the major focus of treatment and the monitoring of treatment. It is here that the staff has at least weekly contact with those in active treatment. Here too, the family learns to know the entire staff. This ensures against their confronting an unknown professional when a team member is away or when the visit is unscheduled. The staff monitors the psychosocial aspects of the activities of the child. Is he in school? If unable to attend, does he have home-bound instruction? How are the brothers and sisters? From this setting referrals to other team members are made. The social worker may contact the school or facilitate contact with community agencies. The nurse in charge of home visits may spend time in the home and then recommend public health nurse help or home-maker service.

The home is the ideal place for a sick child, provided the parents can support it. Because of geographic realities, physicians in their community are often enlisted as adjunctive members of the team, relieving the parents of long and exhausting drives to the clinic. In selected cases, the home can be the best place for the child to die, and it is a team responsibility to help that family who elects to care for the patient there. This decision is made by the family, and the team assists. Under these circumstances, nursing and/or social service provide daily telephone contact in addition to the services of community nursing.

When the child is of school age, every effort is made to return him to school. This coordination is done by the social worker with the advice of the oncologist. Restriction of activity or other special needs are correlated with the principal and, if offered, the school nurse. Many schools are as upset as the parents, and the counseling skills of the social worker can alleviate their anxiety.

Selection of Team Members

Permanent team members must voluntarily elect to work in this clinical area. Age-appropriate personal maturity, a capacity for empathy, and a firm conviction that the treatment and care of malignant disease must include total psychosocial as well as medical needs are essential. They need to appreciate that the family can grow as a result of having experienced the loss of their child-sibling. Whether they are inexperienced students or residents or experienced junior staff, those individuals usually master the art of giving this type of care.

There are life events when temporary withdrawal from the team and transfer to another unit are indicated. A death in their own family or the diagnosis of malignant disease in a loved one is often so draining that temporary reassignment for the duration of their mourning is indicated. Once recovered, their future contributions to the care of malignant disease are considerably enhanced, and they experience themselves as more effective.

Certain personalities prone to depression or to acting out of previous, unresolved losses ought to be counseled to work in another area. They may deliver excellent care but in the process overextend themselves to the point of emotionally becoming "one" of the family and suffering great personal distress. Succinctly stated, they "need" the dying child and his family and use this process of caring to fulfill personal, unmet, and unresolved needs. Psychiatric consultation may benefit them, but it has been my experience that they angrily reject any such offer. They exemplify those who refuse to mourn and cling to the dying process vicariously to avoid the final giving up of their loss. When their own distress cripples them, they may suffer serious depressive episodes and affect the morale of the other staff members. An example of this can be seen in a case of the nurse who eventually became unable to work. When she refused all offers of help, she was forced to go on sick leave. She visited families whose children had died and sought employment at other cancer centers. Although she was an excellent nurse technically, her refusal to mourn rendered her an emotional cripple. She now works in an area of adult nursing that places similar demands on her. It is obvious that she continues to seek and need this type of work.

Individuals with chronic, nonprogressive diseases may find the emotional demands of working with malignancy too great. Although there are no hard and fast rules, it is not advisable to have such members on the team.

The painful aspects of career growth in this area must not be viewed as incipient decompensation. On the contrary, appropriate, free verbalization of painful feelings is a sign of the beginning of the attempt at mastery. With the support of the team, particularly from the senior oncologists, and training in techniques of management, those individuals do well.

In a training center where rotation through a malignant disease service is mandatory, there is something to be learned no matter how reluctant the trainee is. It may be as important to learn that this area of medicine is definitely not for them. Or it may be an orientation so that in whatever field of medicine they practice, they will have an appreciation for the ordeal the family with malignant disease faces. On the occasion of departure of a resident to his next rotation, he was asked what he had learned. He replied simply, "I learned how to be more of myself in my care." No greater tribute can be given to the team than that. They provided the opportunity and support; he made use of it.

The Methods

The team members who are involved with direct clinical patient care are those most in need of support. Those providing invaluable services in the laboratory, x-ray department, blood bank, and administration do not require the same type support; thorough orientation in dealing with distraught parents should suffice in a well-run institution. Hour after hour, the clinical caregivers—nurses, aides, IV team, play specialists, medical students, interns, and residents—encounter the repetitive questions; bear the brunt of complaints, anger, and emotional decompensation; and inevitably have their own feelings aroused.

The social worker interviews all newly diagnosed (or newly admitted, if diagnosed elsewhere) patient's parents. She obtains an overview of the premorbid functioning of the family and the personality of the child. She then shares this with the house officers and the nursing staff, enabling them to better understand the functioning of the family and to appreciate the dynamic aspects of their behavior under the initial shock of diagnosis. In addition the social worker is experienced in crisis intervention therapy and consults frequently with the psychiatrist. Rarely, a parental psychosis reactive to the intolerable diagnosis occurs, and this is referred to the psychiatrist. By sharing of information the staff are helped to anticipate certain difficulties on the ward and to mobilize their skills at dealing with them.

A weekly parent conference is conducted by the senior oncologist, the social worker, and the child psychiatrist. Although attendance is voluntary, all new parents are urged to attend. Other parents who are familiar with the conference attend when they have problems with other children or with understanding the rationale of a new course of therapy or when they have complaints. The conference lasts ninety minutes and is conducted in the outpatient clinic waiting area from 6:30 to 8:00 P.M. This enables working fathers and mothers to attend. It is an open conference insofar as subject matter is concerned and topics vary widely. The more information the parents have been given (and assimilated), the more comfortable they feel with their now-enforced relationship with the service.

At these meetings the services of the team are explained. Perhaps most important, the conference provides unhurried access to the oncologist, social worker, and the child psychiatrist. Nurses and IV team members, along with selected students, may also attend. How then does this support the staff? Immediately, it provides them with parents who have at least an intellectual understanding of the service operation. The parents now know to whom to go with certain problems. When parents wish to complain about any aspect of the service, they may do so without burdening the nurses.

A weekly conference devoted to the emotional-psychological management of patients and their families is conducted by the child psychiatrist. Nurses, house officers, oncology fellows, medical nursing students, psychiatrist fellows, a senior oncologist, and nursing supervisor attend. When certain problems involving the children they work with are discussed, the play specialist and the IV nurse attend. The conference begins with a review of the previous week's discussion to encourage feedback and continuity. New management problems are presented by the nurse and the house officer. The social worker contributes background information. Psychological issues around the management problems are discussed and treatment approaches are formulated. Certain issues are used for teaching psychodynamic aspects of human behavior under intolerable stress, and the defensive nature of the observed behavior is elucidated. With the participants voicing their feelings, a wide range of expression becomes evident. For the younger team members, identification with the adolescent patient stirs unresolved fears of death; often, they are impotent to set limits that will comfort the adolescent, rationalizing, "I don't blame him." Thinly veiled anger is occasionally directed at the psychiatrist because he is unable to "come up with an answer." Interpretations are never made. Instead, an attempt is made via the use of identification to promote empathy. If the team member is frustrated because a child will not talk, it can be pointed out that talking may seem too threatening, that silence is preferred. Thus, to talk is not essential; nonverbal communication by the use of caring acts, for example, reading, sitting and relaxing, or appropriate touching behavior, may relieve the caregiver of his frustration over not being able to understand the meaning of silence. If a child resists care, often including him in a piece of that care, for example, selecting the IV site or holding the swab, may foster his identification with the caregiver. Anxiety-binding mechanisms should be supported and a degree of compulsivity and obsessive behavior tolerated and recognized as adaptive coping responses under these circumstances.

After a series of deaths, a nurse said that she had no trouble with identification with the child but that she was torn when identifying with the parents. She did not allow this to interfere with her care, and parents were supported by her empathy and, I suspect, also with the pain of her identification. The group gave her warm support when she was in tears. Like the parents, she was able to grow through this experience and take pride in her capacity to function effectively under such external and internal stress.

Great effort is expended to focus on the total family unit. Each family member reacts to the vicissitudes of the disease. Familiarity with their coping patterns and progress lends the necessary perspective for total care. Again, the nuclear family is the unit of intervention.

In addition to the structured meetings, there ought to be periodic social occasions including spouses. This enables the team to experience each other in a pleasurable manner and with no problem to encounter. Additionally, it permits nonclinical team members to mix with clinical team members, and each group becomes more aware of role differences and the important contribution each makes.

When team members leave for professional reasons (promotion, completion of training, etc.) or for personal reasons (marriage, pregnancy, etc.), the occasion ought to be marked by a social affair. Their departure represents a loss to the team that needs to be acknowledged. New members, likewise, ought to be introduced at some informal occasion, for entry into a well-functioning team can be difficult. By the same token, the team is temporarily wary of new members. These are natural group reactions, and a well-functioning team smoothly adapts.

Summary

Malignant disease treatment teams require emotional support to deliver effective medical and psychosocial care. The support is provided by the following:

the concept of the nuclear family as the unit of intervention

treatment planning that encompasses the psychosocial needs of the family

structural design that acknowledges the emotional needs of the caregivers

structural organization that implements specific methods to ensure that the emotional needs are met

· 19 ·

Psychosocial Interactions of the Dying Child, His Parents, and Health-Care Professionals

GEORGE W. MARTEN AND ALVIN M. MAUER

Providing medical care and emotional support to the dying child is one of the most difficult of human experiences. The stresses imposed by this situation can adversely affect communication among the child, the parents, and the professional health-care team (physicians, psychologists, psychiatrists, and nurses) and may, therefore, alter the ability of professionals and parents to meet the emotional needs of the child. Although the feelings and attitudes of fatally ill children and of their parents are well described in the medical and psychologic literature, much less is known about the interactions among those responsible for the care of a dying child. What, for example, constitutes helpful interaction? Can one pattern of interaction be recommended over another? Published opinions on these and other questions are drawn mainly from the experience of practicing physicians and other health-care professionals and thus are open to systematic research by objective methods. The purpose of this article is to review critically the prevailing attitudes toward interactions of the health-care team both with the dying child and among themselves. By being aware of the pitfalls inherent in dealing with a fatally ill

Supported by Grants CA21765, CA20180, CA23099 from the National Institute of Health, and by ALSAC.

child, we may be able to overcome communication barriers and interprofessional tensions that arise frequently during care of the patient.

Catastrophic illness and death of the child is a severe, stressful situation not only for the patient and his family but for all other adults involved. While much literature is concerned with the child's feeling and needs (Richmond and Waisman 1965, Green and Solnit 1974, Green 1961, Howell 1966, Moore et al. 1969, Tavormina et al. 1976, Goggin et al. 1976, Kellerman et al. 1977, O'Malley n.d., O'Malley and Koocher 1977, Spinetta et al. 1973, Spinetta and Maloney 1974), with the needs of the family for support (Goldfogel 1975, Friedman 1967, Langsley 1961, Nolfi 1967, Tisza 1962, Knudson and Natterson 1960, Foster n.d., Murstein 1960), and with the needs of the siblings for understanding and communication (Gogan, n.d.), there is relatively little literature concerning the need of the therapeutic team, dynamics of interaction among the members of the team, and the necessary energy-saving support of team members by each other and by the team leader.

The Child

During different stages of catastrophic illness, the needs of the patient and his family change, and demands on caring personnel change in quantity and quality. The goal of management is not only to decrease pain, anxiety, guilt, and distress but also to help the child cooperate with the treatment regimen and maintain maximal functioning under the circumstances and an acceptable self-image and to attain a "dignified death" (Schoenberg 1970).

One of the important tools for dealing with such tasks is an open communication not only with the family but also with the child. In the past some professionals dealing with a child suffering from fatal illness have been hesitant to discuss procedures, diagnosis, and prognosis candidly with preadolescent children. We know now that information has been individualized according to the level of the child's sophistication, his momentary physical condition, and his readiness to tolerate the impact of the bad news. We also know that a young child six years old sooner or later becomes aware of the diagnosis and prognosis of his illness (Spinetta et al. 1973, Spinetta and Maloney 1974), that he has a need to discuss his fears and worries, and that fantasies about his illness may be more frightening than the reality. Although the family has the right to choose denial, we have to offer the information again and again.

We know that the receptivity to truth changes in different stages of the child's disease, and communication of such information has to be given gently and gradually. Some hope should always be given to the child and the adults around him. We also know now that the silent child who does not ask questions does not necessarily mean to deny but is willing to pass all the concern to the parents while maintaining a regressive, dependent, passive attitude.

Attempts of the professional personnel to shield children from knowledge about their illness, diagnosis, and prognosis come from their own discomfort about a subject. They usually succeed in communicating their anxiety to the children, who are then afraid to ask in fear of losing the favors of the adults they greatly depend on (Waechter 1971).

The child needs friends and does not want to antagonize the staff and other important adults and remain silent (Vernick 1973). We know now that if children are encouraged to ask questions about their illness, they overcome their hesitancy and ask more questions, to the benefit of their emotional adjustment, and the better functioning of the staff (Karon and Vernick 1968, Vernick 1973). The children who can talk about their illnesses are less anxious and depressed (Kellerman et al. 1977) and possibly may even have fewer physical complications (Bedell et al. 1977). The open and free communication between staff and the child is necessary to decrease the child's anxiety and guilt and free his energy for struggle with the part of reality that we have no information to offer about—the death itself.

However, there are many aspects of illness and dying we can help the child with, and many children will ask many questions. It is important to go into detail where detail is requested, because the child needs a predictable environment. Even painful procedures are tolerated better if the child is prepared for it in a detailed sequence of events. Patients in this way quickly develop trust in the professionals if they do experience the events in the exact sequence as told. The nurse or a child-life worker might supply such explanation in advance of the medical procedures.

The Parents

Parents benefit from individual and possibly later group discussion of their cognitive and affective reaction to the stress of their children's fatal illness (Goldfogel 1975, Tisza 1962, Solnit and Green 1959). Denial is a normal reaction against the fear of being overwhelmed by the unexpected and devastating facts of their child's diagnosis and prognosis. Gradually, with the attending physician's patience and in repeated sessions, the fact of the fatal illness dawns on them, together with the need of facing it constructively. Of course, a few of them do choose protective attitudes toward their child, and the so-called conspiracy of silence develops between the parents and the child. Each does not want to hurt the other one by mentioning the bad news, but both know. Such a situation is destructive psychologically in most cases because silence erects the barrier between the patient and his environment that contributes to feelings of isolation and prevents the child from expressing his feelings (Schoenberg 1970). If the parents themselves abstain from talking to each other and the patient's siblings at home, behavior and school problems may develop in the siblings. Denied and repressed feelings of parents come to the surface in the form of depression or suspiciousness and projection at the time of the death of their child.

Fortunately, most of the parents are able to deal well with the impact of the diagnosis and prognosis. After initial anxiety, parents accept the routine of examination and treatment for their child. Their emotional upheaval gradually subsides to a chronic state, with a mixture of apprehension and hope that the child will become one of the successes of modern therapeutic approaches (Powazek et al. 1978). Of course this is an oversimplified statement. For many mothers every infection or indisposition of a child, which normally would be ignored by the family, becomes, under the circumstances of latent malignancy, a source of renewed anxiety and of fear of relapse, of metastatic process, or of other serious complications.

If the physician attending such a family fosters open communication, a good relationship, and awareness of the emotional impact of the child's malignancy on the patient and his family, he will be able to foresee their potential problems and guide the family through the individual emotional reactions with or without consultation from mental health professionals.

There are crisis situations in families with a history of premorbid emotional maladjustment. Such families may need help from psychiatric professionals. There are parents who decide to interrupt treatment of their child and shop for a better diagnosis somewhere else or to look for help from a faith healer in their community. Some patients have difficulty leaving outpatient care after long chemotherapy sessions and return with complaints showing excessive dependency on the hospital or physician. Instead of being happy about ending the drudgery of repetitive treatment, they ask for continuation of their dependent relationship by developing symptoms that resemble relapse signs (Alby, n.d.). After thorough examination such patients need to talk to a member of the mental health team. Other children have anticipatory vomiting during their chemotherapy or develop anorexia or some other condition puzzling to their physicians and requiring psychiatric consultation.

Of the three most critical times—the times of diagnosis, relapse, and death—the most severe and difficult to deal with is the death of the child. It is difficult not only for the family and for the brothers and sisters of the patient but also for all adults around the child and for the treatment team. The grief reaction frequently starts very early with the phenomenon we call anticipatory grief (Lindemann 1944). When it becomes clear to the family that the treatment is not working and the child might die, the members of the family gradually develop loosening of their emotional ties to their fatally ill child before his actual death. The anticipatory mourning makes the acceptance of the death of the child a little easier, but it does not prevent the devastating impact of the death itself.

The Physician

The physician could be of great help to the family if he is aware of his own feelings during the event. Schoenberg (1970) describes the "feeling of helplessness and ineffectuality," which might lead to anger toward the "disappointing patient," followed by guilt and withdrawal. On the other hand identification with patients might provoke the physician's own feelings of "separation and abandonment," which lead to grief and depression. The family needs their physician's support at this point more than before and suffers if he keeps distance from them because of his own deep-seated feeling of helplessness or abandonment. If the patient puts his physician in a parental role, often quite unconsciously, the physician might use it in a supportive manner rather than allow the patient to regress into childlike behavior and expectation of omnipotence from him (Schoenberg 1970).

At times the physician is tempted to let the house staff take charge of the dying person to protect himself and his feeling. This is a great disservice to the patient, who needs continuity of care, especially at this critical crisis point of his life. His fears of abandonment and desertion are greatly enhanced if he feels his physician increases distance from him. The team members' feelings of helplessness or abandonment have to be anticipated, recognized, and accepted by the medical staff for the sake of good functioning (Easson 1968). Otherwise, tension develops and is expressed by angry feelings projected on one another, on the patient, or on the patient's family.

Such difficulties should be recognized by the head of the treatment team and other members of the team. From time to time one of them will reach the limit of tolerance for such a situation. Such a point expresses itself in manifesting sudden irritability, attacking verbally other members of the team, complaining bitterly about the parents of the patient, withdrawing from the patient, or spending some free time with the patient. Then members of the healing team might be of great help to each other by giving emotional support.

Overidentification or overinvolvement happens more frequently if the dying child reminds the physician of his own child, of his siblings, or of himself, in the case of adolescent patients. The physician's tolerance for emotional stress becomes especially low. Discussion with the team leader is quite helpful if such a situation is recognized soon enough. At times a staff person needs to reinvest his emotion from the dying child, which is most easily done by transferring the emotions to the patient's family. This reinvestment ends occasionally in a close nonprofessional relationship with the family. This stepping out of the professional role into prolonged ties with the family is not helpful to the family or to the child. It prolongs their dependency on the hospital or the staff person, interferes with their grief process by postponing their mourning, and sometimes leads to emotional and interpersonal complications. These complications are not conducive to the growth process that, under normal circumstances, should be taking place as the loss of the child is worked through by the family.

Example: The mother of a child with cancer developed a close relationship to a nurse's aide who was pleased she could offer the unhappy person some "help." After the death of the child a tension developed at home between the mother and the father of the deceased child. During each crisis in the family, the mother left her hometown and traveled to join the nurse's aide for a few days at a time. When the husband urged his wife by phone to return, she misrepresented her situation by claiming to get counseling from her child's former physician. Because of the high esteem in which he held the physician, the husband never questioned this and always gave in to his wife's wishes when she claimed the hospital was on her side. It was not until the physician found out about these visits that he put an end to this practice and the mother started marriage counseling in her community. She had tried to avoid this before with the "help" of the nurse's aide's "friendship."

Intellectualization is a defense against the anxiety and depression produced in physicians and nurses by a dying child. It is well known and frequently observed in hospital units taking care of children with malignant diseases. The tragic event is reduced into a fascinating academic problem and an exercise in maintaining the life in the mind of the helping team member (Eason 1970). On the other hand, it is of no help for the team member to become depressed to the degree of breaking down in front of the family. The family and the patient need the physician to be compassionate and involved but strong and self-controlled. This is a very difficult task because physicians and nurses are frequently troubled by their own fears of death provoked by their close relationship to the dying child. While struggling with their conflicts, they tend to put distance between themselves and the patient and family (Binger et al. 1969). Therefore physicians and nurses have to deal not only with the painful reality of the dying child but also with their own reaction to death at the same time (Easson 1970).

Frequently, in large institutions where many professionals form the team, a rescue fantasy develops between the members of the helping team. It is a totally unconscious notion that one person or group of professionals is more helpful than another and that the other professional or group is harming the patient. Therefore the professionals try to rescue the patient from the other's care or to interfere with their work, totally unaware of the dynamics and consequences of the action. It is not a phenomenon exclusive to the hospital for children with fatal illness but exists in many institutions for children with chronic problems. Open communication between the members of the team usually takes care of such problems.

It is important for the members of the healing team to be aware of these pitfalls and risks of their professional function and to be of help to each other. The leader of the team has a particular responsibility not only for high medical standards but also for the smooth and economical functioning of the team. All of these problems interfere with this smooth functioning and often create unnecessary complications in the delivery of care for the patient and family. Occasionally they also interfere with the emotional adjustment of some member of the helping team who gets so anxious that he has to leave the service, or so depressed that he develops suicidal preoccupation or inability to work. Frequent meetings, with open discussion of one's feelings in a one-to-one situation with the team leader, are usually a good way to prevent such symptoms. In the discussion of the feelings, of course, not only guilt and anxiety but also anger must be ventilated. This is more difficult, anger being socially less acceptable than feelings of guilt. It is especially difficult to discuss anger with one's superior because of the belief that anger is sinful and must be suppressed and handled with guilt and shame. Of course, anticipation of the crisis rather than crisis-oriented management is the best policy. If open discussion is allowed in the team and feelings are discussed, then many of the side effects and symptoms in members can be nipped in the bud.

Mental Health Professional

Interpersonal and intrapersonal problems not only exist in the medical team but also are present in the mental health professional. The usual contact between the nurse and attending physician and the mental health team member is through the consultation. While the reason for referral is usually depression, anorexia, a behavior problem, or high anxiety of the patient or other member of the family, many referrals have a more complicated origin. The consultant must not only focus on the patient's problems but also ask why the consultation was requested and why at this particular time. Patients are referred more for disruptive behavior than for withdrawal and depression. This is not unique in hospitals but is also true for teacher's referrals of pupils to mental health centers. The good patient, just like a good pupil, is one who does not interfere with the work of the teachers and nurses, even if he lives in his own quiet terror or depressive self-absorption. Frequently behind the consultation requests is the expectation to "make the patient behave" (O'Malley, n.d.). At times referral for consultation is made when the staff is overburdened by identification with too many dying children at the same time. The referral has the goal not only of emotional support of the patient in a physical or emotional crisis but also of taking the pressure from a staff person (O'Malley and Koocher 1977) who is overwhelmed and needs to withdraw from the patient emotionally for a while. It is important for the consultant to recognize this and to support not only the overt object of referral but also the staff person in need. At times the referral is made to express anger and rejection of the adolescent by punishing him with psychiatric consultation. If not recognized, such a consultation may only increase the communication gap between the patient and staff.

In general the task of mental health professionals is to maintain or reestablish appropriate communication channels between the child and the surrounding adults (Powazek et al. 1978). They should assist the staff in the more effective management of the patient by modification of the attitudes in one or both parties involved. For example, the patient's complaint might express a plea for sympathy or for reassurance because of his regression to a younger level of psychological adjustment. The complaining is often misinterpreted by the nurses as an expression of ingratitude. They might react angrily to the patient, who then becomes more withdrawn, isolated, and complaining than before. Psychiatric staff members might interfere with these "reverberating or self-defeating circuits" (Schoenberg 1970) and reestablish communication between the patient and personnel. Interpretation of anger of the patient or his parents as a defense against depression prevents the staff from reacting punitively toward the patient, from rejecting him and later feeling guilty about it. Alby and Alby (1973) warn the psychological professional to communicate the "raw material and realistic appraisal to medical staff, otherwise they would consider the report absurd and even offensive." Nicole Alby emphasized that the task of the psychiatrist is helping the communication rather than taking each patient into therapy. She advocates short intervention with some cases but points out how difficult it is for the psychologist or psychiatrist to accept the fact that his role is not to cure the patient but to help him to have a better relationship with his doctor.

The mental hospital professional is not immune to developing symptoms; the difficulty of accepting a role secondary to the patient's physician might surface in the form of depression or feelings of being low on the totem pole or discriminated against or in other projective and angry ruminations. Of course, as long as they can talk about it to each other, they do not need to act it out by an angry written or spoken remark or by angry withdrawal and by forming distance between themselves and their medical colleagues.

At the end of chemotherapy, when adolescent patients have a difficult time separating emotionally from the hospital and doctor, they often develop symptoms aimed at prolonging their dependency. However, there is another outstanding time of crisis—the time of relapse. During the relapse of malignant illness there is "an eruption of catastrophic reaction" (Alby and Alby 1973), especially after long periods of remission. Children and their families become angry with the doctor, whom they considered omnipotent before. "Another remission does not count and the treason cannot be forgotten," state Alby and Alby. Often the physician is drawn into this reaction and an entire team becomes depressed and searches for a scapegoat. "Everyone is vulnerable when a child is dying" (Alby and Alby 1973). At such a time the psychiatrist or psychologist can be of help by interpreting the messages and pointing to the background of feeling and giving support.

When the child's physical strength decreases and it becomes obvious that he or she will die, the psychiatrist should not be called into the situation at this stage, if possible. There is no substitute for the attending physician's relationship to the child and to the family. He should stay with the family, with the psychiatrist in the background counseling him if necessary and guiding him through this crisis with advice and emotional support. In general, psychiatric consultants should impress the team with the important implications of their behavior, but there is no substitute for the attending physician's sole responsibility for a patient. The psychiatrist should avoid the temptation to compete for the attending physician's role (Alby and Alby 1973). But, of course, the members of the mental health team are subjected to the same stresses that the rest of the helping team is suffering and are not immune to the rescue fantasy and acting upon it.

Example: A very competent young member of the mental health team had so successfully counseled the depressed adolescent that the possessive and manipulative mother of the patient became alarmed by her son's independent strivings. During the next hospitalization of her son the mother persuaded the attending physician to postpone the contact with the therapist. Instead of discussing this situation with the attending physician, the mental health professional saw the patient anyway, not realizing that the incident could have created a distance between the attending physician and the mental health service. When it was pointed out to her, she rationalized her action by saying that her "primary duty" was to the patient.

Not only the helping team but also the parents have to be included in each consultation, and the mental health professional cannot talk to the child unless the child, especially an adolescent, is prepared for the referral by his physician and with his parents' approval. The psychiatrist should also clear with the parents issues that might upset the family like expressing anger or talking about dying. Many parents disapprove, especially at the beginning, being afraid to talk about the possibility of death, and are very protective of their child. Such parents would angrily terminate the contact with the psychiatrist or psychologist to the detriment of the child's relationship to all staff members of the hospital (Marten and Mauer 1982).

Of course, when it is indicated, the patient should receive psychotherapy; in such cases, the therapist has to be ready to continue with the patient until the patient's physical deterioration and death. Otherwise, the therapist would confirm the patient's fear of being abandoned by everyone. While therapy should be mostly supportive rather than interpretative, authors agree that the transference relationship, even a quite unrealistic and archaic one, should be supported in the patient (Eissler 1955; Foster, n.d.).

Eissler claims that while therapists should not hide the gravity of the patient's situation, they should somehow convey to the patient an "animistic conviction of patient immortality hoping that, through the transference relationship, a patient who mobilizes archaic trust in the world reawakens to a primordial feeling of being protected by the parental figure of the therapist." In this way Eissler feels the agony of death might be reduced to a minimum. While the recommended attitude seems contradictory, it is not so for the patient, because "it fits his expectation." Eissler also feels that medical training stands in the way of understanding the death because the biological concept of death is only an "absence of something" and there is nothing to be done about "destroyed physical structure." He feels death is "a problem of mind." Religion "equates death with sin which is even less constructive." Eissler recommends that the therapist be aware of sources of pain in the dying person—his envy of the living and his keen perception of the therapist's reaction of "triumph because death stops short of him." Eissler feels that dealing with these sources of pain is very important in therapy of the dying individual.

In conclusion, an important factor must be emphasized. First, the psychodynamic interactions among professionals and with the patient described here are normal occurrences between healthy individuals under the severe stress of having to assist fatally ill and dying children. These are not signs of emotional abnormality in the personnel or patient. Second, it is important to know that the patient can rarely be helped without adults forming a relationship with the child, which means getting emotionally involved. Therefore, the interpersonal tensions and other difficulties in the helping team described can be seen only in personnel who really care about the patient and get emotionally involved. The unconcerned, "job-oriented" professionals who care only marginally about the patient and do not get emotionally involved rarely have the problems described here. The following statement might seem contradictory, but the problem exists only among the dedicated members of the team and in hospitals with high professional standards. In order to overcome the difficulty, all the team members need is to become aware of its existence and to be willing to assist each other with that knowledge. This is the purpose of this article.

REFERENCES

Alby, N. "Ending of the Chemotherapy of Acute Leukemia: A Period of Difficult Weaning." Unpublished article, no date.

Alby, N. and J. M. Alby. 1973. "Doctor and Dying Child." In J. E. Anthony and C. Koopernik, eds., *The Child in His Family*. Vol. II. *The Impact of Disease and Death*, pp. 145–58. New York: Wiley.

Bedell, J. R., B. Giordani, and J. L. Amour, et al. 1977. "Life Stress and the Psychological and Medical Adjustment of Chronically Ill Children." *Journal of Psychosomatic Research* 21:237–42.

Binger, C. M., A. R. Ablin, and R. C. Feuerstein, et al. 1969. "Childhood Leukemia: Emotional Impact on Patient and Family." *New England Journal of Medicine* 280:414–18.

Easson, W. M. 1970. *The Dying Child*. Springfield, Illinois: Charles C Thomas, pp. 83–84.

Easson, W. M. 1968. "Care of the Young Patient Who Is Dying." *Journal of American Medical Association* 205(4):63–67.

Eissler, K. R. 1955. *Psychiatrist and the Dying Patient*, pp. 119–312. New York: International Universities Press.

Foster, D. J. "Surviving Childhood Cancer: Family Coping." Unpublished paper, no date.

Friedman, S. B. 1967. "Care of the Family of the Child with Cancer." *Pediatrics* 40(Suppl):112–22.

Gogan, J. L. "Siblings of Childhood Cancer Survivors." Unpublished paper, no date.

Goggin, E. L., S. B. Lansky, and K. Hassanein. 1976. "Psychological Reactions of Children with Malignancies." *Journal of American Academy of Child Psychiatry* 15(2):314–15.

Goldfogel, 1975. "Working with the Parent of a Dying Child." *American Journal of Nursing* 70:205–11.

Green, M. 1961. "Care of the Child with a Long-term Life-threatening Illness: Some Principles of Management." *Pediatrics* 39(3):441–45.

Green, M., and A. J. Solnit. 1974. "Reactions to the Threatened Loss of a Child: A Vulnerable Child Syndrome." III. "Pediatric Management of the Dying Child." *Pediatrics* 34:58–66.

Howell, D. A. 1966. "A Child Dies." *Pediatric Surgery* 1(1):2–7.

Karon, M., and J. Vernick. 1968. "An Approach to the Emotional Support of Fatally Ill Children." *Clinical Pediatrics* 7(5):274–80.

Kellerman, J., et al. 1977. "Disease-Related Communication and Depression in Pediatric Cancer Patients." *Journal of Pediatric Psychology* 2(2):52–53.

Knudson, G. and J. M. Natterson. 1960. "Participation of Parents in the Hospital Care of Fatally Ill Children." *Pediatrics* 26:482–90.

Langsley, D. G. 1961. "Psychology of a Doomed Family." *American Journal of Psychotherapy* 15:531–38.

Lindemann, E. 1944. "Symptomatology and Management of Acute Grief." *American Journal of Psychiatry* 101:141–48, 194–203.

Marten, G. W. and A. M. Mauer. 1982. "Interaction of Health-Care Professionals with Critically Ill Children and Their Parents." *Clinical Pediatrics* 21(9):540–44.

Moore, D. C., C. T. Holton, and G. W. Marten. 1969. "Psychologic Problems in Management of Adolescents with Malignancy." *Clinical Pediatrics* 8:464–73.

Murstein, D. I. 1960. "The Effect of Long-term Illness of Children on the Emotional Adjustment of Parents." *Child Development* 31:157–71.

Nolfi, N. W. 1967. "Families in Grief." *Social Work* 12:40–46.

O'Malley, J. E. "Long-term Follow-up of Survivors of Childhood Cancer: Psychiatric Sequelae." Unpublished article, no date.

O'Malley, J. E. and G. P. Koocher. 1977. "Psychological Consultation to a Pediatric Oncology Unit: Obstacles to Effective Intervention." *Journal of Pediatric Psychology* 2(2):54–57.

Powazek, M., J. R. Goff, and J. Schyving, et al. 1978. "Emotional Reactions of Children to Isolation in a Cancer Hospital." *Pediatrics* 92:834–37.

Richmond, J. B. and H. A. Waisman. 1965. "Psychologic Aspects of Management of Children with Malignant Diseases." *American Journal of Diseases of Children* 89:42–47.

Schoenberg, B. 1970. "Management of Dying Patient." In B. Schoenberg et al., eds., pp. 238–60. *Loss and Grief: Psychological Management in Medical Practice*, New York, Columbia University Press.

Solnit, A. J. and M. Green. 1959. "Psychologic Considerations in the Management of Death on Pediatric Hospital Services." I. "The Doctor and the Child's Family." *Pediatrics* 32:106–12.

Spinetta, J. J. and L. J. Maloney. 1974. "Death Anxiety in the Outpatient Leukemic Child." *Pediatrics* 56(6):1034–37.

Spinetta, J. J., D. Rigler, and M. Karon. 1973. "Anxiety in the Dying Child." *Pediatrics* 52(6):841–45.

Tavormina, J. B., L. S. Kastner, P. M. Slater, et al. 1976. "Chronically Ill Children, Psychologically and Emotionally Deviant Population." *Journal of Abnormal Child Psychology* 4(2):99–110.

Tisza, P. B. 1962. "Management of the Parents of the Chronically Ill Child." *American Journal of Orthopsychiatry* 32:53–59.

Vernick, J. 1973. "Meaningful Communication with the Fatally Ill Child." In J. E. Anthony and C. Koupernik, eds., *The Child and his Family. Vol. 2. Impact of Disease and Death*, pp. 105–20. New York: Wiley.

Waechter, E. A. 1971. "Children's Awareness of Fatal Illness." *American Journal of Nursing* 1(6):1168–72.

· 20 ·

Care for the Caregivers

EDWARD H. PAKES

As a liaison psychiatrist, I maintain that my task is to "liaise" with others about caring. The caregiver essentially helps a person to see himself in a new illumination. While the caregiver tells the person nothing really new, he provides a supply of stimulation, varied in quantity and technique, throughout the therapeutic relationship. Right timing is important in terms of the onset, duration, and termination of such a relationship. The caregiver clarifies what is expected in terms of time, degree of involvement, and eventual termination but encourages mutual trust between himself and the person he is treating.

The tasks related respectively to the patient, the patient's family, and the professional should not be confused. Questions that clarify these tasks include the following:

1. What is the problem?
2. Whose problem is it (e.g., the patient's, the family's or the professional's)?
3. Can there be a mistaken diagnosis?

How can care be provided for the caregiver? In order to answer that question another must be asked: How can care be provided for patients and their families? Parents asked what message they would like to convey to the medical professions stated that "we are patients too." Not only parents, but also professionals, are patients. Professionals can ask themselves, "How would I approach this parent or colleague if he were my patient?" This means of relating to someone immediately brings a "caring" perspective to the situation. For example, the colleagues of a hematologist who treated many leukemic patients noticed that he would avoid a particular eight-year-old leukemic boy on his rounds. The residents, without saying anything to the hematologist, took over more of the boy's care. After hearing about this, I mentioned to this man that I myself found it difficult to see children with cancer who were near the age of my son. The physician then realized that he had been avoiding the leukemic boy for the same reason, that the boy reminded him so much of how his own son had looked at that age. In this case, I put myself in the role of a "patient." My desire to be understood and to lean upon another person allowed my colleague to do the same and thus brought us closer.

The Selection of Caregivers

Those who care for patients who may die should be selected, if not screened, to see if they are suitable for this stressful, yet potentially rewarding, task. Persons who have survived a loss themselves, just as parents who have survived a loss in their past, often bring a special sensitivity to such a situation. This consideration must be differentiated from a grossly unresolved grief reaction that may be exacerbated on the job.

Furthermore, another consideration is the timeliness of undertaking such a task at a particular time in a person's life. For example, a 21-year-old nurse approached me personally after having worked three months in an isolation unit caring for children with life-threatening immune deficiency diseases. Her boyfriend had become upset by some of the stories she had felt compelled to tell him about the pressures of her work, and she feared her job was threatening their relationship. Because there was no reason to subject this nurse to such an unusually stressful unit at this time in her life, she was transferred. In fact, she thought that at a later time in her life she would probably find working in the children's isolation unit to be a worthwhile challenge.

Matching the Caregiver and the Patient

Each caregiver brings to his work his own specific talents and experiences in life. Some can tolerate the long face of depression, some can wrestle with a family member's anger at the medical professional, while others can give preterminal patients something meaningful to do with their time. An important part of caring for the caregiver is allowing him to perform a task he feels he can perform well and with a good chance of achieving a goal.

If a professional caring for a dying patient appears to be suffering emotional consequences as the result of his task, colleagues should grant his request to transfer. Furthermore, colleagues should attempt to reduce any guilt the professional may have for transferring. As with family members of a dying patient, it is important to follow up the professional with a personal contact to ascertain his ability to cope.

The Task of the Caregiver

Some physicians find treating the terminal patient to be exhausting and frustrating. Others recognize the possibilities for doing something active and useful for the family.

An understanding of the basic psychological aspects of cancer as a life-threatening disease is essential in preparing to deal with it. As cancer research improves the treatment of cancer victims, some patients who were expected to die continue to live for extended years or are cured. Not long ago, death from cancer was more certain—now the uncertainty of the outcome of the disease can produce an emotional cancer just as crippling as the physical one.

The Factors Affecting the Psychology of Cancer in Childhood

Cancer has often been represented by the image of a crab eating away at someone's insides. However, this image is gradually changing into a less ominous one, largely through the efforts of medical professionals.

In their attempts to "catch" the cancer early enough before it devours its host, professionals are searching for an unknown cause. This cause is often portrayed as a virus, but this is sometimes anxiety provoking. The common cold, for which no cure has yet been found, is also caused by a virus. As one may try to avoid "catching" a cold, a layperson may avoid contact with a professional working in the field of cancer for fear of "catching" cancer.

Such anxious reactions to those with contact with cancer extend to the family of a cancer-stricken child. In addition to reacting to the illness itself or to the impaired child, family members sometimes react to problems between themselves, which may aggravate their ability to cope with cancer in the family. The professional must be able to recognize and sort out the problems in order to prescribe appropriate medical and/or psychological treatment.

It is necessary for the caregiver to be aware of a child's conceptualization of his disease. The development stages, which sometimes overlap, are the following:

1. Up to the age of three, the child's main concern is fear of being separated from loved ones.
2. Between ages three and five the child fears mutilation. He worries about the integration of his body and thus about anything that can impair it.
3. The five-year-old believes that there are degrees of illness and of death. He may say someone stabbed ten times is more dead than if stabbed five times. He sees illness as caused by external circumstances and, therefore, reversed by the same.
4. Between ages six and nine, illness is personified as a bogey man who comes to take people away or can magically reverse the event of death. (Adults do not often realize how aware of life and death children are at this age. A vicious cycle can occur in which the parent protects the child, and the child the parent, a relationship resulting in loneliness for everyone involved.)
5. By age nine the child is able to view life and death as concrete entities, that is, as biological processes. For example, a ten-year-old girl likens death to the withering of flowers.

6. To the adolescent, who no longer feels the need for parental protectiveness, a threat to one's health is a traumatic experience. He has difficulty accepting the idea of personal defeat, which may be viewed as the antithesis of independence. Since he experiences such lust for life, he may see illness as punishment for presumptuousness. More than members of any other age group, the adolescent asks, "What have I done to deserve this?" Whereas the young child or mature adult can turn to others for support, the newly "emancipated" adolescent may have too much pride to accept support except from his peers.

During a panel discussion, leukemic adolescent patients stated the following to an audience of parents, professionals, siblings and friends:

1. They resent the sensationalism about their illness (in movies and T.V.).
2. Some major things that bother them are the unpleasantness of vomiting after treatments and the embarrassment of losing their hair. They resent the overprotectiveness of their parents and feel they are often not respected during important communications. For example, if they go to the hospital alone, their parents don't believe what they tell them; if they ask the doctor a question, the doctor directs his answer to the parent; if the doctor asks them a question, the parent answers. Most often they do not feel sick and, therefore, want to be treated normally.
3. They experience some positive effects of their illness, such as gaining insights into life and appreciating what people do for them.
4. In order to improve their own treatment they want straightforward and up-to-date information; resident doctors who do not discuss their cases in their presence because of possible misleading impressions, professionals who do not treat them as specimens, and continued participation in group discussions with other patients, not only cancer patients.

Specific Illness

Leukemia. Leukemia has been somewhat romanticized by the publicity of *Love Story* and *Eric*. Like hysteria, which was originally thought to be a wandering of the womb, leukemia "wanders" through the blood system and cannot be localized to one part of the body. Because of this, many intelligent parents do not really believe it is a cancer. They ask, "Why don't they call it 'cancer of the blood?' " Doctors label leukemia "a blood dyscrasia," a blood abnormality or physiological imbalance. Can doctors expect patients and families to accept this label if they themselves disguise, in their own terminology, the true nature of the disease?

Brain Tumors. The value of intelligence and the fears of mental illness contribute to particular trauma on the part of the family of a child with a brain tumor.

Bone Tumors. Patients and their families who are blue-collar workers may be particularly devastated by the threat of the amputation of a limb.

Wilms Tumor of the Kidney. This disease is now 90 percent curable by surgery, radiation, and chemotherapy. A study conducted two years ago indicates that in half the cases, children were overly aggressive, as if defying someone to knock out their remaining kidney. In the other half of the cases, children were introverted, as if protecting their valuable organ.

One does not necessarily realize the psychological significance of a particular body organ until something happens to it. Sometimes the side effect of drugs may be more disturbing than the actual disease. An 18-year-old girl with a bone tumor was given treatments that would, her mother was told, cause loss of hair. The mother became hysterical because the mother's father used to refer to the mother's hair as her "crowning glory." In this case the patient was not as concerned about her hair as her mother was. In other cases, patients and family members suffer emotional problems even after cancer is cured. In one case, a father felt suicidally depressed because he had delayed noticing his child's eye ailment, which was inherited from him.

Length of Illness

A sudden death, either before or shortly after diagnosis, leaves no time for normal grieving on the part of the parents. Time is extremely important to the family as they cope with their reaction to the loss.

A prolonged illness may cause some of the family or staff to wish the child dead. This may be a source of persistent guilt and may interfere with the completion of the process of mourning. In the case of an extreme reaction, psychiatric referral may be considered.

The Integration of Mental Health Principles into Medicine

The technologies of medicine and psychiatry are often too mechanistic. There are instances in which patients die feeling lonely because doctors seemingly express greater interest in the patient's laboratory findings than in the person himself. Psychiatric patients may be conditioned to concentrate on the particular phobia a professional is interested in treating. There is a need for the investigation of all aspects of every illness, whether medical or psychiatric.

The separate development of psychiatry has led to a more nearly complete understanding of the mourning process. Freud explained how to take into ourselves a lost person as in the digestive process, until either we have resolved our feelings about that person or we need psychic surgery to remove those feelings, which sit there like a lump, unresolved. Bowlby distinguished the stages of protest, despair, and detachment during mourning. Kübler-Ross (1969) made pioneering contributions to our understanding of death, summarized below in medical and psychological terminology:

The first reaction to being told the diagnosis is shock; its psychological equivalent is denial. All systems shut down. The patient reacts, "No, it's not true!" *Examples:* A teenage patient with leukemia absorbed himself with work rather than preoccupy himself with his illness. This, unlike the next example, is healthy denial. The mother of an ill child began fasting as if becoming ill herself would allow her child to get better. Another mother completely denied her child's death; two years after his demise she came to the hospital looking for him. During this stage, treatment consists of supportive care and the sustenance of life forces, including biological, psychological, and financial.

Denial yields to anger and protest. Patients ask, "Why me?" There is an increasing use of projection at an unconscious level, especially with children. Patients experience their affliction as if thrown on them by those around or by God. Blaming is paramount; many patients blame the doctor, who may not have made the original diagnosis as soon as they would have liked. Parents may thereafter isolate themselves from the doctor. This is a difficult stage because it is likely to disrupt the human relationships that are necessary to sustain life. Parents then typically complain. If staff members experience the attacks personally and counterattack instead of giving support or correcting misconceptions, they may increase the parents' suffering.

Guilt is most often associated with this blaming stage. For example, when a young person is ill, the question of who is to blame arises. The 21-year-old parents of an 18-month-old child were separated. The father was caring for the child because he felt that the infant had become ill because of neglect by the mother. One aspect of the parents' marital discord was their displaced anger on each other. This anger must be contained and controlled, as must the disease. The physician might say, "Yes, I agree with your frustrations. I am frustrated too. Let's all do everything we can to help your child and you." The specific plan for treatment should then be outlined, even written down. Following this containment of the disease, as well as the emotions, an important procedure that may be labeled "psychological surgery" is used to excise the emotional metastases related to guilt.

Whose Fault Is It?

The answer to this question is usually that it is no one's fault. Nevertheless, everyone, and especially mothers, suffers from guilt. Such guilt can be excised. If so, chronic depression or other mental illness may be prevented. Guilt must be removed in order to leave as little psychological scarring as possible. Parents are relieved when the psychiatrist does not chastise or blame them for their child's illness. Thus, their burden of guilt can be lifted, leaving them with precious energy to continue.

Common Theories Explaining a Child's Illness

- An indiscretion of one's past, for example, pregnancy before marriage.
- X-rays during pregnancy.
- Pills taken.
- Religious guilt, as from marrying out of the family faith.

Parents often punish themselves financially, or other "accidents" happen if these issues are not addressed. Some families become addicted to one trauma after another, as if by punishing themselves enough, the child might improve.

The third stage is bargaining. "I'll make a deal with you." The bad, angry child remembers that if he is good, he will be rewarded. If parents are religious, they may turn to bargaining, "I'll be a steady church-goer if only you will grant my child another two years." Many bargains are kept secretly or can only be surmised. Promises are sometimes made in response to parents' guilt feelings, either about their personal past or about the child's present illness. Therefore, leading the conversation around to the promises and finding their source helps to relieve the pressure of parental guilt.

An interesting phenomenon often occurs in response to the crisis of cancer. Some families with a leukemic child make a drastic change in their lives, as if by doing so the child's illness might change. One parent radically changed his career, another moved to a new home, one became religious, and another exiled his mother-in-law from his home. It is best at this time not to make any drastic change in one's lifestyle without considering it seriously. Any further change creates an additional burden.

Fourth, after a cancer victim realizes that bargaining is not entirely successful, a profound but necessary depression takes over. Both psychological and material losses, in addition to physical losses, are experienced. A healthy child loses his normal functioning, parents may lose their self-esteem, and costly medical attention depletes savings. It is important for professionals to know when to give material (financial) support and when to just be there.

There are two kinds of depression: In the first, losses can be replaced. For example, a wig can replace hair for a girl proud of her hair. An incapacitated child, by watching others play, can play vicariously. The second kind of depression, in contrast to the first, is usually silent. Patients may not talk much, but they respond to knowing looks and having someone sit with them. Responding to their questions, for example, about the details of a possible funeral, may relieve their anxiety.

Fifth, acceptance of the illness usually means having traversed most of the aforementioned emotions and being able to put the illness in the back of one's mind in order to carry on living.

Sixth, hope is, of course, a constant force throughout the whole process. Hope is encouraged by the work of doctors, nurses, and organizations like the American Cancer Society.

Representative reactions to these phases in the mourning process are the following:

Patient's Reaction
- DENIAL: "No, it's not me! You looked at somebody else's blood."
- ANGER: "You're murderers! It's not the disease that is killing me, it's your treatments."
- BARGAINING: "If I'm good, will you reward me with a longer life?"
- DEPRESSION: "Yes, it's me. I can't do what I used to. How sad I am."
- ACCEPTANCE: "I guess I have to accept it. I can't do it anymore. My time has come."
- HOPE: "I can still enjoy some things."

Family's Reaction
- SHOCK: "Why us? What did we do to deserve this?"
- DENIAL: "The doctor made a mistake. I'll ask another specialist." (An extraordinary number try to deny the shock with alcohol.)
- ANGER: "It's not my fault, it's the doctors', nurses', neighbors', God's fault."
- BARGAINING: "I'll go to church more. Give my child another year."
- DEPRESSION: "It's like losing part of me."

ACCEPTANCE: "We can't fight it anymore. We'll have to accept it."
HOPE: "The doctor says they are doing research. Maybe they'll find an answer in time for my child."

While parents are caring for their ill child and attempting to survive themselves, it is difficult for them to support their other children as much as they would want to do. Jealousy between siblings occurs. The healthy children may think it is an advantage to be ill. If a child's illness is prolonged, siblings are capable of such extreme behavior as wishing this child dead, in addition to feeling guilty about it. Preadolescents who are told the truth may depend on their good peer group relationships, manage well, and become more mature in the process. If a child is not told the truth about a sibling's illness, he may misinterpret that the parent is ill, a fact more threatening to his security and mental health than if it is the sibling.

Using Dr. Kübler-Ross' stages of mourning, I present the following representative reactions expressed by the caregivers.

Oncologist's Reactions

SHOCK: "Here's another case! How shall I handle it?"
DENIAL: "Maybe I'm wrong about my diagnosis. I'll show the slide to my colleague." (Avoidance of psychological impact is sometimes indicated by the statement; "That's an interesting lab finding.")
ANGER: "Why are they being such difficult parents? I've worked hard on this case. They have no right to be angry. They probably didn't give the medication as I ordered. Maybe they went to Dr. So-and-so before and he couldn't handle them and sent them to me. I get the most difficult cases."
BARGAINING: "I promise to read my journals every night; just don't refer another cancer case for awhile."
DEPRESSION: "I wonder why I feel so low today. All my patients are dying. The statistics I read in cases being treated at other centers show better results. Are we doing enough?"
ACCEPTANCE: "I've tried my best. I guess it is a difficult disease to treat."

HOPE: "That was a great remission. I hope it lasts. I heard about a new drug. Maybe we should try it on our patients."

An important process, almost impossible to do on an individual basis, is that the physician taking part in a parent group is knocked off his pedestal. For example, a mother pulled out a medication mistakenly prescribed for her daughter and accused the doctor of wrongdoing. Once this frustration was aired, the group saw the doctor not as a technician pushing pills but as a person with feelings. However, they put him on a pedestal again with the hope that this would cure their child.

Surgeon's Reactions
SHOCK: "This mass is not what I assumed."
DENIAL: Intellectually a doctor may know the real diagnosis even before seeing the microscopic section, but emotionally he cannot yet admit it.
ANGER: "Those bastards in x-ray. Why didn't they visualize it properly?" Or, "That damned G.P., why didn't he detect this earlier?" Or, "Those parents are neglectful." (Occasionally, a doctor may lose emotional control in the operating room; for example, the instruments don't suit him, or the resident doesn't hold the retractor properly. The loss of control may be related to a fear of the loss of self-esteem.)
BARGAINING: "If only we could get a grant for that research lab."
DEPRESSION: "Look what this day has done to me. I think I'll go to Florida to golf for the weekend."
ACCEPTANCE: "I've done as well as I could. I learned from this case and hope we'll catch the next one earlier."

Nurse's Reactions
SHOCK: "God, another one, what a shame! I didn't think it was such a common disease."
DENIAL: "Maybe they made the wrong diagnosis."
ANGER: "Why are these such difficult cases? That doctor isn't around when he needs her."
BARGAINING: "I'll go on night duty; just don't let another child die on me."

DEPRESSION:	"Why did I ever agree to work on this ward? I think it's time to transfer." "It's okay if they die during the day. I can cry about it on the ward and talk with the other nurses. But if they die in the late afternoon, I carry it home with me to my husband, I don't want to burden him with it. Then he won't want me to work."
ACCEPTANCE:	"We did as much as we could. That child died without suffering much at the end."
HOPE:	"That new drug they are using seems to work."

Psychiatrist's Reactions

SHOCK:	(To the doctors) "You can't do anything to help. We'll send the patient to a social worker."
DENIAL:	"No, it can't happen."
ANGER:	"Why don't they know how to listen and talk to people? I'll show them how."
BARGAINING:	"If you'll only listen to my lecture, it won't be so hard on us all."
DEPRESSION:	"I wouldn't want this to happen to any child of mine!"
HOPE:	"The staff are becoming more aware of what they are capable of doing emotionally for the patients, families, and themselves."

If a person has experienced a recent loss, he usually trusts that the psychiatrist has a sympathetic ear. What equips someone to do this kind of therapeutic work? Good training includes personal experiences, unique for each professional, in which the person has had to cope with grave and uncertain situations.

Risks of Working in Our Field

I have intimated that the psychological stress for working with children who may die is higher than from working with the average medical patient. There is need for organized support, education, and provision of individual psychological assistance for those working with the terminally ill. At one institution, nurses had to petition for the assistance of a psychiatrist. At another hospital, both physicians and nurses jointly realized that they needed psychological assistance.

The Evolution of a Mutual Support System

In 1969, the hematologists and nurses at the Hospital for Sick Children, Toronto, requested a study of the reactions to leukemia on the part of a victim's family and the professional staff. Eventually, the breakup of several marriages and the frequent absence of fathers motivated those conducting the study to initiate parent groups, which were held for eight weeks. These were attended by parents, a psychiatrist, the physician whose patient was involved, an oncology resident, a clinical nurse, and several nurses from the ward. These groups developed a supportive, emotive, and experiential educational experience par excellence. Each physician agreed to do at least two of them, and they were as exhausting as they were educational.

These groups evolved into the Family Leukemia Association, which is essentially a self-help association with strong ties to the medical personnel in the hospital. It is for families with a living child who is a patient, as well as for families with a deceased child. The Association helps families to face the reality of a loss and to survive and continue to grow despite the death of their child. Physicians initially opposed the Association, feeling it would complicate their work. In fact, it has undoubtedly lightened their load because many parents are able to help each other in certain ways better than professionals can help them. The Association as an organized process of self-help is an excellent channel for the expression of the mourning anger of the parents who participate. The Family Leukemia Association is still in the process of evolution. Followup studies on the participating families have been conducted on an informal basis. A chaplaincy student whose child died of leukemia has been significantly responsible for the project. The emphasis is on the prevention of emotional illness in the survivors of a child's death that occurs in the hospital. Once an ill child dies, the family members continue to participate in the program. Once the parents know that professional care for them goes beyond the death of their child, they are supportive of the continued efforts of the staff. Indeed, this is their way of caring for the caregivers! There is a cycle of caring!

A professional may often call a parent to ask for assistance in counseling a family who is ethnically, socioeconomically, or otherwise similar in lifestyle to that parent. Such a parent usually phones the professional to inform him on how well he is doing, rather than call only in the event of trouble.

In conclusion, the essential elements of a supportive and caring system for the caregivers include the following:

1. A screening of the professional personnel so that those who may be particularly vulnerable to excessive stress do not fall ill themselves.
2. A group support system for both doctors and nurses that allows reasonably free exchange of emotion, viewed as part of the work without jeopardizing the work (for example, time for crying when a child dies).

   A nurse once explained that working with children who have cancer is different from working with adults with cancer. The adults depend upon the professionals for "nursing." The children depend upon her for a parental kind of support. The child's emotional needs are vital. If a professional gets the child's trust at the beginning of the treatment, she can do almost anything procedurally and the child will accept it, as if coming from a parent. The system must accommodate the flexibility of an immediate kiss and hug for a child, as well as a brief time off for a nurse who has just lost one of her cares.

   In the more successful units, there is someone who is able to bring comic relief to a trying situation. Such a person is likely to be a head nurse who accepts guff from both parents and other nurses without taking it personally, who helps with routine nursing tasks, who has the ability to listen and understand what her charges are saying, and who is willing to give extra personal time and energy from time to time.
3. The involvement of someone who is partly outside the system so that an individual on the team can consult with him personally without fear of the loss of confidentiality.
4. A *definite* organized followup system for the "survivors" of a child's death, including staff, so that the results of one's efforts can be seen at intervals after the event of death.

It is important to distinguish between care and treatment for the caregivers. If active psychological treatment for caregivers is needed, it should be mostly outside the system. It may be the role of someone like a psychiatrist to make referrals for assistance.

Care, in these circumstances, is the spontaneous giving of oneself on the part of co-workers and parents. It is an experience that brings all closer in a unique way, which is the reward for any unusual suffering a person may encounter in work with cancer patients who are children.

Finally, as the illnesses of yesterday are being beaten today, professionals are devoting more time and attention to studying family and staff reactions to a health crisis, a child stricken with cancer. In the process professionals are learning much about what environmental factors contribute to mental stress and illness surrounding a health crisis. If the physician, the team, and all others deal actively and appropriately with cancer patients, these professionals can contribute effectively to the immunization of emotional problems in the patient and his family, as well as in the hospital staff caring for them.

REFERENCES

Kübler-Ross, E. 1969. *On Death and Dying.* New York, Macmillan.

· 21 ·

Children With Cancer in Group Therapy

CLYDE H. FLANAGAN

"No doubt, in time, the surgeon will consider the psychic response of his patient before, during and after the operation as intimate a part of his problem as the surgical technic itself" (Levy 1945). Although understanding of the severe nature of children's reactions to hospitalization and surgical procedures has become more prevalent, this forecast is far from fruition. From a retrospective study, Levy (1945:12) found that, when an operation is followed by another operation when fears were still manifest from the first, serious emotional sequelae resulted. In another classic paper, Bowlby, Robertson, and Rosenbluth (1952) reported on the filming of a two-year-old's reactions to hospitalization. A reaction of protest and despair leading to detachment was evident with prolonged separation from the psychological mother. Jessner et al. (1952), studying children's reactions to tonsillectomy, stressed the need for psychic "inner preparedness," that is, "the extent to which the child has been able to master his anxiety and marshall his defenses to cope with impending danger—that affects the final outcome." Prugh et al. (1953), reporting on a study of 200 children, stated, "the objectively verifiable aspects of the stress encountered during hospitalization bore little specific relationship to the degree of reaction on the part of the children." This is consistent with Anna Freud's (1952) observation that the painfulness of a procedure is directly proportional to anxiety, which is proportional to the psychic preparedess of the child for the experience. Prugh and his co-workers, finding that all children in the study showed observable reactions to the experience of hospitalization and treatment procedures, concluded, "Although a persistently traumatic effect of an emotional nature arising from hospitalization does not seem to be inevitable, the possibility of such an effect appears great enough to warrant the application of special prophylactic measures." Stocking and co-workers (1972:664) reported a high incidence of missed psychopathology by a pediatric ward staff, unnecessary hospitalization, and a high incidence (63.7 percent) of significant psychopathology that would warrant psychiatric consultation, but only 11.3 percent were referred. This group recommended activity group therapy for preadolescent children in pediatric ward settings.

The information gained by these studies is consistent with the knowledge that when a child perceives intense, diffuse, sudden, and unexpected stimuli, the capacity to maintain psychic equilibrium is severely impaired. In the service of mastery, synthesis, and integration, play is one of the most powerful tools available to the child's ego. In play, the child is in complete control. Experiences received in a passive, helpless state can be acted out with the child in the active role. The world around, which is perceived in a visual, sensorimotor manner, is stored in memory traces of this kind (i.e., sensorimotor). These can be expressed in play with a gradual integration comparable to the verbal catharsis and working through of adults. When the child is ill and requires hospitalization, many factors combine to contribute to an overwhelming of the ego's capacity to cope successfully. Parents are not able to protect the child from pain and suffering, and often he cannot run and play, or play capacity is disrupted, just when it is most needed. Thus, it is evident that much support is needed.

All of these considerations become multiplied many times over with children found to have cancer. Often the illness is acute, and the hospitalization is accompanied by intense anxiety over multiple surgical procedures. The coping-adaptive mechanisms of the child and family are severely tested, if not overwhelmed. In recent years, the experience of this author, consulting to the pediatric wards of a major Army hospital for children with cancer, has supported a need for more support of these children. Many people express an interest in the subject "Death and Dying," but when confronted with the child with cancer, many factors contribute to a neglect of these children's emotional needs.

The medical team caring for these children become incredibly emotionally involved. This contributes to a strong dependent relationship of child and family upon the physician, eventually leading to overprotection and competition within the medical-nursing support staff. The price of admittance of other supporting staff members to the "club" is most often too high. In more sophisticated terms, a massive resistance to a deeper understanding and greater availability of help to this group of children is evident.

From September to July, the author and an art therapy student conducted an activity group using art materials on the pediatric ward of an Army Medical Center. Membership in the group was open to any patient on the ward; however, the primary membership and goal of the group consisted of children on the oncology service. The ward consisted of two sections, one for boys, another for girls, aged 3 to 13 years. Occasionally, an older adolescent was admitted to the ward. The ward is a pediatric ward with children admitted to numerous services in the hospital: general surgery, ophthalmology, orthopedics, urology, and pediatrics. Arrangements were made with the chief of the Pediatric Oncology Service, Department of Pediatrics, to have all children on the service meet in the group for twice a week for one hour. It was decided to meet with the group in a space on the wards that served as a play area, waiting room for parents, and sometimes as space for a bed.

Although a great deal of time and effort was spent getting support and making arrangements for the group, many problems were encountered with the actual weekly support to have the children with cancer actually brought to the group. For example, initially, meetings were held with the chief of the service, who thought the idea of working with these children was a good one and introduced the therapist to the assistant chief of the service, who was very supportive and introduced the pediatric oncology fellows, who were responsible for the day-to-day medical care for these children. It was suggested, however, that the responsibility for getting the children to the group and arranging for space would fall to the nursing staff on the ward.

A meeting was arranged with the head nurse on the ward, who was very receptive to the plan and agreed to support the group by having the oncology patients in the group. The time was arranged for Wednesdays and Fridays from 8:30 to 9:30 A.M.—this being a time following the morning baths, breakfast, and doctor rounds. In addition, the Department of Pediatrics had a daily seminar from 8:00 to 9:00 A.M., which meant the pediatric oncology fellows would not be wanting to see the children during this time. Details of these arrangements are given because the issues of who was to be in the group, who was to get them there, priority for appointments (consultations, lab work, etc.) became the focus of major problems with confusion and intense affective exchanges.

Who was to discuss the group with parents and respond to parental questions became a major problem area. After some time, a meeting was held with the head nurse, who was surprised to hear the author say that all children on the oncology service were supposed to be in the group. The nurse noted that no doctor's orders were ever written on this. Another round of meetings with the assistant chief of the service resulted in the decision to write up a standard operating procedure (SOP) for the group that included the statement, "Orders will be written by the child's physician for those children on the pediatric hematology-oncology service, or on whom the oncology service has received a consult, to attend the group," and "When a child is admitted to the ward on the oncology service, the parents' orientation to the ward is to include an introduction to the therapy group and informed of the child's attendance every Wednesday and Friday." This was signed by the assistant chief of the pediatric hematology-oncology service and the author, chief, child psychiatry consultation-liaison.

This did not solve the problem of attendance: Should a child be required to attend when he or she is "not feeling well" or does not want to attend? Orders were never written and conflicting appointments were not unusual. There were a few children who never attended the group, because of conflict among parent-child-parent-nursing staff-nursing staff-physician. Intense conflict developed with the chaplains and between the co-therapists around the issue of feelings of abandonment and the family of an acutely ill child by the psychiatrist who had to be out of town on business.

The child psychiatry consultation-liaison section has a training program for first-year child psychiatry residents, social work fellows, and postdoctoral fellows in psychology in observing and interviewing children who are hospitalized. Over the years, a major focus of this program has been children with cancer. It was decided to concentrate the focus of this program on these children so that more information could be obtained for understanding and helping the children in the group. Much resistance was encountered within this group of trainees to becoming involved with these children and parents. It was also often difficult for the nursing staff to have the children available for prearranged interviews.

It was with much effort and perseverance, therefore, that the group did meet each week at the appointed time. Frequently only one or two children were present. There developed a relationship with four children who were followed in the group from the time of their first admission for evaluation of symptoms, the diagnosis of cancer, and subsequent treatment.

Patient A is an 8-year-old, Caucasian boy who was admitted to the hospital three weeks after he fell while skating and injured the left knee. When routine x-rays revealed lytic lesions in the proximal left tibia, he was admitted to a local hospital. X-rays of the left foot revealed demineralization in the os calcis, a bone in the foot. A bone biopsy was diagnosed as osteogenic sarcoma, and the patient was referred to the medical center for further evaluation and treatment. The diagnosis was confirmed, and a left, above-the-knee amputation was made and chemotherapy initiated. He came to the group on his second day of hospitalization and drew the picture shown in fig. 21.1. This is a clown on a tightrope with a net underneath. There are grandstands off to the corner. The left leg and foot of the clown is much larger and placed in a tenuous position holding up the clown on the rope.

Figure 21.1

The legs are colored with black cross-hatching and colored in black. The self-projection is evident, and the position of the clown reveals the knowledge that this boy has about his uncertain future. As far as is known, at that time he had not been told his diagnosis (since it had not been confirmed) and no discussion of amputation had occurred. By the next group session, five days later, the diagnosis had been confirmed and a decision to amputate had been made with surgery scheduled in two days.

After several unsuccessful attempts, he produced the drawing in fig. 21.2. This is a scene with Charlie Brown, who lives in the house on the right with a black, cross-hatched foundation, going out to feed Snoopy. He remembers he had already fed him and

Figure 21.2

found he had locked himself out of the house. His mother comes home, is angry, and punishes him. All the objects in the drawing were outlined with a black felt pen prior to coloring in the details. He commented he did not like the green, grassy part of the picture. The color, design, and placement (foundation) of the area beneath the house suggest a representation of the left leg (in the previous drawing). The themes are of punishment and orality. The tree on the left has two blunted limbs that look like a "stump" following amputation. This picture reveals intense anxiety concerning the pending surgery, oral regression, with anxiety related to oral dependency on a punitive mother.

The next drawing was made five days following amputation of his left leg (fig. 21.3). He talked about the surgery and recalled seeing a bright light in the operating room before a mask was put over his face. Feeling somewhat weak, he asked for help in coloring in the black in the picture. He described the drawing as a spaceship on a planet close to the sun surrounded by "deep space." The large oval white area is a receptor for catching the solar energy that powers the spaceship. As he worked on the

Group Therapy 273

Figure 21.3

drawing, pointing to his bandaged left leg, he told of the artificial leg he was getting. This picture is filled with bright light and dark black. Like the space explorer, this boy was beginning a journey into unknown space. The spaceman is safely inside the spacecraft looking out through a periscope. The source of energy is separate from the spaceship and looks strangely like the shape of a leg-knee to foot (refer to fig. 21.1 and the shape of the foot). He has now lost his source of power (his leg). In this powerless, castrated condition what does the future hold for him?

Two days later he drew the picture in fig. 21.4. This is a puppet sitting on a horse with balloons at each end of the horse. Again, a cross-hatched area, red now, was placed on each corner. Above, the place for the puppeteer is empty, or is the puppeteer hidden from view? The day of the drawing, his mother had not wanted him to come to the group, because she and his father were leaving for a visit home (500 miles away) later that day, but he wanted to come and make this drawing. He worked without talking. The small puppet is astride a horse (wooden?) that is lifted with the help of balloons. Is the puppeteer the cancer, phy-

Figure 21.4

sicians, nurses, parents? Compare this drawing with the first one and note what a change is evident. The left lower leg is now gone, to be replaced by a wooden artificial one. The small puppet, controlled from above, is astride a horse with no life, no power of its own, needing balloons for "lift power."

Figure 21.5 is a drawing made five days later. This is the third painting made with the introduction of paints in the group. The first efforts consisted of experiments with the paints by smearing with a brush; the second was more controlled abstract design of square patches of brown and green. This is the third painting, and it was followed by a story about the picture. This is an Indian in a canoe. Becoming "messed up" and "covered over," he changes into a cowboy in a box. The cowboy cuts his way out of the box and saves the treasure, which had fallen out of the canoe (the blue area), off a "stump" in the river. The theme here is "conversion" (Indian to cowboy). The cowboy apparently is a more active, aggressive person than the captured Indian. Does this mean that this boy was leaving a passive, dependent position and moving to a more active one, taking some control, saving his treasure? Also, one can see the wish to break free from his

Group Therapy 275

Figure 21.5

present "boxed in" position and rescue the treasure fallen from the stump, that is, the lost leg. The Indian was captured and boxed in, set adrift, and a treasure is lost; in an identification with the aggressive, cutting surgeons, he can break out and rescue it.

In fig. 21.6, done two days later, he returns to a "Snoopy" drawing. This is the fourth attempt. The first three were rejected when he could not "fix the nose" on Snoopy. In this drawing, Snoopy lies on his house with his food on an elaborate system that protects it from other dogs. On the ward, this patient's mother established a mothering role to a four-year-old boy with leukemia who was also a member of the group. The green line over Snoopy and dividing the drawing represents a force field, protecting Snoopy and Charlie Brown from bad weather. Snoopy and Charlie Brown are also separated by this line; that is, Snoopy is alone with his food. The themes here are the need for protection from other dogs and bad weather and the separation and abandonment (the absent Charlie Brown). The small black tree in one section—is this the lost leg? The big, black tree with the one remaining limb holding the food (compare with the previous

Figure 21.6

Snoopy drawing—the same tree had two limbs). The air is filled outside the force field with "bad" things that must be kept out. Could this represent the "unknown" cause of his illness with intense anxiety concerning invasion and loss of his remaining leg?

Figure 21.7 was done the next week; this was the last drawing. Chemotherapy had been started several weeks before and some hair loss was evident with radical changes in his body image. The lighthouse stands on a rocky shore sending out its light into darkness. There is a sense of strength, completeness, and hope evident in this picture, along with anxiety and depression, which constantly threaten. Following this drawing, the patient was given his new leg and was discharged, to be followed on an outpatient basis.

The next group of pictures were made by Gina, a 6-year-old, Caucasian girl who was admitted to the medical center in September 1977 with a mass in the right leg just above the knee. A diagnosis of osteogenic sarcoma was made, and in October, the leg was removed at the hip. Her postoperative period was a stormy one with phantom limb pain. When she began chemo-

Figure 21.7

therapy, she developed severe nausea and vomiting. All children undergoing chemotherapy suffer these effects, but Gina's were more protracted and severe. She became whiny, demanding, and had frequent temper tantrums.

Figure 21.8 is one of her first drawings made after her bone biopsy but prior to a discussion with Gina of the final diagnosis and decision to amputate. The scene is her home, which is located on the ocean. This is a bright, sunny, happy scene. As with most of her drawings, her name takes a prominent place on the scene. The animal on the tree has a sinister quality to the configuration appearing ready to "pounce." The red dots in the air are also interesting with a black cloud over the entire picture. Gina's mother is in the hospital with her, and Gina is smiling and friendly as she sits in a wheelchair, a bandage on her leg. The house configuration is the dominant theme in all her drawings. This is accompanied by a smaller, protruding, rectangular structure placed upon another larger, squarer structure such as the chimney sticking out of the house or a flag on a boat. Two days later, in fig. 21.9, she is in a car going home from the hospital. Her anxiety

Figure 21.8

Figure 21.9

Group Therapy

Figure 21.10

is more evident at this time. The house is black and the surrounding area is bare. The lines are weak and "shaky," and she wishes to escape her situation and go home.

Five days later (she was to have surgery a few days later), the next drawing was made (fig. 21.10). The "rectangular" structure takes up the entire picture and perhaps the symbolic representation is made obvious, as her name is placed over the upper corner in such a way as to give a torn, ragged, damaged quality to her flag.

The rest of her drawings were made several weeks after her surgery. She had been discharged from the hospital for a visit home, and chemotherapy had been begun. This next drawing (fig. 21.11), when compared to the first one (fig. 21.8), reveals the changed nature of her world. The black cloud has taken over, the picture is blurred, but there is a bright sun over head.

In fig. 21.12 we see the tail end of a whale as it dives for deep water. The next three drawings (figs. 21.13–15) depict ocean scenes and a continuation of the whale theme. In fig. 21.13, a whale is being "shot" and in fig. 21.14, boat and whale are gone. Both these drawings were made on the same day. Is the whale

Figure 21.11

Figure 21.12

Group Therapy 281

Figure 21.13

pulling the boat? Notice the structure in all the last five drawings. In fig. 21.14, it is all that remains. Has the boat sunk with this part protruding above the water?

In the next drawing (fig. 21.15) a boat is missing a major part of its body but remains afloat with a bright sun overhead. She writes "Gina's paper" in black letters, which seems to proclaim, "This is Gina!" In fig. 21.16, the house on the beach scene has quite a changed quality. The blackness is gone but has left behind a rather barren scene with a somewhat "droopy" house and bent chimney.

The last drawing (fig. 21.17) was made after she received her crutches and became quite adept at using them. She had been fitted for an artificial leg and was leaving for home. What is striking is the smallness of the structures; they look far off, but the boat is sailing home.

Roderick is an 11-year-old black boy who was found to have a cranial tumor in his left frontal lobe in October 1974. In December 1974, he had a subtotal resection of the left frontal lobe of his brain. Symptoms recurred in the summer of 1975, and he

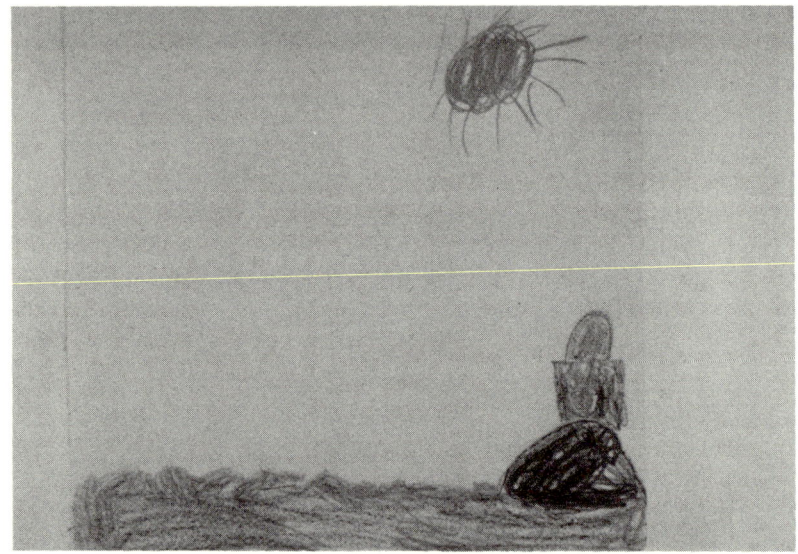

Figure 21.14

Figure 21.15

Group Therapy

Figure 21.16

Figure 21.17

Figure 21.18

received radiation therapy. In the fall of 1976, he was in surgery again for another partial resection of the left frontal lobe. In February 1977 he began chemotherapy. In August 1977 he was discovered to have a cystic mass in the left frontal cranial area with a comatose condition for a week, etiology undetermined. A "diffuse metabolic encephalopathy" was suspected by pediatric neurology. He gradually improved and was beginning another course of chemotherapy when he began therapy in the group.

His first drawing (fig. 21.18) was made using the structure provided by a picture on a can in the play area. It is of note that he picked this picture that places so much emphasis on the head, which is bald except for a "tuft" on top. Rod was losing his hair following chemotherapy. All of Rod's drawings focus on the head.

In the next drawing (fig. 21.19) appears the masked head of the "Super Hero" Spiderman, who is saying, "I think I should go home." The focus of anxiety around the head and the wish to leave the hospital are quite evident. Rod was alone in the hospital, for his parents never visited except when he was ready to

Figure 21.19

leave for home, about 300 miles distant from Washington. Spiderman is a young man who received an accidental exposure to radiation (I believe) producing his extraordinary ability to spin webs of strong material and stick to the sides of buildings. He uses his power to catch criminals. Underneath the mask of the "real" Spiderman is a handsome young man. In fig. 21.20, Roderick portrays what is under his mask and the "monster" self-image. Whether it is the tumor, the treatment, or both, that have converted him is unknown. His anger and wish to strike out are contained in the phrase, "No you are died to." The old Roderick is dead and replaced by a monster. Several months later he made the last drawing (fig. 21.21). Here Roderick sees quite a different image. Is this a projected wish or does it reflect a change in his view and/or fears about himself? I believe that it represents the latter. Roderick had also changed in his interaction with the therapists and with peers. He was friendly, not depressed, and relating well to all around him. He worked on his drawing calmly, slowly, with a general improvement in the way he talked about home and school.

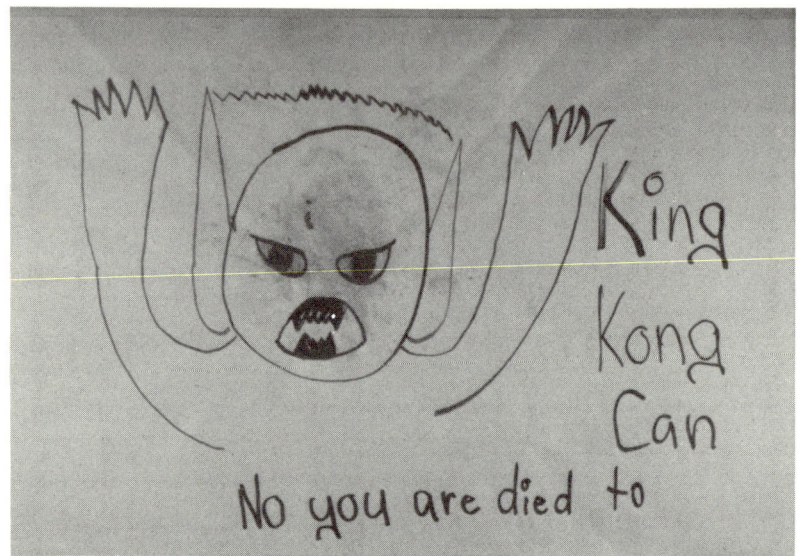

Figure 21.20

Figure 21.21

Figure 21.22

The final three drawings (figs. 21.22–24) were made by Steve, a 4-year-old Caucasian boy admitted to the hospital with enlarged lymph nodes in his neck. Following biopsy and blood studies, he was found to have leukemia. Chemotherapy was begun. The first drawing was made during the first few days of his hospitalization and reflects his projected self-image and anxiety-laden area, that is, his face with "lumps." The next drawing was made several days later following biopsy. He had begun to wet the bed. He suffered severe separation anxiety from his mother, who spent her nights in the guest house. On the days when the group met she came to the ward following the group. The last drawing depicts two people. Most likely this is Steve and his mother leaving the hospital together.

Discussion

The focus of attention on the possibility of serious illness in a family member or on one's own vulnerability mobilizes high levels of anxiety and defenses against anxiety. When the possibility

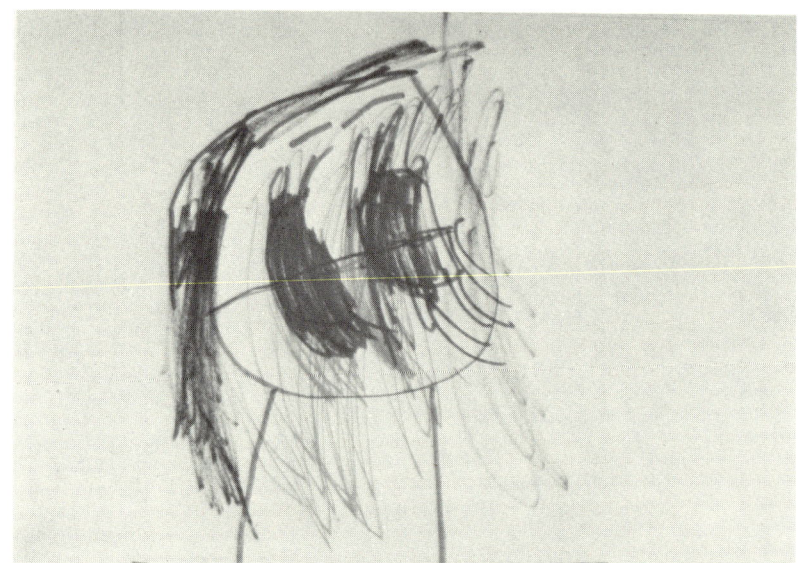

Figure 21.23

Figure 21.24

includes loss of body parts, loss of functions, or death, the intensity of anxiety is greatly increased. Interest in children's reactions to various experiences of loss has been explored by several authors (Bowlby et al. 1952, Jessner et al. 1952, Wolfenstein 1966, Grollman 1967, Furman 1974). Much discussion centers around the child's developmental capabilities in the grief and mourning process. Furman (1974) vividly supports the process of mourning in a child as young as three years of age with the cognitive abilities to understand death as a final loss; that is, the dead cannot return to life. This ability is contingent upon the active support and involvement of a parent who has helped the child to appreciate the death concept in emotionally distant or neutral (uncathected) objects. With these experiences, the young child can understand the irreversibility of a more highly emotionally cathected loss such as of a body part or a parent. Furman defines mourning as an intrapsychic process and grief as the affect produced by mourning.

Wolfenstein (1966) disagrees with the concept that children "mourn" because she proposes that mourning cannot successfully take place until after the work of adolescence.

The work of the children presented in this paper demonstrates the complex intrapsychic processes accompanying loss of an important body part. The interpretation of the illness as punishment is seen in Patient A. Intense castration and separation anxiety are evoked and a new internal body image must be evolved. Before this can take place, the mourning for the lost body part with expression of grief takes place. This mourning process involves a hypercathexis of the lost part and/or function with a gradual decathexis. Once this process has occurred, the realistic potentials and limitations of the "new" body can be internalized.

In order to work through this process in a healthy, adaptive fashion, much support and guidance for the child and parents are necessary. Grollman (1967) stresses the frequent mistakes made when children are assumed to be too young to assimilate information about issues related to death. Children then develop fantasies that are related to their understanding of how the world about them functions. Adequate information (by adequate is meant phase-specific) needs to be provided and time spent listening to the child's processing of this information. Most frequently, on a pediatric ward, children are not given information in such a way as to foster understanding and adaptation. The inconsistencies thus encountered are remarkable. For example, often the child is present when a group of physicians are discussing his illness. This approach is usually related to the idea that the child can understand nothing of what is being discussed. Another aspect of this is that charts and x-rays are frequently left available to the child.

In addition, the death of a child on the ward is frequently not discussed with the other children on the ward, because of attempts to "protect" them from "trauma." The children on the ward are left without support in coping. Waechter (1971), in a study of 16 children aged 6 to 10 years with a fatal illness, found that two had been told their diagnosis and "prognosis," but 63 percent of the group told stories with death as a central theme. Waechter concluded: ". . . knowledge is communicated to the child by the change in affect which he encounters . . . and by his perceptiveness of other non-verbal clues. It also implies a deepening of isolation when the child becomes aware of the evasiveness which meets expression of his concern." The group therapy experience, using art as an activity upon which to structure and focus attention, provides a medium for allowing the child to work through what he is experiencing and gives the therapist an understanding of just where the child is focusing with anxiety and concern. There is an opportunity for rapport with an accepting adult, and the group experience fosters peer interaction and is an added dimension to understanding the child. In this group, children discussed their illness and procedures and shared an understanding with each other. All the children with cancer had received the same diagnostic evaluation, such as bone marrow biopsy, numerous x-rays, and intravenous procedures. They helped each other understand when information was incomplete or distorted. However, sometimes no one in the group had sufficiently accurate information, and a group-projected fear would be shared. It is here that intervention of the therapist is needed.

Silberer (1951) discussed the unique ways in which symbols express phenomena beyond mental capacities. The use of art for the activity group provides a medium for the symbolic expression of affects, conflicts, and perceptions of inner awareness that are beyond developmental cognitive abilities of the child to understand and express verbally. These children demonstrate in the drawings strong adaptive capacities to the experience of loss of major body parts and function while experiencing painful procedures such as multiple bone marrow studies and intravenous chemotherapy.

The reactions of the therapist to these children were extremely intense. This was manifested in constant conflict between nursing staff and therapist. The co-therapist engaged in frequent hostile, angry exchanges. It would appear that these children create intense feelings of helplessness, rage, and guilt that are defended against by mechanisms such as projection, displacement, denial, intellectualization, and withdrawal. The use of the therapy facilitated much interaction with the staff of the pediatric ward serving as a bridge from psychiatry to the medical care team.

The drawings are a permanent record that can be presented and discussed, and thus conviction can be gained about the need for more direct support for these children.

REFERENCES

Bowlby, J., J. Robertson, and D. Rosenbluth. 1952. "A Two-Year-Old Goes to Hospital." *The Psychoanalytic Study of the Child,* Vol. 7. New York: International Universities Press, pp. 82–94.

Freud, A. 1952. "The Role of Bodily Illness in the Mental Life of Children." *The Psychoanalytic Study of the Child,* Vol. 7. New York: International Universities Press, pp. 69–81.

Furman, E. 1974. *A Child's Parent Dies.* New Haven and London: Yale University Press, p. 34.

Grollman, E. A. 1967. *Explaining Death to Children.* Boston: Beacon Press, pp. 3–27.

Jessner, L., G. E. Blom, and S. Waldfogel. 1952. "Emotional Implications of Tonsillectomy and Adenoidectomy on Children." *The Psychoanalytic Study of the Child,* Vol. 7. New York: International Universities Press, pp. 126–69.

Levy, D. 1945. "Psychic Trauma of Operations in Children." *American Journal of Diseases of Children,* 69:7–25.

Prugh, D., E. M. Staub, H. H. Sands, R. M. Kirschbaum, and E. A. Lenihan.

1953. "A Study of the Emotional Reactions of Children and Families to Hospitalization and Illness." *American Journal of Orthopsychiatry*, 23:70–106.

Silberer, H. 1951. "On Symbol-Formation." In D. Rapaport, ed. *Organization and Pathology of Thought*, pp. 208–233. New York: Columbia University Press.

Stocking, M., W. Rothney, G. Grosser, and R. Goodwin. 1972. "Psychopathology in the Pediatric Hospital—Implications for Community Health." *American Journal of Public Health* (April), pp. 331–444.

Waechter, E. 1971. "Children's Awareness of Fatal Illness." *American Journal of Nursing* (June), pp. 1168–72.

Wolfenstein, M. 1966. "How Is Mourning Possible?" *The Psychoanalytic Study of the Child*, Vol. 21. New York: International Universities Press, pp. 93–123.

· 22 ·
The Child Life Worker's Contribution Within an Oncology Setting

Carolyn A. Larsen

In 1976, a child life worker was added to the team in our hematology oncology clinic, which as of 1979 served approximately 150 children with leukemia or tumors requiring chemotherapy or radiation treatment. The outcome, observable particularly in the transformed social environment of the waiting room, has been dramatic in a positive sense. Further, the fact that the child life worker providing this program in the clinic is the one who works primarily on the ward to which the majority of these children would be admitted when necessary has markedly enhanced the quality of support available to the children and their families.

Anxiety and the Waiting Room

The heavy emotional burden imposed on families of a child with a terminal illness is not difficult to appreciate. What was less evident to some of us until quite recently is the role that the repeated clinic visits play in bringing the many painful feelings to the fore, serving as regular reminders of the seriousness of the illness and of the necessity for the child to incorporate into his everyday life submission to painful procedures. Hoffman and Futterman (1971) advanced an argument for the therapeutic use of the outpatient waiting time, regarding it as an ideal opportunity for assessing, as well as fostering, the family's ability to cope. Spinetta and Maloney (1975) documented and discussed the higher and increasing level of anxiety evident in children and youths attending oncology clinics, in comparison with that experienced by those attending clinics for treatment of other serious chronic conditions that are not fatal.

A 15-year-old girl who has been treated through our hematology clinic for several years described to us some of the impact that the regular clinic visits had had on her as a young child. She vividly remembers regularly being sick to her stomach and vomiting while walking up the hill toward the hospital with her mother on the way to her clinic appointments. She also recalled how angry she felt at the doctors, rejecting sullenly any attempts on their part to be friendly with her following treatment. This same girl now usually remains for the duration of the morning, long after the completion of her own monthly checkup, to play with the younger children and help the worker put everything away when the clinic is finished. Although the resolution of her earlier fears and the growth of positive feelings toward the medical staff were evident before the new program was established, the program still seemed to provide an important resource for her. She readily identified its potential positive effect on the feelings and reactions of younger children.

A Résumé of the Child Life Oncology Clinic Program and Its Outcomes

The child life service was extended to the clinic in an effort to relieve some of the anxieties activated by these visits and at the same time to create a milieu in which children, families, and staff members could communicate with greater ease. The younger children have the opportunity to relax and feel more in control through involvement in play, and the families' abilities to cope with the various difficult challenges could be fostered. Moreover, the quality of the child support would be enhanced through knowing the children and families better as people and being more exposed to their ways and needs.

The program has had a particularly obvious impact on the social atmosphere of the clinic, particularly within the enclosed waiting room, which adjoins the examination and treatment area. The "before" scene had been described by permanent members of the staff as a tense, ominously quiet atmosphere. The children for the most part remained passively close by the parents' sides waiting for their names to be called and hearing the cries of other children already called to the treatment area. Staff members said that they experienced this waiting room environment as a psychologically uncomfortable space to enter. The "after" is a relaxed atmosphere in which the majority of children, patients and siblings alike, readily involve themselves in a play activity and in renewing contact with the child life worker.

In the hallway approaching the clinic entrance one young boy, about 3 years of age, could be seen to be "dragging his heels," frowning while clutching his recently pricked finger. His mother was urging him on saying "Come. I smell coffee, Jan must be there!" Part of the change included the setting up of a beverage cart with coffee, juices, and milk. Parents can be seen chatting over a cup of coffee with fellow parents, the child life worker, or other members of the team. They may join their own or another child at the play activity table. Or they may take advantage of the opportunity to escape somewhere briefly, to cope in private with overwhelming feelings. Our experience of such a marked change in the waiting room atmosphere seemed to parallel that reported by Hoffman and Futterman (1971), the room coming alive with activity, each person free to be involved or not.

It is mostly the preschool and school-age children who become readily involved in both play activities and social contact. The adolescents may or may not be directly involved, but they seem to benefit vicariously, having something to watch and feeling more at ease in the livelier atmosphere. Posters, the children's creations, displayed liberally, contribute to the impression of a more personal, humane, and informative environment.

Important needs of the child, youth, or family often become known to the child life worker in this setting. Over several visits, one mother expressed increasingly the tensions caused by the lack of open discussion with her teenage son about the nature of his illness. Another family appeared to be expecting too much of their two healthy teenagers while seeming to have unlimited tolerance of the young afflicted child. These and similar observations about family life and child-rearing issues, shared with the other team members, can help all concerned to make their attention and interventions more personally supportive.

Child Life—a Brief Description

For those who might not yet be acquainted with the child life discipline, a brief description is in order. This specialty, not yet a full-fledged profession, has mushroomed particularly during the past two decades as knowledge of child development and awareness of the impact on the child of hospital- and illness-related experiences have become more widespread. Associated most readily with play programs within hospital wards, child life staff members are increasingly sought for their ability to help the child achieve greater emotional stability and/or developmental progress, at times in the face of formidable barriers. Through the skilled use of activities, normalization of the milieu, and sharing directly with the child many of his or her hospital experiences, the child life worker, equipped increasingly with a strong background in child development, can also make a significant contribution to the team's assessment of behavior and functioning. It must also be admitted that at times their services are sought more for the goal of maintaining order and of keeping the children happily, safely, and constructively occupied. At any rate the workers usually assume a Pied Piper quality, having a following of children once they arrive on the ward.

Timmy, not yet three, newly diagnosed with leukemia and isolated in a single room for initial treatment, illustrates well the trusting attachment frequently formed. On the occasions when it was necessary for his mother to leave his bedside an immediate call would go out for Jan, the child life worker. A favorite play activity during these times was to reenact a happy family experience such as a picnic, using a play house with little family figures.

The main features of the child life worker's role include the skillful provision of pleasurable activities through which a variety of needs can be recognized or met, a regular supportive contact fostering security, and assistance in the psychological mastery of difficult experiences.

Although the service is available in some way to all the children of a given clinical area, there are always a few children with whom a close helping relationship is particularly instrumental to their well-being. In such instances the child life worker may become the most significant source of emotional support to the child. In other instances he or she may provide additional support for a child whose primary nurse or other person assumes this role.

The nature of the work with the children also favors close ties with the parents, the latter often feeling free to express their concerns in the relaxed atmosphere of the playroom to the person with whom their child relates so comfortably.

As in most large pediatric hospitals, our child life service has a long history of involvement in the inpatient care of children with terminal illnesses. During the initial admission when leukemia is first diagnosed, a positive relationship has frequently been established. The value of this early meaningful contact was always apparent when the same child required hospital care later on. However, like the ward nursing staff, we did lose track of the child and family who were treated largely on an outpatient basis and, as a result, were unaware of the child's development and of the effects of the illness or the continuing treatment in the months or possibly years between admissions. The young child might not, in fact, on readmission, be able to remember those whom he had come to trust previously.

Development of the Outpatient Clinic Services

Our services to the outpatient areas of the hospital at large had been requested for several years to help make the waiting time a more tolerable, constructive experience for children and parents and the environment more tolerable for staff. However, there seemed to be no comparison between the needs in this area and those presented by hospitalized children, faced with the stresses and deprivations related to separation, shock, immobilization, pain, and disfigurement. Not yet staffed adequately to meet the hospitalized children's needs, a developed outpatient service seemed years away. However, during the summer of 1975 money became available specifically for a temporary project of serving the children in the outpatient area.

Our goal was to offer support to those children and families likely to be experiencing the most stress. Help from the nursing staff in particular soon pinpointed the hematology clinic as one of the prime areas. The two workers, both new college graduates with student experience in the department, began to provide play activities and emotional support for children and parents within the waiting area. Some children with whom a meaningful rapport had been established during the play activity were accompanied to the treatment area for continued support during a dreaded procedure such as a lumbar puncture. This seemed to foster increased teamwork with the medical staff.

As the project neared an end, the nurse coordinator of the clinic requested that the service become a permanent one, stating that a great need had been filled. She noted that the workers' knowledge of children's needs and reactions to hospital procedures, coupled with their ability to use play activities to help children express their anxieties and concerns, had provided an essential outlet for the children to express their anxieties and frustrations related to medical treatment. She felt that the children were much less anxious when seen by the doctors. She referred to the frequent expression of relief by parents that their children now had something pleasant to look forward to when coming to clinic. She added that the additional knowledge and understanding of the child and family gained by the worker and shared with other team members enabled her to give better nursing care.

However, despite this and an equally supportive statement by the physician director of the service at the time, who felt that the program had enhanced parent-doctor relationships, the hospital administration could not see a way of increasing the department's staff budget to permit continuation of the program.

The service thus ceased, and we became engrossed in the constant and challenging needs presented by other children in the hospital. Whereas, without the continuing contact with these children and their families, we could partially forget about them, those continuing to work in the clinic could not and were unwilling to accept a return to the former status quo.

Over the next several months the nurse in charge of the clinic, supported by the nursing administrator in the outpatient service, made frequent representations to the child life service urging us to find a way to staff the clinic. Although no solution appeared immediately, our commitment to finding one was strengthened. Within the child life service we began to explore how we could possibly extend coverage to this area two full mornings per week without increasing the overall number of staff. Although sympathetic, there were doubts on the part of some of the inpatient child life staff about this area's relative priority, the children being visualized as accompanied by a parent and remaining a relatively short time before returning to the security of home and normal life routines. However it was agreed to reallocate, on a trial basis, a half-time worker's position to the medical ward for children from 3 through 11 years and thus free this ward's regular full-time worker to attend the clinic two mornings each week without jeopardizing the needs of the ward children.

The Link Between Clinic and Ward

The service that thus took shape was not simply the addition of a regular child life worker to this clinic's team. Rather, we reorganized in such a way that the particular child life worker on the inpatient unit serving most of these children was the worker who saw them during their regular clinic visits. We were very soon made aware of the dramatic increase in the measure of security this afforded children and families. Just as they seemed relieved to discover this familiar person in the clinic on their first visit following the initial diagnostic and treatment session in hospital, likewise admissions during crisis periods seemed to be more palatable for children and families cared for primarily on an outpatient basis.

During the last few days of eight-year-old Allison's life, which were spent in the intensive care unit in protective isolation, much pleasure was derived from a cookie-baking session with her long familiar child life worker from the ward and clinic alike. The knowledge that their daughter had been able to have this kind of an experience, and the souvenir photographs of it, were deeply appreciated by the parents.

Two-and-a-half-year-old Sandra, whose diagnosis of leukemia was confirmed half a year previously, was readmitted for 24 hours of treatment. Although this was her first experience with the ward, she moved with ease into the playroom, spending a great part of her day there. She already knew the child life worker through her clinic visits and knew what she could expect of her. Her admission behavior contrasted considerably with that of most two-and-a-half-year-olds, who are usually visibly overwhelmed in this situation and who need time to size up the safety of the new milieu.

Continuity of care is also supported through the worker's efforts to keep the ward nursing staff informed about patients and families the nurses have come to know on the ward. Foley and McCarthy (1976) described how ward nurses can increase care continuity by regular visits to the clinic.

Assessing the Program

There was agreement that if a permanent program were to be started, the "before" and "after" differences should be documented. Thus, together with the two nursing representatives we sought the advice of two experienced researchers in the hospital, one a pediatrician, the other a psychologist.

We thought that it would be helpful both to document general humanitarian differences that might occur and to measure specific outcomes, for example, possible changes in the child's ability to accept and cooperate with treatments, or in the parents' ability to support the child, or in parents' relationships with the medical staff. The use of videotaping to study the children's play behavior or other behaviors defined later could not be reconciled with the need for a comfortable environment. We wrote to Hoffman and Futterman in the hope of being able to take advantage of the simple scoring system they reported they were developing but were disappointed to learn that they had not been able to complete this tool.

Finally, as is often the case, the mechanics of carrying out a study of scientific merit began to look increasingly complex, and the delay in providing a service already recognized as helpful to families became more intolerable. We thus decided to begin the program without the benefits of measuring specific outcomes, except in our respective subjective ways.

From the early months of the program's inception, the worker involved, others in the child life service, and I have never questioned the validity of our own realigned priorities. We had progressed from being relatively oblivious to the needs of families in this setting, and of our own potential contribution, to seeing the service as one of high priority.

After one year of its existence the worker drew up a brief questionnaire seeking an assessment of the role of the child life worker in the clinic by the medical and nursing members of the team. With the exception of one new member to the team who stated "I am somewhat uninformed," the other five respondents perceived the role as providing a valuable component of the overall care. Specific descriptive phrases included were: "decreases tension and anxieties before the children are seen by the doctors," "opportunity for families to expose and cope with the turmoil within," "the 'life-line' between the parents, children and the other clinic staff," "helps bridge the communication gap in the parent-doctor relationships," and "very supportive following treatments or procedures."

The messages from the children and their families seem very clear. A nine-year-old girl was recently observed insisting on continuing to play for a complete hour after the medical aspect of their visit was over. She continued to play after putting her coat on while her mother good-naturedly commented on how hard it was to drag her away, comparing this new behavior to that of a few years earlier when her daughter couldn't leave quickly enough following the medical attention.

REFERENCES

Foley, G. V. and A. M. McCarthy. 1976. "The Child With Leukemia in a Special Hematology Clinic." *American Journal of Nursing* 76:1115 (July).
Hoffman, I. and E. H. Futterman. 1971. "Coping With Waiting: Psychiatric Intervention and Study in the Waiting Room of a Pediatric Oncology Clinic." *Comprehensive Psychiatry* 12:67.
Spinetta, J. J. and L. J. Maloney. 1975. "Death Anxiety in the Outpatient Leukemia Child." *Pediatrics* 56:1034 (December).

· 23 ·

The Child with Cancer Returns to School: Preparing the Teacher

PATRICIA DESY-SPINETTA AND
JOHN J. SPINETTA

Children are living with cancer. As recent medical advances have increased the long-term survivor rate, the child and family must learn to live with the disease for much longer periods. During this time, the child with cancer continues to grow and develop in most aspects of life just like any other child. Thus, the environment surrounding the child must allow normal development under abnormal circumstances (van Eys 1977).

A major part of normal growth and development for all children, including the sick child, involves school. For a child with cancer a return to school represents a continuation of life, hope for the future, socialization with peers, and an attempt to reestablish equilibrium—an equilibrium that does not deny the fact of the cancer but encompasses a new reality base.

Most pediatric hematology-oncology teams make great efforts to maintain good communication among the physician, nurse, social service personnel, parents, and the child. Research has demonstrated that the child, even the young child, with a diagnosis of cancer is concerned about the illness. Even though this concern may not always take the form of overt expressions about impending death, the more subtle fears and anxieties are nonetheless real, painful, and very much related to the seriousness of the illness that the child is experiencing (Spinetta 1974). Older children and adolescents are typically very aware of their illness and its consequences (Vernick and Karon 1965). Further research has also shown that even younger children with cancer, as young as six, were found to resolve the issues surrounding their diagnosis, treatment, and prognosis more effectively when allowed to speak openly about the cancer (Spinetta 1978). Children with cancer return to school with these awarenesses and their accompanying concerns. School personnel play a crucial role in determining whether or not the child with cancer can live a normal life, since so much of the child's day is centered around school. Teachers, counselors, school nurses, and administrators must be prepared to deal with this added responsibility.

A return to school for a child with cancer involves personal interaction with typically one teacher at the elementary school level, five or more at the secondary level, and school nurse, counselor, administrator, in addition to peers. Each person brings to the understanding of the child with cancer her own philosophy of life, attitude toward death, and understanding of cancer (Spinetta 1979a). Furthermore, each school and each district often has a distinctively identifiable attitude toward working with any child with a medical problem in the regular classroom. It is, therefore, imperative to prepare significant school personnel for the reentry of the patient-student.

So, since diagnosis, the child with cancer has received the best possible medical care from his physicians, and love and concern from his family. When he is considered medically ready to return to school, it is important to prepare the school environment to receive and nurture that child. Not to prepare the school adequately, the environment in which he spends an average of five to six hours per day, is to jeopardize the child's attempt to cope with his school life within the context of his diagnosis (Spinetta 1979b).

Teacher Preparation

Philosophy of Death

While individuals associated with the medical aspects of cancer realize that children with cancer are living longer, professionals outside this environment frequently equate cancer with death. Because this equation of cancer with death is not always accurate, this attitude must be addressed if teachers are to be adequately prepared. Just as each member of the medical staff has his own philosophical position on death, so too does each member of the school staff. Each individual teacher's manner of facing death, manner of placing meaning to the mystery of death, may be long-standing within the traditions of past generations, or of a brief standing within the context of a new found cosmology, or even lacking altogether for want of ever having had the need or courage to face the issue previously (Toynbee 1976). A specific teacher's philosophy of death may differ from that of colleagues and from that of the parents of the child with cancer. Nonetheless, the presence of a possibly life-threatened child in the classroom causes reflection and concern among the school staff. For some, this can be a personally unsettling experience.

Not only do individuals have a personal philosophy of death, they also have an emotional position. How people feel about death is as important as how they think about it. Teachers themselves have all had different experiences with death, and all have different means of coping with their grief. It is important to assist teachers to become aware of both their general and their specific attitudes and emotional responses toward the concept of death.

Children's Understanding of Death

Children's ages, experiences, and levels of development influence their understanding of death. Many books and articles speak to this issue (for example, Easson 1970, Grollman 1967, Hostler 1978, Jackson 1965, Spinetta et al. 1976). To place the topic in proper perspective, we address the issue from the age of six onwards.

Concepts of death are age related in children and differ with intellectual ability and development (Spinetta et al. 1976). From approximately the age of six onward, the child seems gradually to be accommodating herself to the proposition that death is final, inevitable, universal, and personal. Many six- and seven-year-old children suspect that their parents will die some day and that they too may die but only in the very distant future. Children in these early school years show a strong tendency to personify death. As children approach preadolescence, they are equipped with the intellectual tools necessary to understand time, space, life, and death in a logical manner. At about the age of ten or eleven the fact of the universality and the permanence of death becomes understandable.

Studies of six- to ten-year-old leukemic children reveal that, despite efforts by parents and medical personnel to keep the child from becoming aware of the prognosis, he somehow picks up a sense that the illness is no ordinary illness. The fear of abandonment and separation, characteristic of the younger child, has added to it a fear of bodily harm and injury and possible awareness of his own impending death or, at the very least the awareness, at a level preceding his ability to conceptualize it, that something very serious is happening. The awareness of one's own impending death becomes stronger as the child nears death (Bluebond-Langner 1974, 1977; Spinetta, Rigler and Karon 1973, 1974).

Family Coping

While it is an important prerequisite for teachers to come to terms with their own philosophy and emotional stance on death, as well as to gain an appreciation of the child's understanding of death at different ages, it is also necessary to realize that each family has its own manner of dealing with crises. Individuals have different levels of stress tolerance, different levels of ability to deal with stress, and different histories of success and failure in overcoming stress (Selye 1974, 1976). The very diagnosis of cancer itself can shift the family's central survival skills to a newer mode (Spinetta 1979b). The teacher then is working not only with a child but also with a family in crisis.

When communicating with teachers, it is important to help them realize that children, all children—and especially the children with cancer—are very sensitive to nonverbal cues in their environment. The child will sense at a nonverbal level if a teacher is uneasy about his presence in the classroom; he can also sense a warm, caring, supportive attitude.

Importance of Hope

The emphasis to this point has been to help the teacher come to terms with his philosophy and emotional stance on death, understand children's developmental understanding of death and children's affinity for process over content, and appreciate differing family coping strategies. It is equally important to convince the school personnel that even a child with a serious illness continues to achieve and develop and may have years of valuable life ahead. Hope is essential in dealing with these students. Unlike denial, hope does not interfere with healthy adjustment and is entirely compatible with an acceptance of reality. Hope is a sustaining human quality, and the important role it plays in all meaningful behavior is not to be underestimated. It provides strength in maintaining the will to live. To give up hope is to give way to despair and sorrow (Spinetta et al. 1982).

As one mother wrote, "preparing a . . . (life-threatened) child for the future by sending him to school, giving music lessons, asking him what he wants from life, is making him like the (normal) kids, which is what he wants most of all. And if research continues, who knows—he may very well have that fanciful future" (Schweers 1976).

Psychological Euthanasia

As van Eys (1977) states, when caregivers do not expect cure, they hamper development. Some may expect the child to die and therefore do not do what is demanded to help the child develop. This attitude, which van Eys labels, "psychological euthanasia," may serve to protect caregivers but is devastating to the child in the classroom. It is imperative then that teachers be helped to see the child with cancer as a living, growing, developing child valiantly trying to learn in spite of a difficult situation.

School Problems

Every effort is being made through the school liaison program, discussed in detail later, to educate school personnel at all levels and resolve those difficulties that can be handled on a policy level. However, there are some issues that cannot be avoided, owing to the child's hospitalization and absences for illness or clinic and the like. How these specific problems are handled directly reflects teacher attitude.

We have found that most children with cancer have difficulties in school for a variety of reasons. Some children, for example, have reading problems. Teachers who see the child as living with a future refer for appropriate diagnostic evaluation and remediation. Teachers who see the child as dying do not refer, and the child goes from grade to grade carrying the burden, not only of illness, but also of a worsening reading difficulty. Attendance may be a problem because of clinic visits and occasional hospitalizations. Many teachers are very cooperative and flexible and allow the child to make up work. Others, especially at the secondary level, do not. The adolescent's need for privacy, coupled with a teacher's need for an absence excuse, can often conflict, especially when an adequate communication system is not present in the school to inform all teachers not only of the fact of the illness but also of the consequences, as it applies to school work.

A well-prepared teacher is a valuable link in the total care of the child. Prepared to deal with the family in crisis, as well as the child, teachers are in a position to communicate with parents in a way health care professionals might not be. For example, many children with cancer were diagnosed as toddlers and preschoolers. Entering into school is a significant step, not only for these children but also for their parents. If the child is successful, the parents feel rewarded in their efforts to promote normal growth and development in spite of the illness. If the child has problems, parents too frequently link these problems to the cancer and blame the cancer for noncancer-related difficulties. A well-prepared teacher will point out to these parents that many children, and not only a child with cancer, have difficulties at the beginning. This support of the parents at a critical transition time by a competent teacher helps the child. In addition, teachers can help parents recognize developmental problems for what they are. The transition from elementary to junior high school is stressful for all students, not merely for the student with cancer.

School is particularly significant for the adolescent cancer patient. The diagnosis of the disease and its treatment can prevent or impede successful development of autonomy, acquisition of consistent body image and sex roles, establishment of peer relations, and the adoption of future-orientated social and intellectual preparation (Kellerman and Katz 1977).

It is important then to allow the adolescent to maximize her own sense of control. School is one area where the adolescent cancer patient can exercise such control. It is essential that all the school personnel with whom the teenager interacts—teachers, counselors, administrators, school nurse—understand not only the fact of the illness but also its school-related consequences as they apply specifically to the adolescent.

In brief, school is an important part of the life of the child with cancer. A well-prepared teacher, one who is attempting to come to terms with her own philosophy of life; who understands the medical facts specific to her student; who sees the child as living, growing, and developing toward a real future; and who understands the dynamics of the child's family, is in an excellent position to make school a positive, happy place for the child.

School Liaison Program

A model school liaison program was designed in San Diego, California, to work with the pediatric hematology-oncology teams at two hospitals to meet the needs of the child with cancer in the school. The program has four phases: school reentry, school referral, teacher preparation, and research. Each section is discussed below. In each of these areas, especially phase 1, school reentry, and phase 2, school referral, the school liaison works in conjunction with parents and patient, especially the adolescents who are encouraged to make primary school contact. The school liaison serves as a backup, working with, not instead of, parents.

There can, however, be barriers to effective parental communication with the school: emotional involvement with the illness, language, economic and educational differences, and incomplete understanding of the illness and its ramifications. Teachers also feel they need someone outside the family with whom they can communicate. In all phases the school liaison works closely with the physicians, hematology nurses, and social workers assigned to the case.

School Reentry

The specific objective of this phase is to work with the child, parent, and physician to contact the school, transmit accurate and specific medical information, offer support and assistance, and establish rapport. Each case is unique.

For example, some children are medically able to return to school but have lost their hair because of certain medications. The school liaison informs the teacher and suggests that, if the parents are willing, someone explain to the class the fact of the hair loss and the general reasons for it. Many times the parents and child are so well prepared by the physician and nurses that they themselves explain. In such instances, the classmates become a source of support for the child. In this way the physician and school work together to support the child and family in a sensitive transition period.

The adolescent's return to school is handled in a slightly different manner. It is the objective of the program to help adolescents assume as much control as possible, furnish them with necessary information, and act as a backup. The initial reentry then sets the stage for all subsequent interactions among the hospital, home, and school.

When an active-preventive approach to initial reentry is taken, such as the one suggested here, all significant school personnel are made aware of necessary circumstances. They act as a support not only to the patient and family but also to one another. In addition, through the school liaison they have easy access to the hospital, and especially the physician, if they should need it. If a problem does arise, previous communication systems already established facilitate its quick and appropriate resolution.

School Referral

In addition to the school reentry program for the newly diagnosed patients, the school referral phase handles the problems as they arise for those patients in the clinic population previously diagnosed, as well as additional problems following reentry for the newly diagnosed. The main concern for the school liaison is to identify the problems and try to find a solution that will prove the most effective for the child, family, school, and physician. To find a workable solution frequently requires a thorough understanding of the school system at all levels, the dynamics of the particular family, and the medical status of the child. Physicians and the members of the hematology-oncology team are kept current on the status of the referral.

Teacher Education

In addition to contacts with individual teachers through the reentry and referral phases of the program, education of school personnel takes place on a more formal and global basis. It was originally planned to sponsor seminars at the hospital; however, because of an effective school referral program, individual school districts and school nurse groups have requested in-service programs themselves. These programs are designed to attract as broad a group of educated professionals as possible, in order to create a general atmosphere of understanding and acceptance of the child with cancer. A psychologist, pediatric hematologist-oncologist, and school liaison participate. These seminars are excellent vehicles for disseminating accurate medical and psychosocial information, assisting teachers and nurses to consider their own values and attitudes, and promoting communication between the medical and education worlds.

The quality of referral that comes from a teacher who has participated in such conferences differs from that of nonparticipants. They refer quickly when a problem arises, are confident in their own recommendations, and know they will receive the information and support they need from the physician.

Research

A final, but central, aspect of the model school liaison program is research. After the permission and cooperation of more than twenty school districts and the parents involved have been obtained, questionnaires are sent on a yearly basis to the teachers of all the students-patients in the study protocol, to assess both teacher attitude and patient behavior. The results of the questionnaires demonstrated that the children with cancer were seen by teachers as having had significantly greater school problems, as a group, than the controls did (Spinetta 1979b; Desy-Spinetta and Spinetta 1980, Desy-Spinetta 1981).

Conclusion

Children with cancer are living longer and attending school in the regular classroom. It is necessary then to prepare school personnel at all levels to assume an active role in the total care of the child. This preparation goes far beyond the mere transmission of pertinent medical facts. It involves helping teachers, counselors, administrators, and school nurses to come to terms with their own philosophy of life and death, to understand the psychosocial implication of the illness for the child, and to appreciate the stress of the parents. It is essential to convince educators that the child with cancer is a living, growing person with a future. School personnel need to know that the members of the health care team are there to support them and are available to work through any difficulties the teacher, student, or parent may be experiencing.

Since children with cancer are living longer and seeking a normal life by attending school, the school liaison becomes, not a luxury, but a vital and essential member of the health care team. Thoroughly familiar with both hospital and school, the school liaison orchestrates communication between both institutions, translates the idiosyncratic vocabulary of each, works through an appropriate educational program for a sick child, and handles referrals.

Everyone involved benefits from having a school liaison as a member of the team. The child is happy in school; teachers are comfortable in their role; the parents are content that the child is safe, productive, and functioning just like any other child his age; and the physician gets a complete picture of the child.

Teachers and other school personnel play a significant role in the life of the child with cancer. Given adequate preparation, information, and support, they are a valuable link in the total care of the child.

REFERENCES

Bluebond-Langner, M. 1974. "I Know, Do You?: Awareness and Communication in Terminally Ill Children." In B. Schoenberg, A. Carr, D. Peretz, and A. Kutscher, eds. *Anticipatory Grief.* New York: Columbia University Press.

Bluebond-Langner, M. 1977. "Meanings of Death to Children." In H. Feifel, ed. *New Meanings of Death.* New York: McGraw-Hill.

Easson, W. M. 1970. *The Dying Child: The Management of the Child or Adolescent Who Is Dying.* Springfield, Ill.: Charles C Thomas.

Grollman, E. A., ed. 1967. *Explaining Death to Children.* Boston: Beacon Press.

Hostler, S. L. 1978. "The Development of the Child's Concept of Death." In O. J. Z. Sahler, ed. *The Child and Death.* St. Louis: C. V. Mosby.

Jackson, E. N. 1965. *Telling a Child About Death.* New York: Hawthorn Books.

Kellerman, J., E. R. Katz. 1977. "The Adolescent with Cancer: Theoretical, Clinical, and Research Issues." *Journal of Pediatric Psychology* 2(3):127.

Schweers, E. 1976. "Questions Without Answers: A Look at the Human Side of Leukemia Management." Paper presented at Leukemia Society Symposium, Rhode Island Hospital (January).

Selye, H. 1974. *Stress Without Distress.* Philadelphia: Lippincott.

Selye, H. 1976. *The Stress of Life.* Rev. Ed. New York: McGraw-Hill.

Spinetta, J. J. 1974. "The Dying Child's Awareness of Death: A Review." *Psychology Bulletin* 81:256.

Spinetta, J. J. 1978. "Communication Patterns in Families Dealing with Life-threatening Illness." In O.J. Sahler, ed., *The Child and Death.* St. Louis: C. V. Mosby.

Spinetta, J. J. 1979a. "Disease-related Communication: How to Tell." In J. Kellerman, ed. *Psychological Aspects of Childhood Cancer.* Springfield, Ill.: Charles C Thomas.

Spinetta, J. J. 1979b. "Coping with Childhood Cancer: Professional and Family Communication Patterns." In M. Eisenberg, ed. *Communication in the Health Care Setting.* Springfield, Ill.: Charles C Thomas.

Spinetta, J. J., D. Rigler, and M. Karon. 1973. "Anxiety in the Dying Child." *Pediatrics* 52:841.

Spinetta, J. J., D. Rigler, and M. Karon. 1974. "Personal Space as a Measure of the Dying Child's Sense of Isolation." *Journal of Consulting Clinical Psychology* 42:751.

Spinetta, J. J., P. D. Spinetta, F. Kung, and D. B. Schwartz. 1982. *Emotional Aspects of Childhood Leukemia: A Handbook for Parents.* New York: Leukemia Society of America.

Toynbee, A. 1976. "Various Ways in Which Human Beings Have Sought to Reconcile Themselves to the Fact of Death." In E. S. Shneidman, ed. *Death: Current Perspectives.* Palo Alto, Calif.: Mayfield.

van Eys, J. 1977. "What Do We Mean by 'the truly cured child?' " In J. van Eys, ed. *The Truly Cured Child: The New Challenge in Pediatric Cancer Care.* Baltimore: University Park Press.

Vernick, J. and M. Karon. 1965. "Who's Afraid of Death on a Leukemia Ward?" *American Journal of Diseases of Children* 109:103.

ADDITIONAL REFERENCES

Desy-Spinetta, P. and J. J. Spinetta. 1980. "The Child with Cancer in School: Teacher's Appraisal." *American Journal of Pediatric Hematology/Oncology* 2:89.

Desy-Spinetta, P. 1981. "The School and the Child with Cancer." In J. Spinetta and P. Desy-Spinetta, eds. *Living with Childhood Cancer.* St. Louis: Mosby.

Spinetta, J. J. and P. Desy-Spinetta, eds. 1981. *Living with Childhood Cancer.* St. Louis: Mosby.

· 24 ·

Feeding the Dying Child—Ethical Decision-Making in a New Guise

JAN VAN EYS

In a sense, the dying child has slipped away from the care of the parent. The need of the child for parental care is absolute for a prolonged time after birth. For a child to die before all means of care and all modes of protection are exhausted means that some line was drawn between ordinary and extraordinary care. That is often difficult enough to do when adults are critically ill. But for children all care is both ordinary and extraordinary alike, since all care must be given to them. Therefore there must be some process by which the line can be drawn for someone who is in our trust and who trusts us. Discussions around artificial life support have generated principles, but they have also allowed a too ready definition of extraordinary means. Extraordinary means are in many minds limited to the usual extreme modes of prolongation of vital signs. Feeding of children is a focus that touches far more on the dilemmas that the dying child's parenteral care can face than does extreme cardiopulmonary life support. Extreme medical measures can become options even within that basic parenteral care task. This paper examines the modes in which care roles are envisioned and the way such ethical dilemmas with children are approached by parents.

The child is in effect totally dependent on parents for care. If parents abandon their child, other adults must take over that role. Care takes many forms, from the support of the body to the development of the mind; but among these two, the physical care of the child is primary. There are discrete elements in that care; shelter, food, aid in self-help, and environmental protection are the basic components. These are for many years entirely beyond the control of the child. In primitive societies, shelter may be very simple and still be satisfactory. Food may be largely obtained by foraging. There is little self-help in hygiene and clothing demanded, and protection from other human beings is a tribal concern. Therefore, children may become self-sufficient at an early age. But no matter how primitive the society is, how small the demands for survival are, up to the age the child can reason as the adults do, the child has no chance of total independent existence.

In our Western society that age is far older. The complexity of our society is such that substantial knowledge is required before independent survival is possible. It is even discouraged below a certain age by agreement among adults. All parents accept that and, therefore, take on the elements of total care of their children. There are, of course, instances of poor parenting, but such extremes are no argument against the general. The enormity of the task of parenting cannot be accepted in factual quanta. Like all elements of our environment we assimilate the tasks as concepts. Care of the child is executed through the concepts of feeding, of shelter, of self-help development, and of protection. These concepts are completely accepted by parents for the well child. The content of the concept, the actual limits perceived, are variable from parent to parent. They are highly culturally determined, are different between socioeconomic classes, and are even often familial in pattern. But there is more similarity between concept content than there is difference. The sheltering, feeding, protecting, and helping of the child are all done in response to a perceived need. One feeds to keep the child from hunger, not because feeding per se is a drive that has to be fulfilled.

While parents have different contents of their concepts, the concept, once accepted, is an all-or-none element in the care. As the needs of the child change, the mode of feeding, sheltering, protecting, helping changes. We do not set a limit to what we do for children once the concept has been assimilated, though we set limits between concepts. Parents have demands put on them by children that they are not prepared to meet. But that means that the demands do not fit in an accepted conceptual set of care. Within our accepted conceptual set there are no quantitative limits. Feeding the hungry child must be made possible no matter what it takes, sheltering the exposed child must be accomplished by whatever means, and protecting the threatened child will be done no matter what the risk.

The image of the instinctual gesture of the mother is easily called forth in this line of reasoning. But it is not just instinctual and unconscious. Rather, the pressure to fulfill the self-imposed demands within each concept of care is quite conscious and determined. Not to feed, not to shelter is thought to be condemnable in society's eyes as much as it is instinctually wrong. Parents have consciences that do not allow ingrained concepts to be broken.

In this process, concepts can be very complex. A child cannot select shelter for himself, but usually the shelter chosen by parents for themselves is adequate for the needs of the child. However, when the child is handicapped, he needs many adjustments to the shelter to make it functional so that it is not a prison but rather a shelter allowing his full development. As the child broadens his horizons, the concept of shelter becomes more complex. It is expected that the situations the child is placed in provide the shelter during that time. A school is not just an adequate place for learning, but parents expect the element of shelter to be given. A church that parents use for their children's religious education contains the elements of shelter. If it does not, parents will not use it. The concept of caring through providing shelter is therefore a very wide one. If the child is handicapped, all such shelters must be adapted also. There is no quantitative limit within the concept. Society, as the totality of caring adults, accepts this. All society is now adapting to the handicapped at enormous societal cost. This cost must be acceptable because the concept cannot be violated. For example, Public Law 94-142 asks that all children be educated in the least constrictive environment possible. From that idea grew mainstreaming, adapting all school buildings to the handicapped, special resource teachers, and public financing of special medical needs in the name of schooling. The cost to society is already enormous and not imaginable if no backlash occurs. But there is no limit within this accepted concept.

When the child becomes ill, new forces are at work. Initially, with advice, the parent accommodates the "new" child within the concept of caring. When the child becomes sufficiently diseased, to generate the prospect of life-threatening illness, ordinary care is clearly insufficient. Extraordinary care is sought—the concept of medical care. The parents relinquish parental control for the concept of medical science as the caregiver. All the parent contributes to that concept is trust. The basic elements of care continue, of course, but ordinary medical intervention, when perceived as vital, is a concept of care that has its own conceptual constraints but also its own lack of quantitative limits within the concept.

Among all these concepts of care, feeding is the most basic. It is basic, beyond shelter and protection. It is so basic that the psychological concept of *nurture* is derived from that root. Nurture is the sum total of that care: shelter, feeding, protection, physical care, as well as psychological security. It is conceived that it will make a stable, healthy adult-person. But to nurture is not only defined as "to further the development of . . . ," but also "to supply with nourishment." The noun *nurture* is both "training, upbringing," and "something that nourishes, food." This part for the whole that nurture has become is only very slightly generalized in the mind of the population. From the popular image of the mother with the chicken soup panacea to the health food craze we can understand the power of the concept of nutrition as the basic form of nurture.

Therefore, the very sick child is surrounded by nutritional support from the parents. It is so much a concept of basic care that its importance is underplayed in medical circles. Just as the hospital should give shelter, so should it feed as a necessity, and not as part of the medical care concept. Physicians consider nutrition at best a paraprofessional concern. If the medical environment has to take over the total care of the child, the physicians are apt to order "diet for age," and they are rarely very clear on what they ordered. There is a gradual change in that attitude. It is clear that malnutrition is becoming a major source of death among cancer patients. Nutrition is becoming more the concern of physicians than it has been for a long time. With that have come new questions. To what degree is the concept of nutrition without constraints for physicians, and what defines the limits of the concept of nutrition as it exists in society today? That latter question is, of course, different from the scientific definition of nutrition.

The concept of nutrition is becoming very stretched. In the population at large, it is probable that the concept is basically not to allow the child to go hungry. There is a less well-defined idea that the food should be of such quality that the child is not missing disease-fighting components of the diet. The concept is not, in the mind of the population, the preconceived nutritionally complete diet. It is always the demand of the child, not the knowledge of the parent, that determines care. While the outcome of nurture is a healthy and emotionally stable adult, parents do not decide their actions on this ultimate goal. They decide on the care indicated that day. Official public education toward the balanced diet either creates neurosis or is basically ignored because it does not address hunger. And the intuitively felt ability to use nutrition as disease preventative or cure is irrationally maintained in spite of the absence of medical or scientific sanction.

Nutrition is medically defined as supplying all externally required elements of homeostasis or growth. Some elements of the diet are required in complex form. It is desirable to be able to eat food, but if it cannot be supplied in an ordinary diet, many alternatives are open to current medical science. If parents are fiercely protective of their human child, if feeding is the most basic means of protection, and if feeding is a quantized concept without internal limits, the question must be raised when is meeting nutritional requirements a medical artifact and when is it a logical, albeit extreme, step in fulfilling the conceptually defined basic care. The steps in feeding the sick toward artificiality can be graded in the content of the diet: from natural foods to an artificial formula, and by the method of delivery; by independent eating to total parenteral alimentation.

In spite of the natural food craze, artificiality in diet composition is accepted. The number of infants fed on "formulas" is very large indeed, heartily endorsed by parental testimonials to physicians. Tube feeding is a time-tested accepted method, and what is poured down the tube is considered irrelevant if it but contains the needed nutrients.

In that setting feeding by vein is readily sold to parents as a needed way to assist them medically in their basic task of feeding the sick child. It can also be presented and accepted as a medical measure that is extreme and embodies and symbolizes the failure of the parent to meet the most basic of cares. That problem arises when it is the only way to maintain life in a patient unable to eat or tolerate foods in the intestinal tract. Parenteral alimentation in children is safe and effective. It allows growth and development of children. It does not carry the extreme of artificial life support. Children are frequently capable of normal mobility, with only very little limitation from an intravenous line and fluid bag.

The impact of nutrition supportive care is growing rapidly. The effect of nutrition on cancer care has been summarized in the *Cancer Bulletin* (May–June) 30(3):1978, including the great impact of intravenous hyperalimentation on cancer care. A good summary of the advent of parenteral hyperalimentation and its current medical impact is given by S. Dudrick: "The Genesis of Intravenous Hyperalimentation." *Journal of Parenteral and Enteral Nutrition* 1(1):23–29, 1977.

The question of using intravenous hyperalimentation must be posed to parents when this is the next step in medical management. It can be presented in one of two ways: "Do you want your child to starve to death?" or "Do you want your child to be kept alive by artificial means?" Do you allow the parent to incorporate this new approach to care in the concept of feeding or do you allow it to enter the concept of extreme life support measures?

Herein lies the dilemma. Total parenteral hyperalimentation is a reality that is within the financial limits acceptable for care and that is well beyond the experimental. Any ethical debate that would be generated when it is applied to a given child is solvable only if it is agreed in which conceptual sphere the measure fits. If parents consider it an admittedly extreme component of the basic need for care through feeding, then it will be pursued at all costs until the child is allowed to depart as a dying person. If the physicians consider hyperalimentation an extreme measure belonging in the concept of purely medical intervention and not basic care, then physician and parent cannot debate or agree ethically.

It is not just academic, as the following case illustrates: A 15-year-old boy was successfully treated for extensive Hodgkin's disease with chemotherapy and radiotherapy, which included abdominal fields. While the disease was controlled if not cured, he was not mentally prepared for this normalcy and abused a number of drugs. At the same time, he developed intestinal fibrosis, making him tolerate food poorly—food that was clearly inadequate in quantity. He became malnourished and had severe abdominal complaints, requiring hospitalization. He was placed on parenteral hyperalimentation with good nutritional success. He could not, however, be weaned from hyperalimentation, because the continued combination of depression and inadequate bowel function made oral feeding not only impossible but even revolting to him.

As so often happens in such cases, all anxieties focused on the nutrition. Nutrition is basic, not only to parents but also to the child. Parenteral hyperalimentation was clearly effective and accepted by the patient and probably by the parents as within the concept of feeding. To the doctors it was an extreme measure, beyond feeding. On the other hand, the dietitians and hyperalimentation nurses accepted the parenteral intervention within the concept of feeding.

A long-range solution needed to be found. It was hoped to discharge the patient on home hyperalimentation. This too is technically feasible, though it requires a great deal of sophistication and compliance from the patient. Physicians were anxious because of their fear of drug abuse through this ready-made mainline. The paraprofessional nutritionists feared the parents' and patient's inadequacy to master this mode of feeding but never doubted the ultimate necessity of this approach. However, the life line (as the hyperalimentation catheter is referred to) needed to be removed after several months. The physicians reacted to this as the stimulus to pursue an alternative route to feeding, a more "normal way"—in other words, a method that fell within their concept of feeding. But the patient had accepted hyperalimentation as an effective, if not secure, mode of feeding, and he reacted with severe depression and anxiety to this loss of nurture.

The major psychiatric overtones of the interactions of this boy with parents and personnel clearly precluded ready acceptance of him as a person. He was merely a protected human being, and he made few recognizable efforts to change this mode of interaction, even though he did act out his desires in antisocial ways. While the boy was being fed by nasogastric tube, the tolerated volume was clearly inadequate. The dilemma is not resolved for this patient. It will not be satisfactorily resolved until the boy and the doctors have the same scope in concepts. The patient tried to tell of his dissatisfaction by vomiting. When the physicians did not listen, he made a serious suicide gesture. The limits cannot and will not be altered, because the hyperalimentation is part of two different conceptual spheres. To make the boy, his family, and the nutritional team change their mind would require them to set limits within their concept. They are not ready to do this. To make the doctors change their mind would require them to expand their scope of concept content or transfer a fact within concepts. That is more readily done. However, until they accept hyperalimentation, not as an extreme medical measure, but as a natural extrapolation of feeding, they are not likely to come to a dialogue with the patient that is meaningful. Hyperalimentation is a new fact to the parents that will have to be incorporated into existing concepts. It is not viewed within the discriminating power of medical and nutritional knowledge that aids in placing it in a specific concept area. Parents are not as likely to objectively garner new knowledge that might change the facts about hyperalimentation significantly.

It might, in fact, be reasonably asked whether there ever ought to be a limit within accepted concepts, or whether the solution must always be sought in the process of assigning new approaches to different and separate conceptual spheres, so that society at large and individuals can make decisions. If we were to put limits within a concept, we would be saying that certain forms of meeting care are unsatisfactory and unacceptable in the mind of the caregiver. Suppose that the boy in our example indeed could be given satisfactory care by home hyperalimentation. There would be a growing demand for nutrients if it were successful, and his life would be seriously curtailed. Like the lives of any physically handicapped, it could presumably be adjusted and be admirably productive, but it would be very different from most. The decision that this is an excessive extension of the concept of feeding the dependent child would lie, not in the impulse of the moment—feeding the starved child now, but in the extrapolation of the consequences. The impulse to feed cannot be denied, and therefore, limiting the alternatives that are acceptable would require a large number of self-deluding assurances that one is doing the best one can in feeding the child.

This dilemma is overcome by excluding the extreme of feeding modes: parenteral hyperalimentation is placed outside the definition of the concept of feeding and into the concept of extreme medical measures. The commitment of parents to total care of their children, their human charges, results in a commitment to this concept in a mode of "do what is best." The concept of extreme medical measures defines an area where care demands entrusting the execution of that care to others of defined skill. That concept does not allow active decision making by the parent beyond the decision to place trust. It is, therefore, the physician who makes the decision within this concept to initiate or terminate a procedure. To ask permission of the parents is to ask restructuring of their perception of the world. If parents indeed think in concepts, usually only applied to an immediate situation, it is the concept that must change, because precedent is not set from the situation. It is a truism that physicians only advise and do not decide. However, advice is never totally without value content. Physicians have their own value system, their own biases, their own definition of quality of life that is acceptable. Do what is best means doing what is best in their own eyes. They may ask the permission of the parents or child, but they can often get the answer they want. "Do you want your child to starve to death?" and "Do you want your child to stay alive by artificial means?" will both be answered by: "Of course not!" Physicians are a convenient focus for the medical care system. However, interactions as described here occur at all levels of the medical hierarchy and at all times in parent-staff interaction.

Because the concept of care of the critically ill is a transference of trust rather than an action from the parents, it is important that the limits of the concepts of the patient and their parents be understood. Physicians are not asked to play god, to act unilaterally, or to make extreme decisions without consent. But physicians are asked to enter their opinions on matters that are part of their skill. Their concepts are extremely important. The limits of care set by the concept of the physician determines the outcome as much as his actual skill does. It would be folly to expect a Catholic hospital, for example, to execute an abortion that might be considered medically indicated in other settings. It is not an element in their concept of prenatal management. If the medical situation were approaching a decision that might make an abortion a medically reasonable alternative, all manner of subtle factors would come into play that would affect the management.

Perceptions of quality of life clearly have an effect on the concept of medical care of the child with life-threatening illness. Hyperalimentation is artificial. It is not cheap, but it is safe in the hospital. Physicians often perceive this as counter to a good quality of life, when a child who is possibly dying might be better at home. Others see the malnutrition as a major cause of malaise. They also see any attempt at therapy hampered by the poor physical condition. Therefore, to them the quality of life is improved only by the feeding of the child by whatever means.

There is no right or wrong in this decision-making process. However, it is quite possible that dialogue will totally falter because of lack of agreement on concept content. If a given element of care is assigned to different concepts by those who discuss its application, no satisfactory agreement will ever be possible. Both parties must recognize this problem and then agree how to discuss it. That is not a verbal agreement on definition but an empathy about where each is in his understanding. The concept confusion is far more severe in basic elements of care than in true extremes in care where the parents and the patients have to assign a new situation to an existing concept or have to generate a new concept sphere. If the latter happens, decisions are easily made.

These problems of extreme life support do arise around children, usually without their input. Care for the very young child is total. As already said, ordinary and extraordinary care merge, because the criteria of self-help and self-determination, which usually are the tests applied to medical intervention, are all unusual. However, that does not mean that children have no ideas about these inflicted interventions. They have feelings exactly like adults. What is saddening and frightening to adults is certainly that to children. Loneliness, rejection, helplessness are all feelings of children. However, their concepts are very different in content, even when they might be grouped in sets like adults. Whatever problems might be encountered between caregivers and physicians would be compounded between adults and children. The problem does not lie in the initiation of concepts per se. The same basic sets are present in children.

The concept of feeding is as fundamental to the child as it is to the caring parent. The need to change from a passive, receiving role to an active, procuring role is an expansion and not an alternative of the concept content. A child does not, therefore, reason primitively in that common everyday area. When a new fact needs to be incorporated, however, a great deal depends on the developmental stage of the child. There is an enormous difference between the reasoning path of a two-year-old and a six-year-old child. A fact as complicated as intravenous hyperalimentation would be very unpredictably handled since the basic ideas are not assimilable. First of all, concepts are dependent on language. Vocabulary must be adequate before a concept can be assimilated. You just cannot explain ethics to a Spanish-speaking adult if all your own Spanish is learned from a Berlitz travel vademecum. Children are in the same boat—they often just do not have the language to assimilate new and complicated elements in their concept content.

Furthermore, below a certain age, even basic concepts are not assimilated. The very young do not know *before, after, into*—very basic concepts. Numbers are assimilated as concepts quite gradually. There is an enormous difference in the teaching in prekindergarten and the average first grade.

Parents are confronted with decision making for the young child that cannot be shouldered by the child. If death comes naturally and expected or suddenly and swiftly, the child will meet death like an adult with wonder, fear, acceptance, resignation, joy, and sorrow. But if a conscious decision must be made that fighting death further is not in the best interest of the child, the parents are very alone—more alone than the dying child is. If you are dying and you know it and acknowledge it, there is no crisis. But if you are responsible for the child, you have a crisis that will never be solved except by your own acceptance of the outcome.

Such times of crises are no time to change concepts. When parents do not understand the doctors, because they have different concept content, the fear becomes acute. Doctors have no more limitation on their concept of ordinary medical care than parents have in their concept of feeding. On the other hand, doctors will not go into the sphere of extraordinary care without clear indication or overt pressure. Parents may become bewildered since they begin to generate a picture of their physicians' concepts without ever understanding the complete scope unless it is indeed brought to its limits.

This bewilderment can contribute immensely to the burden of decision making. Children are pulled in to bolster the parents' concepts. Children do feel the impact of such decisions. But the decisions are not made on feelings. Increasing of suffering can demand stopping of medical care. But ordinary care is never perceived as increasing suffering. Ordinary medical care, when entrusted to physicians, is never quantized. No parents bring their child to a hospital and request five thousand dollars' worth of medical care and no more. The parent will ask to do everything possible to reach the desired care.

To feed or not to feed the young dying child is a decision that lies with the parents. But it is not a decision wherein physicians present facts to help parents make up their mind. Physicians have their concepts, and that is what their advice is built on. Parents have their concepts, and that is what their decision is based on. Such dialogue is not simple. There is no ethical structure that allows the decision to be easy and obvious. We must understand this and not be deluded by the usual debates and its conclusions on extreme life-preserving measures.

· V ·
The Sudden Death of a Child

· 25 ·
Perspective on Sudden Infant Death Syndrome

Ralph A. Franciosi

This paper presents the problem of one entity causing death in young children, sudden infant death syndrome (SIDS), in the context of the larger problem of infant mortality. Both scientifically and socially, awareness of infant mortality lags far behind our awareness of adult mortality.

Stickel (1977) estimated the outcome of pregnancy in the United States as follows: 5,168,000 conceptions; 1,221,000 spontaneous abortions; 629,000 induced abortions; and 118,000 fetal deaths. Fetal deaths were defined as in-utero occurring after 20 weeks gestation. His data indicate that 3 out of 5 pregnancies resulted in a live born infant (3,200,000).

In 1975, 40,000 infants died in the neonatal period (less than 28 days). Sixty percent of deaths occurred within 24 hours following birth and 90 percent at the end of one week (Vital Statistics of the United States 1975). This illustrates that most problems of neonatal mortality occur within one week of birth. The majority of deaths occur in premature infants (less than 37 weeks' gestation) and justifies the preeminence given to prevention of premature delivery in the United States; 19,000 deaths occurred in infants after one month of age. The leading cause was SIDS with the predominant causes in the remainder due to congenital malformations, infection, and "brain damage."

Most deaths in childhood are accidental and are related either to vehicular accidents or drowning. Accidents remain the major cause of death in adolescents and young adults. In this age group, however, deaths caused by homicide and suicide are increasing and a matter of deep concern.

There were 1,806,504 adult deaths in 1974, and 127,884 deaths in infants, children and adolescents (7 percent). The magnitude of adult deaths is impressive, and the major causes are heart disease, 38 percent; cancer, 19 percent; stroke, 11 percent; accidents, 5 percent (approximately one-half are vehicular); and various other causes 26 percent (Vital Statistics of the United States 1974). The numbers of adult deaths are initially impressive and have a great deal of impact regarding national funding. However, it is a fact that all people will die, and our concern is about premature death and its prevention. A logical conclusion would be shifting our emphasis to the physical and emotional stresses in early childhood that relate to adult morbidity and mortality.

If an infant dies suddenly and unexpectedly, there is only a 15 percent probability of explaining the death. The explained deaths are due predominantly to infection, for example, pneumonia. The overwhelming majority of sudden unexpected deaths, 84 percent, are SIDS. The remaining 1 percent do not fit the circumstances required for SIDS and remain unclassified (Beckwith 1975). SIDS is the sudden death of an infant, usually between two weeks and 1 year of age, occurring during sleep, that is unexpected from the medical history and that remains unexplained after review of circumstances surrounding death and a complete postmortem examination including autopsy by a qualified pathologist. Most infants are less than six months of age; however, cases are seen up until two years. In reviewing cases, approximately 60 percent of the infants are found dead between 12:00 midnight and 12:00 noon. However, one must consider that this is the longest sleep period for most infants. The death is silent as evidenced by deaths that occur in car seats with parents present and while an infant is being held.

The association with sleep has opened a new area of research into the physiology of the sleep state in infants. One phase of sleep is referred to as rapid eye movement (REM), and many bursts of skeletal muscle activity, as well as changes in heart rate and respiration are noted. The major breakthrough in SIDS is anticipated in the area of ventilation during sleep in infancy.

An observed case of SIDS in hospital is presented here to reinforce the circumstances surrounding death. A male infant was delivered at 40 weeks' gestation, weighing 2900 grams. The Apgar score 1 minute after birth was depressed to 4 but increased to 9 at five minutes. The immediate neonatal course was uneventful, and the infant was discharged home with his mother at five days of age. His mother is a 21-year-old single parent with no family support. The infant remained well until approximately one month of age when the following were noted: crying, flexion of thighs, and a reddish discoloration approximately twenty minutes after feeding. These were interpreted as signs of "colic." Since feedings were given every three hours around the clock, the episodes occurred over a 24-hour period. The mother sought medical help, and these episodes were relieved by phenobarbitol. When the child reached 2½ months of age, the mother indicated she needed help with parenting. The infant was admitted as a "social admission." On admission, the infant was described as vigorous and "healthy." The nurses described some fussiness around feedings but nothing significant. The mother visited frequently and was developing confidence in parenting skills. On the fifth hospital day the infant, who was adjacent to the nursing station, had a sudden respiratory arrest with cyanosis. There was no audible sound or struggle. The infant seemed to go deeper into sleep and then suddenly stopped breathing. Although the pulse was palpable, no spontaneous respirations could be established and death occurred 2 hours later. The postmortem examination showed the typical tissue changes of SIDS, that is, pulmonary edema and intrathoracic petechiae.

The effect of the SIDS death on the floor nurses was similar to that voiced by SIDS parents. The primary care nurse was most affected and expressed fears about errors of omission and commission. She had recurring doubts about her ability to administer nursing care to ill children if an apparently well child under her care died. The other floor nurses blamed the mother for an unnecessary admission and were concerned about a tarnished reputation since other parents on the floor witnessed the death.

In our experience in coordinating the Minnesota SIDS Program two major problems affecting SIDS management have been encountered. The first concerns the diagnosis of SIDS and reflects on the problem of death investigation. Many times the circumstances surrounding death were not communicated to the pathologist performing the autopsy. Since circumstances in addition to postmortem findings are essential for the SIDS diagnosis, this is a major problem. Second, since the preliminary diagnosis of SIDS required up to four days, the acute grief support for the family could not depend on explanation of cause. We concentrated on various community resources, such as emergency personnel, clergy, funeral directors, nurses, and physicians, to provide the support during this critical period. Approximately one week after the death, a public health nurse was available to explain questions about SIDS to the family.

This presentation defined SIDS as a natural but unexplained death in infants that occurs during sleep. Attempts to understand the causes of SIDS are demonstrating our lack of information about the biology of infancy. This effort will not be easy to achieve, since we live in a youth-oriented and not a child-oriented society that does not place infant and childhood problems as a top priority.

REFERENCES

Beckwith, J. B. 1975. *The Sudden Infant Death Syndrome*. DHEW Publication No. (NSA) 75-5137.

Stickel, G. 1977. "Pregnancy Outcome in the U.S.A." March of Dimes Presentation.

Vital Statistics of the United States. 1974. From Mortality Statistics Branch Division of Vital Statistics, National Center for Health Statistics.

Vital Statistics of the United States. 1975. From Mortality Statistics Branch Division of Vital Statistics, National Center for Health Statistics.

· 26 ·

Predicting the Risk of Sudden Infant Death—Dilemma for the Practitioner

SUSAN J. STANDFAST, BARBARA J. KUTER, SUSAN K. JEREB, AND DWIGHT T. JANERICH

Sudden unexplained death in infancy, the sudden infant death syndrome (SIDS), is generally considered by the infant's parents and the medical profession to be unpredictable and unpreventable. Yet, a few recent studies suggest that some infants can be identified at birth or shortly thereafter as being at high risk of sudden, unexpected death. This risk prediction is based on statistical models. The purpose of this paper is to review the current knowledge about SIDS risk prediction in terms meaningful to practitioners.

Background

Froggatt (1970), an epidemiologist from Northern Ireland, first introduced into SIDS research the concept of characterizing infants at high risk of sudden, unexpected death by use of a multifactor statistical method called discriminant function analysis. The purpose of this type of analysis is to identify the combina-

---

The authors would like to thank Margaret Hoff, ScD, biostatistician, Division of Epidemiology, New York State Department of Health, for reviewing the manuscript. The cooperation of the Office of Biostatistics and the county coroners, medical examiners, and pathologists in our SIDS program is greatly appreciated.

tion of characteristics, such as social class, mother's age, parity, and infant's birthweight, that best distinguish babies who die of SIDS from a random sample of babies born in the same population in the same year who have survived to their first birthday. Kraus and Borhani (1972a) did an epidemiological study of 525 postneonatal sudden, unexplained deaths that occurred among the 339,221 babies born alive in California during 1968. Their data were obtained from death certificates and birth certificates, with classification of deaths confirmed by county coroners, medical examiners, and a panel of university pathologists experienced with SIDS. In their first analysis, simple tabulations of several relevant variables were compared for babies dying of SIDS and the total cohort of live-born infants. The second stage of their study (1972b) used discriminant function analysis. The result was the following set of best combined discriminators (in order of importance): age of mother, total live births to mother, birthweight, multiple birth, duration of prenatal care, sex, complications of pregnancy, and illegitimacy. This set correctly classified 66 percent of the SIDS babies and 70 percent of the random sample of live infants.

Protestos et al. (1973) and Carpenter and Emery (1974) carried this idea further in a series of studies in Sheffield, England. These studies fall into three main stages: first, development of a scoring system for identifying infants at high risk of sudden unexpected death based on discriminant function analysis; second, the clinical application of the scoring system in a randomized controlled trial (Carpenter and Emery 1974, 1977); and third, refinement and validity testing of the scoring system (Carpenter et al. 1977). The first study (Protestos et al. 1973) was a retrospective chart review of obstetrical, perinatal, and early postnatal records of 135 babies who died unexpectedly and were autopsied under the direction of an experienced pediatric pathologist (J. L. Emery) at a single hospital over a 12-year period. A control for each case was selected by choosing the next name in the birth register of the hospital where the case was born. Two hundred variables from obstetric and neonatal records were screened. These were first analyzed as single variables. Next 40 variables that could be ascertained at or soon after birth and that looked like good predictors were further studied by stepwise analysis (Carpenter and Emery 1974). This process yielded the following list of best combined discriminators (in order of importance): mother's age, number of previous pregnancies, mother's blood group, breast feeding, urinary tract infection in pregnancy, polyhydramnios in pregnancy, and birthweight. Later, twin birth was substituted for polyhydramnios. The discriminant function process yielded weights for each factor. The sum of the weighted factors gives the score for each child.

Clinical Application

Carpenter and Emery went on to use their scoring system in a second study to identify high-risk infants at birth (1974, 1977). This prospective study was designed as a randomized, controlled clinical trial. All babies born in the three major maternity hospitals in Sheffield during 1973 and 1974 (11,424) were rated within 24 hours after birth by use of the scoring system. Those whose scores fell in the top 15 percent of the distribution of scores from the retrospective study were classified as high risk; the rest were defined as low risk. The high-risk group for the clinical trial was expected to include 60 percent of the sudden explained and unexplained infant deaths that would occur among the total group of newborns during their first year of life. (This was based on the results of the retrospective study.) Sudden deaths from explained causes as well as unexplained sudden deaths were included because these babies were found in the first study to have characteristics very similar to those of infants whose deaths were unexplained and because such deaths are potentially preventable. After elimination of babies with gross congenital deformities, the high-risk group was divided randomly into a study group and a control group. The study group had been followed with physical examinations at specified intervals and biweekly home visits by a public health nurse over a twenty-week period. The control mothers apparently were not informed that their babies were involved in a study. The details of the study design and outcome have been published (Carpenter and Emery 1974, 1977); for the present purpose, it is sufficient to summarize the results in terms of the mortality rates of the subgroups. The postperinatal infant mortality (deaths between 1 week and 1 year of age) for unexpected deaths was 9.76/1000 high-risk controls compared to 1.56/1000 low-risk babies. This difference is statistically significant ($p < .001$) and confirms that the high-risk infants were indeed at greater risk of dying unexpectedly. The scoring system, when applied to the same community in which it was developed, was effective in identifying at birth as high risk 50 percent of the infants who subsequently died suddenly and unexpectedly. The unexpected death rate in the high-risk study group was 3.19/1000 compared to the high-risk control rate of 9.76/1000. This demonstrates that the home visits did reduce the death rate in the study group.

Several questions arise at this point: (1) Is it clinically useful to be able to correctly identify at birth 50 percent of the babies who will subsequently die unexpectedly? If not, can a higher level of prediction be achieved? (2) What about the other 50 percent of unexpected deaths that occurred to infants who were classified as low risk? (3) What happens to the level of prediction when the Sheffield scoring system is applied to other populations?

The Scoring System as Screening Test

In order to answer the first two questions, it is necessary to look at the scoring system as a screening device rather than as a tool for making a definitive diagnosis. We can measure the validity of a screening test in terms of sensitivity and specificity (table 26.1). Sensitivity is defined as the proportion of truly diseased persons who are called diseased by the test—in this case, the percent of infants who died unexpectedly who had been classified as "high risk" by the scoring system. Specificity is the proportion of truly nondiseased or healthy individuals who are correctly called healthy by the test. In terms of the Sheffield scoring system, the specificity is the percent of surviving babies who had been correctly classified as low risk. Ideally, both of these mea-

Table 26.1.
Comparison of Screening Test Results with the True Diagnosis

	True Diagnosis (Outcome)	
Test or Scoring Results	Disease Present (Died Unexpectedly)	Disease Absent (Surviving Babies)
Positive (High Risk)	TP (True Positives)	FP (False Positives)
Negative (Low Risk)	FN (False Negatives)	TN (True Negatives)
TOTAL	TP + FN	FP + TN
Sensitivity	TP/TP + FN	% having the disease that are so indicated by the test
Specificity	TN/FP + TN	% not having the disease that are so indicated by the test

sures should be close to 100 percent, so that the test detects a maximum amount of disease without falsely labeling healthy persons. However, in practice this ideal is seldom achieved. In Carpenter and Emery's first prospective evaluation of their newborn scoring system, the final sensitivity after two years was 56 percent and the specificity was 84 percent (Carpenter et al. 1977). They have subsequently improved on this by expanding the scoring system to a multistage system in which the infants are initially rated within 24 hours after birth for the eight variables listed earlier; then at age one month they are scored on four more variables: cyanotic or apneic attacks in hospital before initial discharge, difficulty establishing feeds, state of repair of home, and interval to previous live birth. The total score is classified into one of three groups: high, intermediate, or low risk. Intermediate-risk babies become high risk if admitted to the hospital at any time up to 21 weeks of age. The effectiveness of the multistage scoring system compared to the birth score was tested in a small prospective study of 76 SIDS cases and 115 controls followed up to two years of age. The sensitivity of the multistage system in this small study was 75 percent, compared to 57 percent for the at birth only system. However, the specificity was only 51 percent for the multistage versus 82 percent for the birth scoring alone. These results illustrate a general problem affecting quantitative screening tests. Improvement in one measure will often adversely affect the other.

Another measure that can be derived from the evaluation of a screening test is the predictive value of a positive test, that is, the proportion of infants with positive test scores who turn out to have the disease (die suddenly and unexpectedly). This value and its corollary, the negative predictive value, may be the ones of most interest to practitioners. However, these values can be calculated only when the screening test results and true diagnosis or outcome have been ascertained for an unselected population—that is, it does not apply to retrospective case control studies. This value will always be relatively low if the disease is one that occurs infrequently in the population (Vecchio 1966). The Sheffield scoring system gave a maximum (including probably unpreventable deaths) predictive value for a positive test of about 2 percent for their clinical trial. Since the overall incidence of sudden unexpected infant death in Sheffield for the 1973-74 study was 2.6/1000 live births, we should not expect a high positive predictive value. The negative predictive value (percent with a negative test or low-risk score who do not have the disease or die) is not significantly affected by the disease rate. For the Sheffield prospective study this value was 99.8 percent. But for the clinician the remaining question may be, is it worth correctly "predicting" two unexpected infant deaths at the expense of falsely "predicting" 98 others? We feel the answer depends on how the scores are used.

Carpenter et al. (1977) point out strongly in the discussion of their results that they have never used the scoring system to tell any parent that their child is at risk of SIDS. The scores have enabled the primary care physicians and nurses in the community to pay more attention to the postnatal course of babies with certain characteristics; such intervention has apparently prevented some deaths. The well-known Apgar scoring system is used in a similar manner by delivery room and newborn nursery personnel. One of the general principles of screening is that one should screen only for those diseases or conditions in which early identification of high risk or diseased individuals can be followed by an intervention program or treatment that significantly improves the patient's prognosis. The difficulty in sudden infant death syndrome is that there is currently only one measure of outcome—whether the baby is alive or dead at the end of one (or two) year(s). Yet it is quite possible—in fact, quite likely—that many of the surviving high-risk infants (false positives) had more episodes of illness and near-accidents than the low-risk babies. If we had a way of adding these episodes into the end results, the positive predictive value of the scoring system might be increased.

With the improved multistage scoring system there were still 25 percent of the unexpected deaths in Sheffield that occurred to babies who had been classified as medium or low risk (false negatives). These are the ones who probably cause the greatest amount of agony and guilt to the physician. They are the atypical, and therefore least expected of the unexpected deaths—the full-term babies with apparently normal prenatal and perinatal courses who had the best of care in the best of families and yet one morning they were found dead. Perhaps these deaths represent a truly unpredictable and unpreventable subgroup. On the other hand they may be a subgroup with different risk factors from the majority, since the Sheffield low-risk death rate of 1.56/1000 is still higher than the Netherlands rate of 0.42/1000 live births (Baak and Huber 1974). Perhaps we need a third-stage scoring procedure to properly distinguish them from the true negatives.

Application to Other Communities

Can the Sheffield scoring system be applied to other communities? Carpenter et al. (1977) warn that it can be a dangerous tool. They point out that even applying it to a new set of cases and controls in the same community tends to show a reduction in its effectiveness. Any use of the Sheffield system in another population should be preceded by testing its validity on a series of local postperinatal unexpected deaths. We have gone through this exercise for a small series of sudden unexpected infant deaths. These cases were reported to our office by coroners/medical examiners and registrars of vital statistics from ten counties in upstate New York from January 1976 through January 1978 and twenty counties from February 1978 through June 1978. Deaths were classified as sudden unexplained infant deaths (SIDS), other sudden deaths, or hospital deaths on the basis of the clinical history, circumstances of death, and autopsy findings. Beginning in February 1978, live control infants were selected at random from the pool of infants born in the same county within three days of the SIDS baby. The information used in the scoring system was obtained from birth certificates and hospital records; in 1978, home visits were made also.

Table 26.2 shows the Sheffield multistage scoring results for the 20 babies who died of SIDS in twenty upstate New York counties during February through June 1978 compared with 43 age-matched infants who were alive during that period. An ad-

Table 26.2.
Comparison of Sheffield Scoring System Results for SIDS Cases and Controls from Twenty Upstate New York Counties, February through June 1978

Sheffield Scoring Result	Died of SIDS (Cases)	Survived (Controls)
(a) Positive (High Risk)	11	4
Negative (Medium and Low Risk)	9	39
(b) Positive (High and Medium Risk)	16	24
Negative (Low Risk only)	4	19
Total Screened	20	43
(a) Positive = High Risk only	Sensitivity 11/20 55%	Specificity 39/43 91%
(b) Positive = High and Medium Risk	16/20 80%	19/43 44%

ditional 8 SIDS infants and 13 control babies from this period had to be excluded because we were unable to obtain their hospital records and/or a home interview. The multistage scoring system correctly identified in retrospect only 11/20 of the SIDS babies as high risk, for a sensitivity of 55 percent compared to 75 percent in Sheffield. Our specificity was better, with 91 percent of the surviving babies correctly classified as negative. We can improve our sensitivity to 80 percent by changing the classification of medium risk from negative to positive, as shown in table 26.2 (b). The price is a sharp decrease in specificity to 44 percent. Carpenter et al. (1977) were able to correctly identify 71 percent of 24 sudden unexpected deaths in a validation of the multistage scoring system in Sheffield while also correctly identifying 79 percent of the survivors. What are the possible explanations for the poorer results in our series? One possibility is the composition of the case group. In Sheffield the cases included all sudden unexpected infant deaths except those associated with congenital anomalies. Our 1978 cases were only those sudden unexpected deaths that were unexplained by autopsy, that is, "true" SIDS. For all sudden unexpected deaths reported during 1976 and 1977 in ten counties of upstate New York the Sheffield scoring system correctly classified as high risk 20 of the 29 infants (69 percent). The sensitivity for the unexplained deaths (SIDS) was 65 percent (13/20) compared to 78 percent (7/9) for infants who died unexpectedly from known causes. The numbers are small but suggest that a larger percent of babies dying of sudden explained death can be identified as positive, that is, high risk, by the scoring system.

Another possibility is that some of the risk factors for sudden infant death may be quite different in upstate New York from those in Sheffield. For example, we know that in our population the rate of SIDS is three times higher in black than in white babies (Standfast et al. 1979). Yet race per se is not included in the Sheffield scoring system. Race was not examined as a discriminating variable by Kraus and Borhani in their analysis of California infant deaths (Kraus et al. 1972b). But they do provide evidence that the relative importance of some discriminating characteristics differs between white and black infants. In regard to mother's blood group, the Sheffield studies showed significantly fewer case mothers with type A. Our 1976–78 SIDS cases show 10 percent more type A than the controls. In respect to duration of second stage of labor, this information was unknown or not applicable in 40 percent (8/20) of our 1978 SIDS cases compared to 26 percent (11/43) of controls. A large part of this difference reflects a considerably higher rate of cesarean section deliveries in our cases (35 percent) than in controls (12 percent). It is likely that cesarean section rates are higher in New York State in 1978 than they were in Sheffield in 1973–74: for live births recorded in upstate New York in 1977, 14 percent were cesarean sections (double the 1972 rate of 6.5 percent); in England and Wales the incidence of cesarean section was about 5 percent of all births in 1970–72, compared to 2.7 percent in 1958. Such a difference could dilute the true contribution of the length of the second stage of labor on the scores.

Our sample is too small to justify detailed analysis of these and other differences between upstate New York and Sheffield. However it serves to illustrate the point that a screening test developed in one community in England cannot be applied unaltered to a different population in the United States with satisfactory results. This point has already been made for other communities in England (Oakley et al. 1978). Probably the best use to which we can put the Sheffield scoring system is as a catalyst to spur us on to develop a method of risk prediction and, it is hoped, prevention based on characteristics of infants at risk of dying suddenly and unexpectedly in our own communities in the United States.

REFERENCES

Baak, J. P. A. and J. Huber. 1974. "Incidence of SIDS in the Netherlands." In R. R. Robinson, ed. *SIDS 1974: Proceedings of the Francis E. Camps International Symposium on Sudden and Unexpected Deaths in Infancy,* pp. 157–67. Toronto: Canadian Foundation for the Study of Infant Deaths.

Carpenter, R. G. and J. L. Emery. 1974. "The Identification and Follow-up of High Risk Infants." In R. R. Robinson, ed. *SIDS 1974: Proceedings of the Francis E. Camps International Symposium on Sudden and Unexpected Deaths in*

Infancy, pp. 91–96. Toronto: Canadian Foundation for the Study of Infant Deaths.

Carpenter, R. G. and J. L. Emery. 1977. "Final Results of Study of Infants at Risk of Sudden Death." *Nature* 268:724–25.

Carpenter, R. G., A. Gardner, P. M. McWeeny, and J. L. Emery. 1977. "Multistage Scoring System for Identifying Infants at Risk of Unexpected Death." *Archives of Diseases of Children* 52:606–12.

"Editorial: Caesarian Section and Respiratory Distress Syndrome." 1976. *British Medical Journal*, April 24, pp. 978–79.

Froggatt, P. 1970. "Epidemiologic Aspects of the Northern Ireland Study." In A. B. Bergman et al., eds. *Sudden Infant Death Syndrome: Proceedings of the Second International Conference on Causes of Sudden Death in Infants*, pp. 32–46. Seattle: University of Washington Press.

Kraus, J. F. and N. O. Borhani. 1972a. "Post-neonatal Sudden Unexplained Death in California: A Cohort Study." *American Journal of Epidemiology* 95:497–510.

Kraus, J. F., C. E. Franti, and N. O. Borhani. 1972b. "Discriminatory Risk Factors in Post-Neonatal Sudden Unexplained Death." *American Journal of Epidemiology* 96:328–33.

Oakley, J. R., C. J. Tavare, and A. N. Stanton. 1978. "Evaluation of the Sheffield System for Identifying Children at Risk from Unexpected Death in Infancy: Results from Birmingham and Newcastle upon Tyne." *Archives of Diseases of Children* 53:649–52.

Protestos, C. D., R. G. Carpenter, P. M. McWeeny, and J. L. Emery. 1973. "Obstetric and Perinatal Histories of Children Who Die Unexpectedly (Cot Death)." *Archives of Diseases of Children* 48:835–41.

Standfast, S. J., S. Jereb, and D. T. Janerich. 1979. "The Epidemiology of Sudden Infant Death in Upstate New York." *Journal of American Medical Association* 241:1121–24.

Vecchio, T. J. 1966. "Predictive Value of a Single Diagnostic Test in Unselected Populations." *New England Journal of Medicine* 274:1171–73.

· 27 ·

Parental Mortification and Restitutional Efforts Upon the Sudden Loss of a Child

Werner I. Halpern

Nay, but I will go down to the grave to my son mourning.   Genesis 37:35
For her soul is bitter within her; and the Lord hath hid it from me, and hath not told me.   2 Kings 4:27

The unexpected death of a young child represents one of the most heartrending experiences for parents. Attitudes toward children that tend to be implicit in their lifetime must suddenly be dealt with precipitously. A person's philosophy of life is tested most severely when a child dies, as if the belief in the innocence of the young as talisman against death had been betrayed. Powerful humbling and mortifying emotional forces are released by the event that may go beyond mourning, particularly if anticipatory grieving could not occur.

Clinical practice offers opportunities for studying parental reactions to the sudden loss of a child and for developing rallying bereavement support services to the sufferers (Cornwell et al. 1977, Mandell and Belk 1977). Sometimes the parents' behavior, unless better understood, acts as a deterrent to intervention. Various communities are in the process of organizing clinicians and services that function in a variety of settings to become more expert in bereavement counseling of parents at the initial crisis (Fischhoff and O'Brien 1976). It must be kept in mind, however, that some parents may require more than crisis aid in guiding them through the bereavement process. Such work has been spurred by the recent interest in the sudden infant death syndrome (SIDS), as well as by SIDS parent groups.

Although SIDS is the most frequent cause of death in the infancy period, there are other causes in infants and particularly in older children. Reactions to stillbirth (Jolly 1976), perinatal death (Morris 1976), and death from trauma such as fire and accidents occur in sufficient numbers to be a focus of concern. Since proper help at the early stages of grieving has both therapeutic and preventive potential for parents and surviving chidren, its value cannot be overstated for sudden death of young children from all causes.

What assumptions do parents usually make about children that surface so dramatically when their existence ceases? The overriding faith that children shall live has the earmarks of a survival credo. Of course, on a personal level, species survival behavior is performed by the individual as part of his or her psychic ontogeny, that is to say that parents think almost exclusively of self-perpetuation through their progeny. However, despite this strong motivation for continuing one's strain, usually little conscious thought is given to the expectation that the child fulfill this implied promise when the child is alive. Only if the child dies unexpectedly does the full realization of this assumption strike the parent, who feels bereft of the child and what the child could have become. It would seem that the child is an extension of self in space and in time. With death, both aspects of the parent's extension are cut off. As long as the offspring lives, the parent's awareness of personal mortality is attenuated if not suppressed. The sudden loss of this cover of one's own finite existence registers alarm, fear, and hopelessness.

Children, whose lives carry the promise of continuity, provide parents with a sense of pleasure that outweighs the often burdensome responsibilities for them. If the child has carried additional parental hopes, for example, that he become someone who the parent could not be, then the unfulfilled longings are doubly thwarted by the death. This also holds true for other, more personal associations that parents may make about particular children. When the patriarch Jacob heard about the presumed death of his favorite son Joseph, he was particularly afflicted in his sorrow to speak of his own death. If there is a death wish, it is expressed most poignantly by the parent at the loss of a much loved or favorite child. Indeed, the experience that something of the self has died is often an explicit statement embedded in the sadness being expressed.

Not only has the promise been stilled through the child's death, but also the parents must reflect on their responsibility for whatever real and fancied failures in maintaining life that could be ascribed to them. The social contract of parenthood stresses the protective function as the ultimate criterion of fitness. A child's death, particularly if accidental or unexplained, implies a lapse in parental protectiveness or of appropriate action vis-à-vis the child.

There is a long history, of course, when child sacrifice and mortal child abuse were commonplace occurrences against which powerful taboos were erected. The concern about a weakening of this taboo enters into people's thinking whenever retrospection can conjure up alternative actions that could have prevented a child's death or when the reason for the death remains mysterious in etiology. Such thinking is particularly prevalent today since unconscious motivation for behavior is now such a commonly shared perspective. Under conditions of unexpected child death, the parents are plagued by thoughts about what they should have done differently to prevent the death and also by the gnawing question of hidden motivation for wanting harm to befall the child. The ambivalence that is a natural constituent of the parents' feelings toward a child, but ordinarily repressed, becomes a strong and sometimes crazed accuser that demands retribution.

In certain instances a parent sees this presumed hostile intent toward the deceased child in the spouse or in an older child who is held responsible and furiously assailed for the fantasied death-dealing intent (Halpern 1972). Such irrational action has the force of an absolute denial that personal ambivalence toward the child is unthinkable at such a time, although frequently a subject of exasperated comic discussion among parents when children are experienced as burdensome or annoying ("Go play in the middle of Main Street!" or "I could kill you for this!"). When these words or thoughts come back to haunt parents upon the unexpected death of a child, a morbid preoccupation with one's badness may turn into an attack on the self that symbolizes the punishment for murder.

Parents who are bereaved by the sudden loss of a child or children are particularly vulnerable to self-mortification, a process of self-blame and symbolic dying that may not be readily visible. It seems that a rationale for the meaningless death of innocents is found in self-accusation. By finding fault with someone, even one's self, existence is not completely senseless. There can be loss of feeling, automatic behavior, detachment, and emptiness to guard against open self-hatred long beyond the usual mourning period. The emotional numbness does not draw attention to the guilt and often terror that is kept at bay by this protective but generally nonadaptive defensive device. Such a parent may not come to clinical attention until many years after the death of the child, requiring patient rebuilding of confidence in the self.

This rebuilding process may occur spontaneously through replacement of the lost child, through memorializing the deceased, and through social action or advocacy that derives its energy from a redirection of investment in the child to children and their parents with whose problems the afflicted parents can identify. Conventional wisdom supports the notion that grieving can be set aside once a replacement child is introduced into the family. Without doubt, this has a powerful assuaging effect on sorrow and emptiness but of equal significance is the potential for redirection of cathexis to a living being. Clinical wisdom cautions against taking hasty steps with regard to filling the dead child's place with a sibling, particularly if the mother's attitude toward the new child may be pathologically affected in an overprotective manner on the one hand or a too detached attitude on the other (Cain and Cain 1964, Legg and Sherick 1976, Mandell and Wolfe 1975, Poznanski 1972).

Because clinicians prefer to err on the side of saving people additional grief, they are likely to advise an indefinite delay of conception for a bereaved couple until they are able to see that no person can take the place of another and that the new child would be an individual in his own right. While such advice may be justified in some instances, it robs others of a coping feature. The risks to the replacement child can be attenuated if the parents' isolation is held down and if the self-mortification is treated with sympathetically corrective and realistic support. Where irrational guilt feelings about the death play a significant role in the maternal morbidity, a well-placed faith by a therapist in the mother's ability to be a good parent has the power to restore self-confidence.

About twenty years ago, I had occasion to become clinically involved with parents whose four children had been conceived and were born following the loss of two very young boys to a fire in their home eight years previously. The identified patient was the second child and first son in the new sibship who bore the names of his two deceased brothers. He was a tense, emotionally constricted, and withdrawn five-year-old whose attempts at self-expression were described as sneaky. The mother was apathetic and depressed except in her overconcern for the children's well-being. She expressed a sense of doom about the son who not only was a replacement, as were his three siblings, but also memorialized the dead brothers by bearing their names. Considerable guilt over the deaths of the children, whom she had been unable to rescue, had left the mother continuously on the edge of panic with their replacements. She wanted her children to experience the necessary risk-taking of daily life, yet she resented their activities, for these jeopardized a tenuous emotional equilibrium that she had achieved through the replacement and memorialization of the lost children. She feared that at any moment another catastrophic death of a child might confirm what she secretly thought about herself, that she was a murderer of children. The older son was particularly vulnerable to the mother's tentative and often contradictory message that he be assertively careful. The lengthy therapy addressed itself primarily to strengthening the mother in her role functioning to the point where she felt secure enough to become a foster mother to many children. Only as the caring role was reinforced by an advocacy function in behalf of children (the mother had once been a foster child) did she become less ambivalent toward children and more secure in her self-definition of a well-intentioned, benign human being.

Not all parents want to or are able to replace the dead child. The tendency to remain fixated on the loss is transformed by some into a "living memorial" through designation of contributions to charity in the memory of the child, through scholarship awards to deserving youth, through giving the child's name to a facility funded by the parents, and through other public and personal acknowledgments that the memory of the dead child remains.

Although this emotional coping strategy is more prevalent when children have died of an identifiable disease, and usually after a long illness, its adaptive potential in the healing process has a place when unexpected death occurs. When a parent designates the child's room as the memorial, or transfers the given name from the dead to the living and thus attempts to keep the child's memory alive in the family, the purpose may be the same and yet could have a very disturbing influence on the psychological growth of surviving children. In these instances, the clinician can be instrumental in guiding the parents toward an appropriate manner of memorializing the child, as well as in protecting parents from exploitation by the unscrupulous. By externalizing the grief work into constructive social behavior, the parents can find meaning in the death that otherwise remains a pointless event.

Another avenue open to parents suddenly bereft of a young child is found in the self-help movement. As the family finds itself increasingly at sea, it is without the social network of relatives, neighbors, friends, and institutions that once bound it close to a secure harbor. Mutual support must often be found through different means today. Parent organizations of people who have shared the same experience are one such device of finding and giving assistance without the stigma of helplessness or illness that attaches to clinical treatment.

One of the most successful parent organizations relates to Sudden Infant Death Syndrome where the uncertain etiology of the syndrome has caused bewilderment in both parents and the public so that a combination of supportive measures and education has been required to deal with the confusion. Through group effort the affected parents correct distortions of self-mortification among themselves and look for the cause of the problem outside themselves in the hope that this scourge can be controlled and prevented. Although the particular emphasis is not exactly applicable to all cases of sudden death, there is sufficient merit to the idea to promote a support group for parents whose children died through a variety of circumstances but particularly for those whose children lost their lives traumatically.

Here, too, the clinician can serve in a consulting role to parent groups in addition to whatever personal counseling for individual parents and families may be required. By joining forces against unknown causations of death or external hazards such as flammable garments, unguarded traffic, and poisons, the sense of individual shortcomings becomes transcended through cooperative action by a commitment to improving the well-being of the larger society.

To survivors, the death of dear ones is an assault on the meaningfulness of life. This challenge to faith is unusually severe when a young child dies in what was or appeared to have been a preventable manner. Thus, the restoration of a belief in life's meaning and of one's own place in the universe is at the core of grief work and is most crucial for parents who have lost children. Those coping mechanisms that normally assert themselves as part of the mourning process must be strengthened and guided whenever clinicians are called upon for succor. Parental mortification following the death of a child requires special attention from clinicians, who should recognize the positive and negative features of restitutional activities such as replacement, memorialization, and advocacy. Although, unlike the prophet Elisha's efforts with the child of the Shunammite woman, restoring children to life is not in the province of clinicians, there remains an obligation to comfort the survivors and to return them to life.

REFERENCES

Cain, A. C. and B. S. Cain. 1964. "On Replacing a Child." *Journal of American Academy of Child Psychiatry* 3:443–56.

Cornwell, J., B. Nurcombe, and L. Stevens. 1977. "Family Response to Loss of a Child by Sudden Infant Death Syndrome." *Medical Journal of Australia* 1:656–58.

Fischhoff, J. and N. O'Brien. 1976. "After the Child Dies." *Journal of Pediatrics* 88:140–46.

Halpern, W. I. 1972. "Some Psychiatric Sequelae to Crib Death." *American Journal of Psychiatry* 129:398–402.

Jolly, H. 1976. "Family Reactions to Stillbirth." *Proceedings of the Royal Society of Medicine* 69:835–37.

Legg, C. and I. Sherick. 1976. "The Replacement Child—A Developmental Tragedy: Some Preliminary Comments." *Child Psychiatry and Human Development* 7:113–26.

Mandell, F. and B. Belk. 1977. "Sudden Infant Death Syndrome. The Disease and its Survivors." *Postgraduate Medicine* 62:193–97.

Mandell, F. and L. C. Wolfe. 1975. "Sudden Infant Death Syndrome and Subsequent Pregnancy." *Pediatrics* 56:774–76.

Morris, D. 1976. "Parents' Reactions to Perinatal Death." *Proceedings of the Royal Society of Medicine* 69:837–38.

Poznanski, E. D. 1972. "A Saga of Unresolved Parental Grief." *Journal of Pediatrics* 81:1190–93.

VI

Parental Bereavement and Grief

· 28 ·
Childhood Bereavement: Preventability and the Coping Process

Larry A. Bugen

Death, as a life stress, has certainly been well recognized for its severity and prolonged impact on persons of all ages. Although life stresses affect individuals in different ways, the relative importance of each seems to be significantly uniform within cultural groups. The widely recognized work of Holmes and Rahe (1967), for instance, has documented the extremely stressful nature of death in the American culture. From a list of 43 life changes, "death of spouse" has been rated number one in regard to needed readjustment, while "death of close family member" has been rated number five. Readjustment within the Holmes and Rahe studies presupposes differential grief patterns, depending upon the specified life event. It thus appears that the death of one's spouse would indicate the most intense and prolonged bereavement pattern. Though this may indeed be the case, it is too simplistic to predict grief patterns solely on the basis of the deceased's role—for example, husband, wife, or child.

This paper suggests a model for understanding human grief that is not tied to a fixed order of emotional states (Kübler-Ross 1969, Kavanaugh 1972) and does not overextend the importance of role relationships. Instead, two dimensions—*closeness of relationship* and mourner's *perception of preventability* of the death—are hypothesized to be major determinants of both intensity and duration of bereavement. The model, which has been described by Bugen (1977, 1979), appears to have exceptional face validity in regard to childhood bereavement. This paper suggests that "closeness of relationship" and "preventability" have special meaning and importance to parents who experience childhood bereavement, particularly in situations involving Sudden Infant Death Syndrome (SIDS). The paper briefly describes the model, describes its validity in regard to SIDS, and critiques suggested coping skills in regard to SIDS on the basis of the model.

The Model

The model is essentially a 2 × 2 matrix (see table 28.1) in which the vertical axis represents the closeness of the relationship between the deceased and mourner, while the horizontal axis represents the degree to which the griever believes the death might have been prevented. Four reactive grief states are generated from

Table 28.1.
Interaction of Closeness of Relationship and Perception of Preventability as Predictors of Human Grief

	Preventability	Unpreventability
Central relationship	Intense and prolonged	Intense and brief
Peripheral relationship	Mild and prolonged	Mild and brief

this interaction, with each reflecting levels of duration and intensity. Four predictions emerge:

1. A griever who considered the deceased to be a central person in his life and also believes that the death was preventable would be predicted to experience both an intense and prolonged grieving process.
2. A griever who had only a peripheral relationship with the deceased yet believed that the death was preventable would be predicted to experience a mild and prolonged grieving process.
3. A griever who considered the deceased to be a central person in

his life and does not consider the death preventable in any way is likely to experience an intense but brief grief reaction.
4. A griever who had only a peripheral relationship with the deceased and also believes that the death could not have been prevented is likely to experience a mild and brief grieving process.

It is evident that the intensity of the grief reaction depends on the closeness of the relationship between mourner and deceased. If the relationship is central, the grief reaction is intense, if the relationship is peripheral, the grief reaction is mild. A number of criteria are needed to define closeness or centrality. Centrality may refer to a person whose presence and importance is so profound that a survivor feels he has no life left without that person. Mourners typically feel a great deal of despair and hopelessness. Future time orientations become vague receptacles as present pains and emptiness are focused on.

Centrality also refers to a person to whom the survivor had become behaviorally committed through daily activities. Memories of washing dishes and clothes, preparing meals, and arranging transportation certainly increase one's feelings of loss for someone who has died. A person who is a symbol for our hopes and beliefs may also be a central figure. Human grief in response to President Kennedy's assassination seems to reflect this.

Peripherality represents the other pole of the closeness dimension. Peripherality may connote a person whose presence is both felt and respected but whose loss is not regarded or experienced as irreplaceable. It may also reflect the behavioral view that our rewards and pleasures are not contingent on the behavior or presence of the deceased.

When we turn to predictions concerning duration of human grief, we must determine whether the mourner believes the death was preventable. If the cause of death is believed to be preventable, duration of grief is likely to be prolonged. Preventability may refer to the "general" belief that the factors surrounding a death may have been sufficiently controlled that the death might have been avoided. This may include doubts regarding the adequacy of medical and paramedical care and/or doubts about the style of life of the deceased. "General" is meant to connote any factor other than the mourner that might have contributed to the death. In addition, preventability may also refer to the "specific" belief of mourners that they themselves contributed to the death either directly or indirectly.

In contrast, unpreventability refers to the belief that (1) nothing could have been done by any mortal to alter the course of events, (2) everything was done to divert the forces contributing to the death, or (3) God, inevitability, luck, or misfortune is responsible.

Obvious directions for grief management can be understood directly from the proposed model. A griever can cope with loss of a loved one by moving from preventability to unpreventability and/or by moving the relationship to the deceased from centrality to peripherality. Preventability beliefs are usually quite resistant to change and require powerful techniques suggested by attitude change research. Empathic listening and acceptance are normally not sufficient conditions for change, though they certainly are necessary. When preventability beliefs do begin to shift, grievers are then more open to reconstructing new patterns of living, and this restructuring underlies the process of detaching oneself from the deceased.

Sudden Infant Death Syndrome (SIDS)

Parents experiencing SIDS are quite likely to grieve intensely and over prolonged periods of time. The centrality of a child in the lives of parents can hardly be questioned. Minimally, a parent is behaviorally committed to a child through the usual caretaking responsibilities, for example, washing, changing, feeding, and playing. When we also fathom the meaning a loved child has to parents regarding future roles and goals, we can begin to understand how intensity of a grief response is likely. The model just described also predicts a prolonged grief response if a death is believed to be preventable. Data (Bergman 1974, Pomeroy 1969) strongly suggest that parents experiencing SIDS feel guilty and believe that in some way they are responsible for their child's death. A prolonged grief response is therefore likely. A brief introduction to SIDS may be helpful at this point.

SIDS kills approximately 10,000 babies each year in the United States and is the major cause of death in infants between one week and one year of age. The chance of any baby's actually dying of SIDS is about 1 in 350. SIDS occurs more frequently during the winter months, has a higher incidence in males and lower socioeconomic groups, and has a peak incidence at three months of age.

The cause of SIDS is unknown, and researchers have been slow to investigate determinants. In the eight years prior to 1972, for instance, the National Institute of Child Health and Human Development (NICHD) devoted only $420,000 out of a budget exceeding $430 million to research on SIDS. In addition to inadequate financial support, grieving family members may be submitted to callous treatment subsequent to a SIDS death.

A study by Bergman (1972) of 158 communities has revealed that only half of the grieving parents were informed that their child had died from SIDS. The others were told that the death had occurred from such "preventable" causes as pneumonia, suffocation, and strangulation in bed clothes. Blacks were interrogated by police officers more frequently than whites and were more likely to be told that their babies had suffocated. Autopsies were conducted in only one-quarter of the unexplained deaths. Some parents had to wait months for autopsy results, and one out of every ten were never given any explanation at all. One can begin to see why such parents will have difficulty giving up their beliefs that the deaths were preventable and may indeed experience prolonged periods of grief.

The emotional/social costs associated with SIDS are tremendous. Some form of stress is felt by all members of the family. This may include husbands, wives, siblings, grandparents, and others who might be close to the family. These stresses, if not coped with adequately, may result in problems of communication among family members, family breakup, relocation, relationship problems with surviving siblings, and difficulties with subsequent pregnancies. Mandell and Wolfe (1975), for instance, showed that more than 60 percent of the mothers who had lost infants through SIDS had difficulty conceiving another child during the intense grief period that followed. They also found that these mothers had more than three times the normal rate of infertility and more than twice the normal rate of miscarriages in the year following their infant's death. The SIDS mothers had a rate of 31 percent. This compares to a normal miscarriage rate of 12 to 15 percent. Data strongly suggest that the intense and prolonged grief response to SIDS is quite significant and must be reckoned with in a systematic fashion.

Coping With Sudden Infant Death Syndrome

The model described earlier suggests that effective management of grief associated with SIDS must actively encourage the mourner to move toward a belief that the death was "unpreventable." In this way, the prolonged agonies of grief may be somewhat abated over time. Coping resources within the individual, as well as those in the community itself, need to be available. Goldston (1976) has reported on the National Institute of Mental Health's concern with developing such resources in regard to SIDS. Educational, counseling, and community organization activities are all needed, and grants have been awarded in this regard.

Programs receiving NIMH support have accepted and implemented the National Sudden Infant Death Syndrome Foundation's "minimum acceptable standards" for handling sudden unexpected infant deaths in all communities in the United States. These include the following:

1. Autopsies should be available on all children who die suddenly and unexpectedly and should be performed by qualified pathologists.
2. The term "sudden infant death syndrome" should be used as a cause of death on death certificates when appropriate.
3. Families should be notified either by telephone or letter of the autopsy results within twenty-four hours.
4. Followup counseling and information about SIDS and the characteristic grief reactions should be provided by a knowledgeable health professional.

It is apparent that the first three guidelines are intended to provide information quickly to the parents in order to challenge their beliefs in preventability. Such information must emphasize that SIDS is a specific disease, SIDS is a common cause of death for infants, death was unpredictable and unpreventable, and there was nothing the parents did or did not do that in any way could have prevented their baby's death. It is important that these facts be conveyed to parents convincingly by authority figures involved with SIDS management. These people might include the attending physician, nurse, police officer, and justice of the peace.

The counseling visit should occur within two weeks following the death of the child. This visit will essentially be a listening visit in which the "helper" attempts to consolidate and validate existing information (or misinformation). Other problems that the family may be encountering can also be identified as they relate to the disease and/or grief process. Every attempt should be made to allow for followup counseling or a referral to a local SIDS chapter, which will serve as a support group.

Management of SIDS in the Austin (Texas) area reflects these concerns and is an excellent example of a systematic community approach to grief management associated with SIDS. The intervention process may be outlined as follows:

1. The justice of the peace brings the child's body and family by Austin ambulance from home to Brackenridge Hospital emergency room.
2. The justice of the peace is responsible for calling the child's physician. The Brackenridge Hospital emergency room physician (and the child's physician, if available) observes the child and, with the justice of the peace, discusses SIDS with the parents. Emergency room nurse and social worker are also available to support parents and provide them with *Facts About SIDS,* an information pamphlet distributed by the National Foundation for Sudden Infant Death.
3. The justice of the peace orders an autopsy and chest x-ray.
4. The justice of the peace then discusses the autopsy results with the family physician (within 24 hours), and together they decide who will contact the parents in order to inform them of the autopsy results.

5. The justice of the peace then calls Austin-Travis County health department and arranges for followup counseling resources. A team of trained professionals is available for this purpose.
6. The public health nurse or a social worker from the health department then consults with the physician in charge regarding special instructions and contacts a representative from SIDRA, a local support group located in Austin.
7. The public health nurse or social worker then calls the family to make an appointment for a home visit within one week after the infant's death.

The goals of this program ensure that parents receive accurate and consistent information about SIDS as the cause of death. Parents are also given specific assurances that they have not caused the death, nor could they have prevented it in any way. They learn that their child died from a disease and that a support group and host of community professionals are available to work with them through an expected intense, but they hope, abated grief process.

Grief associated with centrality and a belief in preventability can be so debilitating that it is sometimes helpful to specify points for discussion. Such a review facilitates successful coping and has been addressed by Pomeroy (1969). Parents should understand that they will have emotional ups and downs, they will experience many "if only's," insomnia and somatic complaints are common, concentration may be affected, anorexia may be experienced, other children may increase irritability, and husbands and wives may grieve in different ways.

While there are many similar patterns in SIDS families in terms of reactions and questions, each family must be considered unique in their perception of the tragedy. The model proposed in this paper predicts that the grief associated with Sudden Infant Death Syndrome is likely to be intense and prolonged. Although the intensity will be exceptionally difficult to assuage, it is hoped that by knowing the effects of "preventability" upon prolonged grief reactions, constructive actions can be taken to attenuate this process. This paper has outlined both guidelines and a model program that may buttress efforts elsewhere in this area.

REFERENCES

Bergman, A. B. 1972. "Sudden Infant Death." *Nursing Outlook* 20:775–77.
Bergman, A. B., ed. 1974. "Sudden Infant Death Syndrome." *Pediatric Annals* 3:5–82.
Bugen, L. A., ed. 1979. *Death and Dying: Theory, Research, and Practice.* Dubuque, Iowa: William L. Brown.
Bugen, L. A. 1977. "Human Grief: A Model for Prediction and Intervention." *American Journal of Orthopsychiatry* 47(2):196–206.
Goldston, S. 1976. "The Mental Health Aspects of the Sudden Infant Death Syndrome: A Federal Perspective." Paper presented to the American Psychological Association Annual Meeting, Washington, D.C.
Holmes, T. H., and R. H. Rahe. 1967. "The Social Readjustment Rating Scale." *Journal of Psychosomatic Research* 11:213–18.
Kavanaugh, R. 1972. *Facing Death.* Baltimore: Penguin Books.
Kübler-Ross, E. 1969. *On Death and Dying.* New York: Macmillan.
Mandell, F. and L. C. Wolfe. 1975. "Sudden Infant Death Syndrome and Subsequent Pregnancy." *Pediatrics* 56:774–76.
Pomeroy, M. 1969. "The Nurse's Visit to a SIDS Family." *American Journal of Nursing* 69:9.

· 29 ·

Mourning the Fatally Ill Child

EDWARD H. FUTTERMAN AND IRWIN HOFFMAN

Whereas death may have been "a palpable reality, an every day presence" in the nineteenth century (Aaron 1977), coping with the fatal illness of a child is one of the most poignant and stressful events encountered by families in our time (Paykel 1970). The crisis precipitated by such an unexpected and harsh threat profoundly affects the immediate and long-range adaptation of family members. There are distinct emotional hazards in coping with such a crisis. Family equilibrium is endangered. Coping strategies and adaptive mechanisms that may have been useful in dealing with previous developmental and adaptive tasks are challenged. Adaptation to the death of a child is marked by a complex combination of regression and growth, disturbance and restitution, failure and mastery.

In order to better understand the nature of the crisis confronting parents and the process of their adaptation over time, we interviewed and observed families of dying children, particularly those with leukemia, during the child's illness and after death. While we were aware of the psychological risks and potential pathological consequences in dealing with such a catastrophe, our efforts were directed toward describing and defining the complex interaction of adaptational processes over time without resorting to concepts of psychopathology and defense mechanisms (Futterman and Hoffman 1970a, 1970b, 1973; Futterman et al. 1972; Futterman 1975; Hoffman 1972; Hoffman and Futterman 1971; Kirkpatrick et al. 1974).

In the course of six years during the mid-sixties, we recorded extensive open-ended interviews with twenty-three sets of parents of leukemic children at various points during the child's illness and after death. Of the forty-five interviews obtained, thirteen were conducted after the death of the child and eight occurred while the child was in medical relapse. Informal contact with these families and with more than one hundred additional families with children suffering from leukemia and other malignancies contributed to our understanding of the process. In addition, data were obtained from observations in the waiting room of the tumor clinic at the University of Illinois Hospital, on the wards, in the clinic examining rooms, and in a preventive group therapy program developed for the parents.

At that time, chemotherapeutic approaches had extended the average life expectancy of the leukemic child to more than two years, and there was a growing number of children who had survived five years or longer. Medical advances had also reduced the morbidity of these children so that long, symptom-free periods of remission were quite common. On the other hand, death was still considered the inevitable outcome of leukemia within a few years of onset, and the unfolding of the illness was predictable with its increasingly frequent relapses and ever shorter periods of remission until the time of death. At present, with further medical advances, the inevitability of a fatal outcome is not so apparent, and prolongation of life, and even hope for cure, can be expected to influence coping. However, the similarity between our observations and those of investigators studying other life-threatening and severe illnesses in children, such as cystic fibrosis (Leiken and Hassakis 1973), suggests that our work is still relevant.

When death is a realistic possibility, despite the wishes of parents to thwart the inevitable course of the disease and to maintain their investment in the cherished child, mourning invariably begins before the terminal phase. Most workers dealing with fatal illness in children have described aspects of anticipatory mourning occurring in parents and other family members (Binger et al. 1969). Our effort is to describe the process over time in relation to adaptation and postbereavement mourning.

The work of mourning involves gradually relinquishing emotional investment in the dead or dying person. Freud wrote: "Mourning occurs under the influence of reality testing; for the latter function demands categorically from the bereaved person that he should separate himself from the object, since it no longer exists" (1917). In anticipatory mourning, the consequences of reality testing are more complicated. Not only is the person present and alive, but also evidence that he will die is often obscure or hidden and must be taken at the word of the physician. Moreover, unlike postbereavement mourning, anticipatory mourning must be balanced against the realistic task of continuing emotional investment in the dying person with even increased energy devoted to his care.

Mourning versus active caring is one of a series of adaptive dilemmas confronting families coping with the fatal illness of a child. They need to work out balances between apparently polar conflicting, adaptive tasks: for example, acknowledging the ultimate loss of the child and maintaining hope, tending to immediate needs and planning for the future, cherishing the child and allowing separations to occur, maintaining day-to-day functioning and expressing disturbing feelings, caring actively for the personal needs of the child and delegating care to medical personnel, trusting physicians and recognizing their limitations, caring for the child and preparing for his death.

In regard to the task of anticipatory mourning, even while maintaining hope and mastery activities throughout the child's illness, the parents in our study usually began disengaging from the child before his death. We have defined parental anticipatory mourning as a set of processes related to awareness of the impending loss, to its emotional impact, and to the adaptive mechanisms whereby emotional attachment to the dying child is relinquished over time. We have identified a series of interwoven and interdependent processes emerging and reaching prominence at different points in time, which, taken as a whole, encompass the course of anticipatory mourning. These processes are acknowledgment, grieving, reconciliation, detachment, and memorialization.

Acknowledgment

Lazarus (1966) has emphasized the importance of cognitive activity in coping, stating that, "For threat to occur an evaluation must be made of the situation to the effect that harm is signified." Acknowledgment, an outcome of such cognitive activity, entails progressive realization of the inevitability of the child's death. This process involves a continual struggle between hope and despair. Ideally, appraisal of reality mediates between the degree of active preparation for death and the amount of hope maintained.

We found that most parents suspected that their child had leukemia or was very seriously ill before the diagnosis was officially presented to them. Persistence of the child's symptoms despite customary therapeutic efforts, accompanied by active searching, reading, and questioning on the part of the parents, led to suspicions and dread in the prediagnostic period. One father said, "I was sure it was [leukemia], and the doctor, I think he was sure but he wouldn't commit himself." These suspicions tended to mitigate the emotional impact when the diagnosis was finally confirmed and presented in the hospital. In some instances, parents reported feelings of relief that at last they knew what was wrong and could do something about it.

Once told of the diagnosis and prognosis, parents indicated recognition of the child's fatal condition. This acknowledgment marked the beginning of anticipatory mourning. Feelings of disbelief were generally quite ephemeral. In fact, although hope was universal, there were no instances of absolute denial in all of our data. When parents seemed to be oblivious of the awesome prognosis, it represented a strategy rather than blanket denial.

Improvement in the child's condition and achievement of remission as a result of treatment heightened the dilemma between acknowledgment and hope by validating the diagnosis on the one hand and discrediting it on the other. The mixed message of reality perception is illustrated in this statement by a mother whose daughter was on the verge of her first remission:

> When your kid looks terrible, it makes you feel terrible. You don't know what it is and it is the unknown that will scare you . . . and then when I saw

her I realized that, well, she looked a little better. And, like right now she looks great. I mean she is pudgy and those signs have disappeared, but still I know that inside she still has all this. I think that she is fooling a lot of people because you can't see it from the outside.

Typically, families exhibited determination to hold onto acknowledgment of the fatal prognosis even when the course of the illness was long and relatively benign. One mother, whose daughter was in her fourth year of virtually symptom-free survival since the time of diagnosis, remarked, "Part of me believes that there is nothing wrong with her. But there is a little part deep in my heart that knows there's got to be something. I'm sure you're not lying to me."

Sometimes insistence on facing the truth had a fierce quality, and false reassurance from relatives and friends was unequivocally rejected. One father reported, "I almost chewed my wife's head off one night when she had the gall to say to me that one of her friends said that our son was well." Parents often felt more comfortable with people, such as other parents with fatally ill children, who shared their level of awareness of the fatal prognosis. The parent who described the "community of spirit" in the clinic was alluding to the common bond described by Henry James consoling a friend as joining an "army of sufferers" (Aaron 1977).

In spite of the persistence of acknowledgment on some level, periods of remission raised parents' hopes that there might have been some mistake or that their child might be the exception to the rule. The mother whose child was in her fourth year of remission also remarked, "This is four years and I don't believe it. I really think I'm going to wake up some day and it's all going to be a dream." Relapse, therefore, came as a blow and reawakened feelings of despair. Typically, over the long course of the illness a series of such remissions and relapses had a cumulative impact upon parents so that their acknowledgment progressively deepened to the point of resignation. By the terminal period, during the final vigil at the child's bedside, only faint residuals of hope remained.

Acknowledgment evolved with continual alterations in levels of awareness tied to reality events. Hopeful statements were often laden with resignation, while pessimistic remarks were tinged with hope. One mother stated, "Each day we accept it more, because each day that he lives we've got a better chance that there is going to be a cure found." A father epitomized the dilemma and the coping that it requires by advising, "Plan for the future, but not with your heart and soul!" Despite the many day-to-day and even moment-to-moment fluctuations in the interaction between acknowledgment and hope, progressive deepening of parental awareness of the fatal prognosis served to facilitate the process of anticipatory mourning.

Grieving

Grieving refers to the process of experiencing and expressing the emotional impact of the anticipated loss. This includes feelings of shock, numbness, confusion, diffuse anxiety, rage, and pain, along with psychosomatic responses and more differentiated, focused sadness or depression. Overt signs of emotional turmoil varied greatly in intensity, form, and timing. Less differentiated and more diffuse forms of grieving seemed to predominate as early reactions to the diagnosis. Shock and numbness were common. As one mother said, "I listened, but I don't know what he (the doctor) said." Numbness quickly gave way to pain, sadness, and crying. Agitation, physical symptoms, and insomnia were also prominent in the first month or two following diagnosis. During this early period of turmoil, work routines and family life were often disrupted. Parents frequently felt overwhelmed, and grieving was primarily reactive and passive. As one mother put it, "When the doctor hit me with the diagnosis, it was like being hit with a brick."

As the initial turmoil subsided, more controlled patterns of overt grieving emerged. Parents were able to actively inhibit, channel, and time their grieving behavior in coordination with other adaptive tasks with which they were confronted. They usually avoided crying in front of the children, minimized displaying anxiety in the presence of neighbors and relatives, shielded the physician from their rage, and underplayed their fears and worries before each other. They were selective in their choice of resources for emotional support, weighing the vulnerability or potential supportiveness of others in deciding how much to confide in them or to shield them. Some parents resolved to do much of their grieving alone. "I have my times when I am low but nobody sees me. I go and have a good cry and I'm okay." But most found some person or persons, whether spouse or others, with whom they shared their deepest feelings. A common attitude was verbalized by one mother who said, "I think that you have to have somebody to talk to, no matter who it is. Someone that you can confide to and who will let you talk. . . . I think that helps an awful lot."

As part of their active regulation of grieving, parents deliberately timed their expressions of grief. An apparent absence of grief might actually entail an intentional postponement or delay of overt grieving in the interest of other coping processes such as activities designed to prolong the life of the sick child or to maintain family routines. "I save my crying until the children are asleep," one mother stated. From a longer term perspective, another mother remarked as follows:

> It's still in there, I know this and I imagine if she ever gets to a bad point again I will probably be more sad about it but I hope I get out of it. I mean, that's the only thing I can do because I still have another child. I don't know if that's right or wrong but I figure I've got two children and not just the one and I can't just sit around and mope that Brenda's got leukemia.

Prolonged delay of catharsis was chosen as part of a long-range adaptive plan even when the parent perceived that immediate overt grieving might bring relief.

Over the course of time, the quality of grief tended to become more differentiated and focused. A more temperate sense of melancholy emerged, accompanied by active articulation and evaluation of the impending loss. This mellowing of grief occurred in conjunction with reconciliation, detachment, and memorialization. The intensity of grief tended to peak at times of diagnosis and relapse and in the terminal period. However, unlike acknowledgment, successive peaks of grief decreased in strength. Through grieving, in association with acknowledgment, parents accepted, expressed, and articulated the emotional impact of the anticipated loss.

Reconciliation

Discovery of a fatal illness in a child threatens the confidence level of parents and can lead potentially to guilt, blame, and bitterness. Reconciliation refers to the development of a perspective that preserves the family's sense of confidence in the worth of the child's life and the worth of life in general despite acknowledgment of the child's fatal illness. This entails a "cognitive reappraisal" in Lazarus' terms (1965), whereby the stress is reinterpreted in a manner that neutralizes some of its potentially damaging psychological force. As part of the mourning process, before parents can let go of a child, they strive to make it all right to let go by assuring themselves that the integrity and worth of self, others, and life in general will not be destroyed by the child's death.

Redefining the child's death in a way that reduced its awesome implications constituted one form of reconciliation. For example, a father stated, "A child is more fit to die than an adult because he hasn't lived long enough to do anything wrong." A widowed mother remarked, "You know that if this child is going to die, at least she is not alone. She is in Heaven with her father." Redefining led some parents to cast the death in positive terms, as a religious event or as a release from a life of suffering.

Other forms of reconciliation involved seeking consolation from the past and present life of the child and "counting blessings." Parents described appreciation of the quality of the child's life, of the care that the child received, and of the duration of his survival from the time of diagnosis. These included statements like, "I don't think we cheated him out of anything." "I'm thankful he has been around this long." They assured themselves that there was still much to live for and savored such things as their other children, their marriage, their friends, their work.

The following is a particularly poignant and integrative expression of reconciliation, reported by a mother retrospectively seven months after her child's death:

When Harold was ill at home, I used to go into the bedroom and sit with him and the baby and talk to them both. I told him about his own birth and I told him how much we wanted him and how proud daddy was that he had sons. I had to cram in a lot of things in a short time. Many times children don't know these little things. You just never get around to telling them. But this was a time when I planned: "What do I want this child to know about us, about himself, about our family, about our philosophy, about our relationship?" And even if nothing else matters, even if all our philosophy and religion or anything is irrelevant, at least I felt that we did the best job that we could do at that time.

While reconciliation often began as early as the period of diagnosis, it became more fully articulated over time. It facilitated the mellowing of grief on the one hand and the process of detachment on the other. It also fostered a critical review of values, goals, and philosophy of life.

Detachment

The work of mourning includes the difficult task of gradually relinquishing emotional investment in the dying child as a growing being with a future. The process is inexorable despite the wish by parents to prevent or to deny the impending loss.

Timing of detachment seemed related to parental expectations about when the child would die. If the child died "on time," detachment was balanced against other adaptive tasks so that care of the child was maintained to the end, even while adequate preparation for the loss was achieved. The emotional hazards of detachment for both parent and child became pronounced when the child survived longer than expected. Premature detachment can lead potentially to neglect of the child's emotional and/or physical needs with concomitant parental guilt during the illness and after the child's death. In one case, a mother expected her child to live eighteen months based on what she had been told at the time of diagnosis. As the child continued to survive beyond that time, she expressed an eagerness to move on and become reinvolved with other aspects of her life as a parent and as a member of the community. She seemed increasingly impatient with the burden of caring for her daughter, as compared with the positive attitude with which she had earlier taken up this challenge. However, she continued to manage her detachment sufficiently well so that neglect of the child's needs never became apparent. On the other hand, if children died sooner than expected, the reaction could be stormy, as when one father felt cheated because his son expired before the three-year period of survival that he had anticipated.

As they struggled with the dilemma of simultaneously retaining and relinquishing investment in the dying child, most parents, at one time or another, clung to the sick child or indulged his needs at the expense of other family members. In one family, clinging led to transient school phobic episodes arising from intense separation anxiety and mutual ambivalence between a mother and daughter, heightened by the threat inherent in the illness. In general, clinging behavior tended to increase at points of relapse or other evidence of deterioration in the child's condition. While other authors have reported considerable difficulties with school phobia during the illness (Binger et al. 1969), we saw separation anxiety only as a temporary coping response, limited by reality testing, rarely causing significant impairment in the child's developmental progress. As an expression of the urge to hold onto an object soon to be lost, clinging most often had the character of embracing and savoring the cherished child prior to saying farewell.

Detachment usually accelerated in the terminal period. At times hospital personnel complained about a family's seeming lack of concern, callous behavior, and disinterest in a child who had been ill for a long time or who underwent a prolonged terminal phase. In one instance, after hospital staff expressed concern about her failure to visit, a mother admitted to one of us that she "could not bear it" any longer and that she had made a conscious decision to devote more time to other family members, relegating care of the sick child to relatives and to the hospital. Another mother became attached to a number of other children on the ward, describing one of them as her "flower child." When her dying daughter became jealous and sought more attention, the mother became irritated and lost her temper.

On the whole, however, even when overt signs of detachment

were present, parents maintained care of their child's physical and emotional needs throughout the terminal period to the point of death. Most parents were active at this time, making sure that everything possible was being done even while preparing themselves for the end. For some parents, home care of the dying child helped to avoid premature detachment and to maintain the balance between caring and mourning. Nevertheless, gradual emotional disengagement from the sick child prepared the family for the actual loss and permitted them to have energy available to deal with other life problems and to reconstitute their relationships with other family members when the child died.

Memorialization

The literature on bereavement is replete with descriptions of the process by which the mourner eulogizes the dead in the transition, in the words of Henry James, "from the changing world of fact to the steady world of thought" (Aaron 1977). We observed these processes beginning before the actual death. Memorialization refers to the process by which the conscious mental representation of the dying child is molded into a relatively permanent form that will endure beyond the child's death. A fixed image of the child is formed and becomes the way in which he is remembered. In the process of memorialization, progressive abstraction occurred, whereby parents began to think of the child in terms of global characteristics or traits rather than in terms of specific behaviors in specific circumstances. In other words, the child's image became more frozen and fixed and less available to reality testing. Along with this, progressive idealization or eulogization occurred whereby the image of the sick child became increasingly positive. Perception became selective and biased, so that negative attributes were deemphasized, ignored, or forgotten.

An illustration of how the quality of portrayal of the child can vary along these dimensions is offered in a pair of statements made by a father early and later in his daughter's illness. His early description was positive but concrete and observational.

"One of the high points in her life was about three weeks ago when she won the citizenship award for the eighth grade in junior high school. After that she told her mother she had been working on that ever since fifth grade." Later, his description was more generalized and eulogizing. "She was good in almost everything she tried." This was a common progression of memorialization through abstraction and idealization.

An extreme form of idealization is enshrinement, which describes the tendency to conceive of the child as having extraordinary characteristics. When a child is enshrined, he is usually viewed as saintly, with wisdom, insight, understanding, goodness, or sufferance far beyond what is normally ascribed to children. Enshrinement often had a religious quality, as exemplified in the following report by a mother of her interaction with her son in the hospital a few days before his death:

> Marshall asked me how Jesus made people and I started to explain like you would normally to a four-year-old and he said, "No mommy, I know now," and that helped me more than anything anyone could have said or done. I think he was shown a way through God to answer the questions that I could not answer.

Unlike progressive abstraction and idealization, which are observed as gradually progressing processes, enshrinement was often manifested in single dramatic events or extraordinary moments of experience.

With the subsequent death of the child, the fixed images, ascribed meanings, and symbolic interpretations of the child's behavior combined to form the bases of myths about the child that became part of the family's self-image. What began as memorialization influenced the family's philosophy of life and its way of integrating death into its value systems. For example, one mother, seven months following the death of her ten-year-old son, stated:

> In our faith we believe that we can pray for the dead and ask for their intercession. I remembered the moment he died. I kissed him, held his hand for a while and just felt, "Now the child has become more the man." In other words I felt the passing on to another life. He knows more than we do and can perhaps now influence and help us.

Through memorialization the task of detachment was made less painful in that some of the original investment in the child could be transferred to the mental representation of him that endured beyond his death. However, significant investment in the real child was retained until the end, leaving important aspects of the work of mourning to be accomplished after bereavement.

Postbereavement Mourning

After the death of the child, there was usually a deepened sense of acknowledgment of the loss and an upsurge of acute grief, followed by further reconciliation. Grieving at this time testified to the degree of emotional investment in the child maintained throughout the illness, while the limited intensity and duration of post-bereavement turmoil testified to the work accomplished in anticipatory mourning.

We observed few instances of severe psychopathology, severe maladaptive behavior, prolonged turmoil, or permanent family disruption in our group of parents. In those few families showing evidence of severe impairment, signs of disturbance were apparent during the illness, as well as following the death. When maladaptation did occur, the manifestations of anticipatory mourning were often abortive, extreme, or distorted. One father, who began blaming his wife for his daughter's illness soon after the diagnosis, showed signs neither of mellowing of grief nor of reconciliation while the child was alive and had to be hospitalized after the child's death when he threatened his wife with physical harm. Another father failed to progress beyond tenuous acknowledgment mixed with poorly controlled reactive grieving throughout eighteen months of his child's survival. After the death, he became severely distraught and paranoid and for a time was unable to function. He continued to resist genuine acknowledgment, claiming that his son was "healthy except for his leukemia" and blaming the death upon medical mismanagement rather than upon the disease itself.

In a third instance of serious disturbance, a mother who had a history of psychosis and fanatic religiosity refused to acknowledge the fatal prognosis, stating, "As far as I'm concerned, Lila is not sick. . . . I've asked God not to take her and I believe He is not going to take her and I prayed with my minister and that meant two of us had agreed and so she is all right!" Less than two months following diagnosis, the mother withdrew the child from medical care, saying that she was placing her daughter "in the hands of God." The child died at home a few months later. While home care may be helpful for many families, in this instance, home care was no care. Following the death, the mother resorted to an extreme form of enshrinement, describing Lila as "a born missionary" who "reached out into the world and touched a lot of people." This mother's coping resources were not sufficient to deal with the sustained tension associated with the dilemma of anticipating the child's death over a long period of time. Unable to balance caring for the child with anticipatory mourning, her coping was maladaptive and defensive.

These few cases of maladaptation contrast with the adaptive mourning that was characteristic of most parents in our study. In general, the processes of anticipatory mourning were integrated with each other and with other adaptive tasks. The overall course of adaptation was marked by balanced responsiveness to the multiple demands of reality and by progressive change over time. The death of the child, however painful, was adaptively integrated by continuation of the process of mourning in the postbereavement period.

There is some risk in observing successful aspects of adaptation and in generalizing from these, since individual differences may be ignored. In the growing field of thanatology, it is tempting to view exceptional examples of adaptation as models to be followed by others. Workers dealing with death and dying also undergo anticipatory mourning and, by enshrinement, tend to extol the virtues in stoically facing death and to glamorize particular styles of dying to the point where these are offered as prescribed ways of dying and prescribed ways of dealing with dying children, with calm acceptance of death valued as a highly prized goal.

We have tried to characterize the phases of anticipatory mourning, and we have seen that most of the families in our study demonstrated remarkable resources in coping with the fatal illness of a child. We are also aware that any such generalizations do not fully describe differences in family value systems and cultural backgrounds that color the meaning of adaptation to the death of a child. Although we are able to make generalizations about the process of anticipatory mourning, families deal with the tasks and dilemmas in their own ways, according to their own needs in response to the events with which they are confronted.

REFERENCES

Aaron, D. 1977. "The Etiquette of Grief: A Literary Generation's Response to Death." Benjamin Rush Lecture, American Psychiatric Association, Toronto.

Binger, C. M., A. R. Albin, R. C. Feuerstein, J. H. Kushner, S. Zoger, and C. Mikkelsen. 1969. "Childhood Leukemia: Emotional Impact on Patient and Family." *New England Journal of Medicine* 280:414–18.

Freud, S. 1917. "Mourning and Melancholia," Standard Edition, Vol. 14, London: Hogarth Press, 1957.

Futterman, E. H. 1975. "Studies of Family Responses to a Specific Threat." In E. J. Anthony, ed. *Explorations in Child Psychiatry*. New York: Plenum.

Futterman, E. H. and I. Hoffman. 1970a. "Shielding from Awareness: An Aspect of Family Adaptation to Fatal Illness in Children." *Archives of Thanatology* 2:23–24.

Futterman, E. H. and I. Hoffman. 1970b. "Transient School Phobia in a Fatally Ill Child." *Journal of the American Academy of Child Psychiatry* 9:477–94.

Futterman, E. H. and I. Hoffman. 1973. "Crisis and Adaptation in the Families of Fatally Ill Children." In E. J. Anthony and C. Koupernik, eds. *The Child in His Family: The Impact of Disease and Death*. New York: Wiley.

Futterman, E. H., I. Hoffman, and M. Sabshin. 1972. "Parental Anticipatory Mourning." In B. Schoenberg et al., eds. *Psychosocial Aspects of Terminal Care*. New York: Columbia University Press.

Hoffman, I. 1972. "Parental Adaptation to Fatal Illness in a Child." Doctoral Dissertation, Department of Psychology, University of Chicago.

Hoffman, I. and E. H. Futterman. 1971. "Coping with Waiting: Psychiatric Intervention and Study in the Waiting Room of a Pediatric-Oncology Clinic." *Comprehensive Psychiatry* 12:67–81.

Kirkpatrick, J., I. Hoffman, and E. H. Futterman. 1974. "Dilemma of Trust: Relation between Medical Caregivers and Families of Fatally Ill Children." *Pediatrics* 54:169–75.

Lazarus, R. S. 1966. *Psychological Stress and the Coping Process*. New York; McGraw-Hill, pp. 33, 310, 44.

Leiken, S. J. and P. Hassakis. 1973. "Psychological Study of Parents of Children with Cystic Fibrosis." In E. J. Anthony and C. Koupernik, eds. *The Child in His Family: The Impact of Disease and Death.* New York: Wiley.

Paykel, E. S. 1970. "Life Events and Acute Depression" (Paper presented at Annual Meeting of the American Association for the Advancement of Science, Chicago, December).

Index

Abandonment, 116, 143; fear of, 109, 240, 306
Abortions, 331
Acceptance, 141, 259, 260, 261, 262
Accidental death(s), 115, 215, 331-32, 347, 348
Accident proneness, 117
Acknowledgment: in anticipatory mourning, 368, 369-71, 372
Active imagination, 81
Acute death(s), 7, 141
Adaptation to death, 20, 23-24, 112, 268; of child, 366, 368, 371, 379-80
Adolescence, 6, 96, 99, 140, 289, 304; accidental death in, 332; death of parent during, 131-32, 154; dependency on staff, 245; fatal illness in, 212; importance of school attendance in, 309, 310; suicide attempts in, 153; view of illness in, 254
Adults: and bereaved child, 125-26; death of, 332. *See also* Families; Parents
Adverse consequences, theories of, 93-97
Age of child: and ability to mourn, 106-8; and attitudes toward death, 44-46; and awareness/understanding of death, 4-6, 30, 37, 140, 305-6; caregivers' psychological closeness to, 211-12, 251; and home care of child with cancer, 174-75; and reaction to early parental death, 98; and risk of adult psychopathology in childhood bereavement, 91-92, 93
Aggression, 31, 45; as cause of death, 41, 43, 44. *See also* Homicide
American Cancer Society, 262
Anger, 83, 127, 182, 212; of caregivers, re dying child, 214, 215, 218-19; at dead parent, 153; at death of parent, 111, 130; toward deceased, 119; at diagnosis, 141, 212; displaced onto physician, 141-42; toward parents, 115-16, 212; of parents, re dying child, 214, 219-20; staff, 233, 240, 243; stages, 257, 259, 260, 261, 262
Animism, 32
Anorexia nervosa, 6, 239, 364
Anticipation, 22, 23
Anticipatory grief, 142, 239-40, 346; in home care of dying child, 157, 170
Anticipatory mourning, 106, 215, 368; processes of, 368, 369-78; successful, 379-80
Antihemophilic factor (factor VIII), 187
Antisocial behavior, 98, 99, 117
Anxiety, 12-13, 32, 34, 266-67; alleviated by open communication, 237-38; re cancer, 253; caused by religious sacraments, 145; diffuse, 371; mastered through play, 147-48; parental, re home care, 181, 182; physician; 210-11; reaction to serious illness, 288-89; staff, 147, 157; re surviving parent, 131; in waiting room, 293-94, 295. *See also* Death anxiety; Separation anxiety
Apathy, 10, 98, 119
Apgar scoring system, 340
Appetite disturbance, 97, 141. *See also* Eating disturbances
Art therapy, 268-92
Artificiality: in feeding dying child, 319-20. *See also* Life-support systems
Attribution punishment, 31
Austin (Tex.): SIDS management in, 363-64
Automatic behavior, 349
Autopsy(ies), 152-53, 184; in SIDS, 332, 334, 361, 362
Avoidance, 195, 196; of dying child, 137

Bargaining, 258, 259, 260, 261, 262
Bereavement, 89; and adult psychiatric disorder, 90-93; duration, intensity of, 357-58, 359-60; short-term consequences of, 97-99; symptomatology, 97-99, 117, 120-21, 131. *See also* Grieving; Mourning
Bereavement counseling 346-47.. *See also* Counseling; Family, support for; Parents, professional support for
Biotrauma, 21, 22, 23-24
Black children: attitudes toward death, 37, 38-39, 40-44
Blame, blaming, 257, 373
Bone tumors, 254
Brain tumors, 255

Cancer, 216, 258, 265, 332; children with, in group therapy, 266-92; children with, returning to school, 303-14; factors affecting psychology of, in childhood, 252-54; home care for child with, 156-71, 172-79. *See also* Child with cancer
Cancer Bulletin, 320
Candle Lighters, 162
Care, 360; basic, vs. medical intervention, 321-27; for caregivers, 250-65; comprehensive, 225; concept of, 315-18; continuity of, 13, 202, 218, 240; fragmentation of, 218; ordinary/extraordinary (dying child), 315, 318-27; quality of, 213, 214, 215. *See also* Family care
Caregivers, 211-17, 251, 252; care for, 250-65; emotional involvement of, 268, 291; emotional needs of, 252; and home care of child with cancer, 172, 174; insensitivity of, 10; mourning stages of, 260-62; psychological euthanasia by, 307; reactions to death of child, 214-15, 225-26; reactions to dying child, 3; 10; responsibility to parents, 11-12; selection of, 251; support for, 14, 220-21, 226, 263-65; support for adults who nurture bereaved child, 126, 131. *See also* Nurse(s); Pediatricians; Physician(s); Staff
Caring: mourning vs., 368
Catharsis: delay of, 371-72
Causation, wishful, 33, 45, 115-16, 143, 153

Center for Attitudinal Healing, The (Tiburon, Calif.), 80-85
Certainty, 10-11, 12, 15-16
Chemotherapy, 228, 239
Child(ren), 19-26, 326; attitudes toward death, 36-48; capacity to experience grief, 94-96; concept of death, 3-6, 7, 21, 45, 138-40; concept of fatal illness, 253-54; effects of witnessing murder on, 49-74; experience of dying in maturational crises, 20; experience with death, 37, 40-42, 45, 46, 105-6, 127; with fatal illness, 6-15, 366-81; and fear of death, 27-35; fears with parental death, 108; group process for fatally ill, 81-85; learning about death, 37, 43-44, 45-47, 53, 61, 104-5, 126-27; moribund, 148-49; mourning process in, 106-12; needs of, in parental death, 127-28, 154; opportunity to discuss death, 7-8, 61, 104-5; with prolonged illness, 149-50; reactions to diagnosis of fatal illness, 259; reactions to parental death, 89-103, 104-24, 125-33; replacement of lost, 142, 349-51; understanding of death, 3-6, 19-26, 27-28, 29-30, 36-37, 42, 94, 105, 107, 126-27, 289-90, 305-6. *See also* Age of child; Child(ren) with cancer; Death of child; Dying child
Child life (discipline), 296-97
Child life service (oncology clinic), 294-96
Child life worker, 293-302
Child psychiatrist. *See* Psychiatrist, child
Child rearing, 348; during remissions, 150
Child(ren) with cancer; concerns of, 303-4; death at home, 180-86; in group therapy, 266-92; home care for, 172-79; returning to school, 303-14; support for, 294-302
Children's Health Center (Minneapolis), 179
Christmas factor (Factor IX), 187
Chronic (child) death, 141
Classification (defense), 8
Clergy, 162, 174
Clinic visits: anxiety in, 293-94. *See also* Outpatient clinic
Clinical Psychiatry News, 71
Clinicians: role in parent support, 346-53. *See also* Staff

Index

Cognitive activity, 369
Communication, open, 104-5, 114, 121, 127, 129, 145-46, 161, 170, 182-83, 202; with family and dying child, 7-8, 235, 236-37; mental health professionals and, 244; physician/parents, 204; staff, 220, 242. *See also* Dying child, information given to
Community support, 92
Compassion (professional), 13
Competence (professional), 13
Confusion, 371
Conscience formation, 153
Consultants: working with children who witness homicide, 72-73, 74
Consumption of tobacco, liquor, tranquilizers, 97
Control, 116
Conversion symptoms, 98
Coping: with fatal illness of child, 366, 367, 369, 380. *See also* Adaptation
Coping mechanisms, 37, 268, 352
Coping process: preventability and, in SIDS, 362-65
Coping styles, learned, 96
Costs: home care of child with cancer, 178
Counseling, 180, 185; preventive, 105-22; SIDS parents, 363. *See also* Clinicians; Therapy
Course in Miracles, A, 79-85
Courts, intervention by, 11-12
Cultural beliefs, 4, 8, 29, 37, 114; and adaptation to death, 380; and children's attitudes toward death, 42-43; and concept of care, 316; elders and, 76, 77; and funeral attendance by children, 151; life stresses in, 357; and place to die, 156-57
Cystic fibrosis, 4, 367

Death, 34, 105, 247; and the child, 19-26; child psychiatrist's perspective re, 209-23; children's attitudes toward, 36-48; children's concept of, 3-6, 7, 21, 45, 138-40; children's understanding of, 3-6, 19-26, 27-28, 29-30, 36-37, 42, 94, 105, 107, 126-27, 289-90, 305-6; dignified, 236; equated with sleep, 127, 151; emotional meaning of, 28, 30; experience with, 37, 40-42, 45, 46, 105-6, 127; family coping with, in home care, 163-64; finality of, 104, 105, 107, 140, 289; identified with birth, 45; inevitability of, 4-5, 6, 19, 24, 37; in family of hemophiliacs, 187-198; as life stress, 357-58; personal philosophy of, 304, 305; personification of, 5, 21, 32, 37, 42, 43, 253, 306; place of, 15, 156-57 (*see also* Death at home); prolonging, 216-17 (*see also* Life-support systems); reactions to, 256-62, 305, 364; sudden, 141, 255-56, 346-53; universality of, 306; violent, 43. *See also* Child(ren); Death of child; Dying child; Learning about death
Death anxiety, 61, 73; defense against; 45; nonverbal, 29
Death at home, 157, 173, 174-75; for child with leukemia, 180-86
Death of child, 183-84, 225, 239-40; integration of, 379; parental mortification and restitution efforts in, 346-53; physicians' reaction to, 210-11; redefining, in reconciliation, 373; support for parents in sudden, 346-53
Death taboo, 105, 110, 157
Death wish, 348
"Deathman," 41, 43
Decathexis, 112, 119, 289
Defense(s), 8-9, 104-5; of caregivers, 291; in death of sibling, 195; denial as, 113, 145, 148; fantasy as, 30-31; guilt as, 44; infantile dependence as, 24; intellectualization as, 241-42; in parents of dying child, 142
Dehumanization, 9, 15
Denial, 6, 28, 212, 256-57, 259, 260, 261, 262, 291; of anxiety, 140; of death, 20; in death of sibling, 195, 196; as defense, 113, 145, 148; of diagnosis, 141; of finality of death, 104; by parents (diagnosis and prognosis), 204, 238; in physician's facing death, 210; right to choose, 237
Dependence, infantile, 24, 57
Depression, 90, 93, 97, 122, 258-59, 371; in adolescence, 6; in child bereavement, 91, 93; in child's reaction to his dying, 7, 140-41; in infants, 94; linked to

Depression (*continued*)
   learned helplessness, 96; in parents, 238; as reaction to parental death, 99, 113-14, 118-19, 154; as response to inevitability of death, 24; of staff, 214-15, 230, 241-42
Desensitization, 106, 110
Detachment, 266, 349; in anticipatory mourning, 368, 372, 374-76, 378. *See also* Withdrawal
Development: and ability to mourn, 94-96, 289-90; and concept of care, 325-26; and conceptualization of death, 4-6, 9; effect of child's awareness of death on, 19-26; and hospice care for dying child, 201; phobias and ritualistic behavior in, 33-34; and risk of adult psychopathology in childhood bereavement, 91-92; and understanding of death, 253-54. *See also* Age of child
Diabetic coma, 6
Diagnosis; prognosis, 141, 149, 156, 256-57; impact on parents, 212, 238-39, 369-70, 371, 372; of SIDS, 334
Differentiation, 107
Dignity, privacy, 143, 148
Disavowal, 22; 23-34
Disbelief, 182, 369
Discriminant function analysis, 335-37
Disengagement. *See* Detachment; Withdrawal
Displacement, 142-43, 212, 291; onto surviving parent, 153
Disposition of body, 164
Distortions, correction of, 143, 148
Drawing, 147. *See also* Art therapy
Dudrick, S.: "The Genesis of Intravenous Hyperalimentation," 320
Dying: commitment to, 6; concept, 80; process, 199-200; prolonged, 142; ways of, 379
Dying child: awareness of own impending death, 7-8, 138, 138-39T, 140-41, 145-47, 148, 182-83, 202, 204, 213, 237, 306; care phases, 212-17; clinical management of, 3, 143-53, 202-3, 213-14, 236; concept of care held by, 325-26; emotional needs of, 235, 239; ethical decisions re, 315-27; excessive dependency of, 239; and the family, 137-55; hospice care for, 199-206; information given to, 7-8, 106, 114, 121, 127, 129, 145-47, 161, 236-38, 254, 289-90; and mental health professionals, 243-44; quality of care of, 214, 215; participation in own treatment, 148, 202-3, 217, 236; physician's talking with, 143, 145-47; programs for caregivers, 211-17; psychosocial interactions of, with parents and health-care professionals, 235-38; reactions aroused by, 3-4, 6-7, 8; sources of pain in, 247; tasks confronting, 9-10

Eating disturbances, 98, 120
Egocentricity, 115
Empathy, 14, 20, 225, 226, 233; capacity for, 229
Emptiness, 349
Enshrinement, 377, 379
Enuresis, 98
Equipment, furnishings, supplies, 176-77
Eric, 254
Euthanasia, 216; psychological, 307
Experience, 20

Families, 3, 7, 9-10, 137-55, 169, 263; coping ability of, 294, 306-7; dependence on medical staff, 224-25, 241, 268; and early childhood bereavement, 92, 93; effect of fatal illness in child on, 259-60, 366; emotional burden of, 293-94; emotional growth in experience of home care of dying child, 169, 170, 225, 229-30; mourning shared experience of, 109; post-death care of, 169; in SIDS, 334, 362, 363-64; support for, 157-58, 162-63, 169, 170, 236, 263-64, 334, 346-53; as unit of intervention, 225, 233, 234. *See also* Family disruption; Home care; Parents
Family care: comprehensive, 225; in hospice care of dying child, 199, 201-2, 203-4, 205
Family disruption, 92, 96-97, 157, 371, 378; at parental death, 154-55; in SIDS, 361-62, 363

Index

Fantasy(ies), 45, 153, 237, 289; and fear of death, 27, 28, 30-31, 33
Fear, 7, 80, 120, 182; of death, 21, 27-35, 44, 46-47, 76; of death before fulfillment, 203, 212; of mutilation, 140, 253
Feeding: dying child, 315-27
Fetal deaths, 331
Fixation, developmental, 118
Foundation for Inner Peace (Tiburon, Calif.), 80
Free association, 24
Freud, Anna, 19, 44, 95, 107, 266-67
Freud, Sigmund, 22, 29, 113, 256; *Interpretation of Dreams*, 19; on mourning, 107, 119, 368; *Mourning and Melancholia*, 93-94
Funeral: child's attendance at, 47, 48, 109-10, 128-29, 151-52
Funeral arrangements: in child's death at home, 183-84
Future time, 84, 211; and child's fear of death, 32-33

Galvanic skin response (GSR) measure, 30
Gender: attitude toward death, 37, 40-42, 46; and reaction to early parental death, 98
Gender-appropriate behavior: childhood bereavement and, 92
Grand mal epilepsy, 12
Grandparents, 75-78, 162
Grief, 93-94, 212; adult, 97; defined, 289; model for understanding, 357-65; patterns of, 357, 364; similar to physical morbidity, 89-90; work of, 352
Grieving, 110; in anticipatory mourning, 368, 371-73; blocked, 114; child, 128; help in, 347; over impending loss, 141; permission for, 130; postbereavement, 378-80. *See also* Anticipatory grief; Mourning
Group therapy: children with cancer, 266-92. *See also* Parent groups
Guilt, 212, 257-58, 291; in child's reaction to death, 32, 140; defense against separation anxiety, 44-45; re dying child, 213-14, 218; induced by surviving parent, 121; irrational, 350; parental, 141, 142, 149, 214, 219-20; 349, 360, 373;

physician, 240; as reaction to parental death, 114, 115-17; survivor, 143

Handicapped (the), 317-18
Health, 21, 81
Health-care professionals: interactions of, 235-49. *See also* Caregivers; Nurse(s); Physician(s); Staff
Heaven, 46, 129
Helplessness, 8, 12-13, 291; learned, 96; professional staff feelings of, 240
Hemophilia, 187-98
Home care, 15, 379; of child with cancer, 156-71, 172-79; of child with malignant disease, 228, 229; emotional issues in, 182-83; hospice programs of, 199, 202; reasons for, 160. *See also* Parents, desire, ability to care for child at home
Home Care for the Child With Cancer research, 172-79
Home visits, 183, 229
Homicide, 332; witnessed by children, 49-74
Hope, 143, 146, 237, 259, 260, 261, 262, 368; in anticipatory mourning, 368, 369, 370-71; importance of, 307
Hopelessness, 98
Hospice care: for dying child, 199-206
Hospice movement, 157, 199, 200
Hospital for Sick Children (Toronto), 263
Hospitalization, 140, 156, 157, 199, 228; reaction to, 206-7, 266
Hypochondriasis, 98
Hysteria, 254-55
Hysterical personality, 90

Idealization, 376, 377; of dead parents, 121; of lost person, 142. *See also* Enshrinement; Memorialization
Identification: with dead parent, 111-12, 119; with dead sibling, 195, 196; with lost person, 142; physician with patient, 240, 241; staff with parents or patient, 226, 233
Illness, 3, 4, 6-15, 258, 366-67; fear of, in child, 131, 132; interpreted as punishment, 289; prolonged, 256; responsibility for, 257-58; shared by siblings, 187-98

Infant mortality, 331, 332, 361. See also Sudden Infant Death Syndrome (SIDS)
Informed consent, 9
Insomnia, 76, 120, 364, 371. See also Sleep disturbance
Intellectualization, 241-42, 291
Interdisciplinary team: need for (hospice), 203, 204-5
Interpretation of Dreams, The (Freud), 19
Intrapsychic dynamics: early parental loss and, 93-96
Isakower phenomenon, 22
Isolation, 182

Juvenile delinquency, 122. See also Antisocial behavior; Social deviancy
Juvenile diabetes mellitus, 12

Kübler-Ross, E., 83, 147, 256; stages of mourning, 260-62

Learning about death, 37, 43-44, 45-47, 53, 104-5, 126-27; schools and, 72, 73
Learning disturbances. See School disturbances
Leukemia, 4, 254-55, 293, 366, 367; death at home for child with, 180-86; reactions to, 263-65
Life: after death, 129; meaning of, 352, 373; philosophy of, 374, 377-78
Life-support systems, 148-49, 315; question of discontinuing, 216-17, 326. See also Feeding
Listening, 218, 360
Loneliness, 256; of dying child, 8, 9, 12-13, 211
Loss, 3; of boundaries (professionals), 14; children's reactions to, 289-90; of feeling, 349; of love objects, 5, 51, 93-94
Love, 80, 84, 85
Lymphomas, 4

Madness, 34. See also Psychopathology
Magical thinking, 5, 6, 28, 30-31, 33, 34, 45
Mainstreaming, 317-18
Malignant disease(s), 4, 224; setting for treatment of, 228-29; structure for treatment of, 226-27, 234

Maternal deprivation, 96
Maturational crises, 20-22, 33
Medical advances, 11, 156, 210, 252, 367
Medical care: home care of dying child, 161, 170
Medical intervention, 318; as opposed to basic care, 321-27; in SIDS risk prediction, 340
Medical training, 210; re thanatology, 217-19
Medication(s): antidepressant, 141; home care of child with cancer, 175-76; home care of dying child, 181-82
Medicine (discipline): cure orientation of, 225-26, 256; and facing death, 209-10; mental health principles in, 256-62
Melancholy, 119, 372
Memorialization, 349, 351; in anticipatory mourning, 368, 372, 376-78. See also Enshrinement; Idealization
Memory, 22, 23
Mental health: integration of principles of, into medicine, 256-62
Mental health professionals, 243-47
Mental illness, 98; hospitalization for, 98. See also Psychopathology
Metabolic disorders, inborn, 4
Methadone, 175
Minnesota SIDS Program, 334
Miscarriages, 362
Mortality, 40
Mother(s), 239, 257, 317; behavior of, and healthy development, 22; loss of, 153; therapy for, 350. See also Families; Parents
Mother/child relationship, 22, 24
Mourning, 51, 53, 89, 93-94, 256; belated, 120; by caregivers, 221; child's capacity for, 289-90; by children, 106-12, 153, 154; coping mechanisms in, 352; defined, 106, 289; development stage and, 94-96; the fatally ill child, 366-81; healthy, 108-9; re impending loss, 141; lack of, 119-20; pace of, 132; postbereavement, 378-80; premature, 142; reactions to phases in, 259-62; of surviving hemophiliac brother, 195, 196-97; work of, 368. See also Anticipatory mourning; Grief; Grieving

Mourning and Melancholia (Freud), 93-94
Myth(s), 23, 43

National Institute of Child Health and Human Development (NICHD), 361
National Institute of Mental Health, 362
National Sudden Infant Death Syndrome Foundation, 362
Near death experiences, 23
Negative hallucination, 23
Neonatal mortality, 331
Neurosis, 20, 21, 24
New York State: SIDS in, 342-44
Nightmares, 98, 111. *See also* Sleep disturbance
Numbness, 371
Nurse(s), 162, 163; effect of SIDS on, 333-34; home visits by, 183, 229; mourning stages, 261-62; role in home care of child with cancer, 172, 174, 177-78, 179. *See also* Caregivers; Staff
Nurture, 318, 319
Nutrition, 318-20, 231

Object constancy, 32, 95, 107
Object relations, neurotic, 24
Oedipal conflict, 95
Omnipotent entity (God), 104
Oncologist: mourning stages, 260-61
Oncology clinic, 293-302
Optimism, 10. *See also* Hope
Organ donation, 152-53
Orphans, orphanhood, 89, 93-97, 98
Outpatient clinic, 183, 228-29. *See also* Waiting room
Overprotection, 109, 114, 118, 142, 268

Pain, 12-13, 371; fear of, 147
Pain management: in home care of child with cancer, 175, 178-79, 181-82; in home care of dying child, 161, 170
Parent, surviving, 92, 96, 121, 154; and guilt in child, 117; physician and, 154-55; and prevention of psychopathology in child, 122; reassurance to child, 108-9, 128; and regression, 118
Parent/child relationship, 92

Parent groups, 162, 182, 184-85, 219, 263; self-help, 351-52; SIDS, 347, 363
Parental death, 153-55; children's reactions to, 104-24; impending, 106; psychiatric literature re, 89-103
Parenteral alimentation, 320-22, 324, 325
Parents, 10, 11-12, 74, 76, 157, 250, 347-49; anticipatory mourning, 368-78; anxiety re children's witnessing violence, 73-74; attitude toward death, 107-9, 163; behavior of, and healthy development, 22; children's perceptions of attitude toward death of, 44; desire, ability to care for child at home, 160-61, 173, 174, 178, 179, 180-81, 229; and discontinuation of artificial life supports, 148-49; explaining about death, 45-47, 77; and feeding of dying child, 318, 319, 323, 326-27; information given to, 143-45, 181, 182, 184, 203, 232; involvement in care and planning for dying child, 219-20; involvement in decision-making re children who witness violence, 72-73; involvement in hospice care of dying child, 204; involvement with pediatric malignant disease team, 231-32; involvement in social action (postdeath), 220, 349, 351-52; loss of fantasied expectations, 142, 360; management of, during prolonged illness of child, 149-50; and mental health professionals, 246; mortification and restitution efforts of, 346-53; in need of psychiatric care, 121, 169, 231-32, 239; omnipotence of, 24; preventability and coping process in bereavement, 357-65; professional health-care givers interactions with, 238-40; professional support for, 180-82, 203-4, 214, 215-16, 219-20, 289, 361-64; reaction to death of child, 138-39T, 141-42; reaction to diagnosis, prognosis, 212, 238-39, 369-70, 371, 372; rebuilding self-confidence of, 349-50, 373; replacing lost child, 142, 349-51; as role models, 91; and school reentry of child patient, 308-9, 310; self-perpetuation through children, 347; self-punishment, 258; in SIDS death, 361. *See also* Families; Parental death

Passivity, 148
Pathology, 34; in reaction to parental death, 112-19. *See also* Psychopathology
Pavor nocturnus attacks, 21-22, 23
Peck, R., 46
Pediatrician(s), 141, 154, 212, 217; and life-support systems, 216. *See also* Physician(s)
Pediatric malignant disease treatment team, 224-34
Pediatric oncology, 156, 163
Pediatric oncology team, interdisciplinary, 158, 169
Peer group relations, 162, 170, 260, 290
Perinatal death, 347
Phobias, 33, 98
Physician(s), 13-15, 133, 145; attending funeral, 151, 184; care phases of dying child, 212-17; and decisions re feeding dying child, 323-24, 326-27; facing death, 209-10, 214; feelings of inadequacy, failure, 211, 225-26; and hospice care of dying child, 202, 203-4; omnipotence, 13, 214, 226, 240, 261; parental anger displaced onto, 141-42; reaction to death of child, 210-11; reaction to dying child, 3, 143; relationship with child, family, 132, 137-55, 204, 239, 240-43, 245; role in home care of child, 163, 172, 174, 178, 179, 182, 183, 184, 229; role with children in parental death, 153-55; and surviving parent, 154-55; talking with dying child, 143, 145-47, 212-13; talking with parents, 143-45, 149-50, 212. *See also* Staff
Play(ing), 53, 147-48, 296; in clinic waiting room, 295, 298; as expression of anger, 111; as reaction to parental death, 113, 130; in service of mastery, synthesis, integration, 267
Pregnancy(ies), 331, 361-62
Preventability: and coping process, in parental bereavement, 357-65
Prognosis. *See* Diagnosis, prognosis
Projection, 111, 257, 291
Protection, 316. *See also* Overprotection
Psychiatric literature: re adult psychiatric disorders for early parental death, 122; black (re death), 43; re fear of death, 27-35; re management of dying child, 3; re needs of dying child, 235, 236; re needs of family, 236; re parental death in childhood, 89-103
Psychiatric referrals: for caregivers, 264-65
Psychiatrist, child, 141, 147, 154; and care of caregivers, 220-21; on facing death, 209-23; mourning stages, 262; pediatric malignanat disease team, 232-33
Psychiatry, 210, 256
Psychic preparedness, 266, 267; for life or death, 3-18
Psychic trauma: experienced by children who witness violence, 50-51, 52-53, 54, 57, 70, 73
Psychological euthanasia, 307
Psychoneurosis, 90
Psychopathology: caused by lack of grieving, 110; childhood bereavement and, 89, 90-93, 94, 99, 119-22, 153; in hospitalized child, 267; inability to mourn and, 94; in postbereavement mourning, 378-79; in siblings, 187-98
Psychosis, 122
Psychosocial factors: family, 224; interactions of dying child, parents, and health-care professionals, 235-49; staff, 227, 229-31, 232-34
Psychosomatic disturbances, 155, 371
Psychotherapy, 243-47. *See also* Therapy
Public health nurses, 176; support for family in SIDS, 334
Public Law *94-142,* 317
Punishment, 143, 153; attribution, 31; illness as, 289

Quality of life, 323, 324, 373; in home care, terminal childhood cancer, 156, 157-58, 160, 170

Rage, 32, 291, 371
Reaction formation, 142
Reality, 31, 34, 79; distortions of, 113; new concept of, 80
Reality testing, 154, 368, 375; in anticipatory mourning, 368, 369
Reconciliation: in anticipatory mourning, 372, 373-74
Regression, 95, 121, 148; in child's reac-

Index

tion to his dying, 140; as reaction to parental death, 117-18, 131
Regressive behavior, 32, 53, 62
Relapse(s), 228, 245, 370, 372, 375
Relationships, closeness of: and grief, 357, 358-60
Relief, 142; feelings of, at death of child, 184, 215-16
Religion, 4, 27, 37, 46, 195, 247; and autopsy permission, 152; elders and, 76, 77; in enshrinement, 377; honesty re, 129
Religious sacraments, 145
Remission(s), 150, 367, 369-70
Remorse, 142
Repression, 31, 114-15; of fear of death, 31, 34
Resignation, 141
Retrograde amnesia, 23
Ritualistic behavior(s), 30-31, 33
Role models, 74, 91

Sad mood, 98, 119, 130, 153, 182, 195, 371
St. Christopher's Hospital for Children (Philadelphia): hematology-oncology program, 180, 183, 184
St. Louis Park Medical Center (Minneapolis), 179
San Diego, California: school liaison program, 309-12
Schizophrenia, 34, 90, 122
School(s): child with cancer returning to, 303-14; for child with malignant disease, 228, 229; and learning about death, 72, 73. *See also* Teachers
School counselor(s), 304
School disturbances, 98, 154, 155, 162, 308-9; in death of parent, 131; in death of sibling, 190-91, 192, 195. *See also* School phobia
School nurse, 229, 304
School personnel: preparation of, for reentry of student-patient, 304-9
School phobia, 53, 59, 70, 375
Seattle Pain Clinic, 175
Self, omnipotent, 33, 34, 45
Self constancy, 32
Self-derogation, 117, 119
Self-help, 263, 316, 351-52

Self-mortification, parental, 349, 350, 351, 352
Sensitivity, 338
Separation, 32, 94, 154, 266; from dying child, 141; fear of, 253, 306; in hospitalization, 140
Separation anxiety, 30, 32-33, 61, 98, 120, 375; guilt as defense against, 44-45
Separation individuation, 24
Separation tolerance, 92
Sexual identity, 153, 154. *See also* Gender
Sheffield (England) scoring system, 337-44
Shelter (concept), 316, 317
Shock, 141, 371
Siblings, 81-82, 163, 229, 351, 361; and death at home of child with leukemia, 182; hemophiliac, 187-98; jealousy, resentment in, 143, 260; management of, in death of child, 150-52; needs of, 236; participation in care of dying child, 162, 170; reaction to death of child, 138-39T, 142-43, 164; stresses of terminal childhood cancer on, 157
Sibships, 92
SIDS. *See* Sudden infant death syndrome (SIDS)
Simplification(s), 8-9
Sleep, 28; in infants, 21, 332-33
Sleep disturbance, 57, 97, 141, 155, 364
Social deviancy: early parental death and, 92-93. *See also* Antisocial behavior
Social work counseling, 180
Social worker(s), 229; in pediatric malignant disease team, 231-32; role in home care of dying child, 162, 163, 182, 183, 184
Sociopathic personality, 90
Specificity, 338
Spouse(s); bereaved, 97-98; death of, 357. *See also* Parent, surviving
Staff: ambivalence in emotional reactions to dying child, 216-17; conflict, tension within, 216, 236, 240-41, 268; and discontinuation of life-support systems, 149; emotional problems of, 242-43; and home care of dying child, 183, 184-85; and hospice care of dying child, 202, 204-5; on pediatric malignant disease team, 229-31; reaction to

Staff (*continued*)
  death of child, 138-39T, 143; rescue fantasy of, 242, 245; selection of, 264; structure for treatment of malignant disease, 226-27, 234; support for, 230-31, 232-34, 241; and terminally ill child, 157; thanatology training for, 220; understanding of child's level of awareness, 146-47. *See also* Caregivers; Nurse(s); Physician(s)
Stepparents, 132
Stillbirth, 347
Stranger anxiety, 21
Stress: in care for dying child, 235, 236; coping with, in death of sibling, 195-96; in coping with fatal illness of child, 366; death as, 357-58; of hospitalization, 266; of orphanhood, 93-97; of parents, 238; in physician's facing death, 210; reinterpretation of, 373; staff, 225; in SIDS, 361; in terminal childhood cancer, 155, 157-58; in working with terminally ill children, 262
Substitute relationship(s), 112, 116
Sudden infant death syndrome (SIDS), 331-34, 347, 362-64; defined, 332; minimum standards for handling, 362-63; model for understanding grief re, 358, 360-62; parent groups for, 347, 351-52, 363; predicting risk of, 335-45
Suicide, 98, 119, 122, 153, 332
Suppression, 114-15, 195
Surgeon: mourning stages, 261
Surgery, 266
Survivors, 352; prevention of mental illness in, 263, 264. *See also* Families; Parent, surviving
Symptom management, 13; in home care of dying child, 181; in hospice care, 199, 205; in terminal phase, 228. *See also* Pain management
Symptomalogy, 97-99; in child's reaction to parental death, 117, 120-21, 131

Talionic law, 31, 116
Teachers, 47, 150; of children with cancer, 303-14; preparation for reentry to school of patient-student, 304-9, 311-12
Teresa, Mother, 80
Terror (of death). *See* Fear, of death
Thanatology, 209, 379; defined, 19; teaching about, 217-21
Therapy: and home care, 173; group, 13, 266-92. *See also* Parent groups
There Is a Rainbow Behind Every Dark Cloud, 82
Treatment, 9, 144, 149, 257; altered appearance from, 161; for caregivers, 264-65; for childhood cancer, 156; child's participation in, 148, 202-3, 217, 236; decisions re, 11-12, 326; of malignant disease, 224, 226-27, 228-29, 234; new, 12; painful, 293, 298; side-effects of, 161, 255; for terminally ill, 200. *See also* Life-support systems
Trust, 296, 297; loss of, 120. *See also* Communication, open
Tumors, 293

Ulcerative colitis, 6
Uncertainty, 3; rational approach to coping with, 12-13
United States: death stress in, 29, 357
University of California Medical Center (San Francisco), 158
University of Minnesota, 169
  Home Health Services Department, 179
  Hospitals, 174, 178

Values, 374, 377, 380
Violence: television, 47, 57, 58; witnessed by children, 49-74

Waiting room: anxiety in, 293-94, 295, 298-99
Weight loss, 97
White children: attitudes toward death, 37, 39-40, 41, 42-44
Will to live, 79
Wilms Tumor of the Kidney, 254
Withdrawal, 7, 10, 142, 215, 291, 368; in hospitalization, 140, 141; of physician, 143, 240
Working through, 53, 289-90

Yale-New Haven Hospital, 209

Contributors

John E. Schowalter, M.D., Professor of Pediatrics and Psychiatry, Yale University School of Medicine; Chief of Child Psychiatry, Yale University Child Study Center, New Haven, Connecticut

Paul R. Patterson, M.D., Professor Emeritus of Pediatrics, Albany Medical School of Union University, Albany, New York

Margot Tallmer, Ph.D., Professor of Psychology, Hunter College of the City University of New York, New York

Austin H. Kutscher, D.D.S., Professor of Dentistry (in Psychiatry), Department of Psychiatry, College of Physicians and Surgeons, Columbia University; Professor of Dentistry (in Psychiatry), School of Dental and Oral Surgery, Columbia University; President, The Foundation of Thanatology, New York, New York

Stephen V. Gullo, Ph.D., Assistant Clinical Professor, School of Dental and Oral Surgery, Columbia University, New York, New York

David Peretz, M.D., Assistant Clinical Professor, Department of Psychiatry, College of Physicians and Surgeons, Columbia University, New York, New York

A. R. Ablin, M.D., Clinical Professor of Pediatrics and Head of Pediatric Clinical Oncology, University of California at San Francisco

C. M. Binger, M.D., Clinical Professor of Psychiatry, University of California at San Francisco; Training Director and Clinical Coordinator of Child and Adolescent Psychiatry Service, Langley Porter Psychiatric Institute, San Francisco, California

Robert W. Buckingham, Dr. P.H., Associate Professor, Department of Family and Community Medicine, University of Arizona, Tucson, Arizona

Larry A. Bugen, Ph.D., Co-Director of Mental Health, Prucare/Austin Regional Clinic, Austin, Texas; Faculty Member, Central Texas Medical Foundation, Austin, Texas

Tecla Critelli, M.D., Chief, Child and Adolescent Psychiatry Clinic, St. Vincent's Hospital and Medical Center, New York, New York; Clinical Assistant Professor, Department of Psychiatry, New York Medical College, New York, New York

Bruce L. Danto, M.D., Associate Professor, Department of Psychiatry, Wayne State University School of Medicine, Detroit, Michigan

Patricia Desy-Spinetta, M.A., M.S. Adjunct Professor, Department of Psychology; Principal Investigator and Project Director, School Intervention Program for Children with Cancer. San Diego State University, San Diego, California

Clyde H. Flanagan, M.D., Colonel, U.S. Army Medical Corps; Chief, Community Mental Health Activity, U.S. Dewitt Army Community Hospital, Fort Belvoir, Virginia; Assistant Clinical Professor of Psychiatry, Uniformed Services University of the Health Sciences School of Medicine, Bethesda, Maryland; formerly, Chief of Pediatric Consultation-Liaison, Child and Adolescent Psychiatry Services, Department of Psychiatry, Walter Reed Army Medical Center, Washington, D.C.

Ralph A. Franciosi, M.D., Chief of Pathology, Minneapolis Children's Health Center and Hospital; Director of the Minnesota SIDS Program, Minneapolis, Minnesota

Edward H. Futterman, M.D., Clinical Professor of Psychiatry and Pediatrics, Yale University Child Study Center, New Haven, Connecticut

Richard A. Gardner, M.D., Associate Clinical Professor, Department of Psychiatry, College of Physicians and Surgeons, Columbia University, New York, New York

Werner I. Halpern, M.D., Director, Children and Youth Division, Rochester Mental Health Center, Rochester, New York; Clinical Associate Professor of Psychiatry, Department of Psychiatry, University of Rochester School of Medicine and Dentistry, Rochester, New York

Irwin Hoffman, Ph.D., Assistant Professor of Psychology, Department of Psychiatry, Abraham Lincoln School of Medicine, University of Illinois School of Medicine, Chicago, Illinois

Gerald G. Jampolsky, M.D., Psychiatrist, Tiburon, California

Dwight T. Janerich, D.D.S., M.P.H., Director, Division of Community Health and Epidemiology, New York State Department of Health, Albany, New York

Susan K. Jereb, A.B., Student, Physician's Assistant Program, Hudson Valley Community College, Albany Medical College of Union University, Albany, New York

Charles R. Koch, M.D., Director, Child and Family Mental Health Service, Hall-Mercer CMH/MRC of Pennsylvania Hospital, Philadelphia; Clinical Assistant Professor, Division of Child Psychiatry, School of Medicine, University of Pennsylvania

J. H. Kushner, M.D., Clinical Professor of Pediatrics, University of California at San Francisco

Barbara J. Kuter, M.P.H., Epidemiologist, Division of Virus and Cell Biology Research, Merck Institute for Therapeutic Research, Merck Sharp and Dohme Research Laboratories, West Point, Pennsylvania

Lillian G. Kutscher, Publications Editor, The Foundation of Thanatology, New York, New York

Carolyn A. Larsen, B.Sc.N., Director, Child Life and School Services, The Montreal Children's Hospital, Montreal, Quebec, Canada

Dorothy Otnow Lewis, M.D., F.A.C.P., Professor of Psychiatry, New York University School of Medicine, New York, New York

Melvin Lewis, M.B., B.S. (London), F.R.C. Psych., D.C.H., Professor of Pediatrics and Psychiatry, Yale University School of Medicine; Director of Medical Studies, Yale University Child Study Center, New Haven, Connecticut

George W. Marten, M.D., Professor of Psychiatry and Pediatrics, University of Tennessee College of Medicine; Chief of Psychiatry, St. Jude Children's Research Hospital, Memphis, Tennessee

Ida M. Martinson, Ph.D., Professor and Chair of Family Health Care, School of Nursing, University of California at San Francisco

Åke Mattsson, M.D., Professor of Psychiatry and Pediatrics; Director, Division of Child and Adolescent Psychiatry, New York University Medical Center, New York, New York

Alvin M. Mauer, M.D., Professor of Pediatrics, University of Tennessee College of Medicine; Director, St. Jude Children's Research Hospital, Memphis, Tennessee

Nelli L. Mitchell, M.D., Fellow, American Psychiatric Association and American Academy of Child Psychiatry; Supervising Psychiatrist, Rochester Mental Health Center; Clinical Assistant Professor, Department of Psychiatry, University of Rochester School of Medicine and Dentistry, Rochester, New York

Edward H. Pakes, M.D., D. Psych., F.R.C.P. (C), F.A.P.A., Assistant Professor of Psychiatry, University of Toronto; Senior Psychiatrist, The Hospital for Sick Children, Toronto; formerly, Liaison Psychiatrist, Department of Haematology-Oncology, Hospital for Sick Children and Princess Margaret Hospital (Ontario Cancer Institute), Toronto, Ontario, Canada

G. A. Perin, R.N., M.S., Clinical Nurse Specialist, University of California at San Francisco

Joan Taksa Rolsky, M.S.W., Director, Family Support Program, Hematology/Oncology Department, St. Christopher's Hospital for Children, Philadelphia, Pennsylvania

Karen R. Schulman, M.A., Research Assistant, Department of Psychiatry, University of Rochester School of Medicine and Dentistry, Rochester, New York

Albert J. Solnit, M.D., Sterling Professor of Pediatrics and Psychiatry, Yale University School of Medicine; Director, Yale University Child Study Center, New Haven, Connecticut

John J. Spinetta, Ph.D., Professor of Psychology, San Diego State University, San Diego, California

Susan J. Standfast, M.D., M.P.H., Research Physician, Division of Community Health and Epidemiology, New York State Department of Health, Albany, New York

Max M. Stern, M.D., Clinical Associate Professor Emeritus, State University of New York, Downstate Medical Center, Brooklyn, New York; Lecturer and Training Analyst Emeritus, The Psychoanalytic Institute New York University, New York, New York

Jan van Eys, Ph.D., M.D., Mosbacher Professor of Pediatrics; Head, Division of Pediatrics, The University of Texas System Cancer Center, M.D. Anderson Hospital and Tumor Institute, Houston, Texas

Morris A. Wessel, M.D., Clinical Professor of Pediatrics, Yale University School of Medicine; Consulting Pediatrician, Clifford Beers Child Guidance Clinic; Founding Member of Board, The Connecticut Hospice, Branford, Connecticut

April R. Zweig, Ph.D., Institute for Juvenile Research, Chicago, Illinois

Columbia University Press Foundation of Thanalology Series

Teaching Psychosocial Aspects of Patient Care
Bernard Schoenberg, Helen F. Pettit, and Arthur C. Carr, editors

Loss and Grief: Psychological Management in Medical Practice
Bernard Schoenberg, Arthur C. Carr, David Peretz, and Austin H. Kutscher, editors

Psychosocial Aspects of Terminal Care
Bernard Schoenberg, Arthur C. Carr, David Peretz, and Austin H. Kutscher, editors

Psychosocial Aspects of Cystic Fibrosis: A Model for Chronic Lung Disease
Paul R. Patterson, Carolyn R. Denning, and Austin H. Kutscher, editors

The Terminal Patient: Oral Care
Austin H. Kutscher, Bernard Schoenberg, and Arthur C. Carr, editors

Psychopharmacologic Agents for the Terminally Ill and Bereaved
Ivan K. Goldberg, Sidney Malitz, and Austin H. Kutscher, editors

Anticipatory Grief
Bernard Schoenberg, Arthur C. Carr, Austin H. Kutscher, David Peretz, and Ivan K. Goldberg, editors

Bereavement: Its Psychosocial Aspects
Bernard Schoenberg, Irwin Gerber, Alfred Wiener, Austin H. Kutscher, David Peretz, and Arthur C. Carr, editors

The Nurse as Caregiver for the Terminal Patient and His Family
Ann M. Earle, Nina T. Argondizzo, and Austin H. Kutscher, editors

Columbia University Press/Foundation of Thanalology Series

Social Work with the Dying Patient and the Family
Elizabeth R. Prichard, Jean Collard, Ben A. Orcutt, Austin H. Kutscher, Irene Seeland, and Nathan Lefkowitz, editors

Home Care: Living with Dying
Elizabeth R. Prichard, Jean Collard, Janet Starr, Josephine A. Lockwood, Austin H. Kutscher, and Irene B. Seeland, editors

Psychosocial Aspects of Cardiovascular Disease: The Life-Threatened Patient, the Family, and the Staff
James Reiffel, Robert DeBellis, Lester C. Mark, Austin H. Kutscher, Paul R. Patterson, and Bernard Schoenberg, editors

Aucte Grief: Counseling the Bereaved
Otto S. Margolis, Howard C. Raether, Austin H. Kutscher, J. Bruce Powers, Irene B. Seeland, Robert DeBellis, and Daniel J. Cherico, editors

The Human Side of Homicide
Bruce L. Danto, John Bruhns, and Austin H. Kutscher, editors

Hospice U.S.A.
Austin H. Kutscher, Samuel C. Klagsbrun, Richard J. Torpie, Robert DeBellis, Mahlon S. Hale, and Margot Tallmer, editors

The Child and Death
John E. Schowalter, Paul R. Patterson, Margot Tallmer, Austin H. Kutscher, Stephen V. Gullo, and David Peretz, editors